Huebner School Series

PLANNING FOR BUSINESS OWNERS AND PROFESSIONALS

Thirteenth Edition

Ted Kurlowicz

HS331-13

This publication is designed to provide accurate and authoritative information about the subject covered. While every precaution has been taken in the preparation of this material, the authors, and The American College assume no liability for damages resulting from the use of the information contained in this publication. The American College is not engaged in rendering legal, accounting, or other professional advice. If legal or other expert advice is required, the services of an appropriate professional should be sought.

270 S. Bryn Mawr Avenue
Bryn Mawr, PA 19010
(888) AMERCOL (263-7265)
theamericancollege.edu

Library of Congress Control Number 2011903180
ISBN-13: 978-1-58293-049-7
ISBN-10: 1-58293-049-X
Printed in the United States of America

HUEBNER SCHOOL SERIES

Individual Health Insurance Planning
Thomas P. O'Hare and Burton T. Beam, Jr.

Financial Planning: Process and Environment
Craig W. Lemoine

Fundamentals of Insurance Planning
Kevin M. Lynch and Glenn E. Stevick, Jr.

Fundamentals of Financial Planning
David M. Cordell (ed.)

Fundamentals of Income Taxation
Christopher P. Woehrle and Thomas M. Brinker, Jr. (eds.)

McGill's Life Insurance
Edward E. Graves (ed.)

McGill's Legal Aspects of Life Insurance
Edward E. Graves and Burke A. Christensen (eds.)

Group Benefits: Basic Concepts and Alternatives
Burton T. Beam, Jr.

Planning for Retirement Needs
David A. Littell and Kenn Beam Tacchino

Fundamentals of Investments for Financial Planning
Walt J. Woerheide

Fundamentals of Estate Planning
Constance J. Fontaine

Estate Planning Applications
Ted Kurlowicz

Planning for Business Owners and Professionals
Ted Kurlowicz

Financial Planning Applications
Craig W. Lemoine

Advanced Topics in Group Benefits
Juliana York and Burton T. Beam, Jr.(ed.)

Executive Compensation
Paul J. Schneider

Health and Long-Term Care Financing for Seniors
Allen C. McLellan

Financial Decisions for Retirement
David A. Littell (ed.)

The American College® is an independent, nonprofit, accredited institution founded in 1927 that offers professional certification and graduate-degree distance education to men and women seeking career growth in financial services.

The Center for Financial Advisor Education at The American College offers both the LUTCF and the Financial Services Specialist (FSS) professional designations to introduce students in a classroom environment to the technical side of financial services, while at the same time providing them with the requisite sales-training skills.

The Solomon S. Huebner School® of The American College administers the Chartered Life Underwriter (CLU®); the Chartered Financial Consultant (ChFC®); the Chartered Advisor for Senior Living (CASL®); the Registered Health Underwriter (RHU®); the Registered Employee Benefits Consultant (REBC®); and the Chartered Leadership Fellow® (CLF®) professional designation programs. In addition, the Huebner School also administers The College's CFP Board—registered education program for those individuals interested in pursuing CFP® certification, the CFP® Certification Curriculum.

The Richard D. Irwin Graduate School® of The American College offers the master of science in financial services (MSFS) degree, the Graduate Financial Planning Track (another CFP Board-registered education program), and several graduate-level certificates that concentrate on specific subject areas. It also offers the Chartered Advisor in Philanthropy (CAP®) and the master of science in management (MSM), a one-year program with an emphasis in leadership. The National Association of Estate Planners & Councils has named The College as the provider of the education required to earn its prestigious AEP designation.

The American College is accredited by **The Middle States Commission on Higher Education**, 3624 Market Street, Philadelphia, PA 19104 at telephone number 267.284.5000.

The Middle States Commission on Higher Education is a regional accrediting agency recognized by the U.S. Secretary of Education and the Commission on Recognition of Postsecondary Accreditation. Middle States accreditation is an expression of confidence in an institution's mission and goals, performance, and resources. It attests that in the judgment of the Commission on Higher Education, based on the results of an internal institutional self-study and an evaluation by a team of outside peer observers assigned by the Commission, an institution is guided by well-defined and appropriate goals; that it has established conditions and procedures under which its goals can be realized; that it is accomplishing them substantially; that it is so organized, staffed, and supported that it can be expected to continue to do so; and that it meets the standards of the Middle States Association. The American College has been accredited since 1978.

The American College is located at 270 S. Bryn Mawr Avenue, Bryn Mawr, PA 19010. The toll-free number of the Office of Professional Education is (888) AMERCOL (263-7265); the fax number is (610) 526-1465; and the home page address is theamericancollege.edu.

CONTENTS

PREFACE

Because business planning is a complex and dynamic pursuit, it is generally impossible for business owners or professionals to perform the entire planning function alone. Their task is typically delegated to a team of financial services professionals who specialize in various aspects of business planning. The business planning team might include professionals in the areas of law, accounting, investments, employee benefits, and insurance. Although several fine books are available covering one or more of the aspects of business planning, no one book was deemed either complete or concise enough to be appropriate for our purposes. Consequently, the authors have developed this textbook as part of the Huebner School Series in response to our particular needs. The authors hope that they have hit the mark in developing a concise treatise covering the many areas of planning for business owners and professionals in a manner appropriate for the needs of the Chartered Life Underwriter (CLU) curriculum.

ACKNOWLEDGMENTS

The author is grateful for the contribution of previous authors whose material this textbook still contains, especially former American College faculty James Ivers and John McFadden. The author has updated the material substantially and is responsible for any errors in it.

I would also like to express appreciation to Todd Denton and Jane Hassinger, for putting the mauuscript in final form and to Emily Schu for production assistance.

Ted Kurlowicz, JD, LLM, CLU, ChFC, AEP, CAP, is the Charles E. Drimal professor of estate planning at The American College, where his responsibilities include preparation of courses in estate planning and planning for business owners and professionals. He has helped to develop insurance agent licensing examinations for numerous states and has addressed the national conferences of the Society of Financial Service Professionals, the IAFP, AICPA, NAEPC, and MDRT. Ted has appeared on *Your Money*, a business news broadcast on CNN, and *The Financial Advisers*, a business and financial planning program on PBS.

Ted is an adjunct faculty member at Widener University and Philadelphia University, where he teaches in the Master of Taxation program. He holds a BS from the University of Connecticut, an MA from the University of Pennsylvania, a JD from the Delaware Law School, and an LLM from the Villanova University School of Law. He is a member of the Pennsylvania Bar Association and the American Bar Association. Ted was inducted into the Estate Planning Hall of Fame in 2008 by the National Association of Estate Planners and Councils

Charles E. Drimal Estate Planning Professorship Endowment Fund

This permanently restricted chair was established in 1999 to support a professorship. The holder of this professorship is responsible for the development, promotion, and implementation of The American College's programs within the field of estate planning. Ted Kurlowicz, Professor of Taxation, currently holds this Chair.

COMMON BUSINESS PROBLEMS AND PLANNING OBJECTIVES 1

Special Note to Readers Enrolled in American College Courses

Many readers of this book are using it as part of their work for courses in designation programs of The American College (TAC). If you are one of these students, you need to be aware that the book is used in conjunction with materials that are found on The American College Online. It is important that you use this site for additional study materials and instructions on how to prepare for your course. If you have not received instructions on how to access The American College Online, contact Professional Education Services at 1-888-AMERCOL (263-7265).

Learning Objectives

An understanding of the material in this chapter should enable the student to

1. Determine the goals of a business owner in selecting a form of organization with respect to start-up costs, control over the operation of the business, personal liability for business operations, and flexibility in operation of the enterprise.
2. Describe the basic tax treatment of the various types of business entities.
3. Explain the causes of business termination resulting from the loss of an owner.
4. Describe how owners of sole proprietorships, partnerships, limited-liability companies, and corporations are compensated.
5. Identify the potential risk exposures of a typical closely held business.

The owners of a closely held business enterprise face numerous problems. Some are inherent in the organizational structure of the small business and others exist in enterprises of all sizes. Many problems facing the business owner, such as survival in the business marketplace, are obvious. Other problems, such as the reduction in business income resulting from the loss of a key employee due to death, disability, or termination of employment, may not be recognized by the business owner until the incident occurs.

Many problems facing the business owner can be avoided, or at least mitigated, through proper planning. To plan intelligently to avoid or handle future problems, it is necessary to identify the potential problems and form objectives.

The role of the financial services professional is to help business owners or professionals recognize these problems and to assist in formulating plans that are appropriate for the special needs of each client. The purpose of this chapter is to discuss typical problems faced by the closely held business owner or professional. Possible solutions to these problems will be discussed in subsequent chapters.

CHOOSING THE FORM OF BUSINESS ORGANIZATION

Business owners are faced with a number of choices when selecting the form of enterprise. They may elect to operate unincorporated, as a sole proprietorship, a partnership, or a limited-liability company (LLC); or they may incorporate—as a regular (C) corporation or as an S corporation. The choice of ownership form is revocable, and owners of existing businesses often decide to change the form if circumstances so dictate. For example, the sole proprietor might wonder if the benefits of switching to the corporate form of ownership are worth the costs of incorporation. Or perhaps the owners of an existing closely held corporation are considering what the tax advantages would be if they switched to a subchapter S form of business.

The choice of a form of ownership is a complex decision facing all business owners because it will have a significant impact on the initial start-up cost, the control and flexibility in management, the taxation of the business and individual owners, the ability of the firm to raise capital, and the business risks absorbed by the individual owners.

Since it is unlikely that any one form of enterprise will be most advantageous in all aspects, a decision should be made after weighing all factors. An incorrect selection is typically reversible; however, it will often be a costly planning mistake. As a result, the decision regarding the form of ownership should be made in the early planning stages of the business with professional advice from an attorney, a tax adviser, and a financial services professional.

Forms of Business Organization

- Unincorporated
    - Sole proprietorship
    - Partnership
        - General partnership
        - Limited partnership
    - Limited-liability company
- Incorporated
    - C corporation
    - S corporation

Goals of the Business Owner

Owners often have several objectives when selecting the form of ownership under which the business will operate. The priority ranking of these goals might differ from one individual to the next, but all are shared to some extent by the typical closely held business owner or professional.

Minimum Start-up Costs and Formalities of Operation

There are typically few statutory formalities involved in forming unincorporated businesses—proprietorships and partnerships. An unincorporated business might have to register the name of the business with the state government authority, and a search should be made to ensure that the name chosen is not already in use.

Since the proprietor is the sole owner of the business, there is no reason for any agreements to be drafted at formation, except perhaps employment contracts for certain hired employees. In contrast, a partnership should be formed with a formal written partnership agreement. These agreements can range in complexity from a simple agreement for a two-partner firm to a complex agreement similar to a corporate charter or bylaws. Professional help is recommended in drafting these agreements regardless of complexity. Obviously the cost of the agreement will depend on the amount of legal assistance required for its drafting. In the case of a large professional partnership the cost may equal or even exceed the cost of a simple incorporation.

limited-liability company (LLC)

The *limited-liability company (LLC)* is a relatively new form of entity. Authorized in all 50 states and the District of Columbia, the LLC is the fastest growing form of enterprise. LLCs are formed under the auspices of an enabling state law. The members file articles of organization with the state authorizing the business. They form an operating agreement to list the specifics of their association. The operating agreement will be a complex document and professional fees will be incurred. Generally, the start-up costs will exceed those of a simple partnership or corporation.

The formation of a corporation is, like an LLC, governed by statutory formalities. The process is regulated by the state of incorporation and always involves specific required procedures and costs. For example, the articles of incorporation and bylaws must be drafted. The articles must be filed with the state, and stock certificates for all classes of stock to be issued must be prepared and distributed. Employment contracts for employees, particularly owner-employees, must be prepared. Subscription agreements might be formed with the original stockholders, or in the case of a formation of a larger corporation shares of stock will be issued through the services of an underwriter or an investment banker.

For any incorporation, even the most basic, certain filing fees and/or taxes must be paid to the state. Legal fees will be required to pay for advice and document drafting. The cost of the appropriate professional help for the incorporation is money well invested. A typical complaint of shareholders of closely held corporations is that they received bad advice at the inception of the corporation. In any event the cost of incorporation is several hundred dollars at a minimum and may run much higher in more complex cases.

The cost of forming the business enterprise is not significant in the long run. Although incorporation generally involves higher start-up costs and more formalities than other ownership forms, these factors usually do not dissuade owners from forming a corporation. However, the owners of a relatively simple business or professional practice may decide that the costs and formalities of incorporation are an unnecessary expenditure.

Control of the Closely Held Business

closely held business

Owners of a *closely held business* usually hope to maximize their control over the business. The sole proprietorship has only one owner who may run the business without any interference from others and holds powers limited solely by the laws of the state. The proprietor loses control of the business only upon its liquidation.

A partnership is formed under the voluntary association of two or more partners. Inherent in this type of organization is an agreement by the partners on the basic business purpose of the partnership and sometimes the sharing or delegation of specific control functions among the partners.

Each partner typically has the authority to represent the partnership in business matters. This means that an individual partner is capable of frustrating the others by representing the partnership in a manner contrary to their wishes. To avoid such potential conflict, the control of the partnership could be spelled out in the original agreement. However, any partner who becomes dissatisfied may have the right to force dissolution of the partnership by terminating the voluntary agreement to associate with the other partners.

Fortunately the original partners cannot lose control to outsiders against their wills. The sale of a partnership interest to a third party does not automatically create a partnership with that third party since all existing partners must agree to accept the buyer as a partner. Therefore the original partners can ensure that their control of the partnership will not be diluted by outsiders.

An LLC is formed and governed by its articles of organization and operating agreement. Similar to a partnership, management control will depend on the operating agreement. Generally not all members will have the authority to represent and control the business. Subject to some tax choices, discussed in chapter 2, the control may be centralized under the guidance of one or more members.

Most LLCs will not permit completely free transferability of the ownership interests. Usually restrictions on transfer will occur and membership will not automatically be conferred on a transferee of an ownership interest. Because of these factors, the control of the current owners should be fairly certain in an LLC.

The control of the corporation is vested in the board of directors, which oversees the management of the corporation. The election of the board of directors can generally be dominated by the majority shareholder. Unless minority shareholders can gain representation on the board, the closely held corporation will be under the continuous control of the majority shareholder.

Difficulties occur in the control of the corporation when there is no clear majority owner. For example, the corporation could be owned by a number of individuals or two 50 percent owners. Or a corporation might find it necessary to dilute the control of a majority shareholder by issuing new stock to outsiders to raise badly needed capital. In these instances there are some planning techniques available to the shareholders seeking control of the corporation. In any event the control of a corporation depends on its individual characteristics.

In summary, the proprietor generally has the maximum control over a business. A partnership can effectively prevent outsiders from exerting control over the partnership. However, the partnership situation presents the possibility for a deadlock in control by existing partners that can be solved only by terminating the partnership.

Closely held corporations can typically be controlled by the majority shareholder. However, in the absence of any restrictions on the transfer of stock, the original owners of the corporation may transfer stock to outsiders and introduce a new voice into the control structure of the firm. The original controlling shareholder group may be able to retain control over the board of directors, but the additional new shareholders may become a hindrance and a source of future conflict.

Flexibility in Business Operations

Sole Proprietorship. Flexibility in the operation and management structure of the business is generally a desirable characteristic. The owners desire the ability to grasp business opportunities quickly or to abandon losing enterprises. Again, the proprietor has the maximum flexibility to make these decisions. He or she is free to enter a new line of business without conflict from other owners. This could be accomplished by simply opening a new shop while maintaining or abandoning the old line of business. The proprietor's actions in the management and operation of the business are unrestricted.

Partnership. Although a partnership offers considerable flexibility in the operation of a business, it is more limited than a proprietorship since the agreement of all partners is required for any major business decisions. The typical partnership agreement limits the activities of the firm to specific types of enterprise. The partners are free to change this agreement, which can be accomplished with little effort or loss of time. However, it is important to note that this action must be approved unanimously.

Limited-Liability Company (LLC). Similar to a partnership, an LLC will provide flexibility in the original organizational form. Management, compensation, and other characteristics can be selected by the owners in the operating agreement. However, unless otherwise provided, the operating agreement can generally be amended only with the consent of all members.

Corporation. The corporate form of ownership offers the least flexibility in operation of any type of business. For example, the powers of a corporation are limited by its original charter, and actions outside these powers may be beyond the authority of the firm. Although modern corporate law provides the corporation with broad, but not unlimited, powers, major corporate actions must be approved by the board of directors (and possibly shareholders). This requirement in itself limits the flexibility of a corporation since the board can take action only at specified times and subject to various restrictions. Obviously it is more difficult for a corporation to make fundamental changes in the operation of the firm.

Some states have special closely held corporation statutes that provide a closely held corporation with operating flexibility similar to that of unincorporated businesses. These statutes might allow a corporation to act without a board of directors, for example. Even in the absence of a closely held corporation statute, many closely held corporations operate without the formalities required by law. This could be dangerous since the IRS or third-party claimants might successfully challenge the corporate status of the business.

The Ability of the Business to Raise Funds

The ability to raise capital is limited in any small business, regardless of the form of ownership. There are some distinctions worth mentioning among the various forms of ownership with respect to both the method and the ability to raise capital.

Sole Proprietorship. The simplicity of a proprietorship is a double-edged sword. The operating formalities are less burdensome, but the owner's independence can become a drawback for some purposes such as raising capital.

A proprietorship is formed when the owner begins operation by putting personal assets to use in the business. The capital of the proprietorship consists of the proprietor's assets plus any additional amounts the proprietor can obtain through borrowing. Whatever credit is available to the proprietor depends solely on the proprietor's personal financial position, including, of course, the proprietor's business interest. Obviously there is a built-in limit on the amount any one individual will be able to borrow from commercial or private sources. Extremely wealthy individuals, who might otherwise have substantial ability to raise funds, are more likely to form businesses as corporations than as proprietorships for a variety of other reasons discussed later.

By definition a proprietorship is not permitted to raise funds from an important source available to other forms of ownership—the expansion of the equity base by adding new owners. If a proprietor finds it necessary to expand the equity base of the business by soliciting capital contributions from new owners in exchange for an equity interest, the proprietorship is transformed into another form of ownership—either a partnership or a corporation.

Partnership. Although a partnership has limits similar to a proprietorship in its ability to raise capital, it does have a potentially larger equity base on which to raise capital since it has at least two owners. If the partners have substantial personal assets and are willing to guarantee a loan, a lender is more likely to extend credit to the partnership. It is also easier for a partnership to expand its equity base by taking on new owners. However, this requires the original partners to accept new partners who have all the rights and responsibilities of the original owner.

limited partnership

Limited Partnership. All states have laws permitting the creation of special limited partnerships, which are composed of active participants (general partners) and passive investment partners (limited partners). The general partners all retain personal responsibility for business operations, while limited partners are at risk only to the extent of their investment in the business. Regular (general) partnerships are owned solely by general partners. Limited partnerships can raise capital by selling partnership interests to limited partners in exchange for capital contributions without diluting the control of the general partners. The limited partners invest capital in return for a share of future income and growth of the business but are not burdened with unlimited personal liability for the operation of the partnership. For this reason many risky ventures requiring large amounts of capital are formed as limited partnerships.

Limited-Liability Company (LLC). All states currently have statutes permitting the formation of LLCs. This form of organization is particularly advantageous with respect to the ability to raise funds. An LLC features several favorable characteristics of other types of organizations in one enterprise. It provides pass-through tax treatment without requiring that any members retain unlimited liability. It permits an unlimited number of members, unlike an S corporation. For business owners who are concerned about liability from business operations but would like to raise capital from passive investors, the LLC is an excellent choice.

Corporation. In theory the corporate form should be selected for a business that will require substantial capital and expand rapidly. A corporation is a separate legal entity and may own assets in its own right. The corporation can borrow in its own name and may be able to use the various sources of commercial credit to raise any needed capital.

A small closely held corporation with limited assets is unlikely to be able to borrow large amounts secured by corporate assets alone. Commercial lenders are likely to require the individual shareholders of the closely held corporation to personally guarantee loans made to the corporation. In this respect a small closely held corporation is similar to unincorporated businesses in its ability to raise funds.

A distinct advantage of the corporate form over other forms of business enterprise is the ability to raise capital by expanding the equity base. A corporation can take on additional owners to expand its equity capital simply by exchanging equity (newly issued stock) for capital contributions. In addition, this increase in the ownership base of the corporation may allow it to increase its debt while maintaining a safe debt-equity ratio. For these reasons the corporation is generally superior to other forms of ownership for a business that will grow and have large capital needs.

One problem associated with the issuance of stock to new investors is the potential loss of control by the current shareholders. Techniques can be used to perpetuate the control of the current majority shareholders under these circumstances. Of course, it may be difficult to attract investors unless some control is relinquished, but investors may be willing to take a noncontrolling interest for the opportunity to share in the corporate earnings and appreciation in stock value if business prospects are favorable.

Issues in Selecting Form of Business Organization

- Ease and expense of formation
- Control
- Flexibility in operations
- Ability to raise capital
- Liability of owners
- Income taxation
- Compensation and fringe benefits for owners

In selecting the form of ownership it is critical that the business owner consider the future capital needs of the business. For a business that will remain small, the unincorporated form should be sufficient to handle future capital needs. Any enterprise that anticipates rapid growth or has large initial capital needs should be organized in a form that facilitates the expansion of the equity base—a corporation or perhaps a limited partnership.

The Limited Liability of Owners From Business Operation

The operation of a business creates risks from which both the business and the owner need protection. There is the obvious risk that business failure will render the firm insolvent. Furthermore, the operation of a business creates potentially large risks. For example, there are many dangers, both hidden and obvious, on the business premises that could cause injury to employees or third parties. There is the risk that a business's defective products will create liability by causing injury to consumers. Finally, there is the possibility that a business will become liable for injuries caused by its agents and employees.

Sole Proprietorship. The proprietor faces the greatest risk exposure of any business owner since the business and personal assets of the proprietor are legally indistinguishable, so that the debts of the proprietor's business are also his or her personal debts. Therefore the failure of the proprietorship enables the business creditors to satisfy their claims from the proprietor's personal assets. Misfortunes of the proprietor's business can lead to the proprietor's personal financial ruin.

General Partnership. The general partnership exposes the partners to a liability danger that is similarly unlimited. One characteristic of the partnership form is that more than one owner will share in the losses. The liability of the partners for partnership losses is " joint and several." That is, each partner is liable individually and as a member of the group for any claims against the partnership. Partners sued individually by the business creditors may, however, seek contribution from the other partners for their share of any amounts that were expended to satisfy the claims. A partner's share of any partnership loss depends on the underlying situation. Although the initial partnership agreement should specify the percentage share of each partner of any claims against the partnership, all general partners are ultimately liable.

All individuals, including partners, are personally responsible for their own actions. If the negligent act of a partner results in a lawsuit against the partnership, the partnership and other partners are liable if the action took place within the scope of the partnership business. The negligent partner will be liable to the partnership and the other partners for any funds paid to satisfy the claim. For this reason the nonnegligent partners will not suffer a loss for claims arising from the acts of a negligent partner to the extent that the negligent partner remains solvent.

An obvious question is whether the personal liability of a general partner can be limited by the partnership agreement. For example, can the agreement state that a specific partner does not share in any losses of the partnership? The answer to this question is no. The doctrine of joint and several liability provides that the general partner is always ultimately individually liable for claims against the partnership.

Limited Partnership. As a relief from the harshness of unlimited liability in general partnerships, all states permit the formation of limited partnerships. The advantage of the limited partnership lies in the fact that some investors—the limited partners—may contribute capital and participate in the profits without unlimited personal liability. The limited partners may suffer losses, but only to the extent of the capital contributed to the partnership.

The law requires that each limited partnership have at least one general partner. The general partner, of course, is exposed to unlimited personal liability for claims against the limited partnership. To prevent any one individual from absorbing this risk, some limited partnerships are formed with a corporation as the general partner.

limited-liability partnership (LLP)

A relatively new form of partnership is the *limited-liability partnership (LLP)*. LLP or RLLP (registered limited-liability partnership) laws have now been enacted in all states. An LLP is a partnership that has filed or registered under the state's enabling law to operate with for all partners. The distinction between the LLP and the limited partnership is that an LLP can be a general partnership and all general partners have limited liability. Under LLP or RLLP laws in general, limits are placed on the liability of partners from the unsatisfied debts and obligations of the firm arising from the negligence and misconduct of other partners. The assets of the partnership itself remain at risk; thus each partner's liability is limited to his or her investment in the partnership. In addition, many states restrict the types of entities that can form as LLPs or RLLPs. For example, some states prohibit the practice of law under this organizational form.

Limited-Liability Company (LLC). The LLC is a relatively new form of enterprise that was developed primarily to address the liability concerns of would-be entrepreneurs. This liability protection is the most important characteristic of the LLC and a key distinguishing factor from a partnership, which provides limited liability only for its limited but not its general partners.

The LLC is the only business entity that allows every member, including managing members, to enjoy limited liability while the entity is treated as a partnership for federal income tax purposes. This insulation is particularly important if the underlying business or asset may involve environmental claims, product liability claims, or similar exposures.

Corporation. The corporate form of ownership provides its owners (shareholders) with personal protection that is unavailable to proprietors or general partners for liability stemming from the operation of a business. Corporate shareholders contribute capital in exchange for equity. Theoretically the capital contributed by a shareholder is the limit of his or her liability for the risks of running the business. The liability arising from the operation of a corporation is satisfied out of corporate assets, regardless of whether they are sufficient to satisfy all claims.

The corporate form is not always a panacea for business owners seeking limited liability, especially in the case of a closely held or professional corporation. Business creditors of these corporations are unlikely to accept solely the corporation's signature on loans to the corporation unless it has substantial assets. For this reason shareholders of a closely held corporation often find that they must personally guarantee the loans extended to the business. To the extent of their personal guarantees, the shareholders remain personally liable for the debts of the corporation. Since corporate shareholder-employees remain personally liable for their own actions, they are not protected from the consequences of these actions, even if occurring in the scope of their employment. This is particularly important in the professional corporation, where malpractice liability for the individual shareholder-employee is a significant risk. The professional is unable to use the corporate form of ownership to protect personal assets from liability caused by his or her own professional malpractice.

The corporate form of ownership does, however, provide significant liability limits for its owners. First, a closely held business with substantial assets may be able to obtain credit solely in the corporate name. The shareholders are liable for debts of an insolvent corporation only to the extent of their capital contribution.

Shareholders are also not personally liable for many of the risks associated with the operation of the business. For example, individual shareholders will not have to satisfy personal injury liability suits against the business not arising from the actions of the individual shareholder. This is a significant liability shelter in the modern liability theater, where courts and juries have taken an expansive view of the law concerning personal injury lawsuits.

Liability of Owners

- Proprietors—unlimited
- General partners—unlimited
- Limited partners—limited
- Members of LLCs—limited
- Stockholders—limited

In selecting the form of business ownership, limited liability is always preferable, to the extent that it is available. The need for and the ability to achieve limited liability depend on the actual business being formed. Obviously, passive investors obtain limited liability by (1) purchasing shares of stock in a corporation, (2) investing in a limited partnership interest, (3) investing in an LLC interest, or (4) where permissible, investing in an LLP.

However, owners who actively participate in business activities face a different situation. First, an owner who is actively involved in the business cannot be a limited partner. An owner of a closely held corporation or LLC is often forced to take personal risk for any credit obtained by the corporation or LLC. To this extent even an LLC or corporation does not completely shelter the closely held business owner from liability.

The decision of a professional as to the form in which to operate a professional practice may not be influenced to any great extent by unlimited personal liability. The primary risk of a practice is malpractice liability. Since all individuals remain personally liable for their actions, the professional cannot limit liability for his or her own malpractice by operating as an LLP or LLC or by incorporating. (Note that the state's LLP, LLC, or corporate law must authorize the professional to adopt such organizational forms.) A professional corporation, LLP, or LLC does, however, limit the liability of an owner-employee for actions of others in the enterprise performed while not under the direct supervision of the owner-employee. Since this also shields one professional from liability for the malpractice of another, this limitation can be significant.

The liability risks faced by business owners for the operation of a business are a highly significant concern. The risk of personal financial ruin resulting from losses or liabilities of the business is not a welcome prospect, but the desire to limit liability should not be the sole factor in selecting the form of organization. Many of these risks can be shifted through the purchase of insurance.

The Minimum Overall Tax Burden

Business owners and professionals are likely to derive most of their total income from their business or professional practice. The overall tax burden resulting from business- or practice-generated income will depend on the form of organization in which the business or practice operates. The progressive nature of federal income tax rates means that overall taxes will be lower if income can be divided between an owner and an entity. Regular C corporations are the only form of business entity with income tax liability separate from the owners. Business owners or professionals who choose to incorporate can often select between individual and corporate taxation of business income. Adding to the complexity of this situation is the fact that federal income tax rates and brackets differ for individuals and corporations.

Sole Proprietorship. Sole proprietorship income is taxed to the individual owner as self-employment income. The business does not have a separate tax status and does not file a tax return. Expenses incurred in the operation of the sole proprietorship are deductible from the owner's gross income under normal tax rules related to reasonable and ordinary business-expense deductions. The tax picture of the sole proprietorship is relatively clear, and it is encompassed in the overall personal tax planning of the owner.

pass-through entity

Pass-through Entity. Partnerships, LLCs, and S corporations have a somewhat unusual tax situation. These business organizations are not separate taxable entities, and their earnings are allocated among the business owners and taxed at their individual rates. Items of taxable income, capital gain, tax-exempt income, losses, deductions, and credits resulting from the business operations generally pass through in relation to the owners' relative interests in the business. The business owners take these items on their individual returns as they would any personal tax items.

Partnerships, LLCs, and S corporations do have separate entity status for some tax purposes. For example, they have separate tax-accounting methods from the owners. The entities must file an information return that provides each partner or S corporation shareholder with the appropriate share of tax items.

Pass-through entities are quite popular despite the fact that there is little or no difference between individual and corporate income tax rates. This is particularly true when the business owners want to take business losses or deductions on their individual returns. In addition, retained corporate earnings and appreciated corporate property will potentially face a double tax (tax at the entity level and at the individual level) that is not possible in a pass-through entity.

Corporation. The corporation is a separate legal entity with its own tax status and tax rates. It receives gross earnings and calculates its taxable income according to a set of rules applicable specifically to corporations. The shareholders of a corporation are taxed on the corporate earnings only when these earnings are distributed to them. The taxable distributions can take two forms. A shareholder-employee can be paid wages that are usually deductible by the corporation and taxable income to the employee. The corporation can also distribute earnings in the form of dividends to shareholders. However, dividends are nondeductible and still represent taxable income to the shareholder.

The tax treatment of dividends was made more favorable for "qualified dividends income" by the Jobs and Growth Tax Relief Reconciliation Act (JGTRRA) of 2003 and the Tax Increase Prevention and Reconciliation Act (TIPRA) of 2005. Qualifying dividends will be taxable at the capital gains rate before 2013. However, closely held corporations will generally avoid the distribution of dividends if possible.

Closely held corporations are composed of shareholders who are also the primary employees of the business. This structure facilitates potential income-splitting strategies. The shareholder-employees might set their salaries at a level where some earnings will be taxable to the shareholders and some income taxed and retained by the corporation. The shareholders' salaries can be set at a level to minimize the total tax liability, taking into consideration the tax at both the shareholder and corporate level.

Of course, compensation levels are subject to restrictions. First, salary levels must represent reasonable compensation to the shareholder-employee to be deductible by the corporation. Nondeductible salary payments to shareholders will be treated as dividends. Second, close cooperation between the shareholders is obviously required, since income retained by the corporation is not earmarked for individual shareholders and its future receipt is uncertain. Therefore the strategy of splitting taxable income between the corporation and its shareholders is best employed in the corporation held in equal shares by the owners. In this case it makes little difference from a practical standpoint whether income is paid out or retained by the corporation since all rights to the income (liquidation rights) are vested equally in the shareholders. Finally, nontax considerations, such as the adequacy of a shareholder-employee's salary, are of primary importance and may weigh against the minimum tax strategy.

One additional consideration is that personal service corporations are subject to a flat 35 percent tax rate—a marginal rate that may be less than that imposed on highly compensated professionals for some or all of their taxable income on their individual returns.

Of course, there are many nontax factors discussed above that favor the corporate form of ownership. The income-splitting potential is a significant tax advantage of incorporation. Many small closely held businesses might allow some income to be retained by the corporation to take advantage of lower brackets for some levels of income. This is particularly true if the income would otherwise be distributable to an owner in the highest personal income tax bracket.

Individual and Corporate Marginal Tax Rates. The tax rates applicable to individual and corporate income are presented in the tables below. One modification to the effective rate for business entities involves an incentive for encouraging domestic production. For business entities engaged in "domestic production activities," this provision will permit a deduction of 9 percent of domestic production income.

Table 1-1 Corporate Income Tax Rates

Taxable Income	Rate
$ 0–$50,000	15%
$50,001–$75,000	25%
$75,001–$10,000,000	34%
over $10,000,000	35%
For Taxable Income	
$100,000–$335,000 add	5%
$15,000,000–$18,333,333 add	3%
Personal-Service Corporations:	
All taxable income	35%

Table 1-2 Federal Income Tax Rates on Individual Income for 2011*

	Taxable Income	Rate
Married individuals filing joint returns	$0–$17,000	10%
	$17,001–$69,000	15%
	$69,001–$139,350	25%
	$139,351–$212,300	28%
	$212,301–$379,150	33%
	Over $379,150	35%
Heads of households	$0–$12,150	10%
	$12,151–$46,250	15%
	$46,251–$119,400	25%
	$ 119,401–$193,350	28%
	$193,351–$379,150	33%
	Over $379,150	35%
Single taxpayers	$ 0–$8,500	10%
	$ 8,501–$34,500	15%
	$ 34,501–$83,600	25%
	$83,600–$174,400	28%
	$174,401–$379,150	33%
	Over $379,150	35%

	Taxable Income	Rate
Married individuals filing separate returns	$ 0–$8,500	10%
	$ 8,501–$34,500	15%
	$ 34,501–$69,675	25%
	$69,676–$106,150	28%
	$106,151–$189,575	33%
	Over $189,575	35%

* Applicable to the owner's income from sole proprietorships, partnerships, LLCs, and S corporations. Taxable income brackets are indexed annually.

BUSINESS CONTINUITY

Lack of continuity is a major problem facing a closely held business. There are many reasons for a business to terminate, the most obvious of which is financial failure. However, the death, disability, or retirement of an owner or key employee may also result in continuation troubles for the business.

Common Business-Continuation Problems

A closely held business, regardless of whether it is incorporated, typically relies on the skills and services of relatively few individuals. These individuals have a broad involvement with every aspect of the business and are essential to its very survival. In the absence of proper planning the loss of any of these individuals will usually result in a decrease in income or in termination of the business.

The Death of a Business Owner

In theory the impact that the death of an owner has on a closely held business varies by the type of organization. At the death of the proprietor the business assets will be included in the proprietor's estate along with personal assets. These business assets typically have to be liquidated by the personal representative of the decedent-proprietor for an amount less than fair market value resulting in a reduced distribution to the proprietor's heirs. This situation can be avoided through estate-preservation techniques, such as the prearranged sale of the business as a going concern at the proprietor's death.

termination by operation of law

The death of a partner in a general partnership creates a similar problem. A general partnership *termination by operation of law* occurs at the death of one of the partners.

The surviving partners are faced with a dilemma that threatens the future of the business and the careers of the partners themselves. At the death of a partner the survivors must liquidate the partnership. They are faced with a difficult decision. If the business is terminated, the assets must be distributed according to the relative partnership interests or sold for an amount that might be substantially less than fair market value.

The surviving partners may prefer to form a new partnership and continue the business, but the deceased partner's estate must be paid a fair value for the decedent's interest. The surviving partners are required by law to deal fairly with the estate, even though the surviving partners and the partnership may not have adequate funds to distribute a fair share to the deceased partner's estate without liquidating the business. Without a binding prearranged agreement the surviving partners are also subject to claims of the heirs if the amount of the distribution to the estate is deemed unfair.

The limited partnership provides some relief from the business- continuation problems facing the general partnership because the death of a limited partner has no effect on the business. The limited partnership interest can be distributed to the heirs or sold by the estate, and the business will continue as an ongoing partnership with a new limited-investment partner. The death of a general partner in a limited partnership creates the same situation confronting the general partnership: the partnership is dissolved and its assets must be distributed or sold to provide for the estate and the liquidation rights of the survivors. This situation can be avoided either by (1) forming the limited partnership with a corporation as the general partner or (2) adopting an appropriate continuation plan for the limited partnership.

The LLC generally will have some continuity problems at the death of a member. As with any other business, the death of a key service provider will raise practical problems for the future success of the business. In some instances, an LLC will often provide for termination at the death of a member. As with partnerships, continuation of the business can be provided for under the operating agreement.

The corporation continues in existence as a legal entity beyond the lives of the individual shareholders. Does this mean that the corporation is the solution to every business-continuation problem? For the closely held corporation the answer is probably not.

A closely held business typically relies on the personal services of the individual owners. Their ownership interest in the business typically represents the owners' largest asset. While the corporation has a life independent of its owners, the loss of a significant contributor to the business can cause termination of its activities. Even if the deceased shareholder was not critical to the everyday business operations, the fact that the deceased shareholder's estate holds closely held corporate stock might present problems. If the stock held by the estate is substantial, the personal representative may want to dispose of this stock so that a cash distribution can be made to the heirs. If the deceased shareholder's holdings represent a majority interest, this sale will result in a new majority shareholder, which might change the direction of the corporation or, at the very least, disrupt the lives of the surviving shareholders.

Some problems may also arise at a minority shareholder's death. First, a minority interest will probably have to be sold at a discount. Second, the new minority shareholders, whether the heirs of the deceased shareholder or a subsequent purchaser, may have goals adverse to those of the surviving shareholders.

The Disability of an Owner

The continuation of a closely held business may also be imperiled by the loss of an owner's services for reasons other than death. Although a proprietorship or partnership does not terminate by operation of law upon the disability of an owner, the physical inability of the owner to perform services may have the same practical effect because the disabled owner's services must be replaced in some way. Since the owner probably has some special skill or knowledge of the business, this replacement may be difficult and very costly. The disabled owner might also require continued salary payment from the business for the period of disability. These added costs come at a time when the business income has diminished as a result of the loss of the owner's services.

An unsatisfactory arrangement between the disabled owner and the owners who continue to operate the business will usually result in the termination of the firm. The disabled proprietor, partner, or majority owner of a corporation has the power to force dissolution of the business if the disability income is inadequate. The owners who continue to work may also become dissatisfied with the burden of performing all the services of the business while continuing income payments to the disabled owner. In any event the disability will result in unsolvable continuation problems unless it has been prepared for in advance.

Planning for the contingency of an owner's disability may be even more important than planning for his or her death because the occurrence of a disability of at least 3 months is more likely than death at preretirement ages. A subsequent chapter will deal with plans to cover the disability of the business owner

Retirement of the Owner

The retirement of a business owner can have the same impact on the business as death or disability. If the business is to continue during the retirement of an owner, a replacement must be found if the owner performed essential services. The owner will also typically desire some kind of compensation from the business during retirement, which could be in the form of either continued salary payments, retirement plan benefits, or proceeds from the sale of the business interest. For the reasons mentioned in the discussion of an owner's death and disability, this situation can threaten continuation if not properly preplanned.

Fortunately the owner usually recognizes the need to plan for retirement because retirement is viewed as a certainty, whereas early death and disability are viewed as contingencies and are more psychologically convenient to ignore.

The Loss of Key Employees

key employee

The most significant employees of a closely held business are typically one or more of the owners, but many closely held businesses have nonowner employees who become quite valuable. The value of the *key employee* may result from unique skills, special knowledge of the business obtained through long service, and/or contacts with customers and creditors of the business.

The loss of a key employee can have a detrimental effect on the income of the closely held business and might even threaten its existence. The unique skill of the employee might be irreplaceable, or the replacement employee may have to be paid a higher salary and require costly training. A key employee who has important contacts with the closely held business's customers may terminate employment and work for a competitor. The death or disability of a key employee could result in the loss of customers and consequently business income.

The Adverse Effects of Business Termination

Business-continuation problems can occur for many reasons far removed from simple economic failure. The termination of a business will usually result in a direct adverse impact on all individuals closely affiliated with the enterprise.

The Cessation of Income From the Business to the Owner and Family

It is likely that an owner's interest in a closely held business is the most significant, or at least a major, asset held by its owner. If the owner has an active role in the business, his or her income from the business is probably necessary for the support of the owner and family. If the business terminates while the owner is still alive, a large portion of the business owner's income will also terminate. Until the business owner can find a replacement source of income, this can become a severe financial problem for him or her. The situation may be worse if the business terminates due to the owner's death, leaving the surviving spouse and dependents with no income unless the surviving spouse is substantially employable.

Proper planning can solve most of these problems. A continuation plan might prevent the business from terminating and therefore provide for a continuing flow of income. On the other hand, a properly designed sale of the business, although terminating the owner's interest in the business, could provide adequate proceeds for future support of the owner and family.

Sidetracked Careers of the Surviving Owners and Employees

There are severe problems for the business owner who dies, retires, or is disabled without an adequate continuation plan, but there is another significant problem. When a business terminates, the able-bodied co-owners and employees of the business also lose a major income source. For some, this may not be a problem. For example, employees of a terminated professional corporation or partnership can continue their careers in private practice. Other employees with marketable skills can find equivalent jobs elsewhere. The owners or employees may have unique skills designed solely for the now terminated closely held business. In this case it may be some time before their careers can be continued.

The Discounted Liquidation Value of Business Assets

The termination of a closely held business results either in the sale of the business as a going concern or liquidation of the assets on a piecemeal basis. The forced sale of a business following one of these causes of termination often results in receipt of proceeds that are less than satisfactory for two reasons. First, if a buyer is not found through advance planning, it may be difficult to find the appropriate buyer for the business on short notice. Second, a business terminating after the loss of an owner or substantial contributor has bleak prospects and is likely to be unattractive to potential buyers. A prearranged continuation plan or sale may avoid the possible diminution in value of the business.

When a Small Business Terminates

- Loss of income for owners and families
- Disruption of careers of remaining owners and employees
- Loss of value due to forced sale of assets

COMPENSATION AND FRINGE-BENEFIT PLANNING IN THE CLOSELY HELD BUSINESS

compensation planning

A discussion of the planning issues facing the closely held business owner or professional would not be complete without a discussion of *compensation planning.* The business owner or professional operating a business or professional practice is usually motivated by the desire to earn a living. The purpose of compensation and fringe benefit planning is to maximize the usefulness to the owners of any income earned by the business.

Planning the compensation and fringe benefits package of the organization requires a balancing of many different and often inconsistent goals. For example, investing in the future growth and income potential of a business may require the owner to temporarily accept less current compensation from the business.

Compensating the Owners

The compensation of business owners is frequently not given much thought. For example, the net income of a proprietorship flows through directly to the owner. It is assumed that owners of other types of enterprises who are active in the business will simply divide the profits among themselves. However, the form of organization, the owner's tax picture, the individual needs of the owners, and the needs of the business probably dictate a more thoughtfully designed compensation plan.

The Proprietor

The proprietor is entitled to all the profits of the business. Its income is taxed to the owner regardless of whether the income is retained by the proprietor for personal use or reinvested in the business. The compensation of the proprietor—the net income of the proprietorship—can be viewed as consisting of two components—part compensation for services to the business and part compensation for ownership (equity). The extent to which the proprietor consumes or reinvests the proprietorship income depends on the current and future needs of both the proprietor and the business.

Partners

A partnership by definition is owned by two or more individuals. As with the proprietorship, the partners of a general partnership have the right to all income. The actual share of each partner is determined at the end of the firm's tax year when the net income is calculated.

Partners report their distributive share of partnership income on their individual tax returns. As always, a decision must be made by the partners as to the portion of the distributive share that will be reinvested in the business as additional capital contributions. As we will discuss later, the portion of the distributive share reinvested in the partnership is still taxable to the partners but increases their tax bases in their partnership interests.

The method for determining the distributive shares of the various partners in a general partnership should be spelled out in the partnership agreement. If it is not, the partners will have to decide on the relative shares by negotiation. In the absence of a partnership agreement the IRS will allocate the tax burden ratably according to each partner's relative interests.

guaranteed payments

The circumstances surrounding partnership operations will usually dictate the division of partnership income. For example, the partners who provide substantial services to the partnership should receive a share that reflects their efforts. Service partners often receive fixed payments like salaries but known as *guaranteed payments*.

Partners who provide few or no services to the firm but have contributed large amounts of capital should receive a share of income reflecting their equity interests. The actual distributive share agreed upon may take into consideration the needs of the business and/or the tax brackets of the individual partners. However, the IRS may challenge any partnership allocation that does not properly reflect economic reality. That is, each partner's taxable distributive share must be reasonably related to services or capital contribution.

The partners will probably require cash distributions from the business at regular intervals for living expenses. Partnerships typically make periodic distributions known as draws to partners. The size and timing of these draws should be planned with due consideration to the cash needs of the partners, the cash needs of the business, and the expected annual distributive shares of the partners.

At the close of the partnership tax year the draws taken are compared to the partners' distributive shares. If the distributive shares are larger, partners may receive additional cash distributions. If draws were taken in excess of the distributive shares, the partners will either have to reimburse the partnership or decrease their capital accounts.

Each of these transactions has a potential impact on the tax bases of the partners that should not be ignored. Compensation planning for partners is a complex process and should not be done without thorough consideration of all the factors.

Limited-Liability Companies (LLCs)

The compensation of members of an LLC should follow the rules of a partnership, provided that the LLC elects partnership tax treatment. Thus income will flow out to members of an LLC in accordance with the provisions of the operating agreement. Special allocation of income and loss can be made for specific members. In addition, the service-providing members can receive guaranteed payments for their efforts.

For fringe-benefit purposes, members will be treated as self-employed. Thus the tax-advantaged fringe benefits available to members will be limited, similar to the benefits available to partners.

Shareholders

Compensation planning for the owners and owner-employees in corporations presents more options and more complexity than in the case of unincorporated businesses. Part of this is attributable to the need to compensate passive owners through dividends. However, most of the flexibility available in compensation planning for the corporation results from the status of the corporate entity and shareholder-employees as separate taxpayers.

Compensation planning for the corporation and its owners provides both opportunity and complexity. Fortunately a working knowledge of some of the technical rules provided later in this text along with the knowledge of the individual needs of the business client can result in successful compensation planning for the shareholders of closely held corporations.

The form of compensation to the owners of the closely held corporation may consist of cash (salary or bonuses), fringe benefits, or dividends. Since a corporation is a separate taxpaying entity, the manner in which corporate income is paid out to the owners has significant tax effects.

Salary payment to corporate employees, including shareholders, and most fringe benefit contributions are tax deductible to the corporation. Dividends provided to shareholders and payments to an employee above reasonable compensation levels are nondeductible. This results in the double taxation of dividends—and unreasonable compensation for services. That is, these amounts are taxed at the corporate level when the income is earned and again to the recipient when paid. Reasonable compensation to employees in the form of salary or bonuses is deductible by the corporation and therefore is taxed only once when paid to the employee.

The tax treatment of fringe benefits varies depending on the type of benefit. Some fringe benefits, such as group term life or health insurance, provide the ultimate in tax advantages. These types of benefits are deductible from corporate income while providing no taxable income to the shareholder-employee.

At first glance compensation planning for a closely held corporation appears easy. Why not pay out all corporate income in the form of salaries and fringe benefits and avoid the issues of double taxation and corporate tax altogether? While this may be the optimal plan for some closely held corporations, many factors weigh against this simple approach. Among these are the individual tax brackets of the owners, the needs of the business, the obligation to compensate passive shareholders, and the reasonable-compensation limitations.

RISK EXPOSURES OF THE CLOSELY HELD BUSINESS

In this section we will discuss some of the risks facing the closely held business, many of which can be avoided or handled through such techniques as insurance planning.

Risk exposures of the closely held business can be categorized in four general groups:

- losses suffered by business property
- loss in income or increase in expenses due to losses (consequential or indirect) suffered by the business property
- liability to third parties resulting from business activities
- personnel exposures

Losses to Business Property

The task of identifying the potential property losses of the business owner can be divided into two parts. First, it is necessary to identify the business property and determine the property that is subject to loss. Second, the types of hazards to which each piece of business property is exposed must be determined.

Exposed Business Property

real property

personal property

A good starting point for determining the business property exposed to loss is simply to take into account all the property under the ownership, use, and/or control of the business. Property is divided into two major categories—real and personal. *Real property* is defined as land and any property permanently affixed to the land. *Personal property* is commonly described as movables—anything not affixed to the land.

Generally speaking, most property in the control or ownership of the business is potentially subject to losses that must be borne by the business. Many of these exposures are already obvious to the business owner. For example, it is clear that the buildings and inventory owned by the business may be exposed to damage or destruction. However, the identification of all exposed business property will require careful analysis. Potential losses to some property are often inadvertently ignored when property exposures are being evaluated. For example, accounts receivable are assets of the business that, if destroyed, may be difficult to collect.

In some cases the ownership risks of property are unclear. A good example occurs in the sale of real property. Depending on local law, the risk of loss for real property may shift to the purchaser when a contract for the sale of the property is formed. This may transpire even though the settlement date and the actual transfer of possession occur later. The risk may not be obvious to the purchaser, but it is easily handled if the financial services professional recommends the timely purchase of homeowners insurance.

The sale or purchase of goods by the business is another example of debated ownership. When goods are being shipped to and from the business, the change of title depends on the circumstances of the sale and state commercial law. A business may often bear the risk of loss for goods being shipped to or from the business without actual possession.

The business may also be subject to a loss for property not actually owned at the time the loss occurs. Such a loss can occur in the case of properties that are (1) leased, (2) held for others, and (3) held as collateral by the business.

Although the risk of loss is generally borne by the owner of property, a loss may occur to property the business leases. First, the business is subject to loss on any improvements made to the leased premises. Second, the business may be held legally responsible for loss by the property owner. Finally, the business could suffer some additional expense in securing replacement property.

Many businesses such as furriers, repair shops, and warehouses, commonly have the property of others under their control. The individual who holds property for another is known as the bailee and the property held as the bailment. Should the bailment be damaged while in the hands of the bailee due to the bailee's negligence, the bailee's business will bear the risk of the loss. This type of loss can occur in any business that occasionally holds the property of others. In any event possible exposure to bailee liability should be examined and protection secured.

Exposure may also arise if business sales are transacted on a credit basis. It is not uncommon for the purchaser of the business property to secure the credit by pledging property as collateral. The creditor has an interest in and bears a risk of loss to any property used as collateral. The amount of the loss will be equal to the unpaid balance of the loan to the purchaser.

It should be clear at this point that all possible property exposures of the business are not easily identifiable at first glance. Consequently it is recommended that the business owner seek the assistance of a professional in identifying possible property loss exposures in both the business's customary operations and any unusual, but foreseeable, operations.

The Causes of Loss to Business Property

Once this first step of the procedure—identifying the business property subject to loss—is complete, the next step in the process of managing risks is to identify all the possible causes of loss.

Many potential causes of loss are obvious and will not be listed here in an extensive fashion. All business owners know that any owned business premises and contents are subject to many direct losses. Buildings, inventory, and fixtures are subject to loss from fire, explosion, lightning, theft, and employee dishonesty. These risks can be handled by insurance.

Many risks of loss depend on the specialized nature of the business; for example, a business that ships products to customers may be exposed to transportation risks not common to other businesses. Perhaps the business makes a product that must be maintained at specific climate conditions. This type of business bears a specialized risk because of the possibility of failure of refrigeration or heating equipment. It is important for the owner of a business to seek professional advice for managing such risks. It is equally important for professionals to be familiar with the businesses of owners they advise and experienced in the various types of insurance products used to handle these risks.

Consequential Losses

consequential losses

Consequential losses are losses that decrease the net income of a business as a result of a direct loss. Net income can be decreased for either of two reasons. First, the gross receipts may be reduced if operations are curtailed due to a direct loss. Second, a firm may be subject to increased operating expenses as a result of a direct loss.

Decrease in Gross Receipts

One type of indirect loss resulting from damage to business property is a decrease in receipts because of a shutdown or slowdown in operations while the damaged property is repaired or replaced. Diminished gross receipts are typically categorized in two types of exposure—business interruption or dependent business interruption.

Business Interruption. Losses to business property may cause a business to suspend or decrease operations while the damaged property is repaired or replaced. In evaluating this type of exposure, the business owner should consider (1) the decrease in receipts that will occur and (2) the time period during which the income will be decreased. The types of losses that can occur should be determined in full when the business owner evaluates all the property subject to loss exposure.

The time needed to repair or replace the damaged property will indicate the duration of this indirect business-interruption loss. Among the types of indirect losses that can occur during the period of interruption are (1) lost sales during the period of shutdown, (2) lost profit on finished goods destroyed by a direct loss, and (3) lost rental income during a period that rental property is uninhabitable.

Specifics of the individual business must be examined to determine the possible interruption losses. For example, a firm in the business of renting real estate is subject to the loss of rental income if any of the property is damaged. Provisions of the leases used by the business and local law should be examined to determine whether the rental payment will cease during the period the building is uninhabitable. To establish the business-interruption loss in a manufacturing business, it is necessary to know the profits expected from sales lost during the possible periods of interruption. Although this process may sound complex, a professional trained in analyzing this type of risk should be able to estimate potential business-interruption loss exposure.

Dependent Business Interruption. Dependent business-interruption exposure is a loss that is easy to overlook. This type of loss occurs when a business suffers a decrease in income as a result of a loss at the premises of another business. To be exposed to this loss, a business must rely substantially on another firm for its income. As an example, the business may purchase all of a key raw material from a single supplier, or the business might sell all of its products to one major customer.

A direct loss resulting in a shutdown or curtailment in the key dependent firm's operations may have a substantial impact on the income of the business that is being examined. As discussed earlier with business interruption, the duration and magnitude of the dependent business-interruption exposure must be determined.

Extra Expense

Some businesses must remain in operation whenever possible following a loss. For example, newspapers, banks, or professional practices will suffer a loss of customer goodwill if shutdowns occur for any length of time. Their solution is to remain open and absorb any necessary additional costs. New premises or equipment may have to be secured at a premium on short notice. In this respect there is no interruption of business receipts, but income decreases by the amount of extra expenses incurred.

A business that is shut down following a loss will also incur expense costs. Many business expenses, such as business overhead expenses and salaries of key employees, may have to be continued during a temporary business interruption. The expenses represent an interruption loss to the business since they are incurred while the income flow to the business has ceased.

Property Loss Exposures

- Loss of value of owned assets
- Loss of value of nonowned assets
  - Assets bought or sold
  - Assets leased
  - Assets held as bailee
  - Assets held as collateral
- Consequential losses
  - Reduced income
  - Added expenses

Liability to Third Parties

In general the liability risks faced by businesses are the most complex and substantial with which to deal. The liability we are concerned with here is the duty of the business or business owner to indemnify third parties for injuries suffered as a result of operations for which the enterprise is legally liable. The trend in the courts is to award extremely high monetary liability judgments, thus imposing a broadened duty on businesses to respond to injuries that are suffered by members of society resulting from their operations.

Liability exposures are sometimes obvious but in other cases may arise in surprising situations. In the next chapter we will discuss the situation in which a business entity will become liable for the acts of both its owners and hired individuals. The types of liabilities faced by a business depend a great deal on its specific operations. Common examples of liability exposures include

- *liability for the operation of a business.* There are several types of specific liability risks within this general category. First is the liability for injuries to third parties suffered on business premises. Second is the liability of the business for acts of its agents and employees. Third, the business is subject to the so-called products-liability risk. In these cases the business is legally liable for the negligent manufacture of products. In some cases the business may be strictly liable (liable even without fault) for injuries resulting from its products. Finally, the business may become liable to other businesses for such things as unfair trade practices or patent infringement.
- *automobile liability.* A business that uses vehicles in the normal course of operations is subject to a substantial risk of automobile liability. This is particularly true if the firm uses traveling salespersons or delivery vehicles.
- *professional malpractice liability.* A growing area of concern to many businesses, particularly professional practices, is the area of professional malpractice liability. The malpractice standard is being applied to a growing list of professions and imposes a requirement of skillful practice by the professional toward clients.
- *liability of directors and officers.* A growing trend in corporate law is to judicially test the actions of directors and officers while acting on behalf of the corporation. A negligent director or officer may become liable to the shareholders. This type of liability may be a particular concern to the closely held business if director actions are performed with the intent of enhancing the interest of majority shareholders while circumventing the rights of the minority.
- *personal liability.* Personal liability includes injury for such events as false arrest, defamation, and invasion of privacy.
- *specialized liability exposures.* Some businesses may be exposed to specialized liability risks that must be investigated and handled.

For example, aviation liability or ocean marine liability may be incurred by businesses involved in those activities.

- *workers' compensation and employee liability*.

Personnel Exposures

Workers' Compensation and Employer's Liability

Workers' compensation is liability imposed by statute on employers for injuries or illnesses of employees arising out of employment. All states have workers' compensation statutes that provide the coverage and benefit amounts available to employees. The liability imposed on employers for employee injuries or illnesses is on a strict or no-fault basis. That is, the employer must provide the benefits regardless of the absence or presence of negligence on its part.

Virtually all types of employers treated in this text are covered by workers' compensation statutes. The employer may be proprietor, partnership, or corporation, whether nonprofit, municipal, or government agency. The statutory definition of the employer-employee relationship essential to impose workers' compensation coverage arises out of common law. The employer has the right to control the actions of the employee, and the work is being performed as part of the regular business of the employer. Independent contractors are not included in this definition and therefore are not covered by the workers' compensation statutes.

Some employees are excluded from coverage of the state workers' compensation laws. For example, most states provide exclusions for farm workers, domestic employees, and casual employees. A number of states have exclusions for small businesses, typically allowing the exclusion of firms with fewer than a minimum number of employees (for example, two to five).

In evaluating the workers' compensation risk for the small closely held business, the appropriate state statutes should be examined. Any employment settings excluded by workers' compensation statutes are still subject to traditional legal action by employees. That is, employees in excluded employment may assert a claim based on normal negligence standards limited by the common-law defenses of the employer.

In general, all injuries or illnesses that are causally related to employment are covered by the statutes. The typical law provides for benefits in the following categories:

- medical expense benefits, usually without limits
- weekly indemnity benefits to replace lost income limited in benefit amount and duration
- death benefits for the worker's survivors
- scheduled benefits for specific permanent injuries
- rehabilitation benefits

Death or Disability of Key Employees

The death or disability of a key employee may have an effect on a closely held business similar to a property loss in that the key employee's services may be critical to the income of the firm. The permanent or temporary loss of a key employee may result in a decrease in income and/or an increase in expenses to the employing firm.

The business may find that the key employee's special skills are irreplaceable, and the income decrease may be permanent. Often the employee may be replaced but only at a higher cost resulting in a permanent increase in expenses. In any event the closely held business relying on key employees should be advised of the associated risk and take appropriate action to protect its interests.

CHAPTER REVIEW

Key Terms and Concepts

limited-liability company (LLC)
closely held business
limited partnership
limited-liability partnership (LLP)
pass-through entity
termination by operation of law
key employee
compensation planning
guaranteed payments
real property
personal property
consequential losses

Review Questions

The answers to the review questions are in the supplement. The self-test questions and the answers to them are also in the supplement and on The American College Online.

1. What forms of organization can be chosen by the business to carry out an enterprise? [1]
2. How do the formalities of forming a business differ among sole proprietorships, partnerships, LLCs, and corporations? [1]
3. How is the control of business management established in a corporation? [1]
4. What are the possible restrictions on the flexibility of the owners to alter current operating status quo in [1]
   a. sole proprietorships
   b. partnerships
   c. limited-liability companies (LLCs)
   d. corporations
5. Why might business owners anticipating large capital expansion needs consider the formation of a limited partnership rather than a general partnership? [1]
6. Explain what is meant by limited liability, and identify the types of enterprises that provide this advantage to their owners. [1]
7. Explain what is meant by a pass-through entity for tax purposes. [2]
8. Explain how overall taxes might be minimized through income splitting between a corporation and its shareholders. [2]
9. Why does the loss of an owner of a closely held business represent a threat to business continuation? [3]
10. In the absence of continuation planning, what is the status of a general partnership following the death of a partner? [3]

11. Does a closely held corporation legally terminate at the death of a shareholder-employee? Explain. [3]
12. What burden does a disabled owner-employee place on a closely held business? [3]
13. How might the loss of a key nonowner-employee threaten the continuity of a business? [3]
14. What are two reasons why the forced sale of a business might yield unsatisfactory proceeds? [3]
15. Distinguish between a partner's draw and distributive share. [4]
16. What are the four general categories of risk exposure facing a business? [5]
17. Under what circumstances might the risk of loss of nonowned property become a concern for a closely held business? [5]
18. Explain how consequential losses cause the reduced net income of a business. [5]
19. What are the liability exposures resulting from business operations? [5]
20. What types of employers might be excluded from mandatory state workers' compensation coverage? [5]
21. What are the potential results of the loss of a key employee by a closely held business? [5]

UNINCORPORATED BUSINESS ENTERPRISES 2

Learning Objectives

An understanding of the material in this chapter should enable the student to

1. Describe how a proprietorship is formed and the legal unity of the business and personal assets of the proprietor.
2. Explain how a proprietorship is taxed for federal income tax purposes.
3. Describe the types of partnerships, how they are operated, and how different partnerships affect the liability of partners.
4. Explain how a partnership is dissolved, and distinguish dissolution from winding up and termination.
5. Explain how partners are taxed for income tax purposes and how a partner's income tax basis is affected by partnership operations.
6. Describe the characteristics of an LLC.

Business enterprises can take four basic forms—proprietorship, partnership, limited-liability company (LLC), or corporation. A business owner must decide which form of organization is most advantageous in light of the owner's goals for the enterprise. We will systematically discuss the factors that should be considered in making the appropriate choice.

Of the four types of business enterprises, three are unincorporated—proprietorships, partnerships, and LLCs. In this chapter we will discuss the characteristics of unincorporated enterprises and indicate the advantages and disadvantages of each form to the business owner.

Material presented in the next chapter will cover the corporate form of business ownership. Together the two chapters will provide the financial services professional with guidance to assist the business owner in choosing the appropriate form of organization.

PROPRIETORSHIPS

proprietorship

The simplest and most common form of business enterprise is the *proprietorship*. Recent statistics indicate that slightly less than 72 percent of businesses are operated as proprietorships.[1] However, despite their large numbers proprietorships are relatively small, with only a little over 4 percent of the total gross receipts of all business enterprises.

The simplicity of proprietorships is a result of the unity between the business owner and the business. The proprietor owns the business assets, manages the business, and conducts business affairs. As the business grows, the proprietor typically delegates some of the business transactions to independent agents and employees. This exposes the proprietor (principal) to the risks associated with transacting business through agents and employees since the proprietor has personal liability for all activities within the scope of the business.

The Legal Unity of a Proprietor and a Proprietorship

The formation of a proprietorship is accomplished by the owner's transfer of the necessary assets to the business. With the business assets assembled, all that is necessary for the owner to begin operations is for the proprietorship to hang up the proverbial shingle and open the business doors. The beauty of the proprietorship formation is its simplicity compared to the formation of other types of business enterprises.

A relevant concern at this point is the legal status of the assets converted by the proprietor to business use. From both a practical and a legal standpoint, the assets transferred to the business by the proprietor have not changed status. The owner's interest in the business property remains the same as when the property was a personal asset. The owner has the right to control, transfer, or encumber the property in the same manner as if the property had never been transferred to the business. Should the proprietor decide to cease operations, unencumbered business assets can be withdrawn or disposed of subject to the whim of the proprietor.

The unity between the proprietor and the proprietorship creates a unique liability risk. Since there is no legal distinction between the business and the

---

1. U.S. Bureau of the Census, Statistical Abstract of the United States: 2011 (130th ed.), Washington, D.C., 2011.

personal property of the proprietor, the owner's personal property is exposed to satisfy liabilities incurred in the operation of the business.

Conversely, the assets of the business are likewise exposed to any personal debts of the owner. This unlimited personal liability may be enough to discourage potential business owners from taking the risk necessary to form a proprietorship. From the standpoint of the business, the continuity or expansion of the business may be threatened by the personal financial failures of the proprietor.

The unlimited liability of the proprietor for business debts can be avoided in some circumstances. For example, proprietorship debts can be arranged as nonrecourse obligations. A nonrecourse loan limits the assets available to satisfy the debt to the mortgaged or secured property. In this case the debt liability could be limited to specific proprietorship assets. However, the practical application of nonrecourse financing may be limited since creditors of a small business will typically require the owner to personally guarantee the loans.

The Termination of a Proprietorship

A proprietorship may terminate for several different reasons. First, since the business is under the sole control of the proprietor, it may terminate by the voluntary action of the owner.

Second, the proprietorship may terminate by operation of state law for the following reasons:

- bankruptcy of the proprietor
- legal incapacity of the proprietor
- death of the proprietor
- a change in the law that makes the business of the proprietorship illegal

Termination due to operation of law is the natural result of the legal unity of the proprietor and the proprietorship. Since the enterprise has no separate legal status from the owner, the continued existence of a solvent, competent owner is necessary for the proprietorship to remain in operation.

The continuity problem is another disadvantage of this form of business ownership. A goal of business ownership is to provide a stream of income to the business owner and family. The termination of the proprietorship for any of the reasons mentioned above eliminates the flow of business income to the owner. Often this occurs at a time when the business owner or his or her family can least afford the income to stop—in the event of death or disability of the owner.

Federal Income Taxation of Proprietorships

The taxation of proprietorships illustrates the unity of the proprietor and the proprietorship. Proprietorship income is simply combined with other income to arrive at the proprietor's total income. The proprietorship income is reported on the owner's individual return, and no separate filing by the business is required. Most tax benefits available under the Internal Revenue Code (IRC) to other forms of business enterprises are also available to proprietorships.

Taxation of Income

As stated above, a proprietorship is considered an extension of the owner for federal income tax purposes. The proprietorship's profit or loss is computed on Schedule C of the owner's federal income tax return (Form 1040). The net income (or loss) from the business is then simply added to (or subtracted from) the owner's income from other sources. Business deductions resulting in a net loss for the proprietorship year are taken "above the line" and are available regardless of whether the taxpayer itemizes deductions.

In general most tax benefits available to other businesses are also available to proprietorships. For example, the proprietorship may take depreciation and other forms of business deductions. The deduction against income from domestic production activities is available for proprietorships engaged in such activities. However, proprietorship business deductions are available directly to the owner rather than indirectly through the tax return of a legal entity, as in the case of a corporation.

Profits received from the proprietorship activities flow directly through to the proprietor. The tax rates applicable to the business profits of the proprietorship are the same as those applicable to any other kind of income of the proprietor. Since the proprietorship is not a separate taxable entity, income from proprietorship operations is taxed only once—to the owner—rather than twice, as is the case when a corporation distributes income in the form of dividends to its owners. This proprietorship income is taxed to the owner at individual income tax rates.

Taxation of Formation and Dissolution

In general neither the formation nor the termination of a proprietorship is a taxable event to the proprietor. Since the assets converted to business use by the proprietor remain the proprietor's assets, there is no recognition of gain when the assets are put into use by the proprietorship. Similarly when the proprietorship is terminated, the business assets remain the property of the proprietor and no recognition of gain or loss occurs. However, if the proprietorship assets are transferred, the usual rules for recognizing gain or loss on the transfer of property apply.

The Advantages and Disadvantages of Proprietorships

First and foremost among the advantages of operating a business enterprise as a proprietorship is its simplicity. Since the business is treated as an extension of the owner, there is no separate legal entity. The proprietorship can be set up more quickly and at a lower cost than any other form of enterprise. In the same vein, the proprietorship can change its operations without the necessity of complying with partnership agreements or corporate charters. This allows the proprietor to react quickly to opportunities without the hindrances that could slow or frustrate the efforts of other business owners. The proprietorship is able to respond more quickly than any other type of business organization to changing economic trends or business opportunities. Finally, the proprietor can terminate operations and dispose of business assets without the complexities involved in liquidating a partnership or corporation.

A second advantage is that the proprietor is the sole owner of the business and is generally entitled to all the benefits of its operation. In most cases other forms of enterprise involve the sharing of profits with at least one other, and perhaps many, co-owner(s). From a tax standpoint the profits of the proprietorship are taxable income of the proprietor with no possibility of double taxation as might be the case in the corporate form of ownership. All the tax benefits associated with business operations, such as expense deductions, are also taken directly by the proprietor.

The principle of unity between the proprietorship and the proprietor also results in several disadvantages of the proprietorship form of business enterprise. The first disadvantage is the inherent limit on the potential business growth associated with the proprietorship. Although every business requires an influx of capital to expand or enter new markets, a proprietorship is limited to the capital funds that can be raised by the proprietor. As a result the funds must be either contributed from the personal assets of the owner or obtained through whatever credit is available to the owner. The growth of a proprietorship is limited relative to other forms of business organization where more owners are available to contribute capital. Also other forms of organization are distinct legal entities and may have the ability to raise capital in their own name.

A second disadvantage is that all management responsibilities fall on the shoulders of one individual. Although this gives the proprietorship the advantage of flexible and responsive decision making, it also puts all the business pressures associated with major decision making on the proprietor. The proprietor may operate through agents and employees to whom many day-to-day responsibilities can be delegated. However, the proprietor, as the principal, is ultimately responsible for the actions of these agents or employees acting within the scope of employment. Finally, there are many activities that cannot be delegated, the burden for which must remain with the proprietor.

A third disadvantage is the continuity problem. Since the proprietor and the proprietorship are not legally distinct entities, the proprietor must be solvent, legally competent, and alive for the proprietorship to continue. Although the business-continuation problems associated with the operation of a proprietorship will be discussed at length later in the text, it is worth mentioning now that the proprietorship terminates at the death of the proprietor. Two problems associated with the termination of the proprietorship at death are that (1) all income derived from the operation of the proprietorship ceases and (2) the proprietorship assets must be either sold or distributed in kind to the beneficiaries of the deceased proprietor's estate.

A final disadvantage is the unlimited liability of the proprietor for the operations of the proprietorship. With the exception of nonrecourse proprietorship debt, the proprietor is personally liable for all the obligations and liabilities of the proprietorship. Since no one relishes the thought that his or her ownership of a business will result in personal financial ruin, this is an obvious deterrent to forming the business as a proprietorship.

Advantages and Disadvantages of Proprietorships

Advantages

- Simple and inexpensive to form and to terminate
- Owner has full control
- No sharing of the profits

Disadvantages

- Difficult to raise additional capital
- Wide range of management responsibilities for the owner
- Automatic termination on death, bankruptcy, or legal incapacity of owner
- Unlimited liability

PARTNERSHIPS

partnership

Another major type of unincorporated business is the *partnership*, defined as "an association of two or more persons to carry on as co-owners of a business for profit."[2] The partnership may be distinguished from other forms of enterprise such as joint ventures and nonprofit associations that have characteristics of association but operate for limited time periods or purposes. The focus of our discussion will be the two types of partnerships—the general partnership and the limited partnership.

General Partnerships

general partnership

The typical commercial partnership existing under the principles of common law is the *general partnership*. The partners in a general partnership are typically coequals in the ownership and management of the partnership. Each partner is considered a principal with full authority to act on behalf of the partnership and other partner(s). In this sense general partners are also agents of each of the other general partners. That is, each general partner is a fiduciary of the partnership and the other general partners. The general partners have the duty of loyalty and must exercise good-faith judgment when representing the partnership in the scope of the partnership's business. Each general

---

2. Uniform Partnership Act, Section 6, 1914.

partner is entitled to a share of partnership profits and remains ultimately liable for the debts and obligations of the partnership.

Partnerships are typically governed by statutory provisions adopted under various state laws. The general partnership is governed by the Uniform Partnership Act (UPA) of 1914, which has been adopted by the vast majority of states. The financial services professional should be advised that there are differences in the state laws governing partnerships. Questions about the details of the formation and operation of partnerships should be resolved by seeking legal assistance or consulting local law.

Limited-Liability Partnerships

limited-liability partnership (LLP)

All states have enacted legislation authorizing the *limited-liability partnership (LLP)*. The LLP is a partnership form in which all general partners have limited liability. This is expected to be an extremely popular form of partnership. For example, it is noteworthy that several large accounting partnerships have selected the LLP form of enterprise.

An LLP cannot be formed unless a state statute authorizes its formation and the partnership has made the required filing with the state. It can be distinguished from a traditional limited partnership since all general partners can obtain limited liability. Thus a general partner can have an active role in the partnership and still have the liability shelter. An LLP is also more attractive to an existing general partnership than conversion to a limited liability company (LLC) because the existing partnership agreement and the operating characteristics do not have to be significantly changed. However, be aware that there are differences between state laws, and some states limit the types of professions that can organize as an LLP.

Limited Partnerships

A limited partnership is defined as a partnership that includes at least one general partner and one limited partner. The major distinction between a limited and a general partnership is reflected in the responsibilities of the various actors in the limited-partnership setting. The general partner has responsibilities identical to the partners in a general partnership. That is, the general partner has the everyday decision-making authority for the partnership. The general partner also has unlimited personal liability for the operations of the partnership. On the other hand, the limited partner has responsibilities similar to those of a of passive shareholder in a corporation.

He or she is a capital contributor to the partnership but has no management authority and incurs no liability beyond the initial capital contributed to the partnership and any additional capital contributions required under the partnership agreement.

Limited partnerships did not exist at common law and can be formed only where special statutes have been enacted to permit their adoption. The Uniform Limited Partnership Act (ULPA) of 1916 was a model statute after which most state uniform limited-partnership statutes were designed. All states except Louisiana have adopted some form of the ULPA. Many states have begun to adopt a Form of the Revised Uniform Limited Partnership Act of 1976 (modified again in 1985). Again the financial services professional should consult state law concerning the rules related to limited partnerships.

Role of a Limited Partner

- Provide capital
- Incur limited liability
- Have no active role in operations

Partnership Property

An understanding of the nature of partnership property is essential to the understanding of the partner's rights in the property. Partnership property is any property originally contributed to the partnership by the partners and any property subsequently acquired in the partnership name. Although this rule sounds quite clear, extensive litigation has developed regarding whether property held by a partnership belongs to the partnership or to one or more individual partners. The general rule states that the intent of the partners will control any questions of ownership. This intent should be clearly specified in the original partnership agreement. However, intent of the partners can also be construed from their actions.

EXAMPLE

When Chip and Muffy formed a partnership, Chip contributed $75,000 cash and Muffy contributed property worth $25,000. The partnership agreement provides that Chip is entitled to 75 percent of the partnership profits and Muffy is entitled to 25 percent of the profits.

> Chip also contributed two trucks worth $15,000 to the partnership, for which he is paid an annual fee of $5,000. The question of whether the trucks are partnership property or remain Chip's personal property can be determined from factual evidence. First, Chip is paid an annual fee by the partnership for the use of the trucks. Second, the fixed ratio for division of profits does not reflect the trucks as a contribution of capital. These facts lead to the conclusion that the partners never intended the trucks to become partnership property but, in fact, are leased by the partnership.

The Partnership Interest

tenants in partnership

Once it is determined that property is partnership property, what are the rights of the partners with respect to that property? It is said that the partners hold specific partnership property as *tenants in partnership*, which in effect means that each partner has an undivided interest in each specific partnership asset. This interest gives each partner the right to use partnership property for partnership business. However, it does not give a partner the right to personal use of the property or the right to transfer the property without the consent of the other partners.

partnership interest

Once a partnership is formed and holds property, each partner is said to own a *partnership interest* that is an intangible personal property right. In this sense it is similar to a shareholder's interest in a corporation represented by the ownership of stock and provides each partner with specific benefits and responsibilities. For example, the partnership interest held by a partner provides the partner with a right to share in the profits and surplus of the partnership. The actual amount of profit and distributable surplus that represents each partner's share is determined by the partnership agreement.

The partnership interest is considered personal property and is treated as such for inheritance tax and succession purposes, despite the fact that the partnership may be holding title to real property. As a personal property right, each partner's interest in the partnership is transferable by the individual partner. The partnership interest can be sold, gifted, bequeathed, and used as collateral by the partner. However, it is important to note that the individual partner can transfer his or her interest but has no right to transfer specific partnership property. The actual partnership property is held as tenants in partnership by the partners, and a transfer, other than an ordinary course-of-business sale, cannot be made by one partner individually without the consent of the other partners. An unauthorized transfer of property by a partner may be effective to a good-faith purchaser, but the nonconsenting partners may hold the partner who made the transfer liable for the resulting losses.

assignee in interest

The transfer of a partnership interest does not terminate the partnership. The transferee does not automatically become a partner but holds other rights related to the partnership interest. That is, the transferee of the interest obtains the right to share in the surplus and profits of the partnership. In this respect the interest of the transferee is equivalent to that previously held by the transferor. The transferee who is not admitted as a partner is known as an *assignee in interest*.

EXAMPLE

Moe, Jim, and Curly are equal general partners in a sporting goods partnership. Jim is beset by personal financial difficulties and sells his partnership interest to Larry. Since partnership requires a voluntary association, Larry does not automatically become a partner with Moe and Curly. However, Larry's partnership interest does provide him with certain rights, such as a share of profits and a liquidation share if the partnership is dissolved. Of course, Moe and Curly could choose to make Larry a partner through a voluntary agreement.

In a general partnership, the partnership interest provides all partners with the right to participate in the management of the partnership. This right gives the partner the responsibility for the basic decision-making aspects of running the business. Each partner is a principal with the ability to hire agents and delegate certain ministerial duties to agents or employees. The partner is also a general agent of the partnership and the other partners and has the authority to represent the partnership in the ordinary course of business. Since the partnership interest does not provide the individual partners with rights to specific partnership property, individual partners typically do not have the power to dispose of partnership property. Such property may be disposed of by all the partners acting in concert or by an individual partner acting as an agent for the partnership if the sale is in the ordinary course of business. These restrictions are not present in a proprietorship, in which the proprietor owns the property and retains full dominion and control over business property.

A limited partnership is composed of at least one general and one limited partner. The general partner holds all the rights inherent in the partnership interest mentioned above. However, the limited partner's rights are restricted to a share of profits and surplus as determined by the size of the limited-partnership interest held. The limited partner does not participate in the management of the partnership and has no authority to act on behalf of the partnership. In this sense the limited partner's partnership interest is somewhat similar to a passive shareholder's interest in a publicly held corporation.

The Liability of Partners

General Partnerships

The property interest that a partner holds in the partnership gives the partner not only specific rights but also specific responsibilities. As is the case with proprietorships, a general partner assumes unlimited liability for the partnership business operations and also for the actions of the other partners acting on behalf of the partnership within the ordinary course of partnership business. This unlimited liability extends beyond the partner's capital contributions and share of profit or surplus. The general partner's personal assets may be exposed by partnership liabilities.

The partnership as an operating business creates an exposure to many liability risks. The assets of the partnership, along with the personal assets of any general partner, may be required to satisfy the debts and liabilities of the partnership. The general partners in the partnership are said to be jointly and severally liable for these debts, resulting in the possible exposure of each general partner to unlimited liabilities for the operation of the partnership.

EXAMPLE

Able and Baker are partners in the AB general partnership. While on the road selling AB products, Able drives negligently and strikes a pedestrian with the AB van. The pedestrian sues Able, Baker, and AB for damages and is awarded a large judgment. Since Able was within the scope of the partnership business during his actions, the partnership and all the partners are jointly and severally liable. The judgment could first be settled out of the AB partnership property. If AB's assets are insufficient to satisfy the judgment, Able and Baker are liable for the balance out of their personal funds.

Note: If one partner is sued and pays the judgment out of his or her own funds, that partner may have rights of contribution from the other partners. In the example above, Baker could seek contribution from Able for any personal funds paid to satisfy the judgment since Able's negligence created the liability.

Limited-Liability Partnerships

If the partnership organizes or converts to an LLP, the general partnership can have its normal operating characteristics with the added advantage of limited liability for the owners. Under the most favorable LLP laws, partners are not liable (directly or indirectly) for any debts, obligations, or liabilities of the partnership. The liability protection extends to actions arising from personal injury or contract if the loss was incurred by the LLP. Thus a partner has no personal liability for partnership losses solely by being a general partner or otherwise participating in the conduct of the business.

However, an important concept concerning personal liability must be reinforced. Each partner, employee, or agent of the LLP will be personally liable for any negligent or wrongful act committed by (1) himself or herself or (2) any individual under the partner's direct supervision and control while rendering professional services on behalf of the LLP.

EXAMPLE

Able and Baker are partners in a medical clinic in which they provide medical services. They employ two other physicians who work in the clinic. Since their state law permits, they decide to file for LLP status. Able and Baker each remain personally liable for their own malpractice and the malpractice of any clinic employee when that employee is under their direct supervision. However, each partner is not individually liable for the claims against the partnership caused by the malpractice of another partner or physician-employee.

General and, in some cases, limited partnerships register for LLP status by filing the required documents with the Secretary of State or other state agency and by conforming with statutory requirements for LLP status. It will generally be required that a partnership holding LLP status use some designator (for example, LLP) after its partnership name on its stationery to indicate the partners' limited-liability status to third parties who do business with the LLP.

Limited Partnerships

Limited partnerships are distinguished from LLPs in the liability exposure of the general partners. A major distinction between the general partner and the limited partner in a limited partnership is the exposure to liability from partnership operations. The limited partnership provides relief for the limited partners from the harsh result of all partners becoming liable for partnership debts and obligations beyond each partner's contribution to the firm. Since the general partner retains unlimited liability for the operations of the partnership, at least one partner in the limited partnership is ultimately liable beyond his or her contribution to the partnership. However, the limited partners are typically liable to the extent of the capital contributed and their rights to any profits and surplus of the firm.

Clever schemes have been devised in an effort to limit liability in a partnership setting. For example, a corporation could become a general partner while all individual investors hold limited-partner status. The liability shelter provided to limited partners will be allowed only if the partners are actually limited partners. Courts have devised tests to determine the status of a partner as either limited or general. A purported limited partner may become liable as a general partner if the limited partner's actions extend to the management control of the business.

The extent of control required to impute the status of general partner to a limited partner depends on the facts and circumstances of the individual case. However, it is clear that participation in the major decision-making activities of the firm will remove the limited-liability shield from the limited partner.

Dissolution of the Partnership

Partnerships require the voluntary association of two or more individuals. Inherent in this concept is the necessity of continuing voluntary cooperation between the partners for the success and very existence of the partnership. The failure of the continued relationship is a cause of partnership termination.

The Termination Process

dissolution

Understanding the termination of a partnership requires the knowledge of some basic terminology. The *dissolution* is the point at which the partnership ceases as an entity or is dissolved. This occurs when the relationship of the partners ceases to be a voluntary association to carry on the trade or business of the partnership. Dissolution begins the series of events that lead to the termination of the partnership. Following the dissolution of the partnership, the *winding-up* process occurs. Winding up is the series of events necessary to conclude the partnership activities, such as the completion of partnership contractual obligations, paying off the debts of the partnership, liquidating the partnership assets, and distributing partnership assets to the partners or their representatives. The *termination* of the partnership is accomplished when all events necessary to complete the winding-up process have occurred and the bundle of rights and duties inherent in the partnership form of enterprise ceases to exist.

The Last Days of a Partnership

- Dissolution
- Winding up
- Termination

The Causes of Dissolution

A partnership is a voluntary association of two or more individuals to operate the partnership business. To understand the causes of dissolution, it is necessary to understand the significance of the term *voluntary association*. The partnership must be dissolved when any or all of the partners no longer *voluntarily* operate the partnership business. Typical causes of partnership dissolution include the following:

- The partnership agreement may limit the terms of the partnership to a specific period of time or completion of a specific event. At the end of this period the voluntary agreement to operate as a partnership terminates and the partnership must be dissolved.
- Since most partnerships do not have a specific term and are formed to operate for an indefinite period of time, they can be dissolved by the express will of any or all partners. Since a voluntary association of the co-owners is required to form and operate a partnership, the courts will not typically enforce a partnership agreement to continue for an indefinite period in the face of a demand by one or more partners to dissolve the partnership. This general rule applies to general but not limited partners, who do not have the power to demand dissolution of the partnership.
- The partnership agreement may provide for the expulsion of one partner by the other partners for cause according to the terms set forth in the partnership agreement. This action terminates the voluntary association of the partners and dissolves the partnership.
- The general partnership dissolves upon the bankruptcy, legal incapacity, or death of a general partner but not of a limited partner.

Technical Dissolution Distinguished From Actual Termination

It is obvious that large partnerships, such as law firms, do not terminate with the loss of an individual partner. However, a voluntary agreement between the original partners may provide for the continuation of the partnership at an event that normally results in termination. In a sense the partnership technically dissolves and reforms with the remaining partners continuing the business. The partners should agree in advance to such a continuation plan, and this agreement will generally provide liquidation payments to the withdrawing partner (or his or her estate).

Federal Income Taxation of Partnerships

Partnership taxation follows many of the same principles that apply in the taxation of proprietorships. For example, a partnership is not considered a separate tax entity for the purposes of determining and paying federal income taxes. Income and losses of the partnership are reported directly by the partners. While the partnership is not required to pay taxes, it is required to fill out an income tax return (Form 1065 and Schedule K-1) for informational purposes.

The tax treatment of partnerships presents some unique complexities. First, there is more than one taxpayer involved in the taxation of partnership income. Second, although the partnership is not treated as a separate taxpayer for the purposes of determining income and paying federal income taxes, it is treated as a separate entity for many tax purposes. In this sense partnership taxation is a hybrid between the tax concepts applied to proprietorships and those applied to corporations.

Taxation of Income

Although the partnership pays no federal income taxes, each partner must report and pay taxes on his or her "distributive share" of the partnership net taxable income for the tax year. The net income is the gross income of the partnership less allowable deductions. For example, the deduction against income from domestic production activities is available for partnerships engaged in such activities. The partner's distributive share is the amount of net income that the partner is entitled to receive under the partnership agreement, even if no income is actually distributed to the partner during the tax year. If the partnership has tax losses, a deduction for each partner's distributive share of the losses may be taken on his or her individual tax return. This share of partnership income or loss is reported to the IRS and the partners on Schedule K-1 by the partnership. Income from a partnership reported on Schedule E of Form 1040 is taxed on the partner's return at individual rates. However, there is no potential for double taxation since there is no taxation at the partnership level. This is a distinct advantage over the corporate form if income is to be paid out to passive investment partners.

EXAMPLE 1

The ABC partnership has substantial income to pay out to limited partners. Assume each limited partner is in the top federal income bracket—35 percent.[3] The distributive share to each limited-partnership interest for the year is $10,000. There is no tax at the partnership level, but each partner is taxed $3,500 on a distributive share, leaving $6,500 of disposable income.

EXAMPLE 2

Use the same facts as in the example above, except that ABC decides to incorporate. In this case the limited partner (now a shareholder) receives a dividend instead of a distributive share. The income to provide the dividend (again $10,000) is first taxed at the corporate level at rates of up to 35 percent. This leaves $6,500 available to be paid to the shareholder and taxed at tax rates that depend on whether the dividends received are "qualified dividends" and on the tax bracket of the shareholder. Generally, in this example, the dividends would be taxed at the capital gains rate of 15 percent. In this instance, the same $10,000 of business income will provide $5,525 after taxes to the shareholder, compared to $6,500 to a partner if the partnership is chosen.

A partner's distributive share of income or loss is not initially determined by rules of tax law. Rather, the allocation of distributive shares is determined by the partnership agreement. The IRS will generally abide by the terms of the partnership agreement in this respect, unless it finds that the allocation does not have substantial economic effect. In the absence of a specific agreement as to the allocation of income and loss, a partner's distributive share may be inferred by the facts of the partnership, such as each partner's capital interest in the partnership.

EXAMPLE

Nancy and Tim form a partnership in which Nancy contributes cash of $50,000 and Tim contributes a building with a fair market value of $50,000. The partnership begins operation with no formal agreement as to the allocation of income or loss and earns $60,000 in profit in the first tax year. Based on these facts, it may be presumed that Nancy and Tim will share the profits 50-50 in accordance with their relative interest. This means that Tim and Nancy will have to report $30,000 each of taxable income for the year regardless of whether their share of profits was distributed to them.

3. Based on 2011 individual income tax tables.

The partnership, like any other entity, may receive different types of income. For example, the partnership receives ordinary income from its business operations, and it may receive long-term capital gain from the sale of property. Some partnership receipts may be tax exempt, such as the proceeds from a life insurance policy payable to the partnership. The character of all income is passed through directly to the partner. For example, if the partnership has a long-term capital gain, each partner's share of this gain is also a long-term capital gain to the partner. When the partnership receives the tax-exempt life insurance proceeds, each partner's share of these proceeds is also tax exempt.

The partnership agreement may make a special allocation of the various types of income among partners; for example, one partner may be designated to receive all the capital gains. Generally these allocations will be accepted by the IRS if they have substantial economic effect. To have a substantial economic effect, the allocation should create a real impact both on (1) the partner's *distributive share* of total partnership income regardless of tax consequences and (2) the partner's capital accounts. Because special allocations have been abused by taxpayers, the IRS had promulgated complex and restrictive regulations on the subject. In addition, the allocation income from domestic production activities eligible for the new deduction will potentially create possibilities for tax benefits to be shifted between partners. The IRS is expected to provide rules for allocation of income from partnership activities that give rise to the deduction. The financial services professional should be aware that caution should be used in forming special allocations.

EXAMPLE

Boris and Natasha form a partnership. Among the business assets are tax-free municipal bonds and corporate stock. The partnership agreement gives Boris and Natasha a right to 50 percent of the partnership income (tax-exempt income and dividend income). The agreement further provides that all Boris's share will be designated as tax-exempt interest to the extent the partnership has tax-exempt interest. The IRS will regard this special allocation as having no substantial economic effect because Boris and Natasha's actual distributive shares are not affected by the agreement. The result of that conclusion will probably be that both partners will have to reallocate their shares to include 50 percent of each type of partnership income.

Although every partnership should have a carefully written partnership agreement, a partnership can still exist for tax purposes on the basis of an oral agreement or even an implied agreement. If the parties tend to conduct their affairs as partners, the IRS will treat the business as a partnership. Also if the partnership agreement is silent on some particular matter—for example, the allocation of income or loss—the IRS will, in effect, "fill in the gaps" by imputing an agreement on this particular point. Typically the net result of such an agreement will be to reallocate each type of income or loss proportionally to each partner's interest in the partnership.

Partnership income or loss is reported on each partner's return on Schedule E of Form 1040. In this sense the treatment of partnership income is no different from that of a proprietor's. Income is simply added to or subtracted from the partner's income from other sources in arriving at the partner's adjusted gross income. Partnership capital gains or losses retain their character as described above and are reported by each partner on Schedule D along with the partner's other capital gains or losses.

Income Allocation in a Family Partnership

family partnership

Business owners often want to know if they can gain any tax advantages by designating family members as partners in their businesses. The idea of such an arrangement would be to split the partnership income among several people, thus placing some business income in lower tax brackets. The Code has a number of complex rules dealing with family partnerships. Basically the rules are designed to distinguish bona fide family partnerships from mere tax-avoidance devices that will be disregarded for tax purposes.

If the partnership is one in which capital is a material income-producing factor, any person who owns a capital interest in the partnership will be considered a partner for income tax purposes, even if the partner acquired the capital interest as a gift. Thus in such a partnership it might be possible to split the partnership income among family members and to shift the income to persons in lower tax brackets by making a sale or gift of the partnership interest to the family members. If the family member owning the partnership interest is not providing services to the partnership, the income tax rules related to the unearned income of children under age 18 (kiddie tax) apply. Generally speaking, the unearned income of children under age 18 (24 for some full-time students) will be taxed at the parents' marginal tax rate. Furthermore, these rules apply regardless of how the children receive the partnership interest. The rules will limit the family partnership advantages unless the child is above the age threshold and provides substantial services to the partnership.

If capital is not a material income-producing factor (as in a legal, accounting, or other professional practice), the family member who is designated as a partner will have to perform substantial services in order to be recognized as a partner for tax purposes. If the IRS does not recognize the family member for tax purposes, the distributive share will have to be reallocated to the service partners.

EXAMPLE 1

Mike's construction business operates as a proprietorship and has a heavy capital investment in machinery and equipment. Mike donates a 20 percent interest in the business to his 18-year-old son, Hank. Mike files a gift tax return, pays gift tax on the gift, and carries out all the necessary legal steps to make Hank the true owner of the 20 percent interest. Hank has full control over the exercise of his rights as a partner. Mike continues his active involvement in the business, and he continues to pay himself the same reasonable "salary" as before. (The reason for this is discussed below.) Hank will be recognized as a partner for tax purposes, even though he has no active involvement in the business.

EXAMPLE 2

Brenda, a financial planner, gives her 20-year-old son, Hal, an interest in her practice. Brenda goes through all the formalities of making the gift and pays gift taxes. Hal is an artist who performs no services in her service business. The IRS will probably reallocate to Brenda any distributive share assigned to Hal, who will not be recognized as a partner for tax purposes.

There are some further complications in the rules for family partnerships. In addition to the rules discussed above, the Code provides that a partnership agreement will be disregarded in two specific situations.

First, if the partnership agreement determines the donee-partner's distributive share without providing a reasonable allowance for the value of services performed by the donor-partner, the IRS may reallocate the distributive shares. Therefore if Mike, in the first example above, had cut back his usual "salary" and given a larger share to Hank, the IRS would probably reallocate the usual salary back to Mike.

Second, if the partnership agreement provides that the donee-partner's distributive share is proportionately greater than the donor's share relative to their capital investments, the IRS again may reallocate the distributive shares. Thus in the first example if Hank was given a 20 percent capital interest but was entitled to 50 percent of the profits, the IRS would probably reallocate Hank's share of the profits to 20 percent.

Although the rules discussed above are generally referred to as *family partnership* rules, they actually have broader application. The general tax rules for family partnerships apply to all partnership interests created by gift, regardless of whether family members are actually involved. In addition, special rules apply to interests purchased by one member of the family from another. The interest *purchased* by one family member from another is treated as a gift from the seller. For this purpose the family of an individual includes his or her spouse, ancestors, and lineal descendants, as well as any trusts for the primary benefit of such persons.

Income splitting among inactive family members can sometimes be accomplished by using an S corporation rather than a partnership. As described in the next chapter, none of the restrictive family partnership rules apply, but there are other potential tax problems.

Taxation of Formation

To comprehend the federal income tax treatment of a partnership, it is important to understand two issues. One, we will discuss the tax treatment of the formation of a partnership. Two, we will analyze the events that cause adjustments to the basis of each partner's partnership interest. The basis held by each partner at formation and the subsequent changes in basis are significant for two reasons. First, a partner's basis determines the gain or loss from the sale of the partnership interest. Second, the amount of the partner's basis is the limit on the amount of partnership losses that can be deducted by the partner against personal income from other sources. The latter point is significant since many partnerships are formed for the purpose of flowing deductible losses through to the partners.

Consistent with the tax treatment applied to the formation of most types of business enterprises, the formation of a partnership is encouraged by favorable tax treatment. A partnership is formed when partners contribute money or other property in return for their partnership interests. A partner's contribution may be nominal, but it is the basic initial element in the formation of a partnership. The formation transaction is generally not a taxable event to the partners. That is, the partners generally do not recognize gain or loss when they contribute property to the partnership in return for their partnership interest. This is an exception to the general rule that the transfer of property is a taxable event. Similarly the partners usually recognize no gain or loss on capital contributions to the partnership at other points in time. However, this nonrecognition rule applies only to transactions in which the partner is acting in his or her capacity as a partner. For example, if the partner sells property to the partnership rather than contributing it as a capital contribution, gain or loss on the transfer will be recognized by the partner. Such a transaction will simply be treated like a bona fide sale. In addition, gain recognition could occur if the partners contributed different property and the partnership was deemed to be formed for diversification. Finally, the partnership itself does not recognize any gain or loss in the event of a capital contribution by a partner.

The general rule states that amounts expended to organize a partnership or to promote the sale of a partnership interest are not deductible by the partnership. However, a taxpayer may deduct up to $5,000 of start-up or organizational expenses when forming a business. The deduction is further limited for entities with large amounts of start-up or organizational expenses. The current deduction is reduced (but not below zero) by the amount the organizational expenses exceed $50,000. The organizational expenditures are normally applicable to corporations, partnerships, or LLCs. Any start-up or organizational expenses that cannot be deducted currently under this provision will be amortized over 15 years. To be deductible such expenditures must be incurred within a reasonable period before the partnership begins business and before the partnership's initial tax return is due.

Adjustments to Basis

The tax law views each partner's capital contribution as an exchange for a property interest—the partnership interest. This property interest is similar to that held by a shareholder in a corporation but is not evidenced by any share certificates or other intangible objects. However, this interest may be bought and sold as any other property interest.

Since the partnership interest is considered personal property of the partner, it is important to know its basis for tax purposes. When the interest is transferred, any gain or loss recognizable by the partner will be determined by reference to this basis. A partner acquires a basis by making an initial contribution of capital to the partnership at the time of formation in exchange for a partnership interest. Further capital contributions by a partner after the formation of the partnership result in an increase in the partner's basis in the already existing partnership interest. The partner's basis acquired by the contribution is generally equal to the amount of money contributed plus the partner's adjusted basis in any property contributed. Typically the adjusted basis of such property in the hands of the partner is the original cost to the partner less any depreciation deductions and other adjustments taken by the partner.

EXAMPLE

Carl and Jack form a partnership to carry on their construction business. Each partner agrees to put property worth $5,000 into the partnership. Carl contributes his pickup truck, which has a fair market value of $5,000 and an adjusted basis of $4,000. The basis for Carl's partnership interest thus becomes $4,000. Jack agrees to contribute $2,000 in cash plus tools that have a fair market value of $3,000 and an adjusted basis of $1,000. Jack's basis for his partnership interest is therefore $3,000. Thus although both partners contributed property worth $5,000, Carl's basis is $4,000, but Jack's is only $3,000. Any additional contributions made by Carl or Jack will increase their basis at that time.

The significance of basis is apparent. For example, suppose several years later Carl decides to sell his interest in the partnership to Jack for $10,000. Carl's gain can be computed only if his basis is known. Assuming no further adjustments to Carl's basis after formation (an unlikely event) Carl would have a gain of $6,000 ($10,000 less the $4,000 basis).

The determination of a partner's basis in his or her original interest in the partnership seems simple enough. However, a partner's basis for partnership interest can be subject to constant change as a result of the operation of the partnership. These adjustments are part of the complexity of partnership taxation.

Most of the changes in a partner's basis from the regular operations of the partnership result from three rules provided by the IRC. First, a partner's basis for partnership interest is increased each year by the partner's distributive share of the partnership income. Second, the basis is decreased each year by the amount of any distribution received by the partner from the partnership. Therefore there is no change in the partner's basis for the partnership interest if the partnership simply pays out to each partner his or her distributive share of the partnership's income. That is, the basis adjustments for these events cancel each other out. The third rule provides that the partner's basis is decreased each year by his or her distributive share of the losses incurred by the partnership for the tax year. However, the basis is never reduced below zero.

EXAMPLE

Jane has a basis of $50,000 for her partnership interest at the beginning of this year. This year Jane's share of the partnership's profits is $30,000. She actually withdraws $20,000 of this and leaves the rest in the partnership. Jane's new basis for her partnership interest at the end of this year will be $60,000 ($50,000 plus $30,000 less $20,000). If the partnership has losses next year and Jane's share of these losses is $100,000, her deduction for next year will be limited to $60,000, the amount of her basis, and her basis will be reduced to zero. Jane's remaining $40,000 of losses may be carried over to future years and may be deducted in future years to the extent her basis increases in the future.

Two other adjustments to the partner's interest in the partnership should be noted at this time. First, as mentioned above, a partner's basis in the partnership interest is increased by any further capital contributions made by the partner after the formation of the partnership. Second, a partner's basis in his or her interest includes the partner's share of any indebtedness incurred by the partnership. For example, if a two-member 50-50 partnership borrows $50,000, each partner's basis in his or her partnership interest increases by $25,000.

These rules become significant in a partnership designed primarily to flow deductible losses through to the partners. In these tax-shelter-type partnerships the deductible partnership losses flow through to "shelter" the partner's incomes from other sources. Since each partner's deductions for partnership losses are limited to his or her basis, the increase in basis resulting from the partnership indebtedness is a critical adjustment.

Finally, for tax purposes the partnership itself has a basis in the partnership property contributed by the partners. Among other things, a partnership's basis in its property determines the amount of the depreciation that can be deducted with respect to partnership property. Generally the partnership's basis for the contributed property is a carryover basis. That is, the basis of the property is the same as is adjusted basis in the hands of the contributing partner.

The Advantages and Disadvantages of Partnerships

The first advantage of partnerships is the ease and flexibility associated with the formation and operation of the business. The general partnership requires no filings with the state to begin operation. Many partnerships are established on an informal basis, requiring simply the voluntary association of the owners. Since the owners and managers of the general partnership are one and the same, all that is required to expand or alter the purpose of the business is their continued voluntary association. This allows the owners to grasp new opportunities more quickly and with fewer roadblocks than is the case with incorporated businesses. It is important to note, however, that many partnerships, particularly limited partnerships, have formal agreements similar to the articles of incorporation that may limit somewhat the flexibility of the partnership.

There are many tax advantages associated with the operation of a business in the form of a partnership. First, all the partnership profits flow through to the partners through the operation of the distributive-share principle discussed earlier. Thus the potential for double taxation is eliminated, and income can be passed through to passive-investment partners at a lower total tax cost than would be required to provide a dividend to a corporate shareholder.

A second tax advantage of partnership operation is the pass-through of all losses and tax benefits directly to the owners. A new business with substantial start-up costs and losses in the early years might find the partnership form advantageous. Because the losses flow through to the owners, the partners can use these tax benefits to offset personal income from other sources.

The flow of partnership losses to a partner depends upon unique tax-basis rules associated with partnerships. The most significant of these rules is the adjustment to the partner's basis for debt incurred by the partnership. Tax law provides that each partner's basis in the partnership interest is increased by any debt incurred by the partnership. Since the deductible losses that may flow through to a partner are limited to the partner's basis in the partnership, increases in basis allow the partner to take advantage of the tax benefits associated with the flow through of losses.

To some degree the tax laws limit the benefit of using debt financing to increase basis in a limited partnership. The at-risk rules provide that a partner cannot deduct losses of the partnership beyond the extent of the partner's basis, determined without regard to nonrecourse debt incurred by the partnership. That is, unless the partner is *personally* liable (at risk) for the partnership debt, the partner cannot include the partnership debt in basis for tax purposes. Also any partnership losses that cannot be deducted can be carried forward to future tax years when the partner may have the necessary basis.

Finally, the partnership form of organization may be advantageous from a tax-planning standpoint to an owner who would like to split income among family members in lower tax brackets. The so-called family partnerships are formed for this purpose. If the partnership is the type in which capital is a material income-producing factor, a partner with a significant capital contribution may receive an appropriate distributive share. This rule applies even if the capital contributed was acquired by gift from one of the other co-owners. In this manner an owner who is in a high tax bracket can make a gift or sale of a partnership interest to family members above age 18 (24 for some full-time students) who are in lower tax brackets and effectively shift income to the lower-bracket taxpayers.

There are also several disadvantages to forming a business enterprise as a partnership. The first and foremost among these is the lack of continuity of the business. Since the partnership requires the voluntary association of co-owners to operate the business, any termination of the voluntary nature of the relationship causes the business to dissolve. For example, a deceased partner no longer has legal capacity to form the voluntary relationship so a partnership dissolves at the death of a general partner. In the absence of provisions or an agreement to the contrary, the business terminates at the death of any of the general partners. The continuation problems associated with the partnership form of enterprise will be discussed at great length later in the text. It should be remembered that this problem can be somewhat alleviated by the formation of a limited partnership, which does not terminate at the death of any of the limited partners.

Advantages and Disadvantages of General Partnership

Advantages

- Ease of formation
- No double taxation of income
- Tax benefits passed through to owners
- Enhanced ability to raise capital
- Sharing of responsibilities

Disadvantages

- Unlimited liability
- Sharing of profits
- Dissolution (perhaps termination) when a partner dies or leaves the firm
- Limited marketability of a partnership interest

A second disadvantage is the unlimited personal liability of each general partner for losses incurred by the partnership. The partner's personal assets may be required to satisfy partnership debts and any liability incurred by other partners acting within the scope of the partnership business. Again the limited partnership provides some relief to the harsh unlimited liability normally associated with the partnership form of enterprise. Although general partners are always subject to unlimited liability for partnership operation, the limited partner's liability extends only to the capital contribution and any share of profit or surplus designated to him or her.

LIMITED-LIABILITY COMPANIES (LLC)

LLCs have been adopted in all states as a response to demands by business owners who desire liability protection along with the flexibility of pass-through tax treatment for federal income tax purposes. Taxed as a partnership if appropriately organized, an LLC provides an enterprise that permits special allocations of income and loss, income shifting to inactive family members, and estate-freezing opportunities—without the burden of having a general partner with unlimited liability.

Characteristics of an LLC

members

operating agreement

Although state LLC statutes will differ in some respects, there are some characteristics that are common to most. LLCs must be formed by at least two owners, known as *members*, but there is no limit to the number of members an LLC may have. LLCs may conduct virtually any type of business unless specifically prohibited by state law. An LLC must have an agreement between the members (known as an *operating agreement*), similar to a partnership agreement, that states the terms upon which the organization will perform its business or services. Unless it provides to the contrary, the operating agreement may be modified only by unanimous vote of the members. Most important, all members of the LLC are sheltered from liability for business operations.

Formation of an LLC

Start-Up Entities

To form an LLC, its members contribute cash, property, and/or services in return for membership in the LLC. The members file articles of organization with the state authorizing the business. They form an operating agreement to provide the specifics of their association. Although state statutes provide for substantial flexibility, they do limit the association's possibilities. It is important to note that the federal tax treatment of an LLC will depend upon the choices made for the operating terms. If too many corporate characteristics are selected, the LLC will be taxed as a corporation rather than a partnership.

The cost of forming an LLC will generally be high relative to forming a general partnership or simple corporation. This cost distinction may diminish in the future as attorneys become more familiar with LLCs and the legal research time associated with their formation is reduced.

One-Member LLCs

Since LLC statutes were first enacted, there has been a good deal of discussion concerning the viability of a one-member LLC. In other words, can a sole proprietor gain liability protection by filing the appropriate LLC forms with the state? The answer seems to depend on state law. A majority of states specifically authorize the use of single-member LLCs. Other states either require two or more associates to form an LLC or have statutes that don't address this issue.

A further complication is the uncertain treatment of single-member LLCs that are authorized in one state in the courts of another state that does not specifically recognize a single-member LLC. This is certainly a problem that a single-member LLC that intends to do multistate business must address. At this time, the uncertainty of single-member LLCs seems to indicate caution. If the sole proprietor operates solely in a state where single-member LLCs are permitted, this status appears safe. In other instances, incorporation of the sole proprietorship is more prudent. In any event, substantial liability insurance protection alleviates the concern to some degree.

Converting a Partnership to an LLC

Of course, it is anticipated that many general partnerships will be converted to LLCs to provide liability protection for the owners. The partners should file articles of organization with the state and form an operating agreement for the LLC. Presumably, the agreement will amend the previous partnership agreement in accordance with the state's rules applicable to LLCs.

The IRS previously ruled that a conversion of a general partnership to a limited partnership does not terminate the partnership for tax purposes. Since an LLC is treated as a partnership for federal tax purposes, it is reasonable to assume that the conversion from a partnership to an LLC similarly avoids termination of the partnership for tax purposes. This is important since a termination followed by recontribution of the former partnership property to the LLC might result in recognition of gain by the members for appreciated partnership assets contributed to the LLC.

Converting a Corporation to an LLC

The owners of a corporation may wish to convert to an LLC to receive partnership pass-through tax treatment. The conversion to an LLC will be particularly important for a corporation that is ineligible for S corporation status. (The restrictions for S corporations are covered in the next chapter.) Such conversion may be valuable even for an S corporation since partnership pass-through tax treatment has advantages relative to S corporation tax rules. The shareholders may also wish to achieve the greater estate planning flexibility available through the use of an LLC.

To make the conversion, a corporation would have to file articles of dissolution under its state law to liquidate and distribute assets to its shareholders. Unlike the conversion of a partnership, this liquidation could be a costly event because the gain on appreciated corporate property would have to be recognized at both the corporate and shareholder level. The assets of the liquidated corporation could then be contributed by the members to an appropriately formed LLC. Presumably, the transfer of such assets to the newly formed LLC would avoid recognition of gain since the nonrecognition rules for the start-up of a closely held business entity would be met.

In any event, the assets should have no potential gain since each member's basis in the assets would have been increased to fair market value when the corporation was liquidated, and gain was recognized at that time. Thus the conversion of a corporation to an LLC could be expensive from the standpoint of capital-gains tax if the corporation had substantially appreciated assets.

Management of an LLC

The management of an LLC is provided for in its operating agreement. The LLC can be managed by the owners, similar to a general partnership. However, the members do not have automatic authority under state law to act as agents to represent the LLC. In many circumstances, the LLC will have numerous members, many of whom are passive investors, and member-management would be inappropriate. The LLC will, under these circumstances, be controlled by a management team, essentially the same as a corporation's board of directors. These managers could include both member and nonmember managers. The managers will oversee operations of the business and provide whatever governance is delegated by the members of the LLC in its operating agreement.

Liability of Members

The primary advantage of the LLC is the liability protection provided to its members. All members, whether or not they provide services for the LLC, will be sheltered from liability for business operations. Compare this to the limited partnership, where any partner with management authority will lose his or her shelter from liability. Thus the members of an LLC have only their individual investment in the LLC at risk for claims against the business.

Of course, as stated earlier, there is no shelter from liability for an individual's own actions. Thus a member who provides services for the LLC will be liable for his or her own negligent actions. However, the LLC will shelter members from liability for the actions of other employees and general business operations. For this reason, professionals may consider forming LLCs instead of partnerships if state LLC law permits.

Termination of an LLC

The duration of an LLC will be different based on the operating agreement and the goals of the members. In addition, state law often provides for dissolution of an LLC at specified events or intervals. For example, the LLC could be dissolved upon the first to occur of (a) the unanimous consent of all members, (b) a time specified in the articles of organization or operating agreement (often 30 years), (c) a member's voluntary withdrawal, (d) a member's death, (e) a member's expulsion, (f) a member's bankruptcy, (g) a court decree holding that it is not reasonably practical to carry on the firm's business in conformance with its operating agreement, or (h) the occurrence of an event (such as a loss of a professional license) that would terminate a member's continued ability to actively participate in the affairs of the business.

As with any business entity, the remaining members could agree to continue the operation of an LLC after a terminating event. The private agreement could be a prearranged continuation plan but should not create a perpetual life for the LLC.

Division of Profits in an LLC

The LLC's profits and losses, as well as any distributions to members, will be divided according to the relative value of the members' contributions unless they have provided some different allocation in their operating agreement. Guaranteed payments and special allocations to specific members can be provided in a manner identical to the partnership tax rules.

Transferability of the Membership Interest

Transferability of ownership will typically be restricted in the LLC. For example, the operating agreement will often provide restrictions on transfer by providing an option to the LLC or the remaining members to purchase the interest of a member who wishes to withdraw. Even if transfer is permitted, the transferee will not become a member unless the existing members unanimously consent. Note that this is similar to a partnership, where the voluntary association to act as partners is a requisite characteristic.

Members can generally resign after adequate notice (unless the LLC's operating agreement provides otherwise). At that time, the firm must distribute cash, assets, or both with a fair market value equal to the member's interest within a reasonable time.

FEDERAL INCOME TAXATION OF LLC

The goal of the members of the LLC is generally to be taxed as a partnership. If taxable as a corporation, the LLC will not provide pass-through tax treatment and its flexibility. Since a corporation provides limited liability, the partnership tax treatment represents the only major advantage of the LLC over a corporation.

Income Tax Classification of an LLC

The income tax classification of an LLC (other than a single-member LLC) has traditionally focused on whether the entity should be taxed as a partnership or a corporation. The IRS has long focused on a series of factors to determine whether an entity should be taxed as a trust, partnership, corporation, or otherwise. The IRS could disregard an entity's particular preference for its own tax classification if the entity exhibited more characteristics of a different type of entity. Thus a partnership or LLC that exhibited more corporate than partnership characteristics would be reclassified as a corporation by the IRS.

Check-the-Box Entity Classification Regulations

The IRS regulations—the *check-the-box* rules—generally eliminate entity tax classification testing for businesses that wish to be taxed as partnerships. Under the check-the-box regulations, the entity can choose to be taxed as a partnership or corporation without IRS scrutiny unless the entity is a trust or one of a specific category of entities known as *per se corporations*.[4]

Taxation of Single-Member LLCs. Single-member domestic entities will be disregarded for federal tax purposes unless the owner chooses to be taxed as a corporation. Thus single-member LLCs will report income on the individual member's Form 1040 Schedule C unless the owner decides to be taxed as a corporation. For foreign single-owner entities, the default is corporate taxation only if limited liability exists.

Electing Choices Outside the Default Rules. A change in entity classification election must be made in two circumstances. First, an existing entity might want to change its current classification. Second, a newly formed entity may wish to change from its default classification. An election to change tax classification must be made with the eligible entity's tax return (or with an owner's tax return if the entity does not file) and can be made retroactively up to 75 days. Once a classification change is made, it generally cannot be changed for 60 months.

Tax Accounting Method

One issue facing professional LLCs is availability of the cash method of accounting. It is anticipated that many professionals, practicing as partnerships or corporations, will seriously consider converting to an LLC. Professional malpractice is the most serious concern of these individuals, and the LLC may prove to be an attractive choice of entity. The LLC offers protection from liability unavailable to professional partnerships. An LLC, classified as a partnership for tax purposes, offers tax advantages unavailable to professional service corporations. State law enabling the

---

4. Treas. Reg. Sec. 301-7701-2(b) defines entities that must specifically be taxed as a corporation ("per se corporations") to include (1) an entity organized under state or federal law as a corporation, (2) an association described in the regulations, (3) an entity described as a joint-stock company by state law, (4) a state-chartered banking entity insured by the FDIC or similar program, (5) an entity taxed as an insurance company, (6) a business wholly owned by a state or political subdivision, (7) certain foreign entities, and (8) any entity taxable as a corporation by any other IRC section.

creation of professional service limited-liability companies (PSLLCs) must, of course, be in place before this choice is available to professional entities.

The cash method of accounting is virtually always preferable for a professional service entity. Professional firms generally have significant receivables. If receivables are uncollectible, the use of the accrual method of accounting would create a tax hardship by accelerating unreceived income into early tax years.

However, the cash method of accounting may be unavailable to professionals practicing in the LLC form. Provisions of the tax laws require the use of the accrual method of accounting in certain entities. A recent private letter ruling somewhat clarified the position of the IRS with respect to PSLLCs. Under the facts of the ruling, a law firm converted from a partnership to an LLC. The ruling approved the continuation of the cash method of accounting since greater than 35 percent of losses were not allocated to limited partners or limited entrepreneurs. The keys to the ruling appeared to be that (1) no public sale of the business interests ever occurred (typically such sales will not occur in professional entities) and (2) all members actively practiced law for the PSLLC and had voting rights with respect to its management.

Pass-through of Passive Losses

Losses generated at the entity level can be passed through to the personal returns of the members. (However, planners should remember that such loss deductions may be limited by "at-risk" rules, basis limitation rules, or by passive-activity rules.) An LLC may be more attractive than a limited partnership with respect to passive losses. Passive losses can be deducted by limited partners to the extent that the entity provides passive income. Members of an LLC meet the definition of a limited partner. Limited partners (and, presumably, members of an LLC) can avoid this limitation if they materially participate in the activities of the partnership. Several tests can be met by the members in order to qualify them as material participants. Material participant status can be obtained by limited partners (and presumably members of an LLC) by meeting one of the following three requirements:

- more than 500 hours' participation in the activity during the year
- participation in the activity for any 5 of the preceding 10 tax years
- material participation in a personal-service activity for any of the 3 preceding tax years

Limited partners generally lose limited-liability status if they become material participants in the management of the partnership. However, members of an LLC retain limited liability even if such participation occurs. Thus an LLC will have advantages over a partnership with respect to the pass-through of passive losses.

Note that this advantage is eliminated if state law allows a limited partnership to obtain LLP status. In these entities, a limited partner's material participation will not result in that partner's unlimited liability even if such partner is reclassified as a general partner.

Income Tax Basis

Some authorities feel that the LLC may provide members with an opportunity to increase basis through an allocation of the firm's debt. This could be a significant advantage over the limited partnership, where basis is allocated only to partners who have personal risk for the debt. The reason for this proposed distinction is that in an LLC, all members have limited liability and so all of the debt of the firm could be considered to be "nonrecourse" debt (that is, creditors could go against only the asset purchased with the loan and not against the personal assets of the members). This characterization is favorable because nonrecourse liability of the firm is allocated to the members in accordance with their respective interests in the profits of the organization. Thus all members should be able to increase basis and receive a share of nonrecourse liabilities in the same manner as income and loss are shared by the members.

Of course, additional tax basis is important when the LLC will pass losses through to the members since losses can be deducted only to the extent of the members' basis.

ADVANTAGES OF LLC

The liability protection against creditors and claimants is the most important characteristic of the LLC and is its primary advantage over a partnership, which provides limited liability only for its limited but not its general partners. The LLC is the only business entity that allows every member, including managers, to enjoy limited liability while the entity is treated as a partnership for federal income tax purposes.

The LLC can be a useful family business estate planning technique. Since the LLC generally is structured to be taxed as a partnership, it has many of the same features of a partnership used in business and estate planning. First, there is the avoidance of the double tax at the corporate level. Second, income is taxed directly to members (including those who are not active in the business) and the LLC can shift income to junior-generation family members. Third, similar to family partnerships, interests in a family LLC can be shifted to other family members with little physical or financial cost. This shift makes wealth sharing among family members relatively easy. Finally, the ability to form special allocations of income and loss further assists in planning flexibility in the family LLC.

The LLC provides advantages over the partnership relative to the conversion of passive income or losses. It may be possible for an active participating member of an LLC to convert what might otherwise be treated as a passive loss to a normal loss for income tax purposes. Likewise, passive income can be converted into active income. This potential is not possible for limited partners in a family partnership. Such partners are restricted to passive income and loss treatment.

The LLC may provide an estate-freezing vehicle for family assets since multiple gift or estate tax valuation discounts will be available if family assets are placed in an appropriately structured LLC. If assets such as cash, securities, real estate, a closely held business, or any other asset is placed within an LLC, the value of the assets to an outside buyer may diminish. This reduction in the marketability leads to a valuation discount that is realistic and reasonable

Furthermore, the LLC can be split into pieces of differing ownership interests, and control can be vested in the interest that is held by the senior generation.

In addition, special allocations can be structured to limit the value of certain interests given to family members. Under these circumstances, the donees (presumably junior-generation family members) have little say in cash flow or liquidation decisions, which results in an additional reduction in value for a minority discount. Together, the lack of marketability coupled with the lack of control may result in a discount in excess of 35 percent for gift tax purposes. Shifting wealth and splitting income become more cost effective when such discounts are available.

DISADVANTAGES OF LLC

One disadvantage with LLCs is the lack of track record for such entities. There are few regulations, rulings, or cases on LLCs as entities. Provisions of LLC laws vary greatly from state to state, thus making it difficult for a multistate business operation to function.

Another disadvantage is the problem of a departing member. An LLC is required by most states to buy the interest of any member who desires to leave with very little notice (6 months is typical); thus the business may find itself short on cash or operating assets at a financially inconvenient time.

The LLC is not an answer where a public offering of the business interest will be made. If a public offering is contemplated to raise venture capital, LLCs are not appropriate since most publicly traded partnerships are taxed as corporations.

As with partners and proprietors, members of an LLC are treated as self-employed. Some otherwise nontaxable fringe benefits are not excludible from the income of members because they are not considered employees. These benefits include medical benefits, cafeteria-plan benefits, some meals and lodging, and group term life insurance.

LLCs may be costly to form in some circumstances. They require a partnership-type agreement, which can be complex and expensive to draft. By comparison, S corporations can be set up without the expense of a formal contractual agreement between the owners.

Advantages and Disadvantages of LLCs

Advantages

- Limited liability of members
- Taxed as a partnership
- Possible to shift income to low-bracket family members
- Possible to provide special income and loss allocations
- Possible vehicle for estate freezing
- Possible to have different ownership classes

Advantages and Disadvantages of LLCs

Disadvantages

- Short legal and tax track record
- Requirement that a departing member's interest be purchased
- Not available for raising money through a public offering
- Fewer tax-free fringe benefits for members
- May be expensive to form
- Conversion to LLC may cause adverse tax consequences

In addition, conversion to an LLC may cause unnecessary taxes. A business that is currently existing in corporate form cannot be converted to an LLC without a taxable liquidation, which is a cost that many clients will be unwilling to bear.

CHAPTER REVIEW

Key Terms and Concepts

proprietorship
partnership
general partnership
limited-liability partnership (LLP)
tenants in partnership
partnership interest
assignee in interest
dissolution
family partnership
members
operating agreement

Review Questions

The answers to the review questions are in the supplement. The self-test questions and the answers to them are also in the supplement and on The American College Online.

1. How is a sole proprietorship formed? [1]
2. Are the assets and liabilities of a sole proprietorship distinguishable from the personal assets and liabilities of the proprietor? Discuss. [1]
3. What is the proprietor's personal liability for business operations? [1]
4. What are the causes of termination of a proprietorship? [1]
5. How is the business income of a proprietorship treated for tax purposes? [2]

6. Explain whether the formation or termination of a proprietorship is a taxable event to the proprietor. [2]
7. Identify the disadvantages of the proprietorship form for a growing business. [3]
8. What are the legal responsibilities of a general partner to the other partners and the partnership? [3]
9. Describe the differences between an LLP and a limited partnership. [3]
10. What is a limited partner, and what is that person's usual relationship to the partnership? [3]
11. Distinguish between the property of a partnership and each partner's interest in the partnership. [3]
12. What is the fundamental nature of a partnership that dissolves at the death or withdrawal of a general partner? [4]
13. Distinguish between technical dissolution and the actual termination of the business. [4]
14. Identify the manner in which a partnership is treated as a separate entity from its owners for tax purposes. [5]
15. Do partners have unlimited discretion in determining relative distributive shares of partnership income for tax purposes? Explain. [5]
16. Slick is a partner in a law firm. His son, Junior, is in college. Slick's accountant proposes a plan to transfer a portion of Slick's partnership interest to Junior, giving Junior the right to receive $15,000 of partnership income, the approximate costs of Junior's tuition. (Ignore the fact that state law would probably prohibit a nonattorney partner.) This plan is also designed to shift income to Junior to be taxable in his lower bracket. Explain whether or not this plan will actually lower family tax liability. [5]
17. Is a capital contribution to a partnership by a partner a taxable event? Explain. [5]
18. Ralph and Alice formed a partnership at the end of 2008 each made capital contributions worth $100,000 at that time. Ralph contributed real estate with an adjusted basis of $60,000 and Alice contributed cash. The relevant facts for the partnership operation are as follows:

Year	Ralph's distributive share	Alice's distributive share	Amount distributed to Ralph	Amount distributed to Alice
2009	$50,000	$50,000	$40,000	$25,000
2010	($30,000)	($30,000)	$20,000	$20,000

What are Ralph's and Alice's adjusted bases at the beginning of 2011? [5]

19. Describe the organizational formalities of an LLC. [6]
20. Describe how the check-the-box regulations change during the traditional entity classification rules. [6]
21. Identify the advantages and disadvantages of the LLC as a form of enterprise. [6]

CORPORATIONS 3

Learning Objectives

An understanding of the material in this chapter should enable the student to

1. Describe the nature of corporations and how they are formed
2. Explain how a corporation is managed, and describe the rights and responsibilities of directors, officers, and shareholders.
3. Discuss restrictions that may be placed on the ability of shareholders to transfer their stock in closely held or professional corporations.
4. Describe how a corporation as a separate taxpayer can save taxes by accumulating earnings.
5. Explain the impact of the accumulated-earnings tax and alternative minimum tax.
6. Identify the types of corporations eligible for S election and the possible uses of an S election.

During this century the incorporated form of business organization has become an increasingly important vehicle for carrying out all types of enterprises. Although there are fewer corporations than unincorporated businesses, as we pointed out in the last chapter, the vast majority of business wealth is nevertheless amassed in corporations. While accounting for just over 18 percent of the total number of business enterprises in the United States in a recent year, corporations accounted for approximately 82 percent of the total business receipts.[5] Obviously there are reasons for the enormous concentration of wealth in U.S. corporations.

The types of corporations cover a broad spectrum. At one end of the spectrum are the large multinational corporations that own billions of dollars worth of assets and have numerous owners (shareholders). At the other

---

5. U.S. Bureau of the Census, Statistical Abstract of the United States: 2011 (130th ed.), Washington, D.C., 2010.

end of the spectrum are the small family corporations. We will discuss many aspects common to all types of corporations but will focus primarily on the small to medium-sized corporations that are relatively numerous and likely to have significance for the financial services professional. Specifically, closely held corporations and S corporations will be most often encountered by the financial services professional in the local community. These forms of business enterprise present useful planning options for the small business owner or professional currently operating in the unincorporated form.

CHARACTERISTICS OF A CORPORATION

A corporation exists as a legal entity separate and apart from its owners and is created under the laws of the various states. Each state has statutes enabling the incorporation of a business within its jurisdiction. While these statutes differ from state to state, the statutes all have specific required formalities that a corporation must follow in operation. These required formalities are the characteristics that most clearly distinguish a corporation from the unincorporated business form.

However, this distinction may exist more in theory than in practice for some businesses. You will recall from the last chapter that partnerships may be formed and operate with rigid formal agreements similar to those of corporations. We will also learn that many smaller corporate businesses operate in a manner similar to that of partnerships or proprietorships.

Formation of a Corporation

The formation of a corporation is governed by the laws of the state chosen as the place of incorporation. Formal procedures for incorporation differ from state to state. Legal assistance is typically required; fortunately lawyers have developed procedures to streamline and simplify the process, which is often more complex in form than in substance. Nevertheless, legal expenses and filing fees are necessary costs of incorporation.

It is important for every incorporation to comply with the procedures of state law; otherwise the corporate status may be subject to challenge. Within the formal incorporation requirements are many opportunities for planning. The corporation should be formed with provisions appropriate for the needs of the particular business. In this section we will discuss the basic steps of the typical incorporation and the choices available to the business owner.

Choosing the State of Incorporation

The corporation is incorporated in only one state, which is not always the state in which it does most or all of its business. The choice of the state of incorporation can be extremely complex and involves a consideration of each state's tax and corporate laws. Usually the decision is between incorporating in the state of operation or incorporating in a state such as Delaware, where corporate law is favorable. Although state tax burdens vary tremendously, it is usually the state where the business is located rather than the state of incorporation that determines the primary tax burden.

For simplicity most small businesses incorporate in their "home" states for several reasons. First, it will often be necessary to incur the additional expense of securing legal assistance in both the state of operation and, if different, the state of incorporation.

Second, obtaining a charter in a state where the business does not operate gives the corporation standing to be sued in this state of incorporation. Typically jurisdictional rules require that a corporation be doing at least some business within a state before it can be haled into that state's courts to defend a suit. Chartering a corporation in a state where the corporation will do no business subjects the corporation to an additional jurisdiction in which it may be sued.

Finally, incorporating in another state may subject a corporation to taxes or other expenses required by the laws of the state of incorporation. Should the choice of the state of incorporation turn out to be a planning mistake, it is usually possible to reincorporate later in another state.

Choosing the Corporate Name

There are many state law restrictions on corporate names that must be investigated and complied with. For example, the name must often contain such words as *corporation, company, incorporated,* or *limited.* In addition, the name must not be one that can be confused with another organization. Care must be taken in selecting the name, since confusion with a name of another business firm can result in loss of goodwill or even legal damages. Usually the name must be registered with the state and sometimes with other jurisdictions for a small filing fee.

Organizational Formalities

As mentioned above, all state statutes on corporations require compliance with many formalities in both formation and operation. These requirements include the filing or the maintenance of several types of documents. Although the formalities vary according to the statutes of the state of incorporation, the following are among the typical formalities required by most state laws:

articles of incorporation

bylaws

- Prepare preincorporation subscription agreements or contracts to purchase securities. Among the tasks facing the promoter of the corporation is the raising of capital for the new business enterprise. Initially there should be at least one shareholder who agrees to subscribe to or purchase at least one share of stock at par value. This is typically required as a formality to show that the business will have capital to operate. The statutes of several states make these agreements irrevocable and binding on the subscribers (purchasers) when the business is incorporated. Either a preincorporation subscription agreement or a contract to buy the securities is typically used by the small corporation to capitalize the business upon formation. Capitalizing larger public corporations usually involves the services of an underwriter or investment banker to raise the capital and distribute stock. Regardless of the method used, the consideration received by the corporation in exchange for the stock is normally limited by statute to money, services rendered, or property transferred to the corporation.
- Prepare and file the *articles of incorporation.* The articles of incorporation is a lengthy document describing the name and location of the corporation, its purpose and powers, the capitalization of the corporation (classes of stock, par values, voting rights, preferences, and so on), the powers of the directors and the manner of their election, which acts require shareholder approval, and the like. Standard "boilerplate" forms of the articles of incorporation are available, but the financial services professional should make the business owner aware of the alternative provisions that exist. Many of the standard provisions may be inapplicable to the specific business and should be changed. Certain provisions may be included in either the articles or the bylaws, while other provisions must be contained only in the articles. The planning team for the incorporators should avoid treating these provisions casually. For example, the corporate purpose should be stated clearly and should include all activities the corporation intends to

pursue. The extent of the power given to the board of directors should be carefully considered. In the close corporation setting it may be advantageous to provide for the removal of directors or even the dissolution of the business in the case of an irreconcilable deadlock.

It is typically required that the articles of incorporation be registered and filed with the state, which in turn issues a certificate of incorporation. The filing is usually advertised in both a regular and a legal newspaper. The state filing and advertising costs represent additional fees of incorporation.

- Prepare corporate *bylaws*. The bylaws describe the duties and powers of directors and shareholders, the rules for shareholder and director meetings, and other corporate operating matters. State law generally requires that such powers and meetings be carried out in accordance with these bylaws. However, the form and content of the bylaws is not typically regulated, nor must the bylaws be filed with the state. Although the procedure varies from state to state, the initial corporate bylaws are generally adopted by the directors or, in their absence, by the incorporators.
- Prepare a corporate minutes book, stock certificates, and a seal. "Kits" of these corporate documents may be obtained from commercial legal stationery sources for reasonable fees. Obviously the total charge for these formalities is related to the size and complexity of the corporation.
- Conduct organizational meetings and prepare minutes. At all meetings of the board of directors formalities must be observed and proceedings recorded in the corporate minutes book. At the first meeting the directors usually authorize the opening of corporate bank accounts, elect corporate officers, select the corporate fiscal year and accounting method, consider a Subchapter S election, and so on.
- Issue stock certificates.

The above description is designed to provide a general overview of the actual incorporation process. Other steps may be necessary; for example, state and federal security laws may impose additional requirements. Ordinarily the organization of a small local business does not involve the federal securities laws under the jurisdiction of the Securities and Exchange Commission (SEC), but state securities laws may require additional filings in the state of incorporation. For the routine incorporation of a small business, standard boilerplate form documents can be used with only minor modifications. Since little legal work is required in such cases, fees should be minimal. However, any increase in complexity from the simple form will require the payment of significantly higher legal fees.

Corporate Structure

A corporation is a separate legal entity through which business activities are conducted. The actors in this setting—directors, shareholders, officers, and the corporation—have attributes developed by both statutory and case law. Financial services professionals should be aware of these attributes for the purposes of identifying both the risks and the planning opportunities of the corporate business enterprise.

Powers and Liabilities

The corporate structure imposes both powers and liabilities on each of the participants. In this section we will deal with the powers of each of the participants in the operational setting of the corporation and the responsibilities and liabilities placed on each.

Corporation as Legal Entity. The corporation is a separate legal entity formed under the laws of the state of incorporation. As a separate legal entity the corporation is considered an individual, albeit artificial, for the purposes of law. The corporation is a "person" and as such holds title to corporate property. As a separate individual the corporation gains many of the rights and privileges associated with citizenship. It is subject to the jurisdictional powers of its state of incorporation and, if different, any state that becomes a principal place of business.

The powers of a corporation as a separate entity include

- all powers expressly given to the corporation in its charter
- all powers expressly given to corporations by the state laws on corporations
- the right to sue and be sued as a separate legal entity
- the right to hold, transfer, or encumber property for business purposes in the corporate name
- the right to make bylaws for the operation of the corporation
- any powers reasonably necessary to carry out the express business of the corporation

Modern courts tend to interpret the "reasonably necessary" powers broadly and allow many nonexpress powers by implication. An important implied power of a corporation is the authority to purchase stock in another corporation. This authority is limited to acquisitions that fulfill a proper corporate business purpose. However, the scope of the business-purpose standard is quite broad. Typically a corporation with adequate surplus funds (the excess of assets over liabilities) may acquire stock in another corporation solely for investment purposes. Also the proper corporate-purpose test is satisfied when the corporation acquires stock in another corporation engaged in a related business. These powers are useful if the corporation hopes to expand through acquisition or merger or has surplus funds to invest.

The power of a corporation to acquire its own stock is regulated by state law. Typically the corporation has the power to acquire its own stock if the acquisition (1) serves a business purpose and (2) is not detrimental to creditors or shareholders. The acquisition (redemption) of its own stock will generally not be considered detrimental to the creditors or shareholders if the corporation has adequate surplus. The stock redeemed by the corporation becomes treasury stock in which no shareholder has voting or dividend rights.

The corporation is similar to any other separate legal entity in that it may become subject to liability. As a separate legal entity the corporation can be sued in its own name to satisfy these liabilities. Of course, the corporation may have rights to contribution or indemnity for these liabilities from the guilty agents or employees.

The corporation holds property and has the right to secure credit in its own name. As such the corporation may become liable to creditors through its normal operations. The creditors have rights against the corporation identical to those held by the creditors of any private individual. The creditors have priority rights over shareholders upon dissolution of the corporation, but they cannot interfere with the everyday business operation of the corporation unless the actions of the corporation would defraud the creditors of their rights to corporate property. An example of this fraud occurs when an insolvent corporation transfers assets to a third party to frustrate the liquidation preference of the creditors.

The general rule states that the corporation alone incurs the liability arising from the operation of the business. However, there are exceptions in which the other participants in the corporate setting may become liable for corporate actions.

The Corporate Directors and Officers. Corporate law provides for a board of directors to be elected by the shareholders of a corporation.

Management of the corporation is vested in the hands of the directors. In practice most publicly held corporations are said to be managed under the direction of the board. In these instances the board meets infrequently to make the major planning decisions of the corporation, while delegating the everyday administrative management duties to officers and employees of the corporation. In the case of closely held corporations, discussed at length in a later section, the roles of these participants often merge, and directors typically manage the everyday operation of the business in their roles as officer-employees of the corporation.

The board of directors of a corporation is empowered to manage the corporation's ordinary business operations, but it has no power to make decisions that affect the fundamental structure of the corporation. These fundamental changes, such as business mergers, changes in the nature of the business, issuance of a new class of stock, liquidation of the corporation, or major asset sales outside the ordinary course of business, require shareholder approval. The board of directors is typically empowered to make the following ordinary business decisions:

- hiring and termination of officers
- delegating authority for day-to-day management to the officers
- setting of salaries and fringe benefit plans for officers and employees
- making product, manufacturing, and pricing decisions
- declaring dividends
- securing credit for the corporation

quorum

It is obvious that the board of directors holds broad powers over the activities of the corporation, but the powers of the board are not unrestrained. The board of directors has power to act only as a unit, which requires that the board of directors meet at a valid meeting. The validity of a board meeting depends on compliance with state corporate law. In general the meeting must be either (1) a regularly scheduled meeting or (2) a meeting assembled according to the bylaws of the corporation, with notice provided in advance to all directors. As a final requirement a quorum of directors must be present for the action taken at a board meeting to be valid. A *quorum* is the minimum number of directors (typically a majority) required to be in attendance by the bylaws for a valid meeting. At the board meeting a majority vote of participating directors is usually all that is required to make management decisions.

EXAMPLE

The ABC corporation has nine members on its board of directors, five of whom attend the regularly scheduled quarterly meeting. Since the majority of the board members are present, the quorum is satisfied. Suppose the purpose of the meeting is to set the salary budget for the ABC employees for the following year. Typically a vote of only three of the five members present at the meeting is necessary to make the salary decision.

Note: Some corporate charters provide for greater- than-majority (supermajority) vote to approve extraordinary actions of the board.

The corporate officers—president, vice president, treasurer, and secretary—are selected by the board of directors according to the provisions of the bylaws. In a publicly held corporation it is generally the officers of the corporation who manage the everyday affairs of the business. The officers, said to operate under the direction of the board of directors, are employees of the corporation. The authority delegated to the officers by the board of directors varies according to the provisions of the corporate bylaws. An officer has the power to represent the corporation in any action in which the authority to act is either actual or apparent.

Within the authority typically delegated to the officers is the power to

- enter into business contracts for the corporation
- hire and terminate agents and employees
- delegate administrative duties to agents and employees

The directors and officers have responsibilities to the corporation and may incur liability for breach of these responsibilities. The board of directors is an agent of the corporation and, as such, owes a fiduciary duty to the corporation. This means the board has a responsibility to the corporation to act with reasonable care and skill in carrying out its duties and owes the corporation the highest degree of good faith and loyalty.

business-judgment rule

The directors and officers of the corporation owe a fiduciary obligation to the corporation. The standard by which their duty is measured is known as the *business-judgment rule*. If the actions of the corporate directors or officers fall within the bounds of honest business judgment, no liability will be incurred by the directors or officers for losses. For the actions of corporate fiduciaries to fall within the liability shelter of the business-judgment rule, the fiduciaries in their actions must[6]

- exercise reasonable diligence in ascertaining facts relevant to the decision
- hold the reasonable belief that the actions are in the corporation's best interest
- have no personal interest in transactions dealing with the corporation

Traditional corporate law has maintained a broad view of permissible business judgment. Over the years the courts have exhibited a tendency to view normal management decisions with a healthy deference. Regardless of the detrimental result to the corporation, courts did not "second-guess" discretionary business judgments made in good faith by directors or officers. The current trend in corporate law has somewhat eroded the protection of the business-judgment rule. However, something greater than simple negligence or an honest mistake by a corporate fiduciary is necessary to create liability.

Generally speaking, the actions of a director or officer must rise to a level of either (1) gross negligence or (2) bad faith before the protection of the business-judgment rule is forfeited. Actions that create liability for the director or officer include the gross neglect of the duties of office or self-dealing with the corporation. The threshold that action must reach before it constitutes gross neglect of office for the purposes of the business-judgment rule varies markedly by the facts of each case. Corporate boards may be composed of inside directors—directors with positions with the corporation involving day-to-day contact—and outside directors—directors whose only responsibility is to attend infrequent meetings and who are not involved in the day-to-day activities of the corporation. Obviously the more control a director or officer exercises over corporate affairs, the greater the duty owed to the corporation.

---

6. *Aronson v. Lewis*, 473 A.2d 805 (Del. 1984).

EXAMPLE

Mr. Smith is both a director and operating officer of Smith Co., Inc., and is involved in the corporation's everyday management. Mr. Smith recognizes from the records that substantial funds are being embezzled from the corporation but has taken no action to prevent this. He is also aware of a key employee who has made extravagant expenditures that far exceed the capability of his somewhat modest salary. Again Mr. Smith takes no action in this regard. The key employee, holding substantial sums of the embezzled corporate funds, flees to Argentina. Mr. Smith is liable to the corporation for losses incurred due to the employee's fraud because of Mr. Smith's gross neglect in his position in the firm and his failure to ascertain the relevant facts and prevent the fraud by the employee. However, the outside directors of Smith Co. are probably not liable for the same neglect. If the outside directors did not have the knowledge possessed by Mr. Smith, their failure to prevent the fraud does not rise to the same level of bad judgment as does that of Mr. Smith.

The directors or officers of a corporation may also lose the protection of the business-judgment rule when they breach their duty of loyalty to the corporation. A director or officer may breach the duty of loyalty by (1) self-dealing with the corporation or (2) taking personal advantage of a corporate opportunity. The traditional rule once made all contracts entered into between an interested director or officer and the corporation voidable by the corporation. This harsh rule has eased somewhat today, and it is now possible for a corporation and one of its directors to enter into an enforceable contract in certain situations. First, the interested director is required to make a full disclosure concerning the transaction to the corporation. Second, the contract must be a fair bargain to the corporation and approved by a majority of disinterested directors who comprise the quorum at the board meeting where the contract is discussed.

EXAMPLE

Smith, Able, Rodgers, and Clay are directors of the Sarc Corp. At a regularly scheduled board meeting at which Clay is not present, Smith proposes to sell personally held real estate to the Sarc Corp. This sale is approved by a two-to-one vote with director Rodgers dissenting. The sale is voidable by the Sarc Corp. for two reasons. First, Smith has a personal interest in the sale and cannot vote in her own behalf. Also the board meeting was not formed by a quorum of disinterested directors since Smith was counted in forming the quorum.

Note: The sale could have been approved had the three disinterested directors held the board meeting with only two of the disinterested directors approving the sale.

The director's or the officer's duty of loyalty to the corporation generally requires that opportunities within the scope of the business be offered first to the corporation. That is, the director or officer should not personally take advantage of an opportunity suitable for the corporation unless the corporation is unable or refuses to take advantage of the opportunity.

Jurisdictions differ in the application of this rule. Most states would limit the "corporate-opportunity doctrine" to situations in which a corporation has an existing interest or expectancy in the business transaction. For example, expectancy exists if the contract is formed with a customer of the corporation with a history of similar prior transactions. Other states take a broader view of corporate opportunity. In these states the director cannot take personal advantage of any opportunity within the general line of business of the corporation. In any event the director or officer may take advantage of any opportunity that is first offered to, and rejected by, the corporation with full disclosure of relevant facts.

EXAMPLE

Mitch, John, and Craig are directors of Power, Inc., a corporation engaged in the purchase and operation of health clubs. Mitch becomes aware of a health club available at a bargain price and makes full disclosure of the opportunity to the other two directors at the next board meeting. Because it does not have the funds, Power is unable to take advantage of the opportunity. Mitch obtains the financing personally and buys the health club for his own benefit. The transaction is valid since Mitch fulfilled his fiduciary obligation to Power by first giving the corporation the opportunity to take advantage of the situation.

A corporate director or officer who commits a breach of fiduciary duty becomes liable to the corporation for damages. In the case of gross neglect or mismanagement the corporate director may be required to reimburse the corporation or its shareholders for damages directly resulting from the breach. In the case of a breach of loyalty the director or officer may be required to turn over any profits made through either self-dealing with the corporation or wrongfully taking personal advantage of a corporate opportunity. Some courts have provided that the director or officer holds the property obtained through a breach of a corporate opportunity in the form of a constructive trust for the benefit of the corporation. That is, the director or officer will hold legal title to the property, but all benefits from the ownership flow through to the corporation.

For a director or officer to become liable, it is necessary that (1) there was a breach of the fiduciary duty to the corporation and (2) damages resulting were proximately caused by the breach of duty. Since the fiduciary owed the duty to the corporation, it is the corporation that has the right to sue for damages. Because the director or officer is not a fiduciary of any individual shareholder, individual shareholders do not have the right to sue a corporate director or officer for losses to the value of their investment in the corporation. However, individual shareholders may bring an action, known as a shareholder derivative action, on behalf of the corporation to vindicate the corporation's rights against a negligent director or officer.

The duty of corporate directors and officers of public companies was significantly increased by the passage of the Sarbanes-Oxley Act.[7] This law added regulation to corporate governance to protect shareholders with respect to accuracy of financial information made pursuant to federal securities laws. Corporate directors, officers, and other executives face both civil and criminal sanctions for intentional misstatements on corporate financial statements.

Corporate Shareholders. The shareholders are the beneficial owners of the corporation whose ownership rights are evidenced by the stock certificates they hold. Except in a closely held corporation shareholders typically have no involvement in the corporation except at shareholders meetings. Corporate laws in most states require that the shareholders have at least an annual meeting whose scheduling and agenda are usually provided for in the bylaws of the corporation. The corporate directors generally specify the time and place for the meeting and must provide ample notice to the shareholders. Special meetings of the shareholders may be authorized under the bylaws for some special or limited purpose. It is only through the shareholder meetings that the typical corporate shareholder exercises involvement in the corporation.

Stock in a corporation may be categorized as voting or nonvoting. The shares of a corporation with only one class of stock are usually designated as voting by corporate law. Corporations with sophisticated capital structures may have several classes of stock and securities outstanding, some of which may not have voting rights. The right of a shareholder to vote is one of the most significant property interests he or she can hold in a corporation.

---

7. Pub. L. No. 107-204, 116 Stat. 745, also known as the Public Company Accounting Reform and Investor Protection Act of 2002.

Actions of a corporation that may require shareholder votes for approval include the following:

- election (and perhaps removal) of directors
- proposed fundamental changes to the corporation, such as amendment of the charter, sale of business property out of the ordinary course of business, merger, and liquidation
- establishment of bylaws (corporate charter and state law may provide for bylaws to be adopted by the directors)
- approval of transactions in which directors have a conflict of interest

It is obvious that the exercise of the shareholders' voting rights can have a significant impact on the corporation's basic structure. Some techniques for maximizing the impact of the voting rights serve a useful planning function for the corporation's owners. It is clear that straight voting—one vote for one share on all issues—will perpetuate control in the hands of the majority shareholder, which may be disadvantageous for both the shareholders and the corporation. First, the minority shareholders are likely to be dissatisfied by their inability to gain a voice in management. In addition, the corporation may have difficulty raising its initial capital since the value of the minority shares is dubious. One solution to this problem is to issue different classes of shares—some with and some without voting rights—to the shareholders.

EXAMPLE

Suppose Sniffy, Sleepy, and Grumpy form the Dwarf Corporation. Sniffy will contribute 60 percent of the capital on formation, with Sleepy and Grumpy contributing 20 percent each. Obviously if one class of stock is issued with equal voting rights, Sniffy will control all actions of the corporation. However, suppose the shareholders want each shareholder to have equal voting rights with the others. Dwarf could issue two classes of stock upon its initial capitalization, giving 100 shares of voting common stock to all three shareholders and 200 shares of nonvoting common stock to Sniffy. In this manner all shareholders will have equal voting rights, but Sniffy's extra contribution will be evidenced by a share of nonvoting common stock that increases his dividend and liquidation rights.

cumulative voting

Another method of allocating voting control to minority shareholders is known as *cumulative voting*. Some state corporate statutes require cumulative voting, while most others permit cumulative voting if authorized by the corporate charter. Cumulative voting provides that each share of stock receive one vote for each of the directors to be elected at the meeting. The shareholder may accumulate votes by abstaining from voting for specific directors and then casting all the accumulated votes on the preferred candidate for one director position. Thus, minority shareholders may be able to elect at least some directors to the board of the corporation.

The following formula demonstrates the determination of the number of shares necessary for the minority shareholders to elect a given number of directors:

$$S = \frac{T \times N}{D + 1} + 1$$

$S =$ number of shares needed to elect N directors

$T =$ total number of shares outstanding

$N =$ number of directors the shareholder hopes to elect

$D =$ total number of director postions to be filled

EXAMPLE

A new corporation, ABC, Inc., is formed with 3,000 shares issued and outstanding. The corporation is going to have a board of three directors who will all be elected annually with cumulative voting in effect at the regular shareholders meeting. Johnson, a minority owner, wants to know how many shares she needs to hold to elect herself to one of the three director positions. The application of the above formula is as follows:

$$S = \frac{3,000 \times 1}{3 + 1} + 1 = 751$$

So we see that Johnson would need to own 751 shares to be guaranteed one position on the board of directors.

Note: Care must be taken as to how the votes are cumulated and voted, since the other shareholders have cumulative voting rights also and may cast their votes in a manner that will thwart the plans of other shareholders.

voting trust

Other useful planning devices to increase the effectiveness of the shareholders' voting rights are proxies and voting trusts. A proxy arrangement is one in which the shareholder holding the voting right designates another—the proxy holder—as an agent to exercise the voting rights. In a closely held corporation the proxy may be used as a tool to ensure that the shareholders vote their shares according to the devised planning scheme. Proxy agreements are governed by both state corporate law and federal securities laws.

A *voting trust* is an arrangement in which the trust settlors transfer shares in the corporation to the trust. The trustee of the voting trust holds legal title to the shares, and the settlors receive voting trust certificates that demonstrate their continuing beneficial interest in the shares of stock. The trustee holds the right to vote the shares of stock at the shareholders meeting according to the trust agreement.

This arrangement can guarantee that the trust beneficiaries' shares will be voted according to the prearranged scheme. Failure to vote the shares in accordance with the agreement makes the trustee liable for a breach of fiduciary duty to the trust beneficiaries. Voting trust agreements will be upheld provided they have a proper corporate purpose. An example of an improper purpose for a voting trust would be its use by current management to entrench themselves in their jobs or approve unreasonable salaries for corporate officers and employees.

Corporate shareholders have the right to receive dividends declared by the board of directors. Dividends—distributions from corporate earnings and profits—evidence the shareholders' right to participate in the profitability of the corporation. State corporate law typically provides that dividends be paid solely from current or accumulated earnings and profits of the corporation. This requirement is to protect the creditors of the corporation, whose rights may be endangered should the corporation make a distribution that impairs the firm's capital structure. Dividends may be paid in the form of cash, property, stock in the corporation, and/or stock in another corporation.

Dividends are paid solely at the discretion of the board of directors, whose action in this respect is governed by the business-judgment rule discussed earlier. The decision to declare dividends or retain corporate earnings has many planning and tax implications. Well-founded financial theory states that rational investors would be indifferent about the dividend policy of a corporation. Simply stated, this theory says that higher dividends result in lower capital appreciation of the shares and vice versa. Although this theory may have some value for the investor in large publicly held corporations, it has little application to the close corporation setting where shares of stock may have restricted marketability.

It is quite possible that the desired dividend policy of various shareholders and that of the corporate directors will not coincide. The right to declare dividends is vested solely in the board of directors. The shareholders who are unhappy with the dividend policy have limited choices available to vindicate their interests. First, the shareholder could sell the stock and hope to be adequately compensated by the proceeds. The lack of marketability of minority interests in closely held corporate stock may limit the value of this option. Second, the shareholder can wait until the next annual election and try to elect more favorable directors. However, the minority shareholder may have limited ability to affect the election of directors. Finally, the shareholders can sue the corporation individually to try to force dividend payments.

Courts apply the business-judgment rule to disputes involving the appropriateness of actions of the directors in the management of the corporation, including the declaration of dividends. The courts will generally defer to the directors' decision to declare dividends unless clear abuse of discretion or bad faith exists. The shareholders attempting to challenge the dividend policy of the directors bear the burden of establishing that the directors acted in their own personal interests rather than in the interest of the corporation. This type of dispute arises frequently in the small closely held corporation. Majority shareholders withhold the declaration of dividends in an effort to freeze out minority shareholders. The majority shareholders might be motivated by hostility toward the minority shareholders or by the adverse tax conesquences (discussed later) associated with paying a dividend. Regardless of the reason, it is important to note that shareholder actions to force dividends are generally unsuccessful.

The transferability of shares of corporate stock is governed by both state corporate law and by the Uniform Commercial Code (UCC). In general the laws favor free transferability of property and will construe narrowly any restrictions on the right to transfer stock. Therefore any corporate provision creating an absolute prohibition on transferability of shares of corporate stock is typically void. However, some restrictions on the ability to transfer the shares of stock may be enforceable. For example, shares of stock may become subject to a binding buy-sell agreement, as will be discussed at length in a later chapter. However, any restriction on the transfer of stock should be noted on the stock certificates to provide notice of the restriction to third parties who might otherwise purchase the stock without knowledge of the restriction.

Among the rights available to protect the shareholder is the right to inspect corporate records. Corporations must provide shareholders with the most recent financial statements on request and must automatically provide all shareholders with an annual statement. The shareholder's right to inspect other corporate records is not unqualified. If the inspection is for a proper purpose, the corporation must allow the inspection by the shareholder or the shareholder's designated agent. The proper-purpose test will be met if the shareholder's request is motivated by the investment interest the shareholder holds in the corporation. For example, a shareholder has the right to inspect the books of the corporation to discover mismanagement, the true worth of the corporation, or the ability of the corporation to pay dividends. However, it is not a proper purpose to inspect corporate books to gain a competitive advantage in dealing with the corporation.

A shareholder has the right to bring suit on behalf of the corporation to vindicate the corporation for damages suffered. These actions—shareholder derivative actions—are brought by a shareholder when the current corporate management refuses to bring a suit to protect a corporate interest on behalf of the corporation. The suit may be instituted against third parties that have injured the corporation or against directors or officers who have breached their duty, creating injury to the corporation. Although shareholders bring these suits to protect their investment in the corporation, all benefits of the suit flow to the corporation itself. Shareholder derivative actions may provide a useful device for minority shareholders to protect their investment from abusive action by the majority shareholders.

Rights of Common Shareholders

- Receive notification of/attend annual and special meetings
- Vote for board members and on major issues
- Receive dividends if declared
- Transfer shares to others
- Inspect corporate records
- Receive the annual financial statement
- Bring suit to compensate the corporation for damages
- Share in the residual proceeds, if any, at time of liquidation

The general rule provides that shareholders of a corporation are not individually liable to creditors and other third-party claimants of the corporation. Instead the corporation's property may be consumed to satisfy these claims. Therefore the actual loss that may be suffered by individual shareholders is limited to their investment in the corporation. This limited-liability concept is typically a major driving force in the decision to incorporate a business. Since most individuals prefer to insulate their personal assets from the risks of running a business, the limited-liability protection is a distinct advantage of incorporation.

The financial services professional should be aware that there are exceptions to the limited-liability rule. The courts have "pierced the corporate veil" (ignored the separate legal status of a corporation) in some cases where injuries have occurred and the corporate formalities are subject to question. The courts are more likely to ignore the existence of a corporation and impose unlimited liability on a shareholder when the injured party is led to believe that an individual shareholder, and not a corporation, is transacting the business. This situation occurs when the business functions as an unincorporated business, is undercapitalized, and appears to be the "alter ego" of the principal shareholder. However, when the state incorporation statutes are followed explicitly and the owners are operating the business in the corporate form and not in an individual capacity, the courts are reluctant to find an individual shareholder personally liable for corporate activities. It is important to note that the closely held corporate setting, discussed below, leaves greater potential for unlimited liability to the shareholders for corporate operations. The owners of the closely held business often appear to be acting in their individual capacities instead of following the formalities of a corporation.

Closely Held Corporations

The closely held corporation is a hybrid form of business enterprise. It is incorporated under the laws of the state of incorporation and follows formalities applicable to corporations under state law. However, many of the practical aspects of the operation and management of the firm closely resemble those of a partnership. In the absence of a special statute a close corporation can be defined as one with

- a small number of shareholders
- no readily available market for shares in the corporation
- unity between the ownership, management, and employees of the corporation

The Control and Operation of Closely Held Corporations

The decision to incorporate a closely held business is marked by both planning opportunities and pitfalls. The many advantages of the corporate form—limited liability, continuity of life, and various tax advantages—are attractive to the small growing business. However, the strict formalities of corporate law may prevent business owners from operating the business enterprise on the same comfortable and informal basis as in the past. Quite simply, the shareholders hope to operate the closely held corporation as a de facto partnership. They hope to maintain control among themselves according to the prearranged agreement and prevent outsiders from becoming involved in the business. The shareholders hope to continue the everyday management of the business and operate the business enterprise solely for their personal benefit. The planning problem is to maintain the operating status quo of the partnership while taking advantage of the benefits of corporate form.

Traditional corporate law has developed standards of behavior for the various actors in the corporate setting. For example, the corporate directors owe fiduciary duty to the corporation but not to individual shareholders. The shareholders typically owe no duty to either their coshareholders or the corporation. Traditional corporate law would bring strange results if applied to the closely held corporation because one individual—the majority shareholder—wears several hats in the corporate setting.

Case law has developed to adapt to the unusual setting of the closely held corporation. The trend is to impose fiduciary duty on the shareholders when their action involves management or representation of the corporation. This is a natural extension of partnership law to the closely held corporation. Since coshareholders of a closely held corporation are similar to partners of a partnership, the duties of the shareholders with respect to each other should be no less than those of partners.

The goal of the majority shareholders in most closely held corporations is to vest management control within themselves and to provide little opportunity for intrusion by minority shareholders. To this end, majority shareholders have devised imaginative and elaborate corporate provisions to maintain the status quo. For example, if the corporate charter provides for the staggered election of directors standing for election each year, the benefit of cumulative voting for the minority shareholders can be minimized.

EXAMPLE

The Acme Corporation has 1,000 shares of voting common stock issued and outstanding. Louise, the majority shareholder of Acme, holds 600 shares. The remaining two shareholders, Dick and Jane, hold 200 shares each. Acme's board is comprised of three directors. If all three board positions are eligible for election at each annual meeting, cumulative voting will provide Dick and Jane with the opportunity to combine their votes and elect at least one director. However, if the election of the directors is staggered and only one director is eligible for election each year, the effect of cumulative voting is negated. In this case Louise will be able to elect all the directors and exert total control over the corporation.

Another method used by majority shareholders to maintain control of the closely held corporation is the supermajority requirement. Corporate law in many jurisdictions permits the requirement of a higher threshold than a simple majority of shareholders to approve corporate changes or elect directors. A supermajority provision minimizes the risk that minority shareholders will be able to have an impact on corporate policy.

An important and much litigated method of perpetuating the status quo in management and control of a closely held corporation is the contractual agreement between shareholders. The purpose of shareholder agreements, found almost exclusively in the closely held corporation, is to oblige the parties to vote for directors in a prearranged fashion or to otherwise control the governance of the corporation. These agreements will generally be valid unless they violate state law or prevent directors from exercising independent business judgment. Some states now have special closely held corporation statutes, discussed below, that expressly permit and regulate shareholder voting agreements.

Similar in purpose to the shareholder agreement is the voting trust. This trust is a formal agreement among shareholders in which the shares held by the parties to the agreement will be voted in common by a trustee in a prearranged fashion. Most states have statutory controls over voting trust arrangements. For example, the voting trust may be limited in duration to a time period, such as 10 years. It is also typically required that the voting trust have a proper purpose. A voting trust will not serve a proper purpose if it results in the circumvention of statutory requirements for the operation of a corporation. For example, a voting trust that has the practical effect of removing discretionary business judgment from the board of directors may be declared invalid.

The corporation control devices discussed above provide planning issues for the founders of a closely held corporation. These control devices permit the operation of a closely held corporation to be similar to that of a partnership. The planning consideration involves the drafting of the corporate provisions and shareholder agreements consistent with the desired allocation of control and ownership of the corporation. As in the drafting of a partnership agreement the financial services professional should be aware that competent professional advice must be sought to ensure that the document meets its stated purpose and complies with state law.

Closely Held Corporation Statutes

A minority of states have adopted special provisions in their corporate statutes dealing with closely held corporations. The purpose of these statutes is to recognize the special nature of the close corporation and impose requirements that reflect the hybrid nature of its operation. The special closely held corporation statutes provide for operation of the business with formalities similar to those of partnerships.

Typical provisions in the closely held corporation statutes are the following:

- limits on the number of shareholders
- limits on the duration of the business
- elimination of the board of directors
- operation of the business by the shareholders
- provision for voting trust agreements
- provision for shareholder agreements
- provision for forced dissolution by a shareholder
- provision for substantial restriction on the transfer of shares

Increasing numbers of jurisdictions are adopting closely held corporation statutes. The financial services professional should be aware that the provisions of these laws vary from state to state and that local law should be consulted before forming a closely held corporation.

Professional Corporations

Legal Status

professional corporation

The advantages of the corporate form of ownership have attracted many professionals who have traditionally operated their practices as either proprietorships or partnerships. Today virtually all states have statutes that provide for the incorporation of professional practices and require the *professional corporation* to follow all the formalities typically applicable to all corporations within the state. For example, the corporation should operate under the management of the board of directors, execute business contracts in the name of the corporation, and provide employment contracts and salaries to the member professionals. Some of these formalities could be avoided in states with special close corporation statutes.

Operating Characteristics of a Professional Corporation

Generally speaking, the formalities associated with the operation of a professional corporation are similar to those of any other commercial corporation. The professional corporation is formed as a separate legal entity under state law and provides for a continuity of life beyond that of its shareholders. Since the practice of most professions is governed by various licensing requirements of state law, virtually all professional corporation statutes limit the ownership of a professional corporation to licensed members of the profession. At the death, disability, or termination of employment of a professional, the stock held by the professional can be (1) transferred to another licensed professional or (2) redeemed by the corporation. A problem can arise if no buyer can be found or if the corporation has inadequate surplus for the redemption. To some extent, this may limit the continuity of life of the professional corporation.

The limited-liability shelter of the corporate form of ownership offers a distinct advantage over the operation of the business in an unincorporated form. As with any other corporation, the contractual liability of individual shareholders in a professional corporation is limited to their investment in the corporation. The corporation, as the principal, remains vicariously liable for all acts of the corporation's agents (the professionals) in the ordinary scope of a corporate enterprise. However, this liability is limited to the property of the corporation, and individual shareholder-professionals do not expose their personal assets for corporate contractual risks.

Since individual shareholder-professionals remain liable for their own negligent actions, the professional acting as an employee of the professional corporation retains unlimited liability for professional malpractice. The shareholder-professional also incurs unlimited personal liability for the actions of corporate employees directly under his or her supervision. However, when the shareholder-professional has no control over the actions of coshareholder-employees, there is no vicarious liability for the action of a negligent coshareholder.

Despite the retention of personal liability for malpractice on the part of the professional, the professional corporation provides substantial liability protection not available in the unincorporated form of business enterprise. For example, as noted above, the shareholder effectively limits liability for contractual obligations of the corporation and for the actions of other shareholders and employees. No such limits on liability would exist if the professional practice was operated in the form of a partnership.

In summary, the professional corporation affords shareholder-professionals some advantages that would not be present if the business was operated in an unincorporated form. For example, the benefits of the corporate tax structure are available in most instances. Also the advantages of continuity of life of the corporation and limited liability are available, at least to some extent, to the shareholders. These advantages must be balanced against the costs and inflexibility inherent in the formalities of forming and operating a corporation. Financial services professionals should be aware that the laws of the state control the formalities of incorporating and operating a professional or closely held corporation.

THE TAXATION OF CORPORATIONS

A corporation is a separate legal entity organized and operated under state law. Federal tax law will generally recognize the separate tax status of a corporation and its shareholders. In recent years, most of this scrutiny involved reclassifying partnerships or LLCs as corporations since most business owners sought the advantages of pass-through taxation.

Under entity classification rules, all entities that incorporate under state and federal law will be taxed as corporations. In addition, certain per se corporations will be taxed as corporations regardless of their organization form. These include (1) banks, (2) insurance companies, (3) organizations wholly owned by a state or political subdivision, and (4) certain foreign entities. In addition, other entities such as partnerships or LLCs can elect to be taxed as corporations under the regulations.

The Taxation of Corporate Income

A corporation is a separate taxpayer for federal income tax purposes. The corporation itself must file a tax return and pay federal tax on its taxable income. The owners of the corporation—the shareholders—pay no tax on the corporation's income directly. However, when the corporation distributes income to the shareholders in the form of dividends, the shareholders may pay tax on the dividends, currently at the tax rate for capital gains. In other words, corporate income may be taxed twice, first at the corporate level and then again when it is distributed to shareholders.

In some circumstances a shareholder may receive dividend treatment when corporate distributions are made to the shareholder either (1) in exchange for his or her stock or (2) upon dissolution of the corporation.

The potential for double taxation in the corporate form, while a major planning concern, is not always the obstacle it appears to be at first glance. In many cases it is possible for corporations to minimize the amount of tax paid at the corporate level by minimizing the amount of actual corporate taxable income. In closely held corporations most of the net income from the business can be paid out in the form of salaries, which are deductible in computing the corporation's taxable income. By paying salaries to shareholder-employees the corporation can pass along income to shareholders without incurring double taxation. Note that double taxation is avoided only if the salaries are deductible to the corporation. A deduction is allowed only for "reasonable compensation"; salaries paid to shareholder-employees in excess of reasonable compensation will be treated as dividends that are nondeductible to the corporation.

The question of what constitutes reasonable compensation is frequently a subject of dispute between taxpayers and the IRS. Despite the absence of clear standards a few factors can be noted. If the business is heavily capitalized, then obviously some of the business income must represent a return on capital. In capital-intensive businesses only part of the owner's share of income will generally be allowable as reasonable compensation for services. In a business in which capital is not a significant income-producing factor (personal-service businesses), most or all of the business's income could be paid out to shareholder-employees and deducted as reasonable compensation. This is particularly important in view of the special 35 percent flat rate applicable to the taxable income of personal-service corporations. Based on the goals of the corporation and its shareholders, there may be a tax incentive to overcompensate or undercompensate the shareholder-employees. The factors that should be considered for determining reasonable-compensation levels for employees.

Double Taxation of Corporate Income

- A dollar is earned by the corporation, which pays a tax on it at the corporate rate.
- What's left of the dollar is paid as a dividend to the shareholder, who pays a tax on the dividend.
- The solution: Keep the dollar in the corporation, avoiding taxation at the individual's level; or pay the dollar to the individual as a salary, avoiding taxation at the corporate level.

Furthermore, a corporation is not obligated to pay out its earnings as dividends, so double taxation is not automatic. These earnings may be reinvested in the corporate business or simply accumulated at the corporate level, thereby avoiding a second tax at the shareholder level. The accumulated-earnings tax discussed later is designed to prevent a corporation from accumulating earnings to avoid the declaration of taxable dividends.

Special Deduction for Income Derived From Domestic Manufacturing

The income tax rate for manufacturing and production income for activities in the United States was based on the normal income tax rates. The rate of tax was the same as tax on ordinary income with the rate applicable corresponding to the type of entity. That is, a corporation was taxed under the corporate income tax tables, and owners of sole proprietorships, partnerships, LLCs, and S corporations were taxed on pass-through of ordinary income related to manufacturing activities based on the tables for tax on ordinary individual income. Congress has felt that corporate income tax rates are higher in the U.S. than in other countries and has provided several tax benefits in the past, most notably an extraterritorial income (ETI) exclusion.

The World Trade Organization determined that these tax benefits created a prohibited trade subsidy. The ETI exclusion was repealed and a new tax deduction was created for domestic manufacturers. Beginning with income earned in 2005, a special tax deduction is available for business income derived from manufacturing and production based in the United States. The deduction was 3 percent in 2005 and 2006. The deduction increased to 6 percent for 2007, 2008, and 2009, and it will increase to 9 percent for all years after 2009. This deduction applies, regardless of the form of business entity. For example, the deduction can be taken by an entity that is a separate taxpayer such as a regular corporation. The deduction can also be taken on an individual return against pass-through income from an S corporation, partnership, limited liability company, estate, trust, or sole proprietorship.

Domestic production activities include manufacturing, food processing, film or videotape production, energy production, engineering, construction, and computer software production. The property must generally be manufactured, produced, grown, or extracted at least in significant part within the United States. In the case of films or videos, at least 50 percent of the compensation provided to the actors, production personnel, directors, and producers must be for services performed in the United States. Excluded from the allowable production activities are the sale of food and beverages prepared by the taxpayer at a retail establishment and the transmission of electricity, gas, or water. It is clear that some manufacturers will have both acceptable and excluded activities. For example, an energy producer may also be engaged in the transmission of electricity. The income of such business will have to be divided between the covered and excluded activities, and the expenses will have to be allocated in some fashion to determine the income from the qualified production activities.

The allowable deduction for the year is applied to the lesser of (1) the "qualified production activities income" or (2) the taxpayer's taxable income (determined without regard to the deduction). The deduction is taken against taxable income for corporations and adjusted gross income for individuals (that is, the deduction will not be subject to the 2 percent floor for itemized deductions). The deduction is further limited to 50 percent of the wages paid by the employer engaged in the activity. Wages include normal wages and certain elective deferrals under retirement plan arrangements (that is, Secs. 401(k) and 457 plans and, after 2005, Roth IRA contributions).

The deduction is also allowed against alternative minimum tax (AMT) and similarly reduces income of an individual for AMT purposes. The deduction reduces adjusted current earnings of a corporation in determining corporate AMT (discussed later in this chapter). For corporations, the deduction (available for the tax year) is applied to the lesser of (1) the qualified production activities income and (2) the alternative minimum taxable income.

The Taxation of Dividends Distributed to Shareholders

The Jobs and Growth Tax Relief Reconciliation Act (JGTRRA) of 2003 reduced the individual tax rate for qualified dividends received by an individual shareholder. Qualified dividends are taxed at the rate applicable to net capital gains. For most shareholders, this means that dividends received will be taxed at 15 percent. For taxpayers in the 10 or 15 percent bracket for individual income, dividends will be taxed at zero after 2007. Recent legislation extended this special rate until 2013.

Qualified dividends are dividends received from domestic corporations and qualified foreign corporations if the recipient meets certain holding period rules. Under these rules, qualified dividends do not include dividends if the shareholder did not hold the stock for at least 61 days during the 121 days that began 60 days before the ex-dividend date. In addition, special holding period rules apply to dividends received on preferred stock.

The Reinvestment of Accumulated Earnings

The prospect of accumulating earnings in the corporation for reinvestment or otherwise may produce a tax advantage of using the corporate form as opposed to other forms of organization because there is some possibility of income taxed at lower corporate brackets. In addition, accumulated earnings can avoid the double taxation problem for corporate earnings distributed as dividends. The tax rate schedules for individual and corporate taxpayers were presented in chapter 1.

EXAMPLE

Assume Mike has a home improvement business that currently operates as a proprietorship. Mike has no unearned income, and his business income represents his entire reportable income. His business is currently small, and he intends to reinvest as much of the business earnings into the business as possible. Assume that the business has a taxable income of $150,000 annually and that Mike will file a joint return with his wife who is not employed. The current (proprietorship) picture is as follows:

$150,000	$30,070 federal income tax
Mike's after-tax income to be reinvested	$119,930

Mike decides to incorporate and take a reasonable salary of $75,000. The tax situation resulting is as follows:

corporate taxable income	\$75,000 (\$150,000 – \$75,000)
corporate income tax	\$13,750 [(\$50,000 at 15%) + \$25,000 at 25%)]
tax on Mike's salary*	\$11,000
total tax	\$24,750
funds left to reinvest	\$125,250—in the incorporated form \$119,930—as a proprietorship

*assuming 2011 tables and ignoring deductions

The example demonstrates a fact pattern where corporate rates provide an advantage for a small business. The lower overall corporate rates in this instance will permit a growing business to reinvest earnings at lower after-tax cost and accumulate capital faster under the corporate form than under other forms of enterprise. The dollars can be accumulated and used within the corporation subject to the limits of the accumulated-earnings tax penalty discussed below. The more lightly taxed corporate dollars can also be used to fund a tax-advantaged employee benefit plan with shareholder-employees. In addition, corporate-owned life insurance can be purchased for key person or other corporate purposes with earnings taxed at the lower corporate rates and accumulated in the corporation.

The Accumulated-Earnings Tax

The tax advantage of the corporate tax rates on earnings accumulated by the corporation is limited somewhat by the accumulated-earnings tax. Although shareholders' legal actions to force the payment of dividends have met with limited success, the accumulated-earnings tax provides a substantial incentive to distribute income as dividends. Simply stated, the accumulated-earnings tax is a penalty tax designed to prevent tax avoidance through the accumulation of earnings within the corporation beyond the expected needs of the business.

The mechanics of the accumulated-earnings tax are relatively complicated, but the effect is straightforward. A corporation can accumulate up to a "minimum credit" of \$250,000 of earnings and profits (\$150,000 for a personal-service corporation) without encountering any problem with the accumulated-earnings tax. If a corporation accumulates earnings and profits beyond the minimum credit amount, it must be prepared to demonstrate to the IRS that the accumulation is for reasonable needs of the business. If this cannot be demonstrated, the IRS will impose a tax—the accumulated-earnings tax—on the corporation.

accumulated taxable income

The accumulated-earnings tax is currently imposed at a rate of 15 percent on all accumulated taxable income. [8] The *accumulated taxable income* is basically defined as the taxable income of the corporation less

- corporate tax paid on income
- dividends paid
- amounts accumulated for reasonable business needs or, if greater, the remaining minimum accumulated-earnings credit

EXAMPLE

XYZ, Inc., is a manufacturing business that would like to accumulate income but not for business purposes. It simply wishes to avoid double taxation on the payment of dividends. Assume the following facts:

- accumulated earnings and profits at the end of last year: $236,000
- taxable income this year of $500,000
- no dividends paid in either year

The accumulated-earnings tax is computed by first determining the taxable accumulated earnings. Since $236,000 has been accumulated by the end of last year, the unused credit going into this year is $14,000. For this year, the taxable accumulated earnings is $327,750 ($500,000 less $158,250 corporate tax less the remaining credit—$14,000). The accumulated-earnings tax on this amount could be as much as $49,162.50 if all accumulations have no reasonable business purpose.

Corporate earnings may be accumulated for reasonable business needs beyond the minimum credit amount without the imposition of the accumulated-earnings tax. The Code defines reasonable business needs in a highly circular fashion to include all reasonably anticipated needs of the business. Although the Code is not always helpful for this purpose, there is substantial case law determining what is (or is not) a reasonable business need. Professional advice should be sought before planning to accumulate earnings in a corporation.

---

8. The accumulated-earnings tax rate is set at the tax rate in effect for dividend distributions.

Among the clear reasonable business needs is the accumulation of earnings for anticipated capital expenditures. Another reasonable business need specified in the Code is the accumulation of earnings in the year of a shareholder's death and thereafter to perform a Sec. 303 stock redemption. Sec. 303 redemptions are a special type of redemption that can provide tax advantages for the estate of an owner of a family corporation.

The Corporate Alternative Minimum Tax

In response to the popular perception that many corporations do not pay a fair share of federal income taxes, Congress enacted the complex alternative-minimum-tax provisions. Corporations must pay the alternative minimum tax if it is greater than the regular corporate income tax for the year. To the extent that the alternative minimum tax paid exceeds the regular tax for the year, the corporation may use this excess to offset regular tax liability in future years.

alternative minimum taxable income (AMTI)

The tax is imposed at a rate of 20 percent of the *alternative minimum taxable income (AMTI)* above an exemption amount. The AMTI base is determined by adding certain tax-preference items to the corporation's normal taxable income for the year.

These preferences include the following:

- certain excess depreciation taken by the corporation
- tax-exempt interest on certain private-activity government bonds
- 75 percent of the amount by which current adjusted earnings exceed AMTI (computed specifically without this adjustment)

The current adjusted earnings modification is included in the list since corporations often reflect substantial earnings on income statements reported to shareholders and regulatory authorities that are not included in taxable income. For example, corporate-owned life insurance may increase current earnings and profits without a corresponding increase in taxable income when

- annual increases in cash surrender value exceed annual premiums
- death benefits are received in excess of cash surrender value

Current adjusted earnings are similar to the corporate earnings and profits and are determined by the corporation's accounting method and may or may not be regularly reported in a formal statement by a closely held corporation. There is some flexibility in planning for this adjustment as long as generally accepted accounting principles are adhered to. Closely held corporations rarely prepare audited public income statements, but the Code permits less formal statements to be used for the purpose of this adjustment. For example, it may be permissible for the firm to use a noncertified statement that was prepared by the business for the purpose of securing credit.

The AMT applies only to "large" corporations. An exemption from AMT will apply to a small corporation. A small corporation is defined as a corporation that has gross receipts below a minimum threshold. The minimum threshold rules provide that a corporation is a small corporation if its average gross receipts for the 3-year period prior to the current tax year are $7.5 million or less. If the corporation did not qualify as a small corporation for 1998 (when this exemption was enacted) under these rules, it cannot qualify for the AMT exemption in future tax years.

Taxation of Personal-Service Corporations

personal-service corporation (PSC)

The tax laws provide that the taxable income of a *personal-service corporation (PSC)* will be taxed at a flat rate of 35 percent. This special treatment eliminates the tax benefit of graduated corporate rates for PSCs. The 35 percent flat rate can result in an additional annual income tax above the normal corporate tax rates for lower levels of corporate income.

EXAMPLE

The Investment Adviser Corporation has $75,000 of taxable income. Using the flat tax rate of 35 percent the tax would be $26,250 (.35 x $75,000). However, if the corporation could use the graduated corporate rates, the corporation's federal income tax would be computed as follows:

15 percent of the first $50,000 of taxable income	$ 7,500
25 percent of the next $25,000 of taxable income	6,250
Total tax	$13,750

Therefore the additional tax using the flat personal-service corporation rate would be $12,500 ($26,250 – $13,750).

Since the lower brackets are inapplicable to personal-service corporations, the corporate tax advantages for accumulating income to reinvest at the corporate level will be eliminated. If highly compensated professionals take all income out of the PSC as deductible compensation, the PSC avoids the flat 35 percent rate. However, this salary would be taxed at the individual rates of the professional (perhaps 33 or 35 percent).

For the purpose of PSC flat rate a qualified personal-service corporation is defined as any corporation in which (1) substantially all the activities involve the performance of services in the fields of health, law, engineering, architecture, accounting, actuarial science, performing arts, or consulting and (2) substantially all the stock is held by employees who perform such services for the corporation, any such retired employees, the estate of any such employees, or any beneficiary of the estate of any such employees (but only for the 2-year period beginning on the date of the death of any such employee). Thus the professional corporation will generally be subject to this rate.

Performance of services in the field of consulting means providing advice and counsel. A business activity whose income is derived primarily from commissions is not a PSC.

EXAMPLE

Gail Johnstone is both the sole shareholder and an employee of Feebased Planning, Inc., a C corporation engaged in the practice of comprehensive personal financial planning. Its sole business activity is the preparation of financial plans for an hourly fee. Feebased is a personal-service corporation and is subject to a 35 percent tax rate on all corporate taxable income.

Taxation of Corporate Formation

The formation of a corporation can be carried out free of federal income taxes. Tax law provides that the transfer of business property to a new corporation or an existing corporation in exchange for the corporation's stock or securities can be made without recognition of gain or loss on the transaction if the person or persons who transfer the property are in control of the corporation after the transfer. Control for these purposes means 80-percent-or-more ownership. If the contribution does not qualify as tax free, the contributing shareholder will have to recognize gain on the transfer to the extent that the fair market value of the stock received exceeds the shareholder's adjusted basis in the contributed property.

Note that the stock must be issued in return for cash or "property" contributed to the corporation. This means that stock issued for services will not be received tax free, nor will a person receiving such stock be counted as part of the controlling group for purposes of the 80 percent test.

EXAMPLE

Frank and his employee, Mort, decide to incorporate Frank's grocery store business, which is operated as a proprietorship. Frank will supply all the corporate property and Mort merely agrees to continue working for the new corporation. The plan is for each to receive 50 percent of the stock. This transfer of stock to Mort will not be tax free to him. Furthermore, Mort will not be counted as a controlling shareholder for purposes of the 80 percent test, since he did not receive stock in return for property. Since Frank is part of the control group and receives only 50 percent, the incorporation transaction is fully taxable, and even Frank must pay taxes if gain is recognized on the exchange.

If an otherwise nontaxable corporate formation results in the receipt of money or other property (known as *boot*) along with the stock, the gain, if any, will be recognized to the extent of the value of the boot even if the 80 percent test is satisfied. No loss is recognized in any event.

Sometimes the unincorporated business has liabilities that will be transferred to the corporation. In the tax law if a person transfers liabilities to another, this transfer usually has the same consequences as a receipt of money or property by the transferor, since the transferor is relieved of a financial obligation. However, in a tax-free incorporation the assumption of liability is not treated as boot that results in taxation, unless the liabilities assumed exceed the basis of the properties transferred.

EXAMPLE

Frank has decided to rearrange the transaction and exchange his business assets used in the grocery store in return for 100 percent of the stock. Suppose the assets are worth $100,000, and Frank's basis for the property is $50,000. The store is subject to a $40,000 mortgage, and the mortgage is assumed by the new corporation as part of the incorporation transaction. Because the $40,000 mortgage is not in excess of Frank's basis for the store, it will not be treated as boot. However, if the mortgage amount were $70,000, Frank would recognize a capital gain of $20,000 on the incorporation transaction.

When a corporation is formed, the basis to the shareholders of their shares in the corporation is equal to the basis of the property they transferred to the corporation, decreased by the value of boot received and increased by the amount of taxable gain recognized on the transaction. This is a basis rule similar to the one that applies under the Code to many other types of tax-free exchange, including the formation of a partnership as described in chapter 2. However, unlike the situation in a partnership, the shareholders' bases do not include any part of indebtedness later incurred by the corporation. And also unlike the situation in a partnership, the shareholders' bases do not fluctuate as a result of ordinary business operations.

The *corporation's* basis for the property received will be the same as it was in the hands of the shareholders before the incorporation, increased by the amount of gain recognized to the shareholders. This is the basis that will apply for depreciation and other similar purposes.

A corporation may deduct up to $5,000 of start-up or organizational expenses from current income taxes when the corporation is formed. The tax deduction is limited for large amounts of start-up or organizational expenses. The deduction is reduced (but not below zero) by the amount the organizational expenses exceed $50,000. Any start-up or organizational expenses that cannot be deducted currently under this incentive must be amortized over 15 years.

SUBCHAPTER S ELECTION

For federal income tax purposes there is a fourth form of business organization—the S corporation. An S corporation is a corporation organized in the usual manner under state law, but the corporation has made a special election provided in Subchapter S of the Internal Revenue Code (many states have a similar election for state income tax purposes). The election converts the corporation to a pass-through entity for tax purposes, providing tax treatment similar to that of a partnership.

This pass-through tax treatment became extremely important after the Tax Reform Act of 1986. Now that the 1986 tax changes have been substantially revised and the maximum tax rates are identical for individuals and corporations, the S election may offer fewer benefits solely from an income tax rate standpoint, but most closely held business owners will prefer the pass-through tax treatment it offers.

The Small Business Job Protection Act of 1996 and American Jobs Creation Act of 2004 eased some of the restrictions on S corporation ownership, and it helped to facilitate estate planning for S corporation shareholders. Since there are many corporations that are currently operating with S corporation status and tax advantages of the S election still exist, it remains very important to understand the tax treatment of an S corporation.

Restrictions on S Corporations

Types of Corporations

Only domestic corporations are eligible to make the S election. Although the statute refers to small *business* corporations, there is no specific prohibition for professional personal-service corporations; these entities are eligible to make the S election.

Individual Ownership

In order to qualify for a Subchapter S election, a corporation must conform to a number of formal restrictions imposed by the Code. To make an election under Subchapter S, the corporation must not have ineligible shareholders. The maximum number of shareholders in an S corporation is 100. For this purpose, all family members are treated as one shareholder.[9] In addition, all individual shareholders must be citizens or residents of the United States. The estate of a deceased shareholder may continue to hold S corporation stock for a reasonable period of estate administration.

Requirements for Subchapter S Election

- Must be a domestic corporation
- Must have not ineligible shareholders
- Must have no more than 100 shareholders
- No shareholders may be nonresident aliens

Trusts as S Corporation Shareholders

To facilitate business and estate planning flexibility for owners of S corporations, Congress has provided for several types of trusts to be eligible

9. This change and the increase to 100 shareholders was added by The American Jobs Creation Act (AJCA) of 2004. For this purpose, "members of the family" include a common ancestor and all lineal descendants of the common ancestor (including spouses and former spouses of such individuals). To be counted as members of a family, the youngest generation of such lineal descendants cannot be more than six generations removed from the common ancestor. The beneficiary of a qualified subchapter S trust (QSST) will be treated as the owner and a family member for this purpose."

S corporation shareholders. Transfers of S corporation stock to trusts entail careful planning. It is important to coordinate S corporation shareholders' estate plans with the business ownership because the death of a shareholder could cause the stock held by the decedent to be transferred to testamentary trusts created under the decedent's will. The changes brought about by the Small Business Job Protection Act of 1996 reduce the risk of transfer to an ineligible shareholder by broadening the types of trusts eligible for S corporation ownership.

grantor trust

Grantor Trusts. A common type of living trust known as a *grantor trust* is an eligible shareholder of S corporation stock. A grantor trust is one in which the grantor is treated as the owner for income tax purposes. The typical grantor trust is a revocable trust created as a probate-avoidance device. The grantor places selected assets in the revocable trust, and trust assets pass outside of probate at the grantor's death. Thus an S corporation shareholder can fund his or her revocable trust with company stock without jeopardizing the S election. The new law extends the eligibility to revocable trusts for up to 2 years after the grantor's death. Although the revocable trust is the most common form of grantor trust, the tax rules under Secs. 671–678 provide many other forms of grantor "defective" trusts that could be useful for the ownership of S corporation stock.

qualified subchapter S trust (QSST)

Qualified Subchapter S Trusts. The law also allows the creation of a *qualified subchapter S trust (QSST)* to hold S corporation stock. The QSST is a useful planning device for splitting S corporation income among family members without relinquishing complete control of the stock. The trust grantor can gift stock to the trust and effectively shift the tax burden to the trust beneficiary. The trustee holds and votes stock until the designated trust termination date, however—perhaps when a donee-child or -grandchild reaches the age of majority. The requirements of the QSST are as follows:

- It must distribute all its income to an individual U.S. citizen or resident.Under its terms there can be only one income beneficiary.
- During the term of the trust, corpus may be distributed only to the current income beneficiary.
- Each income interest in the trust must terminate on the earlier of the death of the income beneficiary or the trust termination.
- Upon termination of the trust during the life of an income beneficiary, the trust must distribute all its assets to that beneficiary.

- The beneficiary must make the S election (the election is automatic for successor income beneficiaries unless a successor affirmatively refuses to consent).

electing small business trust (ESBT)

Electing Small Business Trusts. Tax law permits a special election for trust that do not otherwise qualify as eligible shareholders of S corporation stock: an *electing small business trust (ESBT)*. The ESBT overcomes some of the disadvantages of the QSST in that the trust may have more than one current beneficiary and the election is made by the trustee rather than relying on the beneficiary. Eligible beneficiaries include (1) individuals, (2) estates, and (3) a qualifying charity (the charity can only be a contingent remainder beneficiary). Only trusts receiving S corporation stock by gift or bequest are eligible to be ESBTs. Thus the trustee of an ESBT cannot purchase the S corporation stock as an investment.

Unfortunately, the ESBT has some tax disadvantages. The S corporation portion of the ESBT must be treated as a separate trust, and items of income attributable to the S corporation stock are taxed to the trust at the highest individual rates. Therefore S corporation income attributable to the trust is taxed at 35 percent and capital gain at 15 percent. There is no deduction allowable to the trust for distributions to beneficiaries, and the ESBT's distributable net income will not include items attributable to the S corporation ownership. The net effect of these provisions is that the tax on the S corporation income cannot be shifted to ESBT beneficiaries, and the S corporation income passed through to the trust is taxed at maximum rates. Note that a QSST that is permitted only one income beneficiary and allows income to be shifted to the beneficiary cannot be an ESBT.

EXAMPLE

Mom owns 100 percent of the stock in Momco, Inc., an S corporation. As part of her estate plan, she makes a gift of 30 percent of her stock to an irrevocable trust. The trust is a "spray" trust giving an independent trustee the discretion to accumulate or distribute all trust income to the beneficiaries (her four children) in shares to be determined by the trustee. The S corporation has $100,000 of taxable income for the year, and the trustee, as title owner to the stock, receives a K-1 from the corporation reporting $30,000 as the trust's share of the S corporation income. The trust is taxable on this portion of its income at 35 percent, regardless of whether any of the income is distributed to the beneficiaries.

Voting Trusts. The use of a voting trust to ensure that shareholders will vote their stock according to a preconceived plan was discussed earlier in this chapter. It is permissible for a voting trust to be formed by S corporation shareholders; the voting trust is an eligible shareholder.

Testamentary Trusts. Certain testamentary trusts that meet the QSST or ESBT rules are eligible shareholders and can make the appropriate election when funded with S corporation stock by a deceased shareholder's estate. However, the new law also permits other types of testamentary trusts to hold S corporation stock for a period of up to 2 years following a deceased shareholder's death.

S Corporation Subsidiaries

qualified subchapter S subsidiary (QSSS)

Under prior law, an S corporation generally could not be a member of an affiliated group of corporations. An S corporation can own 80 percent or more of the stock in a C corporation, but it cannot file a consolidated return with the C corporation affiliates. In addition, an S corporation is permitted to have a wholly owned *qualified subchapter S subsidiary (QSSS)*. If the QSSS election is made, all assets, items of income, deductions, and QSSS credits are treated as if they belong to the parent S corporation.

Tax Treatment of S Corporations

The tax treatment of an S corporation and its shareholders parallels the tax treatment of partners and partnerships. Each shareholder in an S corporation includes in income his or her share of income items, including tax-exempt income, losses, deductions, and credits. The character of income items—for example, whether they are tax-exempt income or capital gain—carries over to the shareholder. Income items are passed through on a pro rata basis to shareholders, and no special allocations of such items are permitted. Corporate tax provisions that relate to the status of a corporation as a separate tax entity, such as the separate rates, accumulated-earnings tax, personal-holding-company tax, and corporate AMT, are inapplicable to S corporations.

As in a partnership, income items are includible by the shareholder in the income of the taxable year in which the corporation's tax year ends. S corporations must generally use a calendar year for tax purposes, and a shareholder will report the S corporation income on the last day of his or her tax year. If there is a change during the year in a taxpayer's ownership share of the corporation, the amount of each item includible by the shareholder will be adjusted to reflect the number of days in the year that the shareholder held each different ownership interest in the corporation. If the shareholder is employed by and receives a salary from the S corporation, this salary payment is includible in income when actually (or constructively) received. Salary payments are deductible from business income, thus reducing the income that passes through on a pro rata basis to all shareholders at the end of a tax year.

S corporation losses deductible by a shareholder are limited to the sum of the shareholder's adjusted basis in his or her S corporation stock, plus any basis the shareholder has in debt owed to the shareholder by the corporation. If a shareholder's share of losses exceeds this amount, then the losses can be carried forward indefinitely and taken as a deduction in a subsequent year in which the shareholder has an adequate basis in stock or debt. For example, the shareholder hoping to deduct carryover losses might increase basis in a subsequent year by making a contribution to the capital of the corporation. This rule is similar to the one that applies to partnerships. This feature of S corporations and partnerships can be useful in tax planning to make the best use of the timing of loss deductions.

EXAMPLE

Jane's share of the net operating loss of Essco (an S corporation) for 2010 is $25,000. Since Jane's basis at the end of 2009 is $5,000, she can offset her income from other sources by recognizing only $5,000 of Essco's operating loss—the amount of her basis. This pleases Jane, since 2010 was not a banner financial year otherwise. Suppose Jane anticipates a change in fortune in 2011 and expects a large amount of income from various sources. She can increase her basis in 2011 by contributing $20,000 to Essco for additional stock (or she could loan Essco $20,000). Jane is now able to recognize her carryover $20,000 loss to offset her 2011 taxable income from all sources.

The basis for a shareholder's stock in an S corporation is adjusted in a manner similar to that of a partner's basis in his or her partnership interest. The basis of a shareholder's S corporation stock is increased each year by the shareholder's pro rata share of the corporation's taxable income and is correspondingly reduced by the shareholder's pro rata share of corporate losses. Once the stock basis has been adjusted for corporate income and losses, it is further adjusted to reflect any corporate distributions to the shareholder during the year since such distributions reduce the recipient-shareholder's basis. If all of a shareholder's pro rata share of an

S corporation's taxable income is distributed to the shareholder during the year, there is no change in the shareholder's basis. If a distribution from an S corporation exceeds the shareholder's basis for the stock, the excess is taxable to the shareholder as a capital gain. In other words, it is treated as if the shareholder had sold or liquidated stock to that extent.

Although in general an S corporation is treated for tax purposes much like a partnership, there are several significant differences. Two of these involve the treatment of indebtedness of the corporation and the treatment of passive income.

An S corporation shareholder acquires a basis in the debt of the corporation only if the shareholder lends the funds directly to the corporation. If the corporation borrows money from a bank, the shareholder does not acquire any basis as a result of this indebtedness, even if the shareholder personally guarantees the loan. By contrast, a partner's basis is automatically increased by his or her share of any partnership debt, including loans from banks or other outsiders. (Of course, the at-risk rules applicable to partnerships will reduce the tax advantage of this "leverage" in some cases.) Since this leverage is important in a tax-sheltered investment, such investment ventures usually use the limited-partnership form rather than an S corporation.

Another important distinctive feature of an S corporation is the treatment of passive income, which includes royalties, rents, dividends, interest, annuities, and gains from stock or securities.

An S corporation is permitted to have an unlimited amount of passive income unless the corporation originally began as a regular corporation and the corporation has earnings and profits left over from the time before it made the Subchapter S election. If the S corporation has such leftover earnings or profits at the end of each of 3 consecutive years, the S election will terminate if more than 25 percent of the corporation's gross receipts for each of those 3 years is from passive investment income. Furthermore, there is a tax at the entity level at corporate rates on any "excess net passive income" as defined in the Code. Under certain conditions the IRS may waive the tax on the excess net passive income.

Use of an S Election

An S corporation is a bona fide corporation under state law and for most purposes is treated like a regular corporation. All the usual corporate formalities must be observed, and all the nontax advantages of the corporate form are available.

The S election is made strictly for tax purposes, and the tax implications of an S election should be carefully explored by eligible closely held corporations. The tax advantages of an S election over regular corporate tax status include the following:

- Business losses are available as deductions on the shareholder's individual returns.
- Double taxation of corporate distributions is generally avoided.
- The accumulated-earnings, personal-holding-company, and corporate alternative minimum taxes are all avoided.
- Business income can be shifted to lower-bracket taxpayers by gifts of S corporation stock to family members.
- Personal-service corporations that make the S election avoid the 35 percent flat income tax rate.

The S election should be carefully considered since it will not be advantageous in all circumstances. With the enactment of LLC and LLP statutes in all states, pass-through tax treatment is available in several types of entities that provide limited liability, giving a business owner other choices besides the S corporation. Pass-through tax treatment may not be advantageous in all circumstances.

The simplified example below illustrates an unwise use of an S election. The decision is generally complex and should be made with careful consideration of the factors and appropriate professional advice.

EXAMPLE

Bette and Cynthia are equal shareholders in Smart, Inc., a computer sales firm. The corporate net income before salary payments for the current year is $150,000 and a reasonable salary for each shareholder is $50,000. Bette and Cynthia have taxable income from other sources during the year and are both in the 33 percent bracket. The shareholders intend to reinvest $50,000 in the business this year. The tax result under the regular and S corporation forms is as follows:

	Regular Corporation	S Corporation
Net income before salaries	$150,000	$150,000
Salaries to owners	100,000	100,000
Taxable income	50,000	50,000
Corporate tax	7,500	N/A
Tax to shareholders	33,000	49,500

One tax-planning possibility commonly used in an S corporation is the splitting of the corporate income among family members by transferring S corporation stock by sale or gift to family members. This possibility has been enhanced by the changes brought about by AJCA that treat all family members as one shareholder for the 100-shareholder limit. None of the complex rules for family partnership taxation is applicable. Thus shares can be transferred without restriction to family members who are totally inactive in the business. However, there is a limitation on the amount of income that can be diverted from primary income earners to inactive shareholders. This restriction ensures that income that actually results from the personal services of the active shareholder is not passed through to be taxed at the lower bracket of the inactive shareholder.

EXAMPLE

Mike decides to incorporate his construction business and make an S election. He distributes half of the stock to his son, Hank, as a gift. Mike and Hank will thereafter each be taxable on half of the corporation's taxable income. Suppose that for a given year the business has net profits of $150,000 without making any allowance for a salary for Mike. A reasonable salary for him would be $90,000, taxable to him at a 28 percent rate. Thus, Mike receives $64,800 from his salary, net of taxes ($25,200 or $90,000 x .28). In addition, his $30,000 share of the net earnings of the corporation is also subject to a 28 percent tax rate. Hank would also receive $30,000 of taxable income. Suppose Hank is in a very low tax bracket this year. Can Mike reduce his salary to an artificially low level for this year to pass through more income to Hank and thereby lower the overall tax burden on the family? Probably not; tax law permits the IRS to push Mike's salary up to its usual level of $90,000 in order to thwart this particular attempt at tax avoidance.

Despite this problem, gifts of S corporation stock are frequently found to be useful as a financial planning or estate planning device. Because of the possible complexities, however, any such plan must be carefully analyzed to ensure that it will actually provide tax benefits or other benefits for the parties.

ADVANTAGES AND DISADVANTAGES OF CORPORATE ENTERPRISES

The first advantage of the corporate form of ownership is the limited liability of the shareholders for the risks of business operations. In unincorporated forms of business ownership the personal assets of the owners (other than limited partners) become exposed to claimants of the business. The corporate shareholder's liability is limited to any capital invested in the corporation. In other words, the shareholder may lose only what was paid for his or her stock. The corporation is a separate legal entity apart from its owners, and all debts of the corporation are debts solely of the corporation and are satisfied out of the corporate property (not the shareholder's personal assets).

This advantage may be limited somewhat in the closely held corporation since creditors are likely to require that the owners of the closely held corporation personally guarantee the obligations of the corporation. Also it is important to note that an individual shareholder-employee is always fully liable for his or her own actions, thus limiting to some degree the significance of limited liability in the professional corporation where malpractice is an important liability exposure. Of course the shareholders of the professional corporation are shielded from the liability created by acts of other employees not under their control.

The second advantage of the corporate form of ownership is the continuity of life of the corporation. The corporation as a separate legal entity has a life distinct from that of the owners. Unlike partnerships or proprietorships, which dissolve upon the death of the owners, a corporation continues beyond the death of the shareholder. Although for practical purposes the death of a majority shareholder who provides substantial services to the corporation may terminate the effectiveness of the corporation as a business enterprise, a continuation plan such as a buy-sell agreement can provide effective preplanned continuity for the corporation.

In addition to the above-mentioned general advantages, there are also some tax advantages to operating a business in the form of a corporation. As a distinct legal entity a corporation is taxed on its income separately. Corporate tax rates are lower than those for individuals at some levels of income. Within certain limits tax law allows corporate income to be accumulated in the corporation, currently avoiding the separate tax at the shareholder level. Amounts under the minimum accumulated-earnings tax credit may be retained by the corporation without restriction. In fact, the corporation can retain amounts above the credit for valid business purposes. Since the goals of the closely held corporation and those of its majority shareholders are often synonymous, the ability to take advantage of "lightly taxed" accumulated earnings to meet the corporate goals is an advantage that flows directly to the majority shareholder. Finally, there are significant tax advantages for providing fringe-benefit plans to shareholder-employees that are unavailable to self-employed owners.

There are also some disadvantages inherent in the corporate form of ownership of which the financial services professional should be aware. First, the corporation must comply with state law, and many organizational formalities must be followed. Formation of a corporation requires the preparation and filing of various documents. The state typically provides for additional fees to charter a corporation with the state. The cost associated with these formalities, along with the costs of capitalizing, generally makes the corporation the most expensive type of business enterprise to create. The use of professionals such as attorneys, accountants, and investment bankers will probably be necessary to form the corporation. Many of the organizational requirements of the corporation provide for continuing costs, such as state laws requiring corporations to file and prepare various annual financial statements and reports.

The operational formalities of a corporation also provide a certain rigidity to the management and operation of the business. Changes can be effected quickly through the flexible and informal structure of the unincorporated business, but corporate law requires that even the most fundamental changes in a corporation be made only through the observance of certain formalities. For example, directors must be elected by the shareholders at annual meetings. The everyday management of the corporation often lacks the authority to make fundamental business decisions without the specific authorization of the board. It is obvious that a business owner facing the decision to incorporate should be aware of these practical problems before reaching a conclusion.

Advantages and Disadvantages of Corporations

Advantages

- Limited liability
- Continuity of life
- Corporate tax rules
- May be easier to raise capital
- Retained earnings not taxed to owners
- Owner-employees can have tax-free fringe benefits

Disadvantages

- Organizational formalities required
- Ongoing formalities required
- Expenses of formation and operation
- Double taxation of dividends

CHAPTER REVIEW

Key Terms and Concepts

articles of incorporation
bylaws
quorum
business-judgment rule
cumulative voting
voting trust
professional corporation
accumulated taxable income

alternative minimum taxable income (AMTI)
personal-service corporation (PSC)
grantor trust
qualified subchapter S trust (QSST)
electing small business trust (ESBT)
qualified subchapter S subsidiary (QSSS)

Review Questions

The answers to the review questions are in the supplement. The self-test questions and the answers to them are also in the supplement and on The American College Online.

1. List the steps that must be taken to form a corporation. [1]
2. Explain the extent to which a corporation can acquire its own stock. [1]
3. Identify the principal responsibilities of the board of directors. [2]
4. From what source do the officers of a corporation derive their authority to manage a corporation's day-to-day activities? [2]
5. Explain the limitations on corporate officers in their management of the enterprise. [2]
6. Zenk, Inc., a closely held corporation, is being formed with 1,000 shares issued and outstanding. The corporation will have four directors, and cumulative voting will be in effect. Determine how many shares a minority shareholder will need to elect one director. [2]
7. What rights do common shareholders have in a corporation? [2]
8. What is a shareholder's liability for debts of the corporation? [2]
9. In what ways does the management of a closely held corporation differ from that of a publicly held corporation? [2]
10. Discuss the restrictions on transferability of stock in a professional corporation. [3]
11. To what extent does the limited-liability principle shelter professionals who incorporate? [3]
12. Explain what is meant by "double taxation" and how closely held corporations typically avoid this burden. [4]
13. If a taxpayer's business affairs could somehow be arranged so that all his or her business income was earned and retained by a corporation (except for the amount required for the taxpayer's personal needs), the corporate form could provide some tax shelter. Explain the restraints that the tax law imposes on the extent to which this is possible in the case of an active
    a. non-personal-service business
    b. service business [4]

14. Briefly explain the purpose of the alternative minimum tax and its impact on the corporate ownership of life insurance. [5]
15. Personal-service corporations (PSCs) are subject to special tax treatment. Identify the types of activities that will cause a corporation to be treated as a PSC. [5]
16. Explain how a shareholder may contribute appreciated property in exchange for stock when forming a corporation and recognize no capital gain. [5]
17. What are the qualifications that must be met to be eligible for a subchapter S election? [6]
18. Describe the income tax treatment of an S corporation. [6]
19. Discuss the possible uses of an S election. [6]
20. Prepare a checklist of advantages and disadvantages of the corporate form of ownership. [1, 2, 3, 4, 5, 6]

COMPENSATION PLANNING IN THE CLOSELY HELD CORPORATION 4

Learning Objectives

An understanding of the material in this chapter should enable the student to

1. Explain the tax advantages available for providing fringe benefits to shareholder-employees of a regular corporation vis-à-vis other business owners.
2. Describe the considerations for determining the appropriate compensation package with respect to both shareholder-employees and other key executives.
3. Describe in general terms the factors that determine whether the compensation of a shareholder-employee is reasonable and the procedure for establishing a valid bonus agreement for a corporate employee.
4. Explain how the distinctions between qualified retirement plans and nonqualified plans affect a closely held corporation's decision to adopt a retirement plan.
5. Describe the types of nonqualified deferred-compensation plans.
6. Explain the nondiscrimination rules applicable to group term life insurance plans.
7. Describe the mechanics of a Sec. 162 bonus plan used as an executive carve-out to a group term life insurance plan.
8. Identify the differences between traditional split-dollar, equity split-dollar, and reverse split-dollar plans.

INTRODUCTION TO COMPENSATION PLANNING

Designing the appropriate compensation package for the owners and key employees of a closely held business is a critical step in the business planning process. Owners of a closely held business have only three opportunities to receive a *remunerative return* on their investment in the business.

First, the owners of a closely held business can receive passive income for the capital they invested in the business. The passive income flows through naturally to owners of sole proprietorships, partnerships, and S corporations—the pass-through entities. However, the allocation of passive income to the owners of partnerships and S corporations cannot be made without fairly compensating the service-providing partners and S corporation shareholder-employees.

In the regular C corporation the payment of passive income to shareholders is an expensive proposition. Passive income (dividends) is paid out of taxable corporate income and received as taxable income (generally subject to capital gains tax rates) by the shareholder. Thus double taxation occurs when passive income is paid to shareholders in the C corporation. Compensation planning for the shareholder-employees of the closely held C corporation generally focuses on the maximization of deductible compensation and the minimization of passive dividends.

Second, the owner of a closely held business can receive return for his or her investment in the business from the potential gain on the sale of the business. If the business, or any part of the business, is sold at a gain, the seller will receive a return of investment and realize a gain over his or her initial investment. Of course, the sale of the business is a one-time event and will generally terminate the owner's ability to receive substantial future income from the business.

Third, the owner of a closely held business can receive compensation on an ongoing basis for the services that he or she provides for the business. Receiving compensation for services occurs naturally in a sole proprietorship because all the business income, after deductible expenses, is available to the sole proprietor. Thus there is little distinction between the passive and "compensation" income of the sole proprietor. In a partnership, although the partners receive a distributive share of income, the distributive share quite often takes into account the services provided by the general partner. Service partners will often receive guaranteed payments for their services to the partnership.

Compensation planning for shareholder-employees of C corporations presents significantly more problems and opportunities since the corporation is a separate taxpayer from the owners.

COMPENSATION PLANNING FOR BUSINESS OWNER

self-employed business owner

The needs of the *self-employed business owner* will often dictate both the size and form of the owner's compensation. Unincorporated business owners do not have the federal income tax advantages that corporate employees have for many types of fringe benefit plans.

Proprietors' partners (or members in an LLC taxed as a partnership) and more-than-2-percent shareholders in S corporations are not considered employees for fringe-benefit purposes. Such owners are considered self-employed. Therefore contributions to certain fringe-benefit plans—group life or health insurance—made on behalf of these self-employed individuals are not deductible by the business for tax purposes. (Note: There is an income tax deduction for the health insurance premiums paid by self-employed individuals, but this is a personal rather than a business tax deduction.) Despite the fact that premiums paid for group life insurance coverage on behalf of these business owners are not deductible, many individuals find establishing group life insurance plans advantageous because of favorable rates, benefits, and underwriting rules. As opposed to other employee fringe benefits, the retirement plan rules for self-employed individuals provide similar advantages to those provided by corporate retirement plans.

The shareholder-employees of a closely held C corporation have an advantage in regard to fringe benefit plans such as group term life insurance. The corporation is permitted to fully deduct contributions made on behalf of shareholder-employees provided that the reasonable-compensation rules are met.

An employer's compensation package is usually divided into two portions—cash compensation and fringe benefits. A business establishes various types of fringe benefit plans based more on the specific needs of the business owners than on the tax considerations. For example, the need for life or health insurance depends on the age, marital status, and number of dependents of the owners. However, the tax treatment of various types of compensation arrangements is also extremely important. The tax benefits of certain types of compensation include one or more of the following:

- the deductibility of such compensation as a business expense of the corporation

- the receipt of such compensation income tax free by the employee
- the deferral of taxation of the fringe benefit into a later tax year

The purpose of compensation planning is to design a compensation package that meets the needs of both the owners and the business. Some components of the compensation package will be determined by the specific needs of the business owners. In other cases, the tax costs will be the primary consideration, and the owners will maximize their overall compensation by minimizing the costs of providing the components of the compensation package.

Three Types of Remuneration for the Closely Held Business Owner

- Passive income via dividends
- Capital gain on sale of stock
- Cash and tax-free or tax-deferred benefits for services rendered

COMPENSATION PLANNING FOR NONOWNER-EMPLOYEE

Compensation planning for the business's nonowner-employees should not be overlooked. Closely held businesses commonly rely on a few key employees. Although many of these employees are also owners, some of them are not. The compensation package for these few key employees should be sufficient to recruit, reward, and retain long-service key employees. The success of the closely held business often hinges on the continued services of such employees. The employer must consider the changing needs of key employees throughout their working lives and design a compensation package accordingly. The compensation package should not only be adequate in size but also contain components tailored to the key employees' specific needs. Quite often a key employee accepts employment or leaves a firm based on the fringe benefits that are provided in addition to the cash compensation.

Although closely held corporations are unlikely to provide the complex and comprehensive benefit plans often provided in larger corporations, fringe benefit planning is still important for the closely held corporation. Overall, fringe benefits are rising faster than cash compensation in the workplace. In order to retain their key employees, closely held corporations must compete with the larger corporations that provide extensive fringe benefit packages. In many ways the compensation package for nonowner-employees is correlated to the package provided for owner-employees. The federal tax and labor statutes contain numerous complex nondiscrimination rules that provide that most employee benefit plans must be nondiscriminatory in eligibility for participation and/or benefit levels. It is difficult, if not impossible, to provide group term life insurance, group health insurance, or qualified retirement plans for owner-employees if other employees are excluded.

In addition, the benefits provided to owner-employees by these plans cannot be vastly out of proportion with the benefits provided to the nonowner-employees. Generally speaking the nondiscrimination rules provide more flexibility for discriminating in fringe benefit plans provided by smaller closely held corporations. Cost-effective compensation planning involves the maximization of the cash and fringe benefit compensation for the owner-employees and other key executives.

THE REASONABLE-COMPENSATION STANDARD

reasonable compensation

For any compensation plan involving shareholder-employees to be successful, the total compensation package must qualify for a deduction from corporate income tax as an ordinary and necessary business expense. Although the IRS examines the whole compensation package in determining *reasonable compensation*, it is generally year-end bonuses or other discriminatory benefits that are deemed by the IRS to be excessive. If the amount of any bonus or any other compensation benefit is deemed unreasonable compensation, the unreasonable excess of the bonus or the other excessive compensation benefit will be treated as a dividend to the recipient shareholder-employee and no business deduction will be available to the corporation. Thus unreasonable amounts paid to or provided for shareholder-employees will be subject to double taxation.

In addition to the reasonable-compensation standard, IRC Sec. 162(m) limits the deduction for compensation to certain officers of publicly traded corporations to $1 million per officer-employee. This limitation does not include commissions generated directly by the executive's performance and certain other performance-based compensation.

If the reasonableness of the shareholder-employee's compensation is tested by IRS audit or tax litigation, the burden of establishing that the disputed compensation is reasonable falls on the corporation. If the corporation presents substantial evidence of reasonableness, the IRS has the burden of rebutting the evidence to prove that the compensation is unreasonable.

The secret to success for corporations in reasonable-compensation cases is to establish evidence prior to the IRS audit that the compensation is reasonable based on the corporate employment relationship with the participating shareholder-employee. There is no clear standard for establishing the reasonableness of shareholder-employee compensation in specific cases. IRS regulations covering Sec. 162 provide a weak starting point. Most of the reasonable-compensation factors have been developed by case law and IRS publications.

Among the factors for testing the reasonableness of compensation are the following:

- the employee's role in the company. This includes the position held by the employee, hours worked, duties performed, and the general importance of the employee to the corporation's success.
- the employee's qualifications for the specific role that he or she has in the corporation
- the comparison of salary paid to a shareholder-employee to the gross and net income of the corporation
- the comparison of salaries for similar executive positions in similar companies. An employee is allowed to earn a salary that is similar to the salary of an employee in another business whose role is comparable. This evidence may be difficult to find in a small or highly specialized industry but may be included in published annual statements of other firms in the industry.
- factors concerning the character and condition of the company. This includes the prevailing condition of both the national economy and the local economy, the complexities of the business, and the relative size of the company.
- possible conflicts of interest. There cannot be a relationship between the corporation and the employee that would permit the company to disguise a dividend as a deductible compensation expense. The more control the shareholder exerts over the corporate operations, the greater importance this factor will have. The courts might examine the company's dividend-paying history and the salaries paid to shareholders to determine if some earnings normally paid as dividends have become salary to the shareholders.
- evidence of a reasonable, consistently applied compensation plan. It is important to determine a bonus plan and to ascertain the

procedure for calculating the amount of the bonus in advance. Of particular importance is the consistency of the compensation package across all employee groups.

The general consensus of practitioners is that the value of documenting the amount of compensation as a reasonable expense in advance cannot be overemphasized. The starting point for such documentation is the board of directors meeting. The board of directors should adopt the compensation agreement for shareholder-employees and other key executives (presumably the participants in a bonus arrangement or some other discriminatory benefit arrangement) by formal resolution. The establishment of any executive benefit arrangement should similarly be adopted by formal resolution. State law generally presumes that actions taken in this manner by the directors are a result of their fiduciary duty to act in the best interests of the corporation. This presumption is certainly weakened when the shareholder-employees in their roles as directors of the closely held corporation are adopting a compensation plan that primarily benefits themselves as shareholder-employees. However, a formal adoption of the agreement backed by substantial entries in the corporate minutes that specify the factors justifying the reasonableness of compensation will make it difficult for the IRS to reject the plan.

The corporate minutes might justify a particular compensation agreement by indicating that such arrangements are common and necessary to compensate the participating key executives for the following reasons:

- Such plans are common in similar firms in the industry.
- The services of the participating executives are essential to the corporation.
- The skills of the participating executives are unique and contribute to the profitability of the corporation.
- The participating executives could not be replaced without at least the same, if not better, compensation package.
- The participating executives have taken lower than the reasonable limits of compensation in the years prior to the adoption of the compensation agreement.

The corporate minutes, of course, will include the date of the meeting and indicate that the board actually discussed the merits of the adopted resolution.

Establishing the reasonableness of the executive compensation agreement in a personal-service corporation is usually a far smaller burden than it is in a business corporation. Quite simply, virtually all the corporate income of a personal-service corporation is related to the goodwill and billing associated with the shareholder-professionals. The payment of almost all personal-service-corporation income as salaries to employees is usually not restricted by reasonable-compensation issues.

With a business corporation it is assumed that some of the business income is a return on invested capital. The more capital-intensive the corporation, the greater the likelihood that the IRS will be successful in raising reasonable-compensation arguments if extraordinary benefits are provided for shareholder-employees. Even if the corporation is in a somewhat capital-intensive industry, shareholder-employees who are also the key executives generally work long hours and provide skills unique to that particular business. As long as the corporation's capital is allowed a reasonable return, substantial payments to these key executives will generally be deemed reasonable. However, remember that the best defense against an IRS reasonable-compensation challenge is proper corporate documentation prepared prior to the time the benefit is provided.

CASH COMPENSATION AND CASH BONUSES

The most visible and significant part of the employees' compensation package is current compensation in the form of cash and bonuses. To the extent such compensation is reasonable, cash compensation and bonuses provide a C corporation with a deduction as an ordinary and necessary business expense under Sec. 162.

Cash Compensation vis-à-vis Fringe Benefits

Generally speaking all employees (including owner-employees) work to receive current cash compensation to meet their cost-of-living needs. The consideration of any fringe benefits must necessarily result in the comparison of the proposed fringe benefits with the foregone cash compensation, assuming that the employer can afford to provide only a target level of compensation for a specific employee. As previously discussed, the needs of the owner-employees and other key executives must be considered in determining the appropriate levels of cash and other forms of compensation. Certainly from a tax standpoint cash is the most expensive benefit for the employer to provide and for the employee to receive. This is a distinct disadvantage of cash compensation. The employer must provide the cash as a current charge against corporate earnings with a corresponding deduction against taxable corporate income. The employee must report all capital cash compensation as ordinary income in the year of receipt.

However, cash compensation provides many advantages for both the corporation and the employee. For the corporation, cash compensation is fixed at the time the compensation level is determined, thus providing a controllable expense. Other types of fringe benefits, such as self-insured sick-pay or health plans, to some extent provide a variable benefit that is more difficult for the corporation to budget. In addition, cash compensation avoids the burdensome requirements of other types of fringe benefit plans, such as the nondiscrimination rules and reporting requirements applicable to many types of welfare benefit plans.

For the employee, cash compensation provides a predictable and secure benefit. The cash received can be immediately spent or saved by the employee and is not subject to risk or forfeiture. Further, employees can purchase on an individual basis many of the fringe benefits often provided by the employer. For example, a healthy employee can often purchase individual term life insurance at rates comparable to or more favorable than group life insurance provided by his or her employer. Although the tax benefits of employer-provided fringe benefits are often not available on an individual basis, cash compensation provides the employee with the ability to personally select the exact benefits he or she wishes to purchase.

Planning Cash Bonuses

Owner-employees and other key executives of C corporations frequently receive cash bonuses. Such bonuses are generally provided at the end of the tax year and are based on the performance of both the corporation and the individual. Closely held corporations often use bonuses for the following purposes:

- Bonuses can be an incentive for performance if related to the executives' contributions to corporate profits.
- Bonuses can reduce the corporate taxable income since the corporation can deduct a reasonable bonus as an ordinary and necessary business expense. This deduction will prevent the current earnings of a corporation from increasing the accumulated earnings and profits and, therefore, will reduce the exposure to future double-taxed dividends.
- Cash bonuses can be provided on a discriminatory basis to provide the owner-employees and other key executives with cash to

purchase certain individually selected benefits, such as Sec. 162 "executive bonus" or split-dollar life insurance.

Establishing Bonus Arrangements

A bonus arrangement can be either formal or informal depending on the circumstances of the corporation. Generally the bonus should be reasonably documented at the corporate level because this documentation is an important piece of evidence against the IRS in a reasonable-compensation challenge to the bonus.

The starting point for establishing a bonus agreement is the board of directors meeting. The board of directors should adopt the bonus agreement by formal resolution. The type of resolution will vary with the type of bonus. For example, the resolution might establish a Sec. 162 executive bonus life insurance plan. This type of arrangement will set up a bonus for a specific amount of premium dollars to be given as a bonus to the employee.

Other types of bonuses may be incentive-based. The corporate resolution in these circumstances describes the bonus formula to be provided for the executive(s). The formula can be based on the overall performance of the corporation or on the individual performance of the executive.

In addition, a corporation can establish a bonus agreement that pays "past" compensation to the key executive. In this case the resolution states that the key executive is being compensated for previous years of services when compensation was insufficient. In any event it is imperative for tax purposes that such a resolution be established prior to the end of the year in which the employee will receive the bonus.

Timing the Bonus and the Employer's Deduction

Since individuals are cash-basis taxpayers, a bonus is taken as ordinary income by the employee in the tax year in which the bonus is received actually or constructively.

On the other hand, most corporations use the accrual method of accounting for tax purposes although some S corporations continue to use the cash basis. Under the accrual basis of accounting, the employer may take the deduction when the liability to make such payment is fixed. This means that a year-end cash bonus may be deductible in the year in which the bonus accrued (when the related services are provided) even if such bonus is paid in a later tax year. Therefore the bonus agreement should be established in the tax year in which the corporation hopes to accrue the expense.

A year-end bonus paid after the close of the tax year can be treated as deferred compensation. Generally such deferred compensation is deductible only in the year in which the corporation actually paid the compensation. However, IRS regulations permit the deduction of a bonus accrued in a tax year if such bonus is actually paid within 2½ months of the close of the previous tax year in which the services were performed (and the bonus earned). Note that these rules do not apply if the recipient of the bonus is a more-than-50-percent owner of the corporation. In the case of a controlling shareholder, the corporation may take the deduction only in the year in which the bonus is actually paid even if the accrual of such bonus occurred in an earlier tax year.

Reducing the Executive's Out-of-Pocket Tax Liability for Cash Bonuses

zero-tax bonus plan

Since the executive's income tax bracket could be as high as 35 percent (the rate in effect at the time of publication), the bonus may cause some concern over the receipt of taxable income. One method of addressing this concern is to use a *zero-tax bonus plan* (also referred to as a double-bonus plan or tax gross-up plan). Under this arrangement the bonus is large enough to cover both the amount of the bonus and the executive's income tax liability. (Of course, the executive will also have to pay tax on this additional amount of bonus.)

The zero-tax bonus is most often used when the bonus is provided to the executive to meet a specific benefit need, such as executive bonus or split-dollar life insurance plans (both discussed later). The size of the bonus is determined by the following formula:

$$\text{Required bonus} = \frac{\text{TB}}{1-t}$$

where TB = after-tax target bonus

t = executive's marginal tax rate

EXAMPLE

Assume that an executive is in a 35 percent tax bracket and the required bonus for the year is $1,000. A $1,538 bonus will be required to provide the executive with sufficient funds to receive the after-tax target bonus. The corporation will continue to receive the deduction for the full bonus assuming it meets reasonable-compensation standards. This type of arrangement is particularly favorable when the corporation's relative tax bracket is high because the value of its tax deduction is that much greater.

Reimbursement Agreements

Bonuses are the most likely portion of the compensation package to trigger a reasonable-compensation challenge by the IRS. Generally regular salary levels are fairly stable and easy to justify as reasonable. Fringe benefits are usually subject to various nondiscrimination rules. If such nondiscrimination rules are not violated, fringe benefits that are paid to owner-employees and key executives are generally deemed reasonable by the IRS.

However, bonuses can be subject to dramatic fluctuation and may often be used as a tax-avoidance device. In C corporations, bonuses can be used to reduce the taxable income of the corporation and reduce the exposure to future double-taxed dividends. Thus reducing the taxable income to levels at or near zero increases the risk that the IRS will challenge the compensation level of the owner-employee.

This risk increases to the extent that corporate income is produced by sources other than the owner-employees and key executives. Thus, if capital is a material-income-producing factor, some corporate income must be allocated to such capital in the investment component of the shareholder's interests. The risk of challenge is reduced if the income is produced primarily by the owner-employees, such as in the case of a personal-service corporation.

The risk of the reasonable-compensation-plan challenge often causes the corporation and shareholder-employees to form reimbursement agreements. Such agreements require the shareholder-employee to return any compensation deemed excessive if the IRS disallows a deduction for a portion of the employee's compensation because it failed to meet reasonable-compensation standards. Such reimbursement agreements are generally only entered into by shareholder-employees since they will be directly affected by the loss of a corporate deduction through their ownership interest. Any excessive compensation disallowed as a deduction by the IRS will be returned to the corporate assets.

Under the reimbursement agreement the employee gets a corresponding deduction for the amounts returned to the corporation in the tax year in which the funds are returned. This deduction should offset taxable income that the employee had taken in the prior year when the bonus was received unless the employee has different income tax brackets in the year in which the bonus was received and returned. Although the reimbursement agreement provides some evidence to the IRS that the amounts of compensation subject to the reimbursement are excessive, the IRS has generally been unsuccessful in challenging the validity of the reimbursement agreement in court.

DEFERRED-COMPENSATION PLANS

Deferred-compensation plans are an important part of the compensation package for owner-employees of a closely held corporation. Under a deferred-compensation plan, part of the employee's compensation over the employee's service-providing years is deferred until a later period, such as the employee's retirement.

This deferral meets three goals. First, the deferred compensation will provide income for the employee during retirement when the employee's income for services will cease. Second, the deferred-compensation plan will provide a participant with an accumulation vehicle to enhance the participant's normal savings. Third, the deferred compensation meets a tax-planning objective since a properly designed deferred-compensation plan defers taxation until the income is received.

Any benefits of tax deferral will increase as the executive's tax bracket increases. Although the maximum rates are lower following the passage of several tax-reduction packages in recent years, tax-deferral opportunities remain important for highly compensated shareholder- and other key employees.

Deferred-compensation plans are categorized as either qualified or nonqualified plans.

Qualified plans must meet a plethora of federal nondiscrimination and administrative compliance standards. These standards increase the cost of such plans since a broad base of employees must be included in the plan and significant administrative fees must be paid. However, the corporation gets an immediate income tax deduction for contributions to a deferred-compensation plan while the employee's tax on plan benefits is deferred until such benefits are received.

Advantages of Nonqualified Deferred-Compensation Plans
• Employee's receipt of taxable income can be deferred until the money is received. • Employer can avoid the high cost of benefits and plan administration by excluding the rank-and-file employees.

Nonqualified plans provide a similar deferral of the employee's receipt of ordinary income. However, nonqualified plans also cause a deferral of the employer's tax deduction until such benefits are paid. The deferral of the corporate tax deduction is more than offset in the closely held corporation by the fact that the nonqualified plan can be provided without inclusion of the rank-and-file employees. Since closely held corporations often wish to maximize the benefits for shareholder-employees while minimizing benefit costs of other employees, such corporations may find the nonqualified plan to be advantageous.

Qualified Retirement Plans

This discussion will provide only a brief overview of qualified plans. Qualified plans provide the closely held corporation and its shareholders with an important technique of tax deferral. Contributions to the qualified plan are deductible from corporate income tax, and earnings on plan assets are deferred until benefit payments are made to participants. In effect, by participating in a qualified plan, the participants are receiving an interest-free loan from the federal government for the funds invested in the plan. Since the controlling shareholders of a closely held corporation determine its compensation plan, these shareholders are free to choose between taking current cash compensation for services or receiving the tax shelter provided by the adoption of a qualified plan.

The funding rules applicable to qualified plans often permit higher contributions based on the income level and the age of a participant. This means that in a closely held corporation the shareholder-employees and key executives are more likely than the younger, lower-paid employees to receive significant benefits from the retirement plan. This is particularly true if the qualified plan is integrated with Social Security. Therefore, qualified plans can be designed to maximize the portion of the compensation package available to the owners and key executives. Of course, nondiscrimination rules will generally require the participation of some regular employees.

A qualified plan will help the closely held corporation attract and retain employees other than the shareholders. Since closely held corporations must compete with larger publicly held corporations for their employees, a qualified retirement plan may be the key to attracting the employees needed by the closely held corporation.

Defined-Benefit Plans

Qualified plans are categorized as either defined-benefit or defined-contribution plans. A defined-benefit plan indicates a specific benefit that an employee will receive. The contribution that is made on behalf of each employee to a defined-benefit plan depends on the amount needed for each employee to pay the promised benefit. The maximum annual benefit that a defined-benefit plan can provide is 100 percent of the employee's average compensation for his or her 3 consecutive years of highest pay, up to a maximum benefit of $195,000 (2011 figure). The amount is adjusted annually for inflation with rounding to the nearest $5,000 threshold.

The shareholder-employees of a closely held corporation are generally in the position to establish their salary levels within the reasonableness restrictions. However, highly compensated shareholder-employees and key executives are usually limited by the maximum dollar figure in the defined-benefit plan. A defined-benefit plan's benefit formula determines the promised retirement benefit. This benefit is typically pegged to a percentage of the employee's final salary (for example, 50 percent of the employee's average compensation for his or her 3 years of highest compensation out of the final 5 years prior to termination of employment). Because the employer promises a specific benefit under the defined-benefit plan, making additional contributions for underfunding problems is the corporation's burden.

Defined-benefit plans are generally the best choice for a closely held corporation, particularly when the shareholder-employees and key executives are older than the other employees. Under such circumstances the majority of contributions to the defined-benefit plan will be used to fund the promised benefits for older employees. This is due to the fact that there is less time for the contributions and accumulated earnings to grow to the level needed to provide the promised benefit. Defined-benefit plans can also provide for contributions for past service for all participants when the plan is adopted. Since the shareholder-employees and other key executives will most likely have significant past service, the company can legally provide greater contributions for such individuals at the inception of the plan.

Defined-Contribution Plans

A defined-contribution plan is the simplest of qualified plans. Each employee in the plan has an individual account. The corporation makes annual contributions to each account under a contribution formula.

The maximum annual contribution that a corporation can make to a participant's account is the lesser of $49,000 (for 2011) or 100 percent of the employee's salary. Since the contribution formula is based on the employee's current salary, the annual contributions vary with the employee's salary. The benefit received by the employee depends on the amount of contributions and the investment performance of the plan assets over the accumulation period. Thus in defined-contribution plans the investment risk related to assets in an employee's account falls on the employee.

Requirements for Qualified Plans

The current requirements for qualified plans stem from the Employee Retirement Income Security Act (ERISA) enacted in 1974 and amended numerous times. Qualified pension plans are subject to the jurisdiction of the IRS, the Department of Labor, and the Pension Benefit Guaranty Corporation. The rules for adopting and maintaining a qualified plan are costly from an administrative standpoint. Small closely held corporations might adopt standardized or prototype plans and reduce significantly the cost of adopting a qualified plan.

For the closely held corporation the largest expense of the qualified plan results from complying with the nondiscrimination rules. Such rules are in place to prevent qualified plans from prohibitively discriminating in favor of highly compensated employees. Thus the nondiscrimination rules are incongruous with the goals of maximizing the owner-employee's share of the compensation package. Although it is impossible to include the nondiscrimination rules in detail in this brief discussion, the rules can be placed in one of three broad categories as follows:

- The coverage test requires that a certain minimum percentage of nonhighly compensated employees be covered by the plan. The test permits the exclusion of certain younger and minimal-service employees as well as employees who are subject to a collective-bargaining agreement in which good-faith bargaining has occurred with respect to a retirement plan. In short, this test requires that 70 percent of the eligible nonhighly compensated employees be covered by the plan if all highly compensated employees are covered.

- The plan cannot provide benefits on a prohibitively discriminatory basis. In general, this means that the benefits provided to highly compensated employees cannot be unduly favorable relative to the benefits provided to nonhighly compensated employees.
- Contributions to the plan cannot prohibitively discriminate in favor of highly compensated employees. This requirement prevents an excessively disproportionate amount of annual contributions from being made to the accounts of highly compensated employees.

Profit-Sharing Plans

A profit-sharing plan is a form of defined-contribution plan designed to offer the participant a share in the company profits (corporate profits are technically unnecessary to make a plan contribution). From the owners' perspective the profit-sharing plan may be more advantageous than other types of qualified plans in the closely held corporation's compensation plan for the following reasons:

- The plan can be structured to let the employer decide whether or not to make contributions in specific years. The tax rules require that contributions to profit-sharing plans merely be substantial and recurring. Thus a closely held business can avoid plan contributions in years in which the company has cash-flow problems.
- The plan can be designed to provide contributions only when a target profit amount has been reached for the year. This type of plan has a motivational element in that the profits can be correlated with the performance of key employees.The plan can be designed to permit withdrawals from a participant's (including a shareholder-employee's) account after the contributions have been in the account for 2 years.
- The plan can be structured to base contributions on an allocation formula that permits higher contributions based on the participant's salary and years of service. This generally increases the relative contributions of the shareholder-employees and other key executives.

Closely held corporations can use profit-sharing plans to provide a retirement plan that is more flexible with respect to funding. Since closely held corporations may be concerned with the required annual contributions under the previously discussed qualified plans, the profit-sharing alternative may be more attractive to the owners. However, a profit-sharing plan has lower limits with respect to deductible contributions. A profit-sharing plan can be adopted in conjunction with another type of retirement plan if the owners of the closely held corporation want to maximize both flexibility and deductible contributions.

Nonqualified Deferred-Compensation Plans

Advantages of Nonqualified Plans

A nonqualified deferred-compensation plan is an employer-provided benefit plan that defers income tax liability, typically until the participant retires. Nonqualified plans are not required to meet the stringent qualified plan rules. The nonqualified approach may be advantageous from the standpoint of the closely held corporation for the following reasons:

- to exceed the maximum benefit and contribution levels applicable to qualified plans for selected employees
- to provide a retirement plan for owners and other key employees without including rank-and-file employees in the plan
- to avoid the administrative compliance standards applicable to qualified plans
- to permit shareholder-employees or other key executives to temporarily defer taxes on income into a later tax years, which might provide an advantage if the recipient is currently in a high bracket.

Types of Nonqualified Deferred-Compensation Plans

salary reduction

Salary Reduction Arrangements. A *salary reduction plan*, also called an *in lieu of* plan, is an agreement between the employer and the participating employee to either reduce the employee's salary or defer an anticipated bonus and to provide that such amounts be received in future tax years. These plans provide for deferral of compensation that the employee would otherwise receive in cash, and such plans generally provide investment return on the amounts deferred. One type of salary reduction plan, called the *top-hat* plan, is a deferred-compensation plan for a selected group of management or highly compensated employees in which the participant elects to defer the amount that will provide benefits at his or her retirement.

The taxation for such compensation will be deferred only if specific requirements are met. Salary reduction arrangements have decreased in popularity with the reduction of individual income tax rates.

Salary Continuation Plans. Most nonqualified plans fit into the broad category of salary continuation plans. Salary continuation plans can be designed to provide deferred-compensation benefits at the participant's death, disability, and/or retirement. These arrangements have no current cash option available to the employee. The death or disability benefits are a percentage of the employee's compensation, and are provided to the employee or his or her designated beneficiary.

supplemental executive retirement plan (SERP)

Salary continuation plans designed to provide retirement benefits can be categorized as *excess-benefit plans* or *supplemental executive retirement plans (SERPs)*. An excess-benefit plan is a retirement plan in which selected participants, generally shareholder-employees and key executives, will receive retirement benefits in excess of those possible under the qualified plan limitations. That is, these plans provide (1) benefits in excess of the 100-percent-of-salary or $195,000 (for 2011) limitation in defined-benefit plans or (2) contributions in excess of the 100-percent-of-salary or $49,000 (for 2011) limitation in defined-contribution plans.

A SERP is a plan that generally complements the qualified plan benefits for a selected group of participants. Such plans provide benefits for the key executives of a corporation and, unlike excess-benefit plans, supplement the retirement benefits at levels both above and below the qualified plan limitations. These plans will meet the goal of providing discriminatory benefits to shareholder-employees and other key executives. The closely held business can use a salary continuation plan to provide a substantial retirement, disability, and death benefit to the owners without necessitating the costly inclusion of rank-and-file employees.

death-benefit-only (DBO) plan

Death-Benefit-Only (DBO) Plan. A DBO plan is a type of nonqualified plan designed to provide death benefits to a participant's heirs. DBO plans can provide a lump sum to the participant's survivors, but generally they pay installment benefits at the participant's death. Since a DBO is a nonqualified plan, participation can be based on discriminatory factors. Survivor benefits are taxable as ordinary income to the recipient-survivor and are deductible by the corporation when paid to the survivors.

The death-benefit-only plan benefits will be included in the participant's estate unless (1) the decedent participated in no other nonqualified deferred-compensation plan with the employer that provided living benefits and (2) the participant did not reserve the right to change the beneficiary initially designated. If the estate inclusion is a problem, the employer and employee should consider a Sec. 162 bonus plan or a split-dollar agreement with the use of an irrevocable life insurance trust (ILIT).

Requirements for Income Tax Deferral in Nonqualified Deferred-Compensation Plans

AJCA of 2004 made changes to prevent abuses with nonqualified deferred-compensation plans and the IRS followed up with regulations. Distributions must be limited to these specific events:

- the participant's separation from service. A distribution to a key employee of a publicly traded company cannot begin until at least 6 months after separation.
- the participant's disability. Disability is defined under either the strict Social Security definition of total and permanent disability or under the company's accident and health plan.
- the participant's death
- a time or event specified by the plan
- a change in ownership or control of the corporation
- an unforeseeable emergency such as (1) a severe financial hardship to the participant resulting from an illness or accident of the participant, spouse, or dependent, (2) the loss of the participant's property due to casualty, or (3) other similar extraordinary and unforeseeable circumstances beyond the participant's control. The amount cannot exceed the amount necessary for the emergency plus taxes on the distribution.

constructive receipt

economic benefit

The taxation of nonqualified deferred-compensation benefits ordinarily links the timing of the corporation's deduction to the participant's receipt of benefits. The key to success is deferring the income tax liability until the receipt of the benefit. To avoid current taxation on the deferred benefit, the employee cannot (1) be in *constructive receipt* of the income or (2) receive a current *economic benefit* from the deferred amounts.

To avoid constructive receipt the employee's receipt of the income must be

- subject to *substantial limitation or restriction*. This requirement is met if the employee simply has to wait a certain time period (for example, until retirement) for the benefits.
- deferred by binding agreement prior to the time when the employee earns the compensation. The employee cannot choose to take cash when the income is earned. In the salary reduction agreement the employee and employer will agree to defer the receipt of the salary or bonus before the related services are performed.

Any economic benefit currently received from the plan is immediately taxable to the participant even if such benefit is not constructively received. The participant receives an economic benefit if funds are vested or set aside for the employee outside the claims of general corporate creditors. Under such circumstances the economic benefit exists because the employee has a cash equivalency in the form of a secured and funded promise.

An economic benefit exists if the funds are placed in an irrevocable trust in behalf of the participant. The corpus of the trust will be a cash equivalent because the employer has given up control of the assets in the plan. To avoid an economic benefit, the plan assets must be subject to substantial risk of forfeiture. The assets can be set aside in a (1) reserve account held by the employer, (2) revocable trust, or (3) rabbi trust. Under a reserve account or revocable trust there is no economic benefit since all plan funds are subject to the employer's control. In a rabbi trust, since the assets are available to the general creditors of the corporation by the terms of the trust, no economic benefit exists. AJCA of 2004 adds penalties for plan assets placed outside of the United States for domestic participants and triggers that cause vesting of assets as a result of the employer's financial health.

FICA Implications of Nonqualified Deferred Compensation

Salary-deferral plans and nonqualified deferred-compensation benefits meet the definition of wages for FICA purposes. With the hospital insurance (Medicare) tax not subject to any wage base, this could be an immediate and significant tax on otherwise deferred amounts. The nonqualified benefits will be defined as wages at the later of (1) when services are performed or (2) a time at which there is no substantial risk of forfeiture to the participant's rights to the benefits.

LIFE INSURANCE IN THE COMPENSATION PLAN

Qualified Retirement Plans

Life insurance on the life of a participant can be included with the funding of the qualified defined-benefit or defined-contribution plan. The coverage must be based on nondiscriminatory factors. The plan uses the insurance to provide incidental death benefits. The employer receives a current income tax deduction for premium amounts contributed to the plan.

The amount of coverage eligible to be included is limited by the following incidental tests:

- The death benefit cannot exceed more than 100 times the expected monthly benefit.
- The total premiums paid over the life of the plans must be less than (1) 50 percent of the cost of the plan if ordinary life insurance is used or (2) 25 percent of the cost of the plan if term insurance is used.

The economic benefit provided by the coverage for life insurance on his or her life is taxable to a participant each year. This annual taxable amount is limited to the economic benefit cost of the pure insurance element reduced by any contribution the participant made to the plan in a given tax year. The accumulation element in the policy (all amounts other than the pure insurance element) is not currently taxable to the insured.

The beneficiary receives death benefits income tax free to the extent of the pure insurance element and any prior economic benefit costs contributed by the participant. The accumulation element of the policy provided by employer contributions is taxable in a similar manner to the accumulation in other pension investments.

Nonqualified Deferred-Compensation Plans

The employer can finance its obligation in a nonqualified plan through corporate-owned life insurance or annuity policies. This type of financing is attractive since life insurance or annuity financing as an asset is a good match for the type of liabilities created by the various nonqualified arrangements. The accumulation in an ordinary life insurance policy or the benefits of an annuity policy can be useful in the participant's retirement years to provide for any salary continuation benefits offered by the plan. Of course, the primary benefit of the life insurance financing is its ability to meet the death benefit obligation of the employer should the participant die prematurely. The life insurance financing is particularly appropriate to provide benefits in a DBO plan.

The life insurance policies are owned by and payable to the employer. As such, they avoid the constructive-receipt or economic-benefit problems because the general creditors have access to the funding policies. The premiums are, of course, nondeductible; however, the cash surrender value in a life insurance policy builds up tax free, and the proceeds will be nontaxable when received unless the corporate AMT is triggered based on the tax characteristics of the corporation in the year the life insurance proceeds are received. With an annuity policy, the corporation will have to pay tax on the accumulated earnings since the annuity tax-deferral rules do not apply if a nonnatural person (such as a corporation or rabbi trust) owns the annuity. The corporation receives a deduction when the benefits are actually paid to the participant.

Group Term Life Insurance (Sec. 79) Plans

Sec. 79 plan

Group term life insurance is a benefit plan provided by an employer to a group of participating employees. Such plans, also known as *Sec. 79 plans*, provide the employer with a tax deduction for premium payments made in behalf of a participant unless the premium amounts cause the reasonable-compensation limit to be exceeded (which is an unlikely event).

If the plan's coverage is nondiscriminatory, the first $50,000 of coverage is provided tax free to all plan participants. If the plan discriminates in favor of key employees with respect to coverage or benefits, the actual premiums paid in behalf of such key employees will be taxable as ordinary income to these employees. For this purpose the definition of a key employee is the same as under the qualified plan rules, and the definition generally includes the shareholder-employees of a closely held corporation. Thus it is important that the plan qualify as nondiscriminatory under Sec. 79 to avoid the adverse tax treatment of the shareholder-employees. If the plan does not qualify as nondiscriminatory, it would generally be better for the employer to adopt an informal bonus plan. An informal plan permits the shareholder-employees to purchase individual coverage (assuming all can be underwritten on an individual basis) while permissibly discriminating against other classes of employees.

Taxation of Group Term Life Insurance Plans

- Nondiscriminatory plans—Employer-paid premiums are tax free to insured for first $50,000 of coverage. Thereafter, IRS Table I rates determine taxable income.
- Discriminatory plans—Employer-paid premiums or rates based on the IRS Table I schedule, if higher, for all of the coverage are taxable as income for key employees.

The taxable amounts of coverage (that is, amounts above $50,000) are taxed based on the Table I rate schedule provided by IRS regulations. The Table I rates increase progressively in 5-year age brackets up to age 70. The following table provides the Table I rates applicable to group term life insurance, split-dollar plans, and qualified retirement plans containing life insurance.

Table 4-1 Table I Rates

5-Year Age Bracket	Cost per Month per $1,000
Under 25	$.05
25–29	.06
30–34	.08
35–39	.09
40–44	.10
45–49	.15
50–54	.23
55–59	.43
60–64	.66
65–69	1.27
70 and above	2.06

These rates are used to measure the economic benefit provided by the employer for income tax purposes with respect to the employer's contributions to the term insurance component of such employee benefit plans.

EXAMPLE

Suppose a retired executive, aged 65, has $150,000 of postretirement group term life insurance coverage. Since $100,000 of this coverage is subject to tax, the executive has to include $1,524 ($1.27 x 100 x 12 [months]) in income annually at age 65.

Requirements Under Sec. 79

The Sec. 79 coverage is provided under a contract held directly or indirectly by the employer. The coverage must provide the following:

- general death benefits excludible from income tax under Sec. 101(a). Thus travel and accident and health (including double indemnity) policies do not qualify under the group term life rules of Sec. 79.
- coverage to a group of *employees*. Employees must generally be common-law employees. Therefore a shareholder can be covered only if he or she is an actual employee of the corporation. A group is all employees of the employer or fewer than all employees if the group is determined by factors such as age, marital status, length of employment, employment classification, and/or membership in a union subject to collective bargaining. A group must generally include at least 10 employees; however, the special rules discussed below do provide an exception for smaller groups. Subject to the nondiscrimination rules discussed below, the plan can cover fewer than all employees and hold down the overall cost of the plan.
- insurance protection precluding individual selection of coverage amount. It can be based on formulas related to age, service, job classification, and compensation. For example, a plan that provides a death benefit five times a participant's annual salary precludes individual selection.

Nondiscrimination Rules Applicable to Sec. 79 Plans

Groups With 10 or More Members. The nondiscrimination requirements focus on both the coverage and benefits provided by the plan. To meet the coverage test, the plan must either

- cover at least 70 percent of all employees;
- have no more than 15 percent of the participants from the key employee group; or
- benefit a reasonable classification of participants.

For the coverage test the corporation can exclude (1) employees with less than 3 years of service, (2) part-time or seasonal employees, and (3) employees subject to collective bargaining. In general, it is difficult for a closely held corporation to exclude any nonkey employees if the shareholder-employees and other key employees participate.

The *benefits* test requires that the benefits be either a flat amount or a uniform percentage of compensation (for example, 2.5 times current salary). The benefits restrictions permit participants to voluntarily purchase additional coverage.

Groups With Fewer Than 10 Members. The IRS regulations provide more stringent requirements for smaller groups. These groups will lose the favorable tax treatment unless the following requirements are met:

- All full-time employees must be covered. (A 6-month waiting period is permissible.)
- Evidence of insurability can be tested only on the basis of a medical questionnaire.
- The benefits must be (1) a uniform percentage of compensation or (2) in brackets such that no bracket is more than 2.5 times the next lowest bracket and the lowest bracket is at least 10 percent of the highest bracket.

Postretirement Coverage. Although the welfare-benefit-plan rules are not technically nondiscrimination rules, they do apply to postretirement group term provided through retired lives reserves (RLR) plans. These rules make it generally infeasible to prefund postretirement group term life coverage to retired shareholder-employees in excess of $50,000. Unfortunately most of these individuals have substantial estates and desire permanent postretirement coverage of higher face amounts. For this reason, retired key executives often retain their positions on the board of directors to continue to participate in group coverage.

Executive Bonus (Sec. 162) Life Insurance Plans

Sec. 162 plan

One type of employee compensation arrangement that is currently advantageous for shareholder-employees is the executive bonus (Sec. 162) life insurance plan. The primary advantage of a *Sec. 162 plan* is its ability to avoid the nondiscrimination rules applicable to other fringe benefits.

Sec. 162 plans have the additional advantage of simplicity, which holds down the administrative costs. As the earlier material demonstrates, compensation planning and fringe benefits planning are becoming increasingly complex. The discussion of split-dollar life insurance plans at the end of this chapter indicates that a bonus life insurance plan may be the most effective method to provide discriminatory life insurance protection to a select group of executives. Split-dollar faces a risky and uncertain future as a result of recent IRS pronouncements. It is quite possible that some existing split-dollar plans will be converted to bonus arrangements if continuing life insurance is provided to the executive when a specific split-dollar plan is no longer feasible. The executive bonus plan is refreshingly simple and faces a relatively certain tax structure. Shareholder-employees and executives who participate in the plan apply for, own, and name the beneficiary on permanent life insurance policies covering their lives. The personally owned nature of the policy provides the maximum flexibility for the executive. The premiums for such policies are provided through a bonus payment by the corporation. The corporation either pays the premium directly to the insurer or provides the amount necessary to pay the premium as a bonus to the executive, whom the insurance company bills directly.

The income taxation of Sec. 162 plans is also easy to illustrate to clients. The premium amount paid directly to the insurer (or the bonus paid to the employee) is treated as gross compensation income to the employee under Sec. 61(a)(1). This compensation is treated as ordinary income subject to the employee's normal individual income tax rate. Assuming that the bonus and the employee's other compensation represent reasonable compensation, the corporation deducts the amount of the bonus as an ordinary business expense under Sec. 162(a)(1)—thus the origin of the name Sec. 162 plans. Although the tax burden of the bonus is immediate to the executive, the bonus can be designed as a zero-tax bonus, as discussed above, to reduce the executive's out-of-pocket costs. In addition, the executive is the owner of the life insurance policy and can use policy dividends to reduce future premiums (and the need for future taxable bonuses).

The primary reason why closely held corporations adopt Sec. 162 plans is their exemption from the federal nondiscrimination and administrative reporting rules applicable to most other types of fringe benefit plans. The board of directors of a closely held business or professional corporation can choose the participants who will be included and limit the plan to those shareholder-employees who desire individual life insurance coverage. Similarly there are no discrimination rules with respect to benefit limits.

Theoretically the plan can provide any amount of life insurance premium to purchase coverage on the life of a shareholder-employee who desires substantial coverage.

Advantages of Sec. 162 Plans
• They avoid nondiscrimination rules that apply to other fringe benefits. • Plan simplicity keeps administrative costs low.

However, the corporation should be careful in providing unlimited coverage since the corporate deduction for bonus payments to the plan is limited by the reasonable-compensation rules. If the limit is exceeded, the corporate income tax deduction will be lost with respect to the amount of any bonuses to shareholder-employees deemed unreasonable and the excess bonus will be treated as dividend payments rather than compensation. It is prudent for the board of directors of the corporation to adopt the Sec. 162 plan by formal resolution and provide evidence in the minutes to the corporate purpose for establishing the plan. For example, the corporation can indicate the need to retain or attract key executives by offering the Sec. 162 plan as a benefit.

Coordination of the Sec. 162 Plan With the Corporation's Group Term Life Insurance Plan

Do the substantial individual insurance benefits available under a Sec. 162 plan render the Sec. 79 plan obsolete? The answer to this question depends on many factors. Does the corporation already have a Sec. 79 plan in place that benefits employees? Does the current plan meet the nondiscrimination rules? Does the corporation wish to continue to provide group term life insurance coverage to nonhighly compensated nonowner-employees? Generally the group term life insurance plan should not be dropped as a result of the popularity of the Sec. 162 bonus plan.

For plans that meet the nondiscrimination requirements, Sec. 79 plans still offer favorable tax treatment. The corporation gets an ordinary business expense deduction for contributions to the plan, and the employees, including the shareholder and other key employees, receive the first $50,000 of coverage tax free. The corporation may also want to avoid the adverse morale consequences of terminating a popular fringe benefit plan covering a broad cross-section of employees and replacing the plan with a highly discriminatory executive bonus plan covering only a few key employees.

What is generally recommended is that the shareholder and other key employees who require (and for whom the corporation wishes to provide) more substantial life insurance coverage participate in a Sec. 162 bonus life insurance plan for personally owned coverage to supplement a Sec. 79 plan. The Sec. 79 plan can still provide the key employees with the $50,000 tax-free coverage. Under the Sec. 79 plan, however, additional group term coverage provided to these key employees will be taxable to the participant and can be deemed discriminatory, which will result in all benefits becoming taxable to such key employees. This excess coverage can instead be "carved out" of the group term life insurance plan and provided through the Sec. 162 bonus arrangement. Thus the executive bonus plan is also commonly referred to as a Sec. 79 executive carve-out bonus plan. The carved-out portion of coverage is actually superior to what can be provided under a Sec. 79 plan even if nondiscrimination rules were applicable to group term coverage. The key shareholder-employees participating in the plan will receive permanent individual life insurance policies that provide participants with tax-free cash-surrender-value (CSV) buildup and the other flexibilities associated with the ownership of permanent individual life insurance.

Table 4-2 Comparison of Sec. 79 Plan and Sec. 79 Carve-Out Plan

	Sec. 79	Sec. 79 Carve-Out
Coverage	Must meet the nondiscrimination test	Carve out excess coverage on a discriminatory basis
Benefits	Flat amount or uniform percentage	Any amount of bonus for carved-out portion that can be justified as reasonable
Income Tax to Executive	Amounts above $50,000 taxed at Table I costs (all taxable to key employee if discriminatory) and cost rises with age	Amount of bonus taxable, but tax cost is level or might actually be reduced in future years if policy performance permits the premiums to cease
Premium Deductibility	Fully deductible	Fully deductible

The executive bonus arrangement is also more favorable to the shareholder-employee in the postretirement years. The nondiscrimination rules generally limit the funding of RLR plans to $50,000 of postretirement coverage. Executive bonus plans provide the participating employees with permanent coverage (without any $50,000 limitation), which is held individually by the employee and thus available during the retirement years.

Reporting and Disclosure Requirements

It is unclear whether Sec. 162 bonus life insurance plans will be deemed welfare benefit plans under the provisions of ERISA. Since the plan provides taxable benefits to a select group of highly compensated executives, most of the reporting and disclosure requirements will not apply. However, if the plan is deemed a welfare benefit plan, a written plan document must be made available to the Department of Labor on request. As a precaution, there should be a formal corporate resolution that adopts the plan to satisfy the writing requirement. Written notice of the plan in a claims procedure should be given to every participant. Finally, a corporate officer should be appointed as "named fiduciary" of the plan to comply with any applicability of the ERISA provisions.

Estate and Gift Tax Planning Considerations

The Sec. 162 bonus life insurance plan involves the ownership of an individual life insurance policy by an insured-employee. As such, the proceeds of the life insurance will be included in the insured-employee's gross estate under the provision of Sec. 2042. This may not be a desirable result, particularly since the highly compensated plan participants are probably accumulating substantial estates irrespective of the bonus life insurance plan. If the gross estate inclusion is a concern to the participating executive, the plan can be designed with third-party ownership of the individual life insurance policy.

EXAMPLE

The spouse of the insured-employee or an irrevocable trust created by the insured-employee can own the life insurance. If the third party is the initial applicant and owner of the policy, the proceeds will be excludible from the gross estate of the insured even if the insured dies immediately after the coverage becomes effective. If estate tax problems become a concern at a later date, a participant in the plan can gift an existing policy to a third-party owner. In this event the insured will have to survive the 3-year period following the transfer or else the insurance proceeds will be included in his or her gross estate under the provisions of Sec. 2035.

In the example above, the gift tax consequences of such a transfer depend on the circumstances of the transfer. If an individual third-party owner, such as a spouse, is a donee of the life insurance policy, the original transfer of the policy plus any premiums paid by the employer will be treated as a gift from the insured-employee to the third party. The gift in this case will qualify for the annual gift tax exclusion (the annual gift tax exclusion is indexed for inflation and is $13,000 for 2011). Of course, any future premiums paid by the employer will be treated as taxable income to the insured-employee and as gifts from the insured-employee to the third-party owner.

If the policy is transferred instead to an irrevocable trust created by the insured, the transfer of the policy and any premiums paid subsequently by the employer will be treated as a gift from the insured-employee to the beneficiaries of the trust. However, the gifts under these circumstances will qualify for the annual exclusion only if the beneficiaries are given current withdrawal rights.

Split-Dollar Life Insurance Plans

Basic Concepts of Split-Dollar Life Insurance

split-dollar plan

Structure and Purpose of Split-Dollar Life Insurance. A *split-dollar plan* splits the premium obligations and policy benefits of a life insurance policy between two individuals or entities. The parties to a split-dollar agreement are normally an employer and employee. The two parties share the premium costs while the policy is in effect, pursuant to a prearranged agreement. At the death of the insured or the termination of the agreement, the parties split the policy benefits or proceeds in accordance with their agreement.

Because split-dollar plans can be limited to a select group of shareholder-employees and other key personnel, the plans were often selected as a fringe benefit option for closely held corporations. Split-dollar plans have evolved into many forms and have been used to provide life insurance protection and, perhaps, some retirement savings for select participants. In many instances, the split-dollar plan is designed to provide a "rollout" (see discussion below) of the policy to the participant at some point in the future (for example, at retirement).

Split-dollar plans must meet minimal reporting and disclosure compliance requirements. The insurer will handle most of the plan administration. Depending on the employer's and employee's tax brackets, split-dollar plans can be used in a group term carve-out in lieu of a Sec. 162 bonus plan. Because the corporation's tax bracket and the amount of compensation provided to shareholder-employees are largely in the control of the shareholder-employees, selecting the appropriate executive life insurance arrangement can be made optimally at their discretion.

endorsement method

Split-Dollar Life Insurance Policy Ownership. The policyowner of the underlying policy in a split- dollar plan can be either the employer or the insured-employee. The employer owns the policy and has primary responsibility for premium payment under the *endorsement* method. The employer's share of the benefits is secured through its ownership of the policy. The insured designates the beneficiary for his or her share of the death proceeds, and an endorsement is filed with the insurer stipulating that the beneficiary designation cannot be changed without the insured's consent.

collateral-assignment method

The insured is the policyowner and has premium payment responsibility under the *collateral-assignment method.* The corporation loans the employee its share of the annual premium, and the corporate amounts are secured by the assignment of the policy to the corporation. The corporation receives its benefits as assignee of the policy at the earlier of the employee's death or the termination of the split-dollar plan. For the income-tax (but not gift or estate taxes) purposes, the company will be treated as the policyowner in collateral-assignment split-dollar arrangements that do not provide "equity" to the participant-insured.)

Traditional Split-Dollar Plans

In traditional split-dollar plans, a corporation and an employee split a life insurance policy covering the employee's life. The plan can be designed under either the endorsement or collateral-assignment method. The premium can be split in a number of different manners. The employee is, in theory, the contributor of the premium equal to the cost of the net amount at risk (the term portion of the coverage); the corporation contributes the remainder of the premium and is secured by the cash surrender value (CSV). However, most split-dollar plans are noncontributory, and the employee is taxable annually for the corporation's excess contribution under the tax theories discussed below. The death benefit is split between the participating executive and the corporation as follows:

- The corporation receives the CSV (the corporation might have the right to receive back its actual contributions if such contributions are greater than the CSV at the time the corporation is reimbursed).

- The beneficiary named by the insured receives a death benefit equal to the pure amount of risk.

The traditional split-dollar arrangement has the following advantages:

- Discrimination in favor of shareholder-employees and other key executives is permissible.
- The employer can provide a life insurance benefit to selected employees with minimal charge to corporate earnings and with predictable tax cost to the employee.
- The plan is preferable to the Sec. 162 bonus plan if the corporation is in a lower tax bracket than the executive.
- The corporation can help the participating shareholder-employees purchase insurance to fund a buy-sell agreement.

The split-dollar plan will not afford the corporation a current income tax deduction even if the employee incurs taxable compensation. Thus, the corporation has to retain taxable income to contribute its share of the premium. The retained amounts of income can then provide the corporate contributions to a split-dollar plan covering selected shareholder-employees and other executives. Therefore, the use of certain amounts of corporate taxable income for this nondeductible split-dollar expenditure will be less costly from a tax standpoint if the corporation's marginal income tax bracket is lower than the employee's.

From the participating executive's point of view, traditional split-dollar plans continue to be favorable if an insurance benefit is desirable. Although a taxable economic benefit may be incurred and employees will receive taxable income subject to a maximum marginal bracket of 35 percent, a valuable life insurance benefit has been made available that is taxable at potentially low term insurance costs.

The class of employees that the split-dollar plan will cover is another important consideration. If coverage under the plan extends beyond the shareholder group, the split-dollar plan may be more favorable from the corporation's standpoint than the executive bonus plan. This is particularly true if the plan covers younger executives who may not stay with the current employer for their entire working careers. Under these circumstances, the corporation may not want to permanently lose its contributions, which will occur in a Sec. 162 bonus plan. The split-dollar plan gives the corporation a return of its actual contributions (possibly with a return on the invested funds), thus minimizing its charge to earnings for providing a valuable fringe benefit. Of course, it may be possible to design a dual arrangement in which a Sec. 162 bonus plan can be provided for the shareholder-employees and split-dollar coverage for junior executives. Generally speaking, the split-dollar plan is more favorable when lower corporate cost is indicated by such factors as the desire to cover a group larger than the shareholder-employees.

Equity Split-Dollar Arrangements

equity split-dollar plan

An *equity split-dollar plan* has been popular from the employee's perspective because excess cash surrender value builds up for the employee's benefit during the split period. The employee can use the equity in the CSV to supplement retirement benefits. The arrangement works as follows:

1. The employee's premium share is equal to the Table 2001 rates or the insurer's standard term rates, if lower. (Note: The use of PS 58 rates is still permissible in some cases as the discussion below indicates.) In a noncontributory (employer-pay-all) plan, the employee would be taxed on the cost of the economic benefit or under the interest-free loan rules, depending on whether the equity split-dollar is designed as an endorsement-method or collateral-assignment arrangement.
2. The employer pays the remainder of the premium.
3. The employer's share is equal to the lesser of the employer's premium contributions or the CSV.
4. The employee receives the death benefit equal to the excess over the employer's share.
5. During his or her lifetime, the employee builds up an interest in the excess of the policy CSV over the employer's share.

As with other split-dollar variations, the equity method involves careful consideration of all corporate goals, including the reduction of taxes. One obvious advantage of this arrangement is that the corporation receives all its contributions back. This is important for a closely held corporation in which the actual corporate outlay must be minimized, particularly if the plan covers executives outside the shareholder group. In addition, the corporation will not show a profit on its interests in the plan, and the potential impact of the corporate AMT will be avoided.

Some of the federal income tax implications with equity split-dollar arrangements cannot be ignored. First, the employee must furnish the annual term cost with after-tax dollars. Again, the corporation receives no federal income tax deduction for its contribution to the plan. One method of reducing the employee's outlay and coincidentally giving the corporation a valuable tax deduction is to provide the employee with a bonus equal to his or her annual contribution to the plan. A zero-tax bonus can be used to provide the employee with the full necessary after-tax funds to pay his or her annual contribution. The bonus arrangement is more valuable when (1) the corporation is in a higher tax bracket than the participating employee and (2) the plan is limited to shareholder-employees.

Split-Dollar Plans as an Alternative in the Executive Carve-Out Plan

The impact of the nondiscrimination rules on Sec. 79 group term life insurance plans was discussed previously with respect to executive bonus plans. Once again, a carve-out arrangement can be designed to provide substantial levels of life insurance coverage for key executives. Because split-dollar plans are exempt from nondiscrimination requirements and most of the reporting and disclosure compliance rules applicable to many other types of fringe-benefit arrangements, they allow corporate employers to freely discriminate in the class of participating employees and in the level of benefits provided. A discriminatory plan can eliminate all but shareholder-employees and other key executives from coverage. In addition, the split-dollar plan's individual permanent policy provides the popular postretirement coverage currently limited in RLR plans. The plan has the dual advantages of offering low-cost permanent life insurance to select executives while giving the employee an incentive to remain with the corporation.

Nondiscriminatory group term life coverage should still be adopted (or continued) if such coverage is otherwise desirable for the employer. Remember that Sec. 79 provides significant tax advantages to both the employer and the employee. The split-dollar carve-out alternative is simply one way to offer excess (discriminatory) life insurance coverage to shareholder-employees and other key executives without running afoul of nondiscrimination rules. The individuals participating in the split-dollar carve-out plan should still be covered under the group term life insurance plan, but their coverage should be limited to $50,000 or the permissible nondiscriminatory level of death benefits, if greater. If cost is a concern and the corporation does not feel the need to provide life insurance to a broad class of employees, the corporation should avoid the Sec. 79 plan.

Split-Dollar Rollouts

One criticism of the traditional split-dollar arrangement is that the employee receives no living benefits because the CSV remains either (1) directly in the employer's control if the endorsement method is used or (2) assigned to the employer if the collateral-assignment method is used. A second problem is that the annually taxable costs of the economic benefit rise dramatically as the employee's age increases.

split-dollar rollout

The *split-dollar rollout* provides a solution by terminating the split-dollar agreement at some point during the employee's life. The policy vests in the employee, including the unrestricted access to the CSV, and the corporation is repaid for its contributions through policy loans. Because the rollout is financed by (1) a policy loan if the CSV is sufficient, (2) a loan from the employer to the employee, or (3) a bonus by the corporation that relinquishes its rights under the contract, the limitation on personal interest deductions is a problem.

Several alternatives to save the rollout have been recommended. These alternatives should be considered if it otherwise makes sense to transfer the policy outright to the participant after the "split period." One alternative is for the executive to buy out the corporation's interest for cash. This alternative has never been popular, however, because it involves the conversion of substantial personal assets to cash surrender values on an after-tax basis. In addition, the corporation has tied up funds for the term of the split period without any corresponding tax deductions. This cash-out alternative appears to make no more sense than having employees use after-tax income to buy the policy at its inception without a split-dollar arrangement.

Another method is to provide the policy or the funds to pay for the rollout as a bonus to the employee. To minimize the size of the bonus, it might be advisable for the rollout to occur at a relatively early date, such as five years. The size of the CSV (hence the bonus) will be smaller at this time, and the size of the required taxable bonus will be minimized. If reasonable compensation is a question with respect to the size of the rollout bonus, smaller bonuses can be spread over a period of years to finance the buyout of the corporation's interest gradually. The corporation will secure its interest with interest-bearing notes to the employee. The corporation can also provide additional bonuses to pay the interest on the notes.

There are several suggestions for maintaining the low cost of the plan for the employee following the rollout. First, the required annual premium amounts can be paid out as bonuses to the employee under a Sec. 162 arrangement. In addition, the amount of the premium required following the rollout can be minimized by using an abbreviated premium payment approach. Of course, the rollout will have to occur somewhat later if the parties wait until the premium payments cease as a result of policy performance. Other options—for example, the surrender of paid-up additions at the time of the rollout to provide premium future dollars—are often employed.

Reverse Split-Dollar Plans

reverse split-dollar (RSD) plan

As an alternative to the equity or rollout type of split-dollar plans for providing substantial living benefits to executives, the *reverse split-dollar (RSD) plan* has achieved some popularity. In the RSD variation, the corporation and executive roles are reversed. In the basic form of RSD, the corporation pays the pure insurance portion of the premium, measured by PS 58 rates. The executive pays the balance of the premium. Because PS 58 rates are generally higher than the required premiums for the term portion of a policy, the corporation's contributions will cause equity to build up for the employee's benefit. (Note: The IRS has taken the position that PS 58 rates should not be used in an RSD plan. It would appear that the use of the Table 2001 rates applicable to regular split-dollar would be permissible.)

Under the RSD arrangement, the corporation's share at the employee's death is the pure insurance proceeds. The plan is designed so that the executive (or a third party) has individual ownership of the policy and the executive retains all rights in the policy other than the corporation's death benefit. At some point in the future, usually at the executive's retirement, the plan is terminated and the executive receives the policy unburdened by the employer's right to the death benefit.

The RSD plan is designed to meet some specific goals and should be used only when circumstances indicate. First, there should be a corporate need for the pure insurance on the life of the executive. For example, the corporation may be using the death proceeds as key person indemnification, to fund a stock redemption, or to fund a DBO plan.

The split-funding nature of the RSD plan helps hold down the cost for the executive who receives a substantial CSV benefit at retirement when the corporation's interest terminates. The RSD plan presented a good alternative to a traditional rollout or an equity split-dollar arrangement.

An RSD plan is a useful arrangement in some circumstances if the potential income tax problems are avoided. First, the corporation needs temporary life insurance coverage on a shareholder-employee or key executive in many circumstances—key person, 303 redemption, 302 redemption, DBO, and salary continuation. In addition, the ordinary life insurance policy received unencumbered by the employee at retirement is a valuable and popular asset. You will recall from the Sec. 79 discussion that RLR plans are limited generally to $50,000 of postretirement coverage. However, in an RSD plan the postretirement coverage is unlimited, and, what's more, the executive has current access to a substantial growing CSV.

The employee's contribution to the RSD plan can be provided through employer bonuses to take advantage of a tax deduction to the corporation.

Income Taxation of Split-Dollar Plans

Because a split-dollar plan is most often provided as a fringe benefit, it is necessary to discuss the taxation of the plan at both the corporate and employee levels. The taxation of split-dollar life insurance varies, depending on the type of plan, but it has traditionally been based on the general premise that the employee is taxed on the economic benefit that he or she receives annually from the plan. The economic benefit theory will continue to apply to endorsement-method split-dollar and nonequity collateral-assignment arrangements.

Economic Benefit Theory. In Rev. Rul. 64-328, C.B. 1964-2, the IRS ruled that the tax consequences of the basic split-dollar plan are the same, regardless of whether the plan is designed under the endorsement or collateral-assignment method. The economic benefit is the pure insurance element, measured by the cost of one-year term life insurance, conferred on the insured during the year. The term cost is the employee's share of the amount of protection in a given year multiplied by the term rate for the employee's attained age. In Rev. Rul. 66-110, C.B. 1966-1, the IRS ruled that the term cost is the lesser of the PS 58 rates or the insurer's annual renewable term rates offered to the general public. Any contributions made by the employee to the split-dollar plan can be applied against the economic benefit to reduce the tax cost of the plan. One important consideration is that the economic benefit would continue to be taxed at increasing term rates for the life of the plan. This generally indicates that the split-dollar plan be rolled out to the employee or terminated before the employee becomes too old and the economic benefit costs become unpalatable.

The traditional measurement of the economic benefit under a split-dollar plan was modified early in 2001. In IRS Notice 2001-10[10] (hereinafter the "2001 Notice"), the IRS stated its position to change the manner of measuring the economic benefit under split-dollar plans and life insurance contained in qualified retirement plans. Specifically, the Notice indicated that the IRS was withdrawing the PS 58 table as a measure of the economic benefit under the plan. The IRS suggested that the PS 58 costs used in the past to value the economic benefit to the employee-participant for the employer's contributions to the insurance coverage were too high for the realities of the insurance marketplace. (The use of these rates made reverse split-dollar plans, discussed earlier, an attractive employee benefit plan for key employees.) In addition to PS 58 tables, prior rules permitted the use of the insurer's standard term rates to measure the economic benefit provided by the employer's contribution to a split-dollar plan. Because these term rates varied from insurer to insurer, the IRS felt that there was unequal tax treatment among individuals participating in split-dollar plans offered by different insurers.

The 2001 Notice provided Table 2001, to be used in lieu of PS 58 rates. However, the economic benefit could still be measured by the actual term rates if lower than Table 2001 rates. However, the IRS was concerned about the use of special low rates uniquely published by insurers for the measurement of economic value under split-dollar life insurance plans. The 2001 Notice furnished guideline definitions for actual term rates and did not offer much grandfathering relief to existing split-dollar plans.

Table 4-3 Economic Benefit Costs for $1,000 of Life Insurance Protection

Attained Age	Sec. 79 Extended and Interpolated Annual Rates	Attained Age	Sec. 79 Extended and Interpolated Annual Rates	Attained Age	Sec. 79 Extended and Interpolated Annual Rates
0	$0.70	33	$ 0.96	67	$ 15.20
1	$0.41	34	$ 0.98	68	$ 16.92
2	$0.27	35	$ 0.99	69	$ 18.70
3	$0.19	36	$ 1.01	70	$ 20.62
4	$0.13	37	$ 1.04	71	$ 22.72
5	$0.13	38	$ 1.06	72	$ 25.07

10. 2001-5, IRB, 1/10/2001.

Attained Age	Sec. 79 Extended and Interpolated Annual Rates	Attained Age	Sec. 79 Extended and Interpolated Annual Rates	Attained Age	Sec. 79 Extended and Interpolated Annual Rates
6	$0.14	39	$ 1.07	73	$ 27.57
7	$0.15	40	$ 1.10	74	$ 30.18
8	$0.16	41	$ 1.13	75	$ 33.05
9	$0.16	42	$ 1.20	76	$ 36.33
10	$0.16	43	$ 1.29	77	$ 40.17
11	$0.19	44	$ 1.40	78	$ 44.33
12	$0.24	45	$ 1.53	79	$ 49.23
13	$0.28	46	$ 1.67	80	$ 54.56
14	$0.33	47	$ 1.83	81	$ 60.51
15	$0.38	48	$ 1.98	82	$ 66.74
16	$0.52	49	$ 2.13	83	$ 73.07
17	$0.57	50	$ 2.30	84	$ 80.35
18	$0.59	51	$ 2.52	85	$ 88.76
19	$0.61	52	$ 2.81	86	$ 99.16
20	$0.62	53	$ 3.20	87	$110.40
21	$0.62	54	$ 3.65	88	$121.85
22	$0.64	55	$ 4.15	89	$133.40
23	$0.66	56	$ 4.68	90	$144.30
24	$0.68	57	$ 5.20	91	$155.80
25	$0.71	58	$ 5.66	92	$168.75
26	$0.73	59	$ 6.06	93	$186.44
27	$0.76	60	$ 6.51	94	$206.70
28	$0.80	61	$ 7.11	95	$228.35
29	$0.83	62	$ 7.96	96	$250.01
30	$0.87	63	$ 9.08	97	$265.09
31	$0.90	64	$10.41	98	$270.11
32	$0.93	65	$11.90	99	$281.05
		66	$13.51		

The IRS followed this Notice rapidly with Notice 2002-8[11] (hereinafter the "2002 Notice"), which altered some of the harsh implications of the 2001 Notice. Specifically, the 2002 Notice revoked much of the 2001 Notice while retaining the Table 2001 rates to measure economic benefit. The 2002 Notice also provided transitional rules to grandfather split-dollar plans for some issues. For example, the PS 58 rates are still available to plans entered into before January 28, 2002. In addition, the harsher test for using the insurer's actual term rates does not apply to plans entered into before that date. For plans entered into after January 28, 2002, Table 2001 rates or the insurer's actual term rates can be used until final regulations are released by the IRS. After 2003, however, the insurer's term rates can be used for post-January 28, 2002, plans only if the applicable insurer (1) regularly makes the availability of such rates known to persons who apply for term insurance, (2) regularly sells term insurance at such rates to applicants in the insurer's normal distribution channels, and (3) does not commonly sell term insurance at higher rates to standard risks under its most common definition of standard risks.

The IRS then issued final regulations[12] in September 2003, which still do not conclusively determine the taxation of split-dollar life insurance. The regulations provide for an effective date of September 17, 2004, but continue to use some of the principles and transition dates of the 2002 Notice. They indicate that the economic benefit theory will apply in the future solely to endorsement-method and collateral-assignment plans that do not provide equity to the participating executive. The annual economic benefit will be taxable to the employee (and deductible by the employer, if reasonable compensation tests are satisfied). For plans entered into before January 28, 2002, the economic benefit can be measured by (1) PS 58 rates, (2) Table 2001 rates, or (3) the insurer's actual term rates, if lower. For plans entered into after January 28, 2002, the PS 58 rates are unavailable. Under the final regulations, the measure for the economic benefit is not provided, but is reserved for future guidance. Presumably, the economic benefit for new arrangements can be measured by either Table 2001 rates or the insurer's actual term rates, if lower (subject to the restrictive definition of term rates discussed above).

---

11. 2002-4 IRB 398.

12. Treas. Regs. Secs. 1.61-2 and 22; 1.83-1,3, and 6; 1.301-1; 1.1402(a)-18; 1.7872-15, 31.3121(a)-1. 31.3231(e)-1(a)(6), 31.3306(b)-1(l), and 31.3401(a)-1(b)(15)

Under the new version of the economic benefit theory, any equity that does accrue in equity endorsement split-dollar arrangements will not be taxed under Sec. 83 until the policy is transferred to the employee.

EXAMPLE

Suppose the XYZ Corporation offers a split-dollar plan to its sole shareholder and company president, Mr. Joffe, aged 45. If the policy has a $100,000 face amount death benefit and the corporation has the rights to the cash surrender value of $40,000, Mr. Joffe's share, which is the pure amount at risk, is $60,000. The company's accountant has decided to report the economic benefit under Table 2001 rates. For the tax year, Mr. Joffe received an economic benefit of $91.80 ($60,000 multiplied by the Table 2001 cost per $1,000 of $1.53). If Mr. Joffe makes no contributions to the plan, the taxable benefit to him for the year is $91.80.

interest-free loan

Loan Tax Regime. Traditionally, the IRS applied the economic benefit theory solely to the taxation of split-dollar life insurance plans. Congress adopted interest-free and below-market loan provisions into the Internal Revenue Code in 1984, but these rules were not made applicable to split-dollar until the recent IRS pronouncements. Under the new regulations, equity collateral-assignment split-dollar will be treated as a series of *interest-free loans* from the corporation to the participant-insured. Essentially, this tax treatment views the corporation's contributions as loans that will be repaid when the plan terminates. The taxation under the interest-free loan rules is extremely complex and will be oversimplified here. Simply, for a demand loan, the corporation is treated as providing compensation to the participant-insured equal to the forgone interest each year based on applicable federal interest rates. The corporation can deduct this amount as a compensation expense. The employee is treated as receiving ordinary income to the extent of such forgone interest.

Income Taxation of Reverse Split-Dollar Plans

A couple major tax problems with the RSD plan must be considered. Determining the amount that the corporation will be required to pay for its right to the death benefit is a critical decision. The IRS addressed these concerns to some degree in the 2001 Notice. The IRS then perceived abuses in private reverse split-dollar and issued Notice 2002-59[13] that probably signals the end of reverse split-dollar in the future. The Notice provides that

---

13. 2002-36 IRB, 8/16/02.

the party that pays the premium in a reverse split-dollar agreement (that is, the corporation) and keeps the right to the insurance protection can no longer use the rates published for measuring economic benefit (that is, PS 58 or Table 2001 rates) to determine the tax treatment. The Notice does not, however, provide the appropriate tax treatment.

Estate and Gift Tax Considerations of Split-Dollar Plans

The estate tax implications of traditional split-dollar life insurance plans have been well established. If estate liquidity is a concern for the executive participating in a split-dollar plan, some kind of third-party ownership—the executive's spouse or an irrevocable trust—should, in lieu of the insured, enter into the arrangement with the employer at the plan's inception. In this instance, the collateral-assignment method should be used if the participant-insured is a greater-than-50-percent shareholder in the corporation to avoid the attribution of incidents of ownership to the shareholder's estate. As a result of the new regulations, the collateral-assignment split-dollar agreement should be nonequity split-dollar to avoid the adverse tax consequences of the interest-free loan tax regime.

The gift tax issues must be addressed if the participant-insured has allowed an irrevocable trust or an individual third party to hold his or her rights under a split-dollar agreement. Simply, all premiums contributed by the participant to the plan (or amounts of economic benefit taken into income early years of the arrangement, the death benefits will represent the primary by the participant) will be treated as gifts to the third-party owner or the beneficiaries of the irrevocable trust.

Estate taxes are more of a concern with RSD plans. These plans are designed for the insured executive to own the policy from its inception or at least have significant control over the incidents of ownership. Sec. 2042 requires the entire proceeds to be includible in the insured's estate at his or her death under these circumstances. This amount includes the death proceeds payable to the corporation. Thus, RSD can potentially create a huge estate liquidity problem for a participant. That is, the corporation's share of death proceeds will be included in the gross estate for tax purposes, but the proceeds will be in the hands of the corporation and not the executor. In the early years of the arrangement, the death benefits will represent the primary portion of proceeds from the policy, and an early death could create an insolvent estate for the executive.

Table 4-4 Comparison of Methods for Inclusion of Life Insurance in the Compensation Plan				
		Qualified Plans	Nonqualified Plan Benefits	DBOs
1	Corporate Income Tax Deduction	Up to incidental limits	Benefits deductible when paid	Benefits deductible when paid
2	Current Income Taxation to Employee	Table I costs less employee contribution	No	No
3	Employee's Share of Death Benefit	Full proceeds	Full deferred-comp. benefit	Full proceeds
4	Income Taxation of Benefits Received by Heirs	Tax free to extent of amount at risk	Yes	Yes
5	Proceeds in Employee's Estate for Estate Tax Purposes	Yes	Yes	No, unless the decedent possessed living nonqualified benefits
6	Employee Access to Cash Surrender Value	No, unless profit-sharing plan (indirect access through plan loan)	No	No

Fortunately, the IRS alleviated some of this concern in a private ruling. Essentially, the ruling states that

- the policy underlying the RSD plan is in the insured's estate under Sec. 2042 if the insured has incidents of ownership within 3 years of death
- the estate receives an estate tax deduction for any amounts that must be paid to the corporation for its share of the proceeds. This ruling solves the estate tax problems presented above. The estate will effectively be taxed only on amounts available to the executor, which is the employee's share of the proceeds.

The corporation might be using the RSD proceeds to make a DBO or stock-redemption distribution to the estate. In these cases, the liquidity burden of the RSD plan will be lessened. Again, the method for removing the proceeds of an RSD plan from the estate will be to establish the RSD plan with a third-party-ownership arrangement.

	Sec. 79 Plans	Sec. 162 Bonus Plans	Split-Dollar Plans	Reverse Split- Dollar Plans
1	Yes, if reasonable compensation	Yes, if reasonable compensation	No deduction	No deduction
2	Table I costs for coverage above $50,000	Full amount of bonus	Table 2001 (or term) cost less employee contribution or interest free-loan taxation	Uncertain
3	Full proceeds	Full proceeds	Amount at risk (traditional plan)	Cash surrender value (full proceeds after RSD plan terminates)
4	No	No	No	No
5	Yes, unless assigned to third-party owner more than 3 years prior to death	Yes, unless assigned to third-party owner more than 3 years prior to death	Yes, unless assigned to third-party owner more than 3 years prior to death	Yes, unless assigned to third-party owner more than 3 years prior to death (estate gets a deduction for amount of death benefit payable to corporation)
6	N/A	Yes	Yes	Yes, unless restricted by plan agreement

CHAPTER REVIEW

Key Terms and Concepts

self-employed business owner
reasonable compensation
zero-tax bonus plan
salary reduction
supplemental executive retirement plan (SERP)
death-benefit-only (DBO) plan
constructive receipt
economic benefit
Sec. 79 plan
Sec. 162 plan
split-dollar plan
endorsement method
collateral-assignment method
equity split-dollar plan
split-dollar rollout
reverse split-dollar (RSD) plan
interest-free loan

Review Questions

The answers to the review questions are in the supplement. The self-test questions and the answers to them are also in the supplement and on The American College Online.

1. Identify three ways a shareholder of a closely held C corporation can benefit from business ownership. [1]
2. Describe the tax advantages available to shareholder-employees of a regular corporation with respect to fringe benefits that are not available to self-employed owners. [1]
3. Identify the possible tax advantages available with respect to fringe benefit plans. [1]
4. Explain how the type and amount of fringe benefits provided to nonowner-employees are often correlated to benefits provided to shareholder-employees. [2]
5. What factors can be useful in establishing the reasonableness of compensation provided to a shareholder-employee? [3]
6. Identify the possible purposes of providing cash bonuses to shareholder-employees and other key executives. [3]
7. Under what circumstances will a bonus paid to an employee in a given tax year be deductible by the payer-corporation in a previous tax year? [3]
8. Mr. Exec is a key employee of ABC, Inc. The corporation wants to provide him with a bonus that is large enough for Mr. Exec to pay a $2,000 annual premium on a personally owned life insurance policy and pay all federal income taxes imposed as a result of the bonus. If Mr. Exec is in a 35 percent marginal income tax bracket, how large a bonus must ABC provide? [3]
9. Describe the operation of a reimbursement agreement between a corporation and an employee. [3]
10. Identify the three goals of deferred-compensation plans. [4]
11. Explain why a defined-benefit plan might be the optimal choice for a qualified retirement plan for a closely held corporation. [4]
12. Describe the features that make a profit-sharing plan attractive for a closely held corporation seeking maximum flexibility with respect to its qualified retirement plan. [4]
13. Briefly describe the following types of nonqualified deferred-compensation plans: [5]
    a. top-hat plans
    b. excess-benefit plans
    c. supplemental executive retirement plans

14. Identify the circumstances in which the benefits paid from a death-benefit-only plan will be excluded from a deceased participant's estate. [5]

15. Describe the plan design considerations necessary to prevent the tax doctrines of constructive receipt or economic benefit from causing the current taxation of compensation amounts deferred in a nonqualified plan. [5]

16. Describe the limitations on the amount of life insurance that can be included in a qualified retirement plan. [6]

17. Describe the penalty that applies if a Sec. 79 group term life insurance plan discriminates in favor of highly compensated employees. [6]

18. Explain the nondiscrimination requirements that must be met if a Sec. 79 plan is adopted for a group with fewer than 10 members. [6]

19. Explain how a Sec. 162 plan can be used in conjunction with a group term life insurance plan to provide substantial life insurance coverage to shareholder-employees while retaining the tax advantages available in the group term plan. [7]

20. Distinguish between the endorsement and collateral-assignment methods for designing split-dollar life insurance plans. [8]

21. Describe briefly the mechanics of a reverse split-dollar plan. [8]

22. Explain the reporting and disclosure requirements applicable to the employer who adopts a split-dollar life insurance plan. [8]

PROBLEMS IN BUSINESS CONTINUATION 5

Learning Objectives

An understanding of the material in this chapter should enable the student to

1. Explain, in light of the interest of creditors and heirs, the rules that relate to an executor's authority to continue a proprietorship after the proprietor's death.
2. Identify the problems with various plans made by a proprietor for continuation of the business after death, and compare these approaches with an insured buy-sell agreement.
3. Identify the problems that an executor and the surviving partners encounter in attempting to continue a partnership after a partner's death.
4. Identify the problems with various alternatives to the liquidation of a partnership that are (a) improvised *after* a partner's death or (b) set up *before* a partner's death. Compare these alternatives to a partnership buy-sell agreement.
5. Describe the problems arising at the death of a close corporation stockholder, and distinguish those problems that are unique to minority stockholders and majority stockholders.
6. Identify the problems from plans for business continuation that are (a) improvised after a stockholder's death or (b) set up by stockholders prior to death. Compare them with the result of a buy-sell agreement.
7. Describe the estate preservation techniques that can be employed to either (a) decrease estate tax liability or (b) provide estate liquidity.

BUSINESS CONTINUATION AT THE DEATH OF AN OWNER

The death of an owner is typically disruptive and often leads to the termination of the business. There are many obstacles to continuation of a business at the death of an owner, but some planning methods can be employed to facilitate continuation.

The Probate Process

To understand the business-continuation problems at the death of an owner, it is necessary to be familiar with the process through which the decedent's property passes after death. When an individual dies, there are legal procedures for identifying the decedent's property, collecting it, and distributing it to the heirs. If the decedent left a valid will, the property will generally be distributed in accordance with its terms. If no valid will exists, the property will be distributed according to state law governing intestate succession. The method of distribution, whether by will or intestacy, is generally referred to as the *probate process.* The actual process is determined by the laws of the state in which the decedent's estate is admitted to probate.

The property left by the decedent is referred to as the *estate.* Technically speaking, the estate includes all property in which the decedent held an interest at death. The *probate* estate includes property admitted to probate to pass under the laws of wills and succession. For example, a residence left in the decedent's will is part of the probate estate. Property passing by operation of law or contract may be part of the estate but is not part of the probate estate. Life insurance proceeds left to a named beneficiary (other than the estate) are an example of nonprobate property.

What the Probate Estate Includes

- Decedent's property that passes to another under the decedent's will
- Decedent's property that passes to another under the applicable laws of succession
- Decedent's property made payable to estate by beneficiary designation

During the period of estate administration the estate acts as a legal entity in lieu of the actual decedent. That is, the estate can make claims on behalf of the decedent or defend against claims brought against the estate by others.

executor

administrator

Until the estate is distributed to the ultimate beneficiaries, a representative of the decedent must be designated to hold the property. This individual is referred to as the *executor* if he or she is named in a valid will, or the *administrator* if appointed by the court in the absence of a duly appointed executor. For simplicity we will refer to the personal representative of the decedent as the executor, although the discussion would also be applicable to an administrator.

During the period of estate administration the executor holds legal title to the estate's property. The ultimate distributees (beneficiaries) of the estate hold a beneficial ownership interest in the estate property. The legal title enables the executor to engage in transactions with the estate property, but the actions of the executor are often subject to court approval and may expose him or her to personal liability.

The relationship between the executor as legal owner and the distributees as beneficial owners of the estate property is governed by the principles of fiduciary responsibility. As a fiduciary of the estate, the executor has the serious responsibility of handling the estate property in the best interest of the ultimate beneficiaries. As stated in earlier chapters, a fiduciary must avoid conflicts of interest with those relying on him or her—in this case the estate beneficiaries. Consequently the executor should not transact business personally with the estate and cannot profit from transactions entered into in behalf of the estate.

The compensation scheme for the executor of an estate reflects these fiduciary principles. The executor is paid for actual services rendered on the behalf of the estate. In practice the executor is often paid a percentage of the estate's value. A prohibited form of compensation would be a contingent fee based on the executor's success in handling the estate property.

Although the executor may not profit from transactions with the estate property, the fiduciary relationship creates the possibility that the executor could be responsible for losses incurred by the estate resulting from unauthorized activities in the estate administration process. The executor is also liable for losses if authorized actions are performed negligently.

The restrictions imposed on the executor are at the root of many business-continuation problems. For example, the continuation of the decedent's business is typically beyond the scope of the executor's duty. In this case the executor will be personally liable to the estate beneficiaries for any losses incurred during the continuation of the business. Furthermore, the executor cannot personally benefit from any activities necessary to continue the decedent's business. Therefore even if the continuation of the decedent's business would be beneficial to the estate, the executor is unlikely to take the risk.

The Proprietorship

The death of a proprietor presents the most obvious continuation problem since there are no co-owners remaining to operate and wind up the business. The employees of the proprietorship have no authority to continue the operations. The proprietorship is placed into the legal ownership of the executor along with the other assets of the decedent.

Not only is the executor typically unauthorized to continue the decedent's business, but he or she is also liable to the estate for losses incurred if the business is continued except as provided below. The liability is not excused even if the executor is acting in good faith and a continuation was in the best interests of the estate. But the executor is not liable for the reduction in the value of the business that might occur if the terminated business is sold at a forced liquidation. Under these circumstances it is usually not advisable for an executor to continue the decedent's proprietorship without the consent of all potentially affected parties.

Continuation by Consent

trade creditors

An executor may become liable for losses incurred in continuing the decedent's business. The executor who continues the decedent's business may be excused from liability to all individuals who consent to the continuation of the business. In the absence of this consent the parties who may hold the executor liable for continuing the business are the trade creditors, estate creditors, and beneficiaries of the estate, who have interests in a share of the estate assets and could be harmed if the total value of the estate was impaired by the business continuation. The estate creditors include personal creditors and creditors of the decedent's business whose claims arose during the decedent's life. *Trade creditors* are those to whom the business becomes indebted following the decedent's death.

The executor who obtains the consent of the estate creditors and beneficiaries to continue the business is not liable for normal business losses suffered during the period of continuation resulting from causes other than legal fault of the executor. Of course, the executor is still subject to the normal duty of care and continues to be liable for negligent actions or misconduct.

It is often difficult to obtain the consent of all beneficiaries, who face the risk that consent will cause the business to suffer losses and diminish the estate. Furthermore, consenting beneficiaries have no recourse against the executor for these losses since the estate creditors must also be paid before the beneficiaries will receive distributions. Therefore the beneficiaries are unlikely to consent to the risk of additional priority claimants—the trade creditors of the continued business.

The executor should be aware of all potential distributees of the estate who might bring suit for losses suffered by the estate due to the unauthorized continuation of the business. Therefore the executor should admit the will to the probate court to determine its validity and get consent of all possible distributees. If no will exists, or if all or part of the will is declared invalid, the consent of the heirs as determined by the state intestacy laws is necessary to continue the business. The executor should also be mindful of potential will contests or the possibility of an election against the will by the spouse. These actions could lead to unanticipated claims against the estate. A further problem exists if some of the beneficiaries are minors or otherwise legally incompetent at the time consent is given. These parties are incapable of giving a valid consent and may later disclaim their consent and bring a valid action against the executor for losses suffered during the business continuation.

Obtaining the estate creditors' consent to continue a deceased proprietor's business is a complex and difficult procedure. The executor who continues a proprietorship is deemed to be dealing personally with the trade creditors. That is, the executor is personally liable to trade creditors while running the firm. However, the executor who obtains the consent of estate creditors and beneficiaries has the right to be indemnified from the business assets for his or her liability to trade creditors. Therefore consenting estate creditors would have to subordinate their claims to the business assets to the trade creditors—a risk they may be unwilling to take.

In general, the trade creditors of the continued business have no rights to the nonbusiness estate property even if the executor has the consent of estate creditors and beneficiaries. Since the executor is personally liable to trade creditors, any loss in excess of the business property must be satisfied by the executor, so trade creditors may be reluctant to conduct business with the executor. Furthermore, the executor may be unwilling to take the personal risk. It should be apparent at this point that it may be difficult to get the cooperation of all affected parties to continue a deceased proprietor's business. The potential rights facing all the parties for business continuation following the death of a proprietor are summarized in the table below.

Table 5-1 Rights of Parties Facing Business Continuation at Proprietor's Death

	Consents to Continuation	Not Consenting
Heirs	• cannot hold executor liable except for negligence • give executor indemnification rights from business assets for losses to trade creditors • subordinate distribution rights to estate and trade creditors	• hold executor personally liable for business losses • do not give executor indemnification rights for losses to trade creditors • subordinate distribution rights to estate creditors only • limit trade creditors' rights to legal action against executor
Creditors of the Estate	• cannot hold executor liable except for negligence • give executor indemnification rights • subordinate rights to estate business property to trade creditors • have priority rights over heirs to estate assets	• hold executor personally liable for business losses • give executor no indemnification rights • have priority rights over heirs and trade creditors to estate property

Obtaining consent of the affected parties appears to be a formidable task, but there are cases in which it is the appropriate course of action. It may be obvious to the estate creditors and beneficiaries that the forced liquidation of the proprietorship will greatly diminish the estate assets. Under these circumstances the risk of business continuation may be the more favorable choice. Trade creditors may also see the continued proprietorship as a source of profitable business. In this case it is possible that the parties will consent to the executor's continuation of the business. Considering the difficulties in getting all the parties to agree to the business continuation, it is obvious that a continuation plan formed while the proprietor is alive is a safer course of action.

Continuation Under Statutory Authority

The discussion above indicated some of the difficulties in continuing a proprietorship following the death of the owner, but it is unlikely that the immediate cessation of business activities is in the best interests of most of the affected parties or the economy as a whole. In response to the harsh situation facing the executor following the death of a proprietor, many states have adopted some form of the Uniform Probate Code provision that provides as follows:

> Section 3-715. Transactions Authorized for Personal Representatives; Exceptions
>
> Except as restricted or otherwise provided by the will or by an order in a formal proceeding . . . , a personal representative, acting reasonably for the benefit of the interested persons, may properly
>
> (24) continue any unincorporated business or venture in which the decedent was engaged at the time of his death (i) in the same business form for a period of not more than 4 months from the date of appointment of a general personal representative if continuation is a reasonable means of preserving the value of the business including goodwill; (ii) in the same business form for any additional period of time that may be approved by order of the Court in a formal proceeding to which the persons interested in the estate are parties; or (iii) throughout the period of administration if the business is incorporated by the personal representative and if none of the probable distributees of the business who are competent adults object to its incorporation and retention in the estate;
>
> (25) incorporate any business or venture in which the decedent was engaged at the time of his death.

Since not all states have adopted this provision of the Uniform Probate Code, financial services professionals should be aware of the statute as enacted in the appropriate state if continuation-planning advice is given. The provision as stated above typically allows an executor to continue a business for a 4-month period without fear of personal liability for business losses not caused by the action of the executor. Continuation beyond this 4-month period requires the approval of the probate court upon consideration of the interest of all parties involved in the estate and business.

The provisions providing for the incorporation of the business by the executor may be useful but are limited by the problems normally facing incorporation. That is, there must be equity investors, sources of outside credit, and an active management to continue the business. It is clear that these provisions contained in the model act do not solve all the problems facing the business at the death of the proprietor. However, they are useful to protect the executor and the interested parties from the possible detrimental results of immediate termination of business activities.

Lifetime Proprietorship Continuation Planning

Although the postdeath planning devices can be useful to solve some of the problems facing the executor at the death of a sole proprietor, it is dangerous to rely on these devices as a substitute for thorough lifetime planning. The lifetime continuation-planning devices for proprietorship are (1) the use of will provisions, (2) business trusts, and (3) the buy-sell agreement.

Will Provisions. One form of lifetime planning by the proprietor for continuation is to include a provision in the will authorizing business continuation. The typical provision would direct the executor to continue the decedent's business for a specified period of time or purpose. A provision of this type relieves the executor to some extent for the potential liability related to continuing the business. Probate law generally provides that the executor has a right to indemnity from the estate to cover any personal liability incurred by following the provisions of the will. The executor does remain liable for losses incurred above the amount of assets in the estate as well as for any losses incurred due to negligence.

The executor continuing a business under the provisions of a will becomes liable to trade creditors. As discussed previously, the law provides that these trade creditors are deemed to be dealing directly with the executor and as such have no claim on the proprietorship assets unless the estate creditors and beneficiaries have consented to the continuation. In addition, the executor as a fiduciary is not entitled to profits received by the business during the period of continuation, but the will can include a provision for additional compensation to the executor who takes on the challenge of continuing the business.

The increased risk faced by the executor, along with the lack of personal financial incentive, may make the executor reluctant to follow the will provision authorizing continuation. In general, an executor cannot be compelled to follow the directions under the will to continue the decedent's business.

For these reasons it is necessary for the proprietor who includes these continuation provisions in a will to select an executor who is willing and capable of continuing the business. Since the executor is a fiduciary, the individual selected should not be one with a personal interest in either the business or the estate. Otherwise, a conflict of interests might arise that would render the executor ineffective. For example, a trusted employee may be most capable of running the business at the proprietor's death but, if chosen to be executor, would be unable to make business decisions personally affecting the employee—such as decisions about salary or other working conditions. Consequently it is generally recommended that a corporate fiduciary be named as executor or at least as coexecutor.

If it is anticipated that the executor will not have the skill or personal experience to continue the business, an adviser provision should be included in the will. This provision directs the executor to seek the assistance of specified advisers for the management and direction of the business. The executor following this provision will be relieved from liability for actions recommended by the advisers. Again, it is obviously necessary to select advisers who have no potential conflicts of interest. They could be selected from management or business consulting firms and will be liable to the estate if poor advice is given.

A provision directing the executor to continue the proprietor's business should include the authorization to incorporate the business by the executor. The continued business may incur liabilities that cannot be satisfied by the business assets. In this case the other estate assets may become subject to the claimants of the continued business. This presents the unpalatable specter of a substantial diminution of the remainder of the estate as a result of business failure. The incorporation of the business by the executor will limit the liability for the activities of the continued business to the assets of the corporation. This estate-preservation technique should never be ignored when considering a will provision allowing the continuation of an unincorporated business.

Reasons for including a provision in the proprietor's will authorizing the continuance of the business at the death of the proprietor are

- avoiding forced liquidation of a business by allowing it to be sold as a viable going concern
- maintaining the business as a going concern until an heir of the decedent can take control

- providing continued income from the business to the family or other heirs

The use of will provisions as the sole method of lifetime planning for business continuation may be an ineffective method of reaching these goals for several reasons. Finding a buyer for the business as a going concern after the proprietor's death is often difficult. The search process may be lengthy, and the business may have to be continued for a period beyond the normal period of estate administration. The executor may also be subject to personal risk for continuing the proprietor's business. Furthermore, it is quite likely that the success of the proprietorship depended upon the personal skills of the owner. It may be difficult to find an executor who is willing to accept the risk of continuation and possesses the skills necessary to succeed.

These problems will also occur if the executor continues the business either to sustain it until the heirs take over or to provide income to the family. In other words, the executor must succeed in maintaining the business as a viable enterprise if this continuation plan is to work.

Additional problems arise if the business is maintained beyond the period of estate administration. The executor must provide for all debts, taxes, and expenses of the estate from the decedent's assets. Since the proprietorship is likely to be a significant portion of the assets held by the decedent, another problem comes to light: the executor must find a way to pay the estate costs out of the remaining assets of the estate. If the other assets are not sufficient, the executor will have to liquidate the business to meet these costs. Even if the assets are sufficient to satisfy the costs, there may be insufficient property left after the expenses to provide for the heirs who did not inherit an interest in the business. This problem becomes paramount if the decedent has many heirs for whom to provide but intends for the business to be continued by the executor until one specific heir is capable of taking over.

The Use of the Trust in Continuation Planning. The transfer of the business to an inter vivos (living) trust is one method of providing for business continuation at death. The designated trustee holds legal title to the business and may continue the business beyond the lifetime of the proprietor. At first, the proprietor may be named as trustee to maintain the status quo for the management of the business. The proprietor might then name a cotrustee or successor trustee to continue the business at death or retirement. In any event the proprietor may be designated as the income beneficiary from the trust—receiving the income from the business—until death. At the proprietor's death the trustee continues the business either (1) to provide income to the heirs or (2) to maintain the business until the heirs take over.

It is usually advised that the living trust be revocable until the effectiveness of the arrangement can be evaluated. If the trust arrangement proves successful, the owner can make the trust irrevocable at retirement. Since the trustee selected must have the appropriate skills and financial resources to operate the business, it is usually recommended that a corporate trustee be designated. It may also be appropriate to include an adviser provision directing the trustee to seek the advice of an individual designated by the trust settlor to make recommendations to the trustee about major business decisions. As in the case of continuance of the proprietor's business by the executor, the success of this continuation method depends on the ability of the trustee to operate the enterprise.

A testator often creates multiple trusts in a will for estate planning purposes. For example, the will might include marital and family trusts. If the testator owns a sole proprietorship, the business interest may be divided between the trusts. To facilitate the continuation of the business, it has been suggested that the trustees of the separate trusts form a partnership. Of course, this action must be authorized by the trust provisions and by the state law governing trustee action.

Advantages of continuing the business through a living trust arrangement are the following:

- The business owner has an opportunity to observe the continuation plan and the functioning of the successor management in actual operation before making the plan irrevocable.
- The proprietorship can be continued beyond the lifetime of the owner without reliance on the discretion of the executor to act.
- The trust represents a convenient mechanism to provide retirement income to the owner and income continuation to the owner's family after his or her death.
- The transfer of the business occurs without the publicity and expense of probate.

Disadvantages of the living trust arrangement as a business-continuation device are as follows:

- The trustee's fees may be a substantial drain on business income.
- It may be difficult to find a trustee who is both willing to run the proprietor's business and capable of doing so.

- The trustee's management flexibility and operation of the business are limited by both the trust instrument and state laws restricting trustee behavior.

Many of the problems discussed in the previous section can be solved with the use of an inter vivos life insurance trust. For example, life insurance can be purchased by the proprietor and transferred to a trust to provide for the debts, taxes, and expenses of the proprietor's estate. If the proprietor transfers the policy irrevocably more than 3 years prior to death (or the insurance is purchased and owned by the trustee of an existing trust), the proceeds will not be included in the proprietor's gross estate. Furthermore, if the trustee is merely given the discretion to pay the final expenses of the proprietor, the insurance proceeds will be includible in the proprietor's gross estate only to the extent that they are actually used to pay expenses. Also a life insurance trust can be a useful means of providing sizable death proceeds to heirs who do not inherit an interest in the business.

EXAMPLE

Pete owns a sole proprietorship as his only substantial asset. Pete has two children, Amy and Dave, who are to receive equal shares of his estate. Dave has shown no business acumen, while Amy has taken an interest in the business and is Pete's logical successor. Assuming Pete is insurable, he can purchase insurance on his life equal to the value of the proprietorship. The insurance policy and the business can be placed in an inter vivos trust during Pete's lifetime. At Pete's death the trustee will continue the business until Amy is capable of taking over. At that time the trust will be terminated, the business transferred to Amy, and the insurance proceeds, presumably equal in value to the business, distributed to Dave.

Life insurance can also be used to provide for estate expenses through will provisions, but this will cause full estate tax inclusion of the proceeds. The estate tax can be avoided if the proprietor transfers the policy irrevocably to the intended beneficiary more than 3 years prior to death, but this method will not provide the flexibility available by using an independent trustee for the handling of the proceeds.

The Buy-Sell Agreement. In many cases the continuation of the business by the decedent-proprietor's family is not an appropriate alternative. Under these circumstances it is often best to provide for a prearranged sale of the business at the death of the proprietor. The purchaser of the business might be a key employee of the proprietorship or perhaps a long-time suitor of the business property. A binding buy-sell agreement can be executed between the proprietor and the intended purchaser during the proprietor's life. Briefly the agreement requires the proprietor's estate to sell and the purchaser to buy the business at the death of the proprietor.

The buy-sell agreement has several advantages over other types of continuation plans. It typically provides the proprietor's estate with a value greater than would be available if the business was liquidated by the executor. That is, the purchase price is negotiated by the proprietor while the business is a going concern. This technique avoids the problems associated with forcing the executor to continue the business and/or seek an appropriate buyer during the period of estate administration. Cash proceeds received by the estate from the buy-sell agreement provide funds to satisfy the expenses of the estate and allow quick settlement of the estate and prompt distribution to the heirs. The buy-sell agreement provides assurance to the proprietor and the purchaser that the sale will be consummated. This assurance is particularly important if the purchaser is a key employee of the business. The buy-sell agreement will provide the key employee with a continued source of income at the death of the proprietor.

Proprietorship's Lifetime Continuation-Planning Devices

- Will provisions that authorize continuation
- Transfer of the business to a living trust
- Binding buy-sell agreement

The Partnership

The death of a partner involves many of the same problems associated with the death of a proprietor, but the legal framework is different. Partners do not have direct ownership of partnership assets—the assets are held by the partners as tenants in partnership. When a partner dies, the partnership interest is passed to the estate, not to any individual partnership property. The deceased partner's executor is responsible for handling the partnership interest. However, the executor has no control over the handling of partnership property. The property remains the responsibility of the surviving partners.

Death of a Partner Absent Continuation Planning

liquidating trustees

Without prior planning the general rule states that the partnership is dissolved upon the death of a general partner. At this time the surviving partners become *liquidating trustees* and owe a fiduciary obligation to the estate of the deceased partner. They also then have the obligation of winding up the affairs of the partnership and terminating the business. The surviving partners do not typically have the authority to continue the partnership beyond the time necessary for the winding-up process. That is, they can fulfill existing partnership obligations but generally should not enter into new business transactions.

The surviving partners are placed in a difficult situation. As fiduciaries, they are obligated to dispose of the partnership property at the highest possible price and have a duty of loyalty to the deceased partner's estate. That is, they must provide the estate with a fair price for its share of partnership property even though this distribution reduces their own share, thus placing the surviving partners in an unavoidable conflict of interests. The fiduciary obligation will make the surviving partners liable for breach of duty if the deceased partner's estate is not treated fairly.

In the absence of continuation planning the surviving partners are placed in a position similar to that of an executor of a sole proprietor's estate. Because they have no authority to continue the business, continuance exposes them to personal liability. If the business is continued without authority by the survivors, they may be liable to the deceased partner's estate for any loss incurred. Conversely if profits are made from the continued business, the deceased partner's estate must be paid its relative share. Even if no profits are made, the estate may be entitled to a fair rate of return on the value of the decedent's partnership interest that remains invested in the partnership.

To solve some of the problems of forced dissolution, the partnership agreement could authorize the surviving partners to carry on the partnership business for a limited time. However, since the partnership interest is likely to be a substantial part of any partner's estate, most partners will not form an agreement during their life to allow the partnership to continue indefinitely at their death. The partners typically want assurance that their interest in the partnership will be converted to cash and distributed to their heirs at some point following their death.

liquidation

Avoiding Liquidation of a Partnership. Although predeath continuation planning by the partners is the preferable course of action, it is sometimes possible to avoid liquidation in the unplanned situation. Continuation of the partnership without *liquidation* under these circumstances would typically involve one of the following:

- the formation of a new partnership, with the estate, the heirs, or an unrelated party as a successor in interest of the decedent
- the purchase of the partnership interest of the decedent by the surviving partners
- the purchase of the surviving partners' interest by the estate or heirs who intend to continue the business

These methods may be employed when the conditions dictate that the continuance of the partnership is more favorable to the parties than is forced liquidation. For example, the partnership may be highly profitable and possess substantial goodwill. In this case it is likely that the continuance of the business, or a sale of the business as a going concern, would yield better results than the liquidation and piecemeal sale of partnership assets. However, it is important to remember that effecting a continuation of the partnership under any of the above methods is difficult, at the very least, and provides less certainty than the predeath continuation plan.

Obstacles to Continuation in the Absence of a Prearranged Partnership Agreement. A partnership requires a voluntary agreement to associate by all the partners. An unwilling individual cannot be forced to become the partner of another. Therefore the surviving partners cannot be forced to accept the executor or heirs of the deceased partner as new partners. Also the surviving partners must agree to associate with any individual who purchases the deceased partner's interest from the estate. Finally all heirs who receive a partnership interest must agree with the existing partners and other heirs to continue the business.

The partnership may be continued with the executor as a successor in interest to the deceased partner. However, the executor is subject to the usual fiduciary obligations to the estate. That is, the executor who holds the interest of the decedent may be liable to the heirs of the estate if the continuation results in losses. Also the executor who becomes a partner is subject to the usual liabilities of other general partners.

A possible solution to this problem is to convert the decedent's interest from a general to a limited partnership interest. This will relieve the executor from the liabilities of the partnership, but the executor still generally faces the least amount of risk by forcing liquidation of the partnership and distributing the proceeds to the decedent's heirs. Therefore only an executor who is also a beneficiary of the estate has the incentive to consent to the continuation of the partnership.

The most logical alternative for continuing the business is a purchase by the surviving partners of the decedent's interest. In this manner the partnership business and the careers of the surviving partners will be uninterrupted, while the estate of the decedent will receive cash for the partnership interest held by the decedent. Agreement on a sale price may be difficult in the absence of any prior commitment by the partners. The negotiation of a sale of the decedent's interest to the surviving partners presents some unique difficulties. The personal interests of the surviving partners and the estate beneficiaries are in obvious opposition. The estate wants to receive the largest possible amount for the decedent's interest, while the surviving partners hope to hold the purchase price down. The executor negotiating in behalf of the estate faces the least personal risk if the partnership is liquidated and the proceeds are distributed to the estate.

The fiduciary duty of the surviving partners to the decedent's estate requires them to act solely in behalf of the estate when transacting the sale. This means that the surviving partners must pay the highest possible fair price for the decedent's interest. Such a duty is in direct conflict with their own interest in paying the lowest possible price to purchase the interest. It is also in opposition to the relative bargaining strengths of the parties. Usually the surviving partners are in the strongest position when dealing with the decedent's estate. Since the continued business typically has more value than a business subject to a forced liquidation, the executor may be willing to accept anything in excess of the liquidated value.

Ascertaining the fair value for a closely held business is not an exact science. This means that individual opinions as to the fair value of the business will differ, so the surviving partners cannot be certain that the price paid for the decedent's interest will not result in suits by the heirs for the breach of the surviving partners' duty as liquidating trustees.

An additional problem occurs when negotiating a sale with the executor, who generally has no authority to continue the business or even to sell the decedent's interest without the consent of the heirs. The executor is authorized only to demand liquidation of the partnership by the surviving partners. If the executor allows continuance of the business or sells the business interest to the survivors, liability may be incurred if the heirs are dissatisfied with the results.

The sale of a partnership interest negotiated after the death of a partner presents still another problem. Since the sale is unplanned, there is typically no provision for how the purchase price will be paid. It is not likely that the survivors will have a fund set aside to pay the purchase price. To the extent the survivors' personal funds are inadequate, they may be forced to borrow or to offer the estate an installment note. This provides the heirs with uncertain and potentially illiquid proceeds from the estate for the decedent's partnership interest. The payment of the installment obligation may also prove a burden on the continued success of the partnership.

A final problem that exists in continuing partnership activities following the death of a partner is that of replacing the services of that partner. This may be possible when (1) the business is a commercial partnership not relying on the skills of any individual or (2) the partner was a mere capital contributor to the partnership. However, if the deceased partner possessed unique skills necessary to partnership operation, continuing the partnership following the partner's death may be ill advised. Consequently it is usually unwise or impossible to continue the closely held personal service or professional partnership following the death of an active partner.

Lifetime Partnership Continuation Planning

The many obstacles to partnership continuation make advance planning the most certain and viable alternative. Many of the above problems can be avoided by drafting the partnership agreement to facilitate continuation of the partnership at the death of a general partner. For example, the agreement can provide that the surviving partners will accept the executor or heirs of the deceased partner as full partners at the death of a general partner. The partnership agreement can designate a purchase price for the partnership interest at the death of any partner or can specify how the purchase price will be determined to eliminate the potential conflict discussed earlier. In any event it is more likely that the partners will have equal bargaining power if the agreement is formed when all are alive and healthy.

The Effect of Will Provisions. The partnership concept involves the voluntary association of two or more individuals to operate a business. Provisions in the will of one partner are generally inadequate since they cannot bind the other partner(s) to act in accordance. For example, a will provision that calls for continuance of the partnership with the executor as successor to the decedent requires the acquiescence of the surviving partners. Furthermore, no executor or heir can be forced into a partnership agreement with the surviving partners. As discussed earlier, the executor is likely to be unwilling to act since continuing the business will subject the executor to potential liability to the decedent's heirs for any losses incurred. Also a will provision consenting to the continued operation of the partnership by the surviving partners may leave the estate with no legal recourse against the surviving partners for business losses.

Another possible will provision is a directive to the executor to sell the decedent's partnership interest to the surviving partner(s). Such a provision gives the executor authority to sell the decedent's interest without incurring liability for failure to force liquidation. It also provides an opportunity for the surviving partners to purchase the decedent's interest without concern for the potential conflict-of-interest problem discussed earlier. To fully relieve the executor and surviving partners following the directions of the will from liability to the heirs, a purchase price (or a method of determining the purchase price) should be included in the provision. Otherwise the usual negotiating duties, with their respective potential liabilities, fall on the executor and the surviving partners in transacting the sale.

There are some drawbacks associated with the use of will provisions in continuation planning. A will is typically revocable until the death or legal incompetence of the testator. This means that a partner cannot rely on the provision of the other's will for continuation planning. Not only can any partner unilaterally change his or her will provision authorizing the sale of the partnership interest at death, but also there is no guarantee that the surviving partners will purchase the interest. The surviving partners usually have the right to liquidate the partnership at the death of another partner and are not bound solely by the will provisions of the deceased partner. Finally the unilateral nature of these will provisions does not lend itself to monitoring by the other partner. This means that each partner will be uncertain whether the funding necessary to carry out the sale will ever be made in advance by the others. Again the lack of adequate funding will frustrate the ultimate objective of the decedent in selling the interest—to provide liquid assets to the heirs.

Partnership Agreements. Most partners desire the security of a guaranteed continuation plan. Since a partnership interest is likely to be a major portion of a partner's assets, it is essential to know the expected status of the business following death to plan the estate properly. If the interest is to be sold, the form and amount of proceeds should be known in advance. Perhaps instead of selling at death, the partner would like to leave the interest to a successor heir to carry on his or her share of the partnership duties. In such a case, the partner would like to be certain that death will not terminate the partnership. The optimal method of assuring continuation of a partnership is the adoption of a binding agreement by the partners while they are all still alive.

A partnership agreement is generally upheld by the courts as a binding contract. The type of partnership agreement executed by the partners should match the goals of each partner for his or her business interest. A significant problem facing the partnership at the death of a partner is the diminution in value of the partnership if sold in forced liquidation. One possible solution to this problem is for the partners to form a binding agreement that the partnership will be continued for a short period of time until it can be sold as a going concern. The advantage of such an arrangement is that the surviving partners are not bound to dissolve the partnership at the death of a partner and have adequate time to sell the business at fair value. During this time the continued business can provide income to both the surviving partners and the deceased partner's heirs. However, this situation creates a potential dispute between the surviving partners performing all services and the estate over the fair share of profit that should be received by each.

Since most business owners hope that their lifetime efforts will result in a continued income to their heirs at death, they should plan to avoid liquidation of the business at death. A fair share of profit for the partnership interest can then be paid out to the heirs of the deceased partner. Agreements used to achieve these goals include an agreement by the partners to accept the executor as a new partner. Alternatively the partnership interest could be left in trust with the trustee named as a new partner. It is important to remember that state law should be consulted to determine the legality of such an agreement by a trustee. The advantage of these agreements is that the continued business will provide income that can be distributed to the surviving partners and the decedent's heirs. The agreement can also specify the size of the relative shares to be received by each to remove the potential conflict over the compensation paid to the survivors for performing all the services.

These types of arrangements also result in some disadvantages. A partnership agreement, like any contract, is binding only on the original parties to the agreement. Therefore the executor or trustee can be bound by the agreement only if he or she was a party to the agreement. It may be difficult to find individuals who will accept the risk of signing this type of an agreement in advance. Furthermore, since a partnership requires a voluntary association, the courts will not normally enforce this type of agreement, so the party attempting to enforce it will typically be limited to seeking money damages.

Closely held business owners often hope that a family member will follow in their footsteps in the operation of the business. If this occurs, a binding agreement can be formed by the partners to accept a decedent's heir as a successor to his or her interest in the partnership. This type of agreement should be used only in the limited situations in which the successor heir is currently employed by the business or eminently capable of taking over the decedent's responsibilities. In any event the voluntary principles of the partnership relationship will again prevent specific enforcement of these agreements.

The most common type of partnership-continuation agreement is the buy-sell agreement. Basically this agreement is a plan executed by the partners while living that provides that the surviving partners will purchase the interest of a deceased partner. An alternative form of buy-sell agreement provides that the partnership itself will purchase the interest of a deceased partner. The agreement should also bind the estate to sell the decedent's interest and provide for some method of determining the purchase price.

Many of the problems of partnership continuation discussed previously are solved by this type of agreement. The executor satisfies the duty to the heirs by complying with the agreement and selling the partnership interest to the surviving partners. The surviving partners avoid the conflict of interest with the estate since they do not become liquidating trustees and need only pay the agreed purchase price to the decedent's estate. The heirs of the deceased partner cannot frustrate the operation of the plan since their only right is to receive the proceeds of the sale.

The agreement should also include a purchase price or a method for determining the business value at the time of the sale. When the purchase price is agreed on in advance, the parties to the agreement have more equal bargaining power than after the death of a partner. The prearranged price will typically represent a reasonable arm's-length agreement for the sale price of the business. This fact is important for limiting the estate tax value of the business to the price agreed on in the buy-sell agreement. Finally this type of agreement is specifically enforceable against all parties. Therefore the partners know in advance that the partnership-continuation plan will be carried out.

Among the many issues to be considered in forming the buy-sell agreement are the type of agreement to be used, the valuation method, and the funding mechanism to be used.

Limited-Liability Companies (LLCs)

LLCs are generally treated as partnerships for tax purposes. Prior to the "check-the-box" regulations, LLCs were formed with "partnership-like" operating characteristics to avoid corporate tax treatment. Thus, much of the discussion above concerning continuation problems for a partnership is relevant for LLCs. The discussion that follows will address an LLC's unique continuity problems. Please be aware that the author anticipates a dramatic change in both LLC operating agreements and state LLC statutes once the check-the-box regulations are made final. The anticipated changes would remove the inflexibility in an LLC's operating structure and would probably lead to a more corporate-like continuity-of-life characteristic in these entities.

Obstacles to Continuation of an LLC at a Member's Death

Although the check-the-box regulations generally permit pass-through treatment for LLCs, many operating agreements still provide restrictions on transfer of the LLC interest. Quite often, the members will have to consent unanimously to the admission of a new member. This presents two issues concerning the continuity of an LLC at the time of a member's death. First, a prearrangement for continuity at the death of a member may be essential. The survivors would often have to provide for continuity after the fact by, perhaps, a unanimous vote. Thus, a buy-sell agreement that guarantees such continuity may be prohibited.

In addition, the after-the-fact decision to continue the LLC may be impractical unless the liquidation of the deceased member's interest was funded in some manner. Since the estate of the deceased member has to be paid fair value for the liquidation, the LLC and the surviving members may not have the available funds to provide for the payments to the estate without selling or liquidating the LLC's assets.

Closely Held Corporation

Because the legal format of a corporation is different from that of a proprietorship or a partnership, continuation planning is somewhat different. The corporation is a separate legal entity that is authorized and formed under state law. It is common for corporations to have passive owners who take no active role in day-to-day operations. Since the corporate form of ownership does not require a voluntary association among owners, it is more likely that the ownership interest in the corporation (shares of stock) will be freely transferable by an owner than is the case with unincorporated businesses. However, in small closely held commercial and professional corporations the operating practice is similar to that of partnerships, and many of the same continuation problems occur.

Corporation's Continuity of Life

In contrast to unincorporated businesses there is no legally imposed termination of the business entity at the death of a shareholder in a corporation. In theory a corporation has perpetual life under the laws of the state of incorporation. However, as a practical matter this is often not the case in a closely held corporation.

The death of a shareholder in a large publicly held corporation has no impact on corporate activities unless the shareholder was a key employee or officer of the corporation. At the death of the passive shareholder the shares of stock pass to the estate of the decedent and can be sold or distributed to the heirs. The stock in a publicly held corporation tends to be marketable and income-producing. The shares of stock can be readily sold for cash by the executor or passed to the heirs to provide a future income. In general, the publicly held corporation engages in continuation planning only in the unusual case when the corporation's success depends on a few key individuals.

Impact of the Death of a Shareholder

At the death of a shareholder the nature of a closely held corporation typically presents a continuation problem more like that of a partnership than of a publicly held corporation. The success of the business often depends on the talent and experience of one or a few owners. At the death of a key shareholder it is often difficult for the estate to find a buyer for the stock. Since a closely held corporation rarely pays dividends on its stock, it is unlikely that a passive investor will become interested in the corporation. It may also be impossible to find a purchaser who can replace the deceased shareholder's services to the corporation and join the surviving shareholders in the cooperative management of the firm. Therefore many of the usual business-continuation problems exist in a closely held business at the death of one of the owners.

Size of the Deceased Shareholder's Interest. The continuation problems faced by the closely held corporation at the death of a shareholder often vary by the size of the shareholder's interest. Some closely held corporations have only one owner. For example, a sole proprietor might have incorporated to take advantage of limited liability. In the absence of lifetime planning the sole shareholder's stock passes to the estate at death. The corporation survives the shareholder in form but, as a practical matter, cannot operate without its most significant contributor. The executor is bound by the same restrictions that were discussed in relation to unincorporated businesses in that there is no authority to continue the decedent's business in the absence of consent from the heirs and creditors. Therefore the corporation will typically be sold or liquidated to provide for the expenses of estate administration and distribution to the heirs.

Other closely held corporations have more than one shareholder. In these cases the impact of the continuation problems should be evaluated with respect to all the involved parties—the executor, heirs, and surviving coshareholders. The executor is again left with a business interest that must be used to provide for the expenses of the estate and distribution to the decedent's heirs. Unless the decedent's will provides for distribution of the closely held stock to the heirs or all the heirs consent to the receipt of closely held stock in lieu of other bequests, the executor must somehow convert the stock into cash.

The unplanned sale of stock following the death of a shareholder will generally yield disappointing results. The timing puts the executor in an obvious bind. The sale must be completed during the limited time of the estate administration process, during which it may be difficult to find an appropriate buyer. Potential buyers are also aware of the distressed nature of the sale and expect a bargain price. Compounding this problem is the potential liability of the executor if the sale price is deemed inadequate by the heirs.

The size of the decedent's interest will indicate the problems the executor will face. If the interest represents a minority share, it will be extremely difficult to obtain a fair purchase price. The surviving majority shareholders will be able to dominate the board of directors and control the dividends that will be paid to the new shareholders.

The sale of a majority interest by the estate of a deceased shareholder may also present some problems. The surviving minority shareholders must be relied on to continue the business activities, and the survivors will want additional compensation for the extra responsibility of providing the services previously performed by the deceased shareholder. These minority shareholders will not, however, be in a position to determine the dividend and salary policy of the corporation. A conflict between the new majority shareholder and the surviving shareholders may finally result in the loss of the services of the minority shareholders and force liquidation of the corporation.

It is possible for the stock of a deceased shareholder to pass to his or her heirs if the decedent made a specific bequest of the stock to a beneficiary or if the heirs consent to accept shares of stock in lieu of other property to satisfy their bequests. This situation might be favorable to the parties if the executor's efforts to sell the stock for a favorable price end in frustration.

In practice the transfer of the closely held stock to an heir is usually not the recommended alternative. As was the case with the sale of the deceased shareholder's interest to a new shareholder, the heir faces a potential conflict with the surviving shareholders. Unless the heir is capable of replacing the decedent's services to the corporation, the dispute over salaries vis-a-vis dividends will again be an issue. If the decedent's stock represented a minority interest, the surviving shareholders are capable of frustrating the heir by paying no dividends. The heir who inherits a majority interest in the corporation is likely to be faced with disgruntled surviving shareholders whose demands for higher salaries may have to be met for the corporation to be successful.

Conflicts between shareholders in a closely held corporation can result in legal action by the parties. For example, the minority interest can sue to prevent oppressive freezing-out practices by the majority. Since the director-shareholders are bound by a fiduciary duty to the corporation and its shareholders, the directors are subject to challenge by the other shareholders for their business decisions. For example, majority shareholder-employees may be challenged if they use their roles as directors to increase their salaries. The possibility of continual infighting and lawsuits is not an enviable set of circumstances.

Proper planning can ensure that the business will be disposed of in a manner appropriate to avoid these problems. As a general rule a deceased shareholder's interest should not be passed to an heir unless (1) the heir is capable of replacing the decedent's services to the corporation, (2) the stock transferred to the heir represents a majority interest, (3) the surviving shareholders show a willingness and ability to work with the heir, and (4) the decedent leaves other property sufficient to pay the expenses of the estate and provide for other heirs.

Professional Corporations. Continuation planning is essential for theprofessional corporation since shares of a professional corporation may typically be held only by licensed members of the profession. This requirement limits the options available to the professional shareholder in that shares of stock in the corporation may not be bequeathed to individual family members unless they are also licensed members of the profession. In addition, it will probably be difficult to find the appropriate professional to purchase the interest following the death of the professional corporation shareholder.

In the absence of a continuation plan the most likely course of events is the retirement of the deceased professional's stock by the professional corporation, an alternative not without its drawbacks. For example, some states require that the deceased shareholder's interest be valued at book value under these circumstances. Book value will include neither unrealized appreciation in the value of property held by the business nor the value of goodwill likely to exist in a professional practice.

Otherwise state laws require the stock in a professional corporation to be retired at fair market value. Since it is easy to disagree about the fair market value of a closely held business, it may be difficult for the parties to arrive at the purchase price following the death of the professional.

Finally the professional corporation must have sufficient funds to retire the stock; otherwise some type of installment purchase will be required to complete the transaction. This will place a burden on the future cash flow of the corporation and may delay the process of getting cash to distribute to the heirs.

In many states a shareholder in a professional corporation may not retain his or her stock following the termination of employment with the corporation. For this reason continuation planning for the professional corporation should also include such events as disability or retirement.

S Corporations. A unique problem may be encountered at the death of an S corporation shareholder because S corporations are limited in number of shareholders and the types of shareholders eligible to hold S corporation stock. The death of a shareholder in an S corporation may have an effect on Subchapter S status by causing the stock to be transferred to an ineligible shareholder or to so many individuals that the 100-shareholder limit is exceeded. At the occurrence of one of these events the Subchapter S election is terminated. This risk has been mitigated by the new rules that treat all members of a family as one shareholder for this purpose. In addition, a recipient of a majority interest in an S corporation can choose to revoke the election and have the business revert to a regular (C) corporation.

To facilitate the planning for an S corporation, the estate of a deceased shareholder may hold S corporation stock for a reasonable period of estate administration without terminating the election. Perhaps this time period will continue long enough to make installment payments of estate tax under Sec. 6166 (discussed later). In addition, a grantor trust can continue to hold S corporation stock for up to 2 years following a shareholder's death. Furthermore, certain trusts, such as qualified Subchapter S trusts and electing small business trusts (ESBTs), can be used to hold bequests of a deceased shareholder's stock without terminating the election. Despite the expanded categories of eligible shareholders, without proper planning the stock may be transferred at the death of an S corporation shareholder in a manner that will automatically revoke the Subchapter S election.

The Subchapter S election can be a useful device in solving some of the continuation problems facing a closely held corporation. For example, the typical closely held corporation does not pay dividends because of the double taxation problem. The estate and surviving shareholders can make a Subchapter S election so that income from the business can flow through to heirs of the estate as well as to the surviving shareholders without the burden of double taxation. This technique can be extremely useful to an estate that will pay its tax on an installment basis under Sec. 6166. Income from the continued corporation can flow through to the estate to make the installment tax payments without income tax at the corporate level.

Lifetime Continuation Planning for the Closely Held Corporation Shareholder

Despite the fact that the corporate entity does not terminate by operation of law at the death of one of the owners, it is obvious that prior planning for the death of an owner is as essential for closely held corporations as it is for unincorporated businesses. The usual problems associated with the executor's need to pay the expenses and tax imposed on the estate may cause the decedent's interest in the corporation to be sold. Also the surviving shareholders will be forced to deal with the decedent's heirs or new shareholders who purchase the stock from the estate. Conflicts often arise between the existing shareholders and these new unanticipated business co-owners. Depending on the relative percentage of ownership of the parties and the nature of these conflicts, the efficient operation of the business may be affected. Prior planning by the shareholders may prevent these problems by determining the recipients of each shareholder's stock at death in advance.

Will Provisions. In the absence of specific bequests of stock in a decedent's will the executor must typically dispose of the stock to provide cash to the heirs. There is no control over the selection of potential purchasers unless there is some direction in the will about the disposition of the stock. Therefore the shareholder should include provisions for the ultimate disposition of the stock.

If the shareholder wishes to pass the stock to his or her heirs, specific bequests should be included in the will. It is extremely important to provide the executor with directions about the payment of taxes and expenses of the estate; otherwise the executor will not know whether the testator's intent was to have the taxes paid from the stock or from other property passing under the will.

first-offer restriction

Stock-Transfer Restrictions. In general, restraints on transfer are disfavored by the law and construed narrowly by the courts, but several types of valid stock-transfer restrictions are usually upheld by the courts. It is common for closely held corporation stock certificates to contain a *first-offer restriction* requiring the shareholder to offer stock to the existing shareholders first, usually at an agreed price, before selling it to outsiders. This restriction is effective in protecting the existing shareholders from the anticipated addition of new and possibly undesirable coshareholders, as well as being effective against the estate of a deceased shareholder.

The first-offer provision does not solve all the continuation problems discussed earlier. There is no guarantee to the deceased shareholder's estate that the interest will be purchased by the surviving shareholders or that the surviving shareholders will have the necessary funds available. This presents the possibility that a new unwanted shareholder will purchase the decedent's interest.

option agreement

Another type of restriction that has been used to handle continuation problems is the *option agreement*, which stipulates that the surviving shareholders or the corporation itself will have the option to buy a deceased shareholder's stock at a specific price. Again, this agreement is effective in protecting against the addition of unwanted outsiders. However, such a restriction places the discretion to purchase the decedent's stock solely in the hands of the survivors. The agreement may leave the decedent-shareholder's estate without adequate liquid funds unless the sale option is exercised.

The most effective arrangement for handling business-continuation problems for the closely held corporation is the buy-sell agreement, which provides that the surviving shareholders (or the corporation) are bound to buy a deceased shareholder's stock. The agreement also requires the decedent's estate to sell the stock to the surviving shareholders. The purchase price, or method for determining the price, should be included in the agreement.

A properly funded buy-sell agreement gives assurance to all parties involved. The shareholders feel secure that their estates will receive cash for their stock, enabling the shareholders to plan their estates and provide liquidity for estate taxes and expenses. The surviving shareholders are certain that the business will continue without the influx of any unanticipated outsiders.

In states with close corporation statutes, transfer is generally restricted by law. An agreement embodying such restrictions is prudent and may avoid the harsh results of the close corporation statute. For example, some states allow the estate of a deceased close corporation shareholder to force the redemption (or purchase) of the close corporation stock at its fair market value. This could be costly or devastating to the corporation without proper planning. An appropriate shareholder agreement could allay these concerns.

Corporation's Lifetime Continuation-Planning Devices

- Provisions in the will bequeathing the stock to heir(s)
- Stock transfer restrictions
    - First-offer requirement
    - Option agreement
    - Buy-sell agreement

POSTMORTEM ESTATE PRESERVATION PLANNING

Unfortunately many business owners fail to plan adequately before their death for the continuation of the business. This oversight often leads to business termination resulting from the practical necessity of providing for estate expenses.

Since a closely held business interest is typically a major portion of the estate property, it creates much of the estate tax burden. However, the business interest provides no liquid funds to meet the tax burden; hence the need to liquidate the business to meet the costs of the estate. The purpose of this section is to present some techniques available to the executor to provide for estate liquidity while maximizing the value of the business. These techniques can be employed even in the absence of prior planning by the owner.

Liquidation as a Possibility

Liquidating the business at the death of an owner is one method of providing estate liquidity. This is often the executor's only choice if no planning has been done for business continuation, but in some cases liquidation may actually be the favored choice. For example, there may be no logical successor to an owner of an unincorporated business, and it may be best to terminate by operation of law. Although a corporation continues at a shareholder's death, the loss of the shareholder's personal services may make effective continuation impossible. Liquidation may also be the best way to provide funds to the decedent's family members if they are not inclined to replace the decedent in the business.

There are some tax implications associated with liquidation of a closely held corporation at the death of a shareholder. The decedent's family will probably need income from the business, but unless they provide substantial services to the corporation, the family members must be compensated in the form of dividends. This results in double taxation—both at the corporate and the shareholder level. If a stock redemption is not feasible, liquidation of the closely held business may be the best method for providing cash to the family members.

In general, the stock of the decedent will receive a stepped-up basis at death. Since the heirs may have the benefit of the basis step-up in the decedent's stock, they will have limited or no capital-gain tax to pay when cash or property is distributed to them in a plan of liquidation.

When to Liquidate a Closely Held Business Interest

- When there is no other adequate source of estate liquidity
- When there is no one willing and able to continue running the business

Installment Payment of Estate Tax

Congress has recognized the fact that closely held businesses must typically be liquidated to pay estate taxes at the death of one of the owners. IRC *Sec. 6166 installment payments* of estate tax provide relief from this obstacle to business continuation for qualifying estates holding a closely held business interest.

Eligible Estates

The installment method of paying estate tax can be elected if the closely held business interest exceeds 35 percent of the value of the adjusted gross estate. The closely held business can be in the form of a proprietorship, a partnership, or a corporation. In the case of either a partnership or a corporation the decedent must have had a 20-percent-or-more interest in the business, or the business must have had 45 or fewer partners or shareholders. Furthermore, two or more closely held business interests may be combined for the purposes of meeting the 35 percent test if the decedent held 20 percent or more of the total value of each business at the time of death. There are also requirements that the business be an active trade or business.[14] Thus, a family holding company of passive assets (such as the typical family limited partnership (FLP) created for estate-planning purposes) will not qualify.

Mechanics of the Installment Payments

For a qualifying estate the proportional amount of the estate tax attributable to the inclusion of a closely held business interest may be paid in 10 installments. The first installment of principal must be paid 5 years after the date that the federal estate tax return is due, with interest on the deferred amount payable during this 5-year period. Since the first principal payment is due at the beginning of the 5th year after the estate tax return is due and continues for 9 additional years, the maximum total deferral is 14 years.

The interest rate generally applicable to the deferred estate tax liability is 45 percent of the rate generally applicable to underpayments of federal tax. This rate is adjusted semiannually by the IRS. However, an additional benefit of Sec. 6166 is the application of a preferential 2 percent interest rate on the amount of deferred taxes equivalent to a $1 million business interest. The $1

---

14. The tax law changes in 2001 included an amendment to permit qualified lending and finance businesses to qualify for Sec. 6166 tax deferral.

million threshold for the purposes of the special 2 percent interest rate will be indexed for inflation in $10,000 increments beginning in 1999.[15] The interest paid on Sec. 6166 installments is not income tax deductible.

To qualify for the tax deferral under Sec. 6166, the executor must elect to use the deferral method by the time the estate tax return is due (including extensions). A protective election may be filed to preserve the use of Sec. 6166 if the executor is unsure whether the estate will ultimately qualify.

The tax rules provide for an acceleration of the deferred tax liability during the installment period at the occurrence of certain events. Any combination of dispositions of the business interest or withdrawal of funds from the business by the heirs equal to 50 percent or more of the decedent's interest in the business will accelerate the tax due. However, corporate reorganizations or liquidations of the business interest during the deferral period that represent mere changes in form (the business is continued and substantial assets are not withdrawn) are not dispositions for the purposes of acceleration. In addition, the death of one of the recipients of the business interest during the deferral period will not cause an acceleration of the tax due as long as the property passes to other heirs, keeping the business in the family.

The provision for installment payment of estate taxes may be advantageous if the owner of a family business dies and a large portion of the taxable estate consists of the business interest. However, the use of the installment-payment provision prolongs the period of time during which the estate is kept open. At the election of the executor a shorter deferral period can be selected. In any event this deferral method is a useful device to prevent the strain on estate liquidity due to the inclusion of a closely held business interest. If the estate tax burden is large, the tax relief provided by this section may not be sufficient by itself to solve all the continuation problems. However, this method can be used along with other types of continuation plans, such as stock redemptions, to form a complete continuation plan.

Special-Use Property Valuation

special-use valuation

To help prevent the liquidation of a farm or other closely held business property at the death of the owner, the tax laws allow a *special-use valuation* under IRC Sec. 2032A. The purpose of these rules is to allow real property used in a farm or closely held business to be included in the decedent's estate at the value

15. The indexed figure for 2011 is $1,360,000.

of the property as it is actually used in the business. Normal rules would cause inclusion at fair market value. If the farm or closely held business was using the real property at less than its highest and best use, inclusion of the property in the decedent's estate at the fair market value would create an extreme estate tax burden and threaten the continuation of the business. This tax-relief provision requires the heir to continue to use the property for the farm or closely held business.

Qualifying Property

The following conditions must be met before real property qualifies for special-use-evaluation relief:

- The property must be included in the gross estate of the decedent.
- Real or personal property used in the farm or closely held business represents 50 percent or more of the adjusted value of the gross estate of the decedent.
- At least 25 percent of the adjusted gross estate consists of the qualified real property.
- The property must pass to a qualified heir (the decedent's ancestors, spouse, and lineal descendants of either the decedent or parents of the decedent).
- The decedent or a family member must have owned the real property, used it in a qualifying farm or closely held business, and materially participated in the operation of the farm or closely held business for at least 5 out of the 8 years immediately preceding death.

Allowable Reduction in the Value of Special-Use Property

The maximum reduction in value of a special-use property is $750,000. (The $750,000 maximum valuation reduction is indexed for inflation in $10,000 increments beginning in 1999.[16]) This maximum reduction represents the amount by which the fair market value of the property exceeds the value of the property as it exists in the qualified use. The executor must make the election to take the special-use valuation on the decedent's estate tax return. Also a written agreement consenting to the special-use valuation must be signed by and binding against each person having an interest in the special-use property. Once filed, the special-use election becomes irrevocable.

---

16. The indexed figure for 2010 is $1,020,000

The Code provides methods for valuing the special-use property. In the case of a closely held business the Code specifies the following factors to determine the special-use value:

- capitalization of income that the property can be expected to yield in the farm or closely held business use
- capitalization of the fair rental value of the land in the qualified use
- assessed land values in states that provide for special-use assessment
- comparable sales of other real property in the same geographical area and the same qualified use
- any other factor that fairly values the qualified property

The Recapture of the Special-Use Tax Benefit

The relief provisions of Sec. 2032A were designed to facilitate the continuance of the farm or closely held business property by the decedent's heirs. If the property is no longer used in the special use or held by the decedent's heirs, the basic purpose for this relief provision vanishes and the tax rules provide that the tax savings associated with the special-use valuation will be recaptured. Transactions that result in recapture are as follows:

- Prior to the death of the qualified heir he or she disposes of the special-use property to a transferee other than a member of the family within 10 years after the decedent's death.
- The qualified heir ceases to use the property for a qualified special use within 10 years after the decedent's death.
- The qualified heir or a member of the heir's family fails to materially participate in the business's operation for 3 or more years during an 8-year period ending within 10 years after the decedent's death.

The qualified heir is personally liable upon recapture for the additional estate tax due for the loss of the special-use valuation.

To prevent recapture there are some planning techniques that can be employed. A family partnership or corporation can be formed after the death of the business owner to operate the farm or closely held business. The management structure of the business should provide that the qualified heirs participate actively in the management of the business to satisfy the recapture rules. Buy-sell or stock-redemption agreements should also be executed to prevent any dispositions that might result in recapture. Tax rules permit the transfer of the special-use property by the qualified heir in a tax-free exchange (for example, like-kind exchanges) without the trigger of recapture provisions. Therefore potential discord between qualified heirs can be prevented by performing tax-free exchanges to eliminate the association of family members with potential conflicts in the business of the special-use property.

CHAPTER REVIEW

Key Terms and Concepts

executor
administrator
trade creditors
liquidating trustees
liquidation
first-offer restriction
option agreement
special-use valuation

Review Questions

The answers to the review questions are in the supplement. The self-test questions and the answers to them are also in the supplement and on The American College Online.

1. Briefly describe (i) the legal obligations that are incurred by the deceased's executor and (ii) the rights of trade creditors when a sole proprietorship is continued beyond the proprietor's death in each of the following situations: [1]
   a. without proper authority and without the consent of parties that have an interest in the estate
   b. without proper authority but with the consent of the heirs to the estate
   c. without proper authority but with the consent of the heirs and estate creditors
   d. under state statutes similar to Uniform Probate Code Sec. 3-715

2. Proprietors frequently try to arrange for the continuation of their business through will provisions. If the will provides for continuation and the executor elects to continue the proprietorship, discuss the problems that may confront
   a. the executor
   b. the heirs [2]

3. A revocable living trust is an alternative to a will provision that continues a proprietorship as a going concern after the death of the proprietor.
   a. What are the benefits of such a living trust?
   b. What problems may arise in the use of such a trust? [2]

4. Discuss how a buy-sell agreement can solve some of the problems that arise at the death of a sole proprietor. [2]

5. At the death of a partner, the surviving partners become liquidating trustees. What are the duties and responsibilities of liquidating trustees? [3]

6. A member in a three-person partnership died recently. No plan had been made for the continuation of the partnership. The surviving partners are trying to formulate a plan to avoid liquidation of the partnership. Discuss the problems that may arise if any of the following improvised courses of action is adopted: [3]
   a. continuation of the business without authorization
   b. formation of a new partnership with the heir(s) becoming partners
   c. purchase by the heirs of the surviving partners' interest
   d. purchase by the surviving partners of the deceased partner's interest

7. In his will, a partner has directed the executor to form a new partnership with the survivors, and he has further directed that the heirs become partners when the estate is settled and the partnership interest has been distributed to them. Discuss the problems that may arise at the partner's death because of these will provisions. [3]

8. Members of a partnership believe that they can solve the problem created by a partner's death without a buy-sell agreement. Describe the problems that they may encounter at the death of a partner if they adopt an agreement in which the survivors consent to accept the executor as a partner. [4]

9. Discuss how a buy-sell agreement that is made during the lifetime of all partners can avoid some of the problems with other courses of action. [4]

10. In what ways does the actual operation of a close corporation resemble that of an unincorporated business? [5]

11. If there is no will provision authorizing the continuance of a business, discuss the problems that may arise if an executor of a deceased sole stockholder does not liquidate the corporation. [5]

12. Describe briefly how the relative size of the decedent's interest in the corporation affects continuity. [5]

13. What are the special circumstances of professional corporations that make continuation planning particularly significant? [6]

14. Describe briefly the following types of stock-transfer provisions, and discuss their effectiveness for continuation planning: [6]
    a. first-offer provision
    b. options to the survivors
    c. buy-sell agreement

15. Why might liquidation of a closely held business be the recommended alternative for some estates? [6]

16. What requirements must be met for an estate to qualify for installment payments of estate tax under Sec. 6166? [7]

17. Describe briefly the mechanics of the Sec. 6166 installment method. [7]
18. What actions will accelerate the installment payments under Sec. 6166? [7]
19. Sec. 2032A provides for a reduction in the gross estate tax value of certain property if its current-use value is less than its fair market value. [7]
    a. What types of property qualify for special-use valuation?
    b. What are the requirements for an estate to be eligible?

BUY-SELL AGREEMENTS FOR THE UNINCORPORATED BUSINESS

6

Learning Objectives

An understanding of the material in this chapter should enable the student to

1. Describe the purposes and benefits of adopting buy-sell agreements with respect to closely held businesses and their owners.
2. Identify the contents of the typical buy-sell agreement.
3. Describe how a proprietorship buy-sell agreement can be structured.
4. Define the structure of a partnership buy-sell agreement, distinguishing between the entity and cross-purchase methods and the factors that affect the choice between the two.
5. Describe the tax treatment of the transfer of a decedent's interest in a partnership under both the cross-purchase and entity arrangements.
6. Discuss the advantages and disadvantages of the possible funding alternatives for buy-sell agreements.
7. Describe the benefits of an insured buy-sell agreement.
8. Explain how an insured buy-sell agreement is structured both for proprietorships and partnerships.

THE PURPOSE OF THE BUY-SELL AGREEMENT

The unincorporated business enterprise terminates by operation of law at the death of its owner. In the case of a proprietorship the decedent's personal representative will be empowered only to wind up the decedent's affairs by collecting business and personal assets in preparation for distribution to the heirs. This collection and liquidation of business assets will generally result in a distribution to the heirs, which is far less than would be possible if the business could be sold as a going concern. A partnership also terminates at the death of a general partner. In the absence of a continuation plan the surviving partners become liquidating trustees and are entrusted with the process of liquidating the partnership and making distribution to the estate of the deceased partner. Again, the proceeds from liquidation will probably be less than from a sale of the partnership as a going concern. In an LLC, the operating agreement for the entity and, perhaps, state law might provide for the LLC's termination at the death of a member. Some business continuation techniques might be employed to prevent the termination of an unincorporated business. While several of these techniques may be useful in some limited circumstances, the buy-sell agreement is most often the best form of continuation plan.

specific performance

A properly designed buy-sell agreement will require the estate of the deceased owner to sell and the purchaser to buy the business for a prearranged price. The parties to the buy-sell agreement know with a high degree of certainty that the agreement will be carried out. If the buy-sell agreement is valid, the courts will "specifically enforce" the contract. *Specific performance* (enforcement) is a remedy provided by the courts when money damages would be either difficult to determine or inadequate. This is generally necessary when an agreement has been breached for the sale of a unique property. For example, contracts for the sale of real estate and businesses are specifically enforceable since property of this type is unique, and a judgment for money damages will not satisfy the contract expectations of the aggrieved party. Since specific performance is available as a remedy, the buyer is assured that the courts will force the decedent's estate to sell the business interest according to the terms of the agreement. The estate is assured that the sale proceeds will be received from the buyer.

Benefits of the Buy-Sell Agreement

Although the contemplation of death is not pleasant for anyone, proper estate planning employing a buy-sell agreement offers several advantages. Benefits of the agreement can be summarized as follows:

- It guarantees a market for the business interest.
- It provides liquidity for the payment of death taxes and estate administration costs.
- It may establish the estate tax value of the decedent's business interest, making the estate planning process more reliable for the owner.
- It provides that the business will continue and the careers of the surviving owners and/or employees will not be interrupted.

- The business will be a better credit risk since its probability of continuation is enhanced.

CONTENTS OF THE BUY-SELL AGREEMENT

The various types of buy-sell agreements for unincorporated businesses will be covered in detail in later sections. However, the properly designed buy-sell agreement has several typical provisions regardless of the type of agreement. Failure to draft the buy-sell agreement properly may result in the inability of the plan to meet some of its goals or, in the extreme, its failure to be carried out at all. For this reason it is advisable to obtain the services of a competent attorney in drafting the agreement. Typical provisions of buy-sell agreements include the following:

- *parties to the agreement.* This provision identifies the parties to the agreement (that is, who will be the buyer and who will be the seller under the terms of the agreement).
- *purpose of the agreement.* This provision gives a brief statement of purpose of the arrangement. For example, the provision may state that the agreement is being formed to provide for the orderly transfer of the business ownership when triggered by its operative event—the death of the owner (the disability of the owner could also trigger a buy-sell agreement). Should litigation result over the terms of the agreement, the statement of purpose may help clarify the debated issues by providing useful evidence to the court of the parties' intentions when forming the agreement.
- *commitment of the parties.* This provision indicates the obligations of the parties—that is, that the estate will sell the business interest and that the purchaser will buy it according to the terms of the agreement.
- *description of the interest subject to the agreement.* This provision describes the property that will be sold by the estate. This is particularly important in the unincorporated business where operations tend to be informal and it is difficult to differentiate between the assets of the business and the personal assets of the owner. As we will learn later, classifications of the assets as goodwill, receivables, or capital assets may be significant for tax purposes.
- *lifetime transfer restrictions.* This provision, also known as a first-offer provision, prevents the business owner from making a lifetime transfer of the business to anyone without first offering to sell the business to the buyers under the agreement at the

agreed-upon price. This provision serves two purposes. First, the expectation of the buyer cannot be frustrated without the buyer's consent. Second, the provision is necessary to establish the estate tax value of the business interest at the price stipulated in the agreement.

- *method of determining purchase price.* This provision either stipulates or provides a method of determining the contract price for the business interest. This is extremely important since the adequacy of the contract price is necessary both for (1) the satisfaction of all parties to the agreement and (2) the acceptance by the IRS of the contract price for estate tax purposes.
- *funding.* Unless the purchaser has substantial wealth, it may be impractical or impossible to carry out the buy-sell agreement without arrangements for adequate funding. The contents of this provision will depend on the actual funding mechanism chosen. For example, if life insurance will be purchased to fund the buy-sell agreement, this provision should specify such things as the ownership of the policies, premium payment, and beneficiary designations. If the agreement will be financed by installment payments, the provision should include such things as the size of each payment, the duration of the installment period, and the interest rate that the buyer will pay. The methods of funding a buy-sell agreement will be discussed at length in a later section.
- *transfer of the business.* This provision describes the details of the actual transfer of the business interest at the owner's death. That is, the provision should indicate how the proceeds will be transferred to the estate and how the business will be transferred to the purchaser. For example, a trust is often established to carry out the buy-sell agreement. In this case it is usually the trustee who will hold the insurance policies, collect the proceeds at the death of the owner, and transfer the proceeds to the estate in exchange for the business interest. This provision will usually specify that the business interest will be transferred clear of personal debts of the estate. Furthermore, the buyer will typically agree to relieve the estate of any posttransfer liabilities of the business.
- *modification or termination of the agreement.* This provision is included to provide flexibility for contingencies. For example, it may be necessary to add new parties to the agreement if the business grows. The bankruptcy of either party or the failure of the business may make it unnecessary to continue the agreement. This provision of the buy-sell agreement may be drafted to operate

either (1) automatically in the event of some future contingency or (2) by the joint consent of the parties to the contract.

PROPRIETORSHIP BUY-SELL AGREEMENTS

The proprietorship buy-sell agreement has distinct characteristics resulting from the structure of the business—the unity between the owner's business and personal assets. While partnerships or corporations have distinct legal status, proprietorships hold no assets as an entity separate from their owners' personal property. This means that the purchase agreement for the business must specify which of the proprietor's assets are to be sold as business assets. The choice of assets to be sold under the agreement will have an impact on the taxation of the estate and the buyer.

The single-owner nature of a proprietorship results in a unique characteristic of the proprietorship buy-sell agreement. The agreement binds the proprietor's estate to sell and the purchaser to buy specific proprietorship assets. There is no question as to who will be the purchaser and the seller. This arrangement can be contrasted to the partnership or corporate buy-sell agreements that contain a mutual agreement to purchase a deceased owner's share of the business. In the proprietorship agreement there is no need for this mutual relationship since there is only one owner with an interest to sell.

Although the proprietorship is by far the most prominent form of business ownership in terms of numbers, buy-sell agreements for the proprietor are often ignored.

Finding the Purchaser

At the proprietor's death there are no co-owners and quite often no other natural successors to the decedent's role in the business. Therefore lifetime planning by the proprietor is important to locate a successor. Quite often a key employee or group of employees is the logical choice as purchaser. These individuals are familiar with the business and understand its value as a growing concern. Their knowledge and skills will enable them to continue the business at the proprietor's death. Moreover, these key employees may be quite interested in forming the buy-sell agreement to provide for their own security and advancement. This type of arrangement provides the additional benefit of helping the business to retain these key employees during the proprietor's lifetime.

Many proprietors do not have a readily available successor with whom to establish a buy-sell agreement. For example, professionals often practice as sole proprietorships and are limited by law to transferring their practices to other licensed members of their profession. The owner of a regular business proprietorship may also be the only individual currently capable of continuing the business.

In these instances the other party to the buy-sell agreement must be sought for successful continuation planning. It is often recommended that the owner of the business proprietorship hire and provide a training program for an employee who has the potential to take over the business.

The professional proprietor may seek other professionals to formulate a buyout agreement for the practice. This is particularly important since the successful professional practice has typically developed substantial goodwill and a large clientele, which could become worthless at death in the absence of lifetime continuation planning.

Structuring the Agreement

Which Assets Are to Be Sold

A carefully structured provision listing the assets and liabilities to be transferred is extremely important in a proprietorship buy-sell agreement. Since the business assets are not legally distinct from the proprietor's other assets, a general description of the business in the buy-sell agreement may create ambiguities that will slow down the orderly transfer of the business at the death of the proprietor. The careful structuring of this provision will allow both the proprietor and the purchaser to plan in advance for the transfer of liabilities under the contract. For example, the proprietor must know with certainty which liabilities will be transferred or retained by the estate. This facilitates estate liquidity planning for the proprietor. Furthermore, the careful structuring and valuation of assets and liabilities in the proprietorship buy-sell agreement will help establish tax issues associated with the sale.

The Value of a Trustee

A trustee is often recommended as a party to the buy-sell agreement, particularly if the agreement is to be funded with life insurance. The trustee can serve the valuable roles of collecting premium payments from the parties and acting as custodian for the policies. At the death of the proprietor the trustee will collect the proceeds of insurance policies (or collect the purchase price from the buyer if the agreement is not funded with life insurance) and transfer the proceeds to the estate.

The provision of a trustee should be included in the buy-sell agreement since the trustee becomes a party to the agreement. It is also important to add a provision for the replacement of the trustee if circumstances change. Since a corporate trustee has perpetual life, the selection of a corporate trustee adds stability to the agreement.

Trustee in a Buy-Sell Agreement

- Acts as custodian for the life insurance policies
- Collects premiums from appropriate parties
- Pays policy premiums
- Collects insurance proceeds and transfers proceeds to deceased business owner's estate
- Ensures that business interests or assets are transferred to buyer

Tax Considerations

Federal Income Tax. The parties to a proprietorship buy-sell agreement inevitably view the property transferred under the agreement as a separate business entity rather than as a bundle of individual business assets. However, for tax purposes the transfer is treated as a series of individual asset sales. Because of this tax treatment the purchase price in the buy-sell agreement should be carefully allocated to each asset. The taxation of each transfer depends on the nature of the underlying assets.

income in respect of a decedent (IRD)

From the seller's point of view this allocation would be far more significant for a lifetime sale of the assets than for a buy-sell agreement operating at death. The tax law provides that the basis of assets included in the decedent's estate will be stepped up to their fair market value at the time of death. Therefore virtually no gain will be realized on the sale of these assets by the estate. One notable exception to this rule is the treatment of notes or accounts receivable. Amounts received by the estate for these accounts are deemed *income in respect of a decedent (IRD)*. The basis for these assets is not stepped up to the value at the date of death, and any gain is taxable as ordinary income reportable on the estate's income tax return. This tax treatment is particularly significant for the sale of a professional practice when accounts receivable represent a substantial portion of the business assets.

From the buyer's point of view the allocation of the purchase price to specific assets is equally important. Certain business assets, known as Sec. 1231 assets, will provide a depreciation allowance to the buyer when used in the continuing trade or business. This class of assets includes buildings, machinery, fixtures, furniture, goodwill, customer lists, and equipment used in the trade or business. Not included in this class are items such as land, receivables, and inventory or other property held for sale in the ordinary course of business. Whenever possible, it is to the buyer's advantage to allocate as much of the purchase price as possible to the Sec. 1231 assets, thus providing the buyer with a larger basis on which the depreciation deduction will be allowed. Tax regulations limit the amount allocable to each asset to fair market value. Some of the purchase price will have to be allocated to nondepreciable assets of the business. These rules place a premium on the careful description of, and the allocation of purchase price to, all assets sold in the transaction.

Estate Tax. The primary purpose of the proprietorship buy-sell agreement is to provide the estate with fair value in exchange for the decedent's business interest. To provide accuracy for the proprietor's estate liquidity planning, it is necessary to know the estate tax value for the decedent's business interest. A properly designed valuation provision will "peg" the estate tax value of the proprietorship assets transferred under the buy-sell agreement at the purchase price stated in the agreement. To be accepted by the IRS as the estate tax value, the valuation agreement will have to meet stringent rules if family members are involved.

The allocation of purchase price to the various proprietorship assets transferred by the agreement also has an impact for estate tax purposes. You will recall from the section above that certain receivables will be deemed income in respect of a decedent. The portion of the purchase price related to these items must be included in the gross estate of the proprietor. These items of IRD are also included in the income tax return of the estate. Fortunately an income tax deduction is available to the estate or heirs for the additional estate tax created by the inclusion of IRD in the proprietor's estate.

EXAMPLE

Max Fly, CLU, died on June 30 of last year. At the time of Max's death he had earned $40,000 of commissions that had not yet been paid. These commissions were paid to Max's estate by the end of last year and were fully includible (1) in Max's gross estate for estate tax purposes and (2) on the estate income tax return. Suppose the IRD items were left to Max's heirs in a fashion not qualifying for the marital deduction and that Max's estate is in the 50 percent estate tax bracket. The inclusion of the IRD in Max's gross estate will cause $20,000 of additional estate tax. However, this additional estate tax created by the IRD will be deductible from the estate *income* tax return. If the estate cannot use the entire deduction, it is passed to the heirs and the unused portion is available as a deduction on the income tax returns of the heirs.

PARTNERSHIP BUY-SELL AGREEMENTS

The issues in planning continuation for partnerships are in many ways similar to those related to proprietorships. A partnership terminates by operation of law at the death of a partner. Without adequate lifetime continuation planning the value of a deceased partner's interest in liquidation will usually be less than the value of the same interest as a going concern. Furthermore, the goals of the surviving partners are often in conflict with the goals of the estate. As we learned in the last chapter, a binding buy-sell agreement is often the best way to handle the problems associated with partnership continuation.

The partnership buy-sell agreement has an additional consideration not encountered in the proprietorship buy-sell plan. That is, there is more than one owner and the continuation plan must address the possibility that the buy-sell agreement will become operative at the death of any general partner. Furthermore, the agreement is formed when the parties do not know which partner will die first. Therefore partnership buy-sell agreements contain a mutuality that was not present in the proprietorship agreement. That is, the buy-sell agreement will operate at the first death of any of the general partners, and it commits each of them to buy or sell depending on the circumstances.

Types of Partnership Buy-Sell Agreements

A partnership operates as a separate legal entity distinct from the partners. It holds property as a business entity, while the partners hold their interest in the partnership as intangible assets. This relationship creates two possibilities for a partnership buy-sell arrangement.

cross-purchase agreement

entity agreement

First, the partners can form what is commonly known as a *cross-purchase agreement*. This type of agreement is formed between the partners committing the *survivors* to buy, and the deceased partner's estate to sell, the partnership interest of the first to die. Second, the agreement may provide for the *partnership* to buy and the deceased partner's estate to sell. This arrangement is commonly known as an *entity agreement*.

Cross-Purchase Agreements

The cross-purchase plan involves an agreement between the individual partners and not the actual partnership agreement. Each partner agrees to purchase a share of a deceased partner's interest at death. Each partner must also bind his or her estate to sell the partnership interest to the surviving partners. Generally speaking, the agreement should contain a lifetime-transfer restriction preventing any party from transferring a partnership interest during lifetime without first offering the interest to the other partners. The flow chart below demonstrates the operation of the cross-purchase arrangement.

Figure 6-1
Cross-Purchase Plan

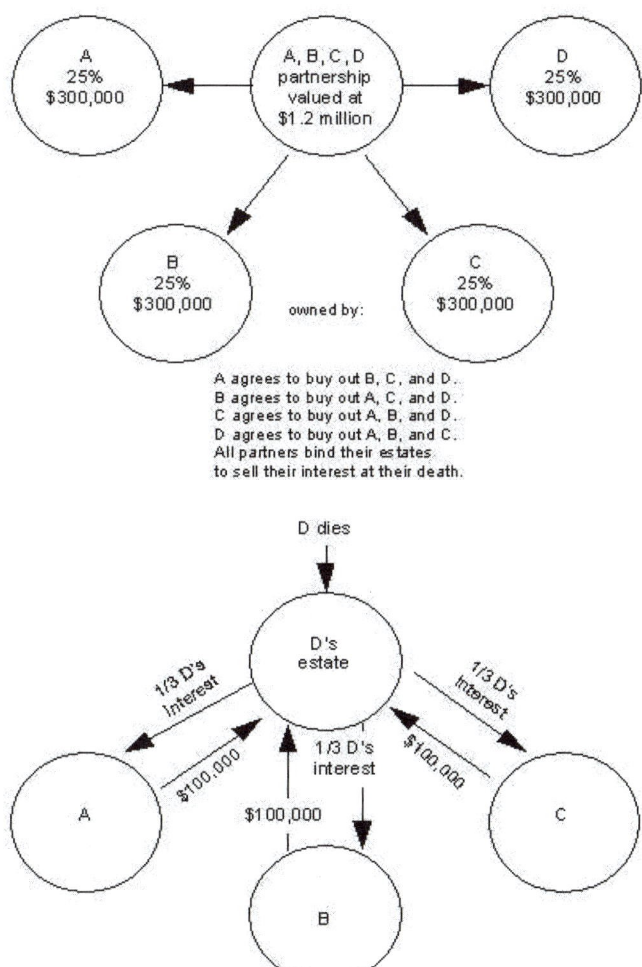

The Entity Approach

Under this approach it is the partnership entity that is obligated to purchase the deceased partner's interest. The agreement provides that the partnership will purchase the interest held by any deceased partner's estate. As parties to the agreement the partners commit their estates to sell their partnership interests to the partnership at death. As we will learn later, the term *purchase* is a misnomer when used in conjunction with the entity approach, since the partnership is actually liquidating the deceased partner's interest under this method. The entity approach is illustrated below.

Figure 6-2
The Entity Approach

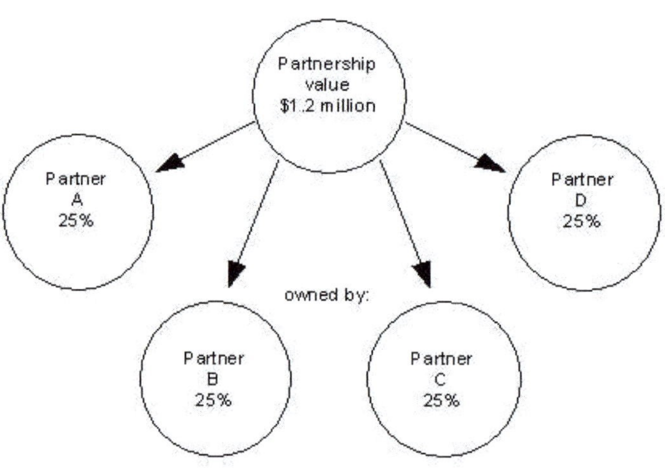

A partnership agreement provides that the partnership will purchase (liquidate) each partner's interest at death. A, B, C, and D form a binding contract for their estates to sell their interest to the partnership at death.

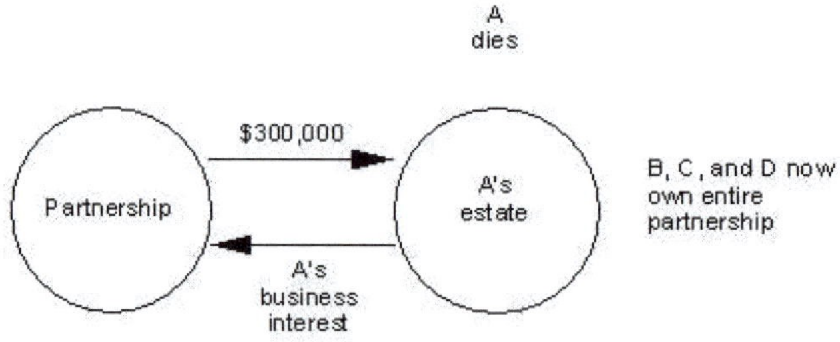

Factors to Consider in Design of the Partnership Buy-Sell Agreement

The partnership buy-sell agreement presents a choice of design options to the individual partners, who can choose either an entity or a cross-purchase buyout. Many factors enter into this decision, and the choice should not be made without considering the circumstances facing the partnership. When designing the buy-sell agreement the financial services professional should consider the circumstances existing in the partnership at the time the agreement is formed and the goals of the partners for the partnership after any buyout is completed.

Number of Partners. As a general rule, as the number of partners increases, the desirability of the entity approach increases also because of the simplicity of the entity approach. At the death of a partner the entity approach involves the purchase by the partnership of the deceased partner's interest. Under a cross-purchase arrangement all the surviving partners will purchase a portion of the deceased partner's interest relative to the size of each one's interest in the partnership. If the partnership has more than a small number of partners, the cross-purchase arrangement can involve several transactions.

EXAMPLE

The TAC company is a general partnership equally owned by eight general partners. If all the general partners enter into a cross-purchase buy-sell agreement, the death of a general partner will commit each of the remaining seven partners to purchase one-seventh of the partnership interest held by the deceased partner's estate. Under an entity approach the death of the same general partner would result in the deceased partner's interest being liquidated by the partnership in exchange for one distribution of cash or property from the partnership in the deceased partner's estate.

The problem created by the greater number of transactions required in the cross-purchase buy-sell agreement is amplified by the funding problem, since the partners don't know in advance who will be the first to die. The cross-purchase arrangement requires that each partner must prepare to buy out any of the other partners at their death. We will discuss the funding of the buy-sell agreement at length later in the chapter, but regardless of the funding mechanism chosen, the cross-purchase arrangement dramatically increases the planning necessary to fund a buy-sell agreement. If a cross-purchase agreement is chosen, the number of funding arrangements needed is as follows:

$$N \times (N - 1)$$

$$N = \text{number of partners}$$

With an entity approach the number of funding arrangements necessary is equal to the number of partners covered by the agreement.

EXAMPLE

Assume the same facts from the example above for the TAC partnership. Suppose the TAC partnership buy-sell agreement is to be funded with life insurance. Under the entity approach, since there are eight partners, only eight policies will be necessary to fund the buyout of the partners by the partnership. However, if the cross-purchase approach is chosen, the number of policies necessary will be 56 [8 x (8 – 1)], because eight partners must purchase seven separate policies to buy out one-seventh of the interest of any of the other seven partners should they die first.

It is easy to see from this example that the cross-purchase arrangement will be impractical for a partnership with more than just a few general partners participating in the agreement.

An additional problem related to the larger number of funding arrangements necessary under the cross-purchase approach is the confidence factor. The success of the buy-sell depends on the ability of each partner to buy out the deceased partner's interest. Therefore the individual partners in a cross-purchase buy-sell must rely on the other partners' abilities to maintain the funding needed for the purchase. The entity plan avoids this insecurity since the partnership controls the funding. For this reason it is generally recommended that a trustee be used to hold the life insurance policies or otherwise monitor the funding of a cross-purchase agreement.

Number of Life Insurance Policies Needed to Fund Buy-Sell Agreement

- Entity plan—one policy for each owner
- Cross-purchase plan—number of partners multiplied by one fewer than the number of owners

A trusteed cross-purchase agreement can also be used to alleviate the problem caused by the large number of policies needed to fund the agreement. The trustee could collect the premiums from the partners and purchase one policy on the life of each partner. At a partner's death the trustee receives the proceeds as the named beneficiary and distributes a proportionate share to each surviving partner. The surviving partners then use the distributions to complete the cross-purchase buyout.

EXAMPLE

Chuck, Sydney, and Paul are equal partners in a firm valued at $3 million. They form a trusteed cross-purchase agreement funded with life insurance. The trustee obtains a $1 million policy on the life of each partner and each partner contributes his share of premiums to the trust. At Sydney's death, the trustee collects the $1 million proceeds and distributes $500,000 to each survivor. Chuck and Paul each pay the $500,000 distribution to Sydney's estate to purchase his interest.

Note: The standard cross-purchase agreement would have required six policies in this case.

Flexibility for Adjusting the Surviving Partners' Relative Interests. A completed buyout under the entity approach will result in the surviving partners holding the same relative interests in the partnership as before the death of the partner. This may not always be the intended result. For example, some of the surviving partners may wish to assume relatively larger roles in the partnership after the buyout, while others may wish to reduce their relative roles. Under the cross-purchase agreement these changes can be incorporated as part of the agreement by obligating some partners to purchase larger interests from a deceased partner's estate when one of the partners dies. Partners who wish to reduce their relative holdings will commit to purchasing a lower share (or none at all).

EXAMPLE

Barbara, Deborah, and Steve purchase a sporting goods store and form their enterprise as a partnership. It is intended that the business will be the primary livelihood for Steve and Deborah, while Barbara contributes capital and will work on a part-time basis for the business. In designing the buy-sell arrangement Steve and Deborah intend to be equal owners of the business if they should survive Barbara. However, she would prefer not to increase her interest above the current one-third should Steve or Deborah die first. Under an entity approach the partnership will liquidate the interest of any of the partners who dies first. Therefore the entity approach will result in a 50-50 ownership arrangement between the survivors whether Steve, Deborah, or Barbara is the first to die.

The partners could reach the intended result quite easily with a cross-purchase buy-sell agreement. In this case Steve and Deborah each commit to buy one-half of Barbara's interest if she dies first. However, Steve and Deborah form a mutual agreement to purchase the other's entire interest if either of them dies first. Under this plan Barbara makes no commitment to purchase anything at the death of either Steve or Deborah and merely commits her estate to sell her interest at death. Using this plan, the partners will achieve their desired results.

Funding Considerations for the Buy-Sell Agreement. We will cover the funding options for the buy-sell agreement at length later in the chapter. There are, however, some funding issues related to selecting the appropriate type of agreement that we will consider briefly here. Quite often, the selection of the appropriate buy-sell agreement must balance the principles of pragmatism and equity.

The funding problems associated with a buy-sell agreement are exaggerated when there is a wide disparity in the partners' ownership shares, ages, and/or health status. In a typical situation the partner with the greatest relative ownership interest is older than the other partners. This means that the younger partners, presumably with lower incomes, have a higher probability of survival and must agree to purchase a larger interest. If a cross-purchase arrangement is chosen, a funding problem will arise because the younger partners must prepare for a fairly large purchase that is expected to occur relatively soon.

If life insurance is chosen to fund the cross-purchase agreement, the younger partners will have to pay premiums based on the older partner's age and the value of the interest. If the agreement is funded by some type of savings or installment payments, the younger partners will have to either save a large sum quickly or forgo a substantial amount of income in the future to fund the buyout of the older larger-interest partner.

On the other hand, it is under a cross-purchase plan that complete equity is achieved. It should be expected that these younger partners will bear a greater burden of the funding since their gain is expected to be greater. If the plan goes as expected, they will receive an increased interest in the partnership, and expected mortality factors indicate that they will benefit from their increased partnership interest for a longer period of time.

Unfortunately the practical considerations often make the more equitable arrangement impossible. The younger partners may find it impossible to fund the buyout of the older partner, particularly if the older partner is uninsurable or substantially rated for life insurance purposes. In this case insurance funding will be unavailable or far too expensive to be practical. Furthermore, if the younger partners are unable to afford the insurance premiums, they will not be able to fund the mortality risk themselves through savings. Although the younger partners may be able to pay the purchase price in installments, this will burden the partnership and the surviving partners' incomes far into the future. In addition, a long installment period may be undesirable to the older partner if estate liquidity problems are anticipated.

Practical considerations often dictate the entity approach when health or other demographic differences exist. Since the entity approach provides funding for the liquidation of the deceased partner's interest through the partnership, the funding burden is borne by the partners in proportion to their relative interests. In this case the older larger-interest partner bears the greatest relative burden of the funding costs. For example, if life insurance is used to fund the agreement, the premiums paid by the partnership on the life of the older partner are far greater than the premiums paid on the younger partners. Since the premium payments made by the partnership are a nondeductible expense, they reduce the partners' distributive shares of partnership income proportionately. Since the older partner has the largest interest, his or her income is reduced the most by this arrangement. In effect, the older partner is providing a subsidy to the younger partners. The older partner is assuming part of the mortality risk and larger purchase price through a larger reduction in distributive share. Despite this fact, the entity approach is often recommended when the ages and relative interests of the partners would make the cross-purchase approach impractical to fund.

The financial services professional should be aware that both practical considerations and equity enter into the design of the buy-sell agreement. When circumstances of age and relative interest create a situation where the partners' interests will be in conflict, it is recommended that each partner obtain independent counsel for designing the agreement.

Valuation—The "Ballooning" Problem. Life insurance is quite often the recommended method of funding the partnership buy-sell agreement (a discussion of funding alternatives is included later in the chapter). The cross-purchase arrangement provides that all insurance policies funding the agreement will be held by the individual partners and not the partnership. The premiums are paid and the proceeds are received by the partners in private transactions. This presents no valuation problem with respect to the buy-sell agreement.

Under the entity approach the insurance policies used to fund the agreement are owned by the partnership, and any proceeds received at the death of a partner become partnership property. The proceeds are then used to liquidate the decedent's interest. However, the policy cash values and proceeds received from the policy "balloon" the value of the partnership. Failure to consider the impact of the life insurance owned by the partnership in the valuation provision will result in inadvertent inequitable treatment of the deceased and surviving partners.

EXAMPLE 1

Larry, Moe, and Curly form the Stooge partnership as equal owners to provide comedy services. The partnership is valued at $300,000 in the buy-sell agreement and the partners form a standard cross-purchase agreement. Assume Moe dies first. Larry and Curly each own $50,000 policies on Moe's life, and each uses the proceeds to purchase his interest. Moe's estate receives the $100,000 and is able to sell or surrender the policies held on the lives of Larry and Curly for the cash values. Larry and Curly each now own a partnership interest valued at $150,000 plus a $50,000 policy on each other's life.

EXAMPLE 2

Assume the same facts as above except that an entity approach is selected for the partnership continuation plan. In this case the partnership owns $100,000 life insurance policies on the lives of each of the partners. At Moe's death the partnership receives $100,000, increasing its value to $400,000. The $100,000 proceeds are transferred to Moe's estate in liquidation of his interest. Larry and Curly now have the last laugh, since each holds a 50 percent interest in a partnership worth $300,000, plus the cash value in the policies on the lives of the survivors. Meanwhile, poor Moe's estate receives only $100,000. The estate never gets the benefit of the increase in value of the partnership due to the proceeds from the policy on his life or the cash values in the policies on the lives of Curly and Larry.

The examples above illustrate the inequities that result from the use of an entity approach funded by life insurance. This does not mean that an entity buyout should not be funded with insurance. However, it is generally recommended that the value of life insurance be included in the purchase price when using the entity approach.

Several approaches have been recommended to consider the insurance value when forming the purchase price. One recommendation is simply for the value of the insurance to be ignored in the valuation provision. At the other extreme it is suggested that the purchase price reflect the full value of the death proceeds. While this method is theoretically fair, a funding deficiency will result unless more insurance is purchased. In the example above this extreme approach would cause Moe's interest to be worth $133,333.33, leaving a funding deficiency of $33,333.33. If more insurance is purchased to cover this deficiency, an additional ballooning problem results.

A more practical method may be for the purchase price in an entity agreement to include the cash values on all the life insurance policies used to fund the entity agreement. This method has some theoretical appeal in that the deceased partner has contributed to the accumulation of the cash values in these policies since the premium payments made by the partnership reduce the partner's distributive shares.

When an entity agreement is funded by life insurance, it is necessary to consider the life insurance policies owned by the partnership in some manner for determining the purchase price. Financial services professionals should be aware that increasing the purchase price in this manner creates a funding deficiency that will have to be resolved. That is, the partnership will have to either (1) liquidate partnership assets to make an additional distribution to the deceased partner's estate, (2) provide the additional amounts to the partner's estate through installment payments, or (3) fund the deficiency in advance through additional life insurance.

Tax Considerations

The tax treatment of the sale or liquidation of a partnership interest is a complex area of tax law. Fortunately within the complexity there are options available for the various planning situations. The material that follows is designed to present the financial services professional with a knowledge of some of these choices without an overabundance of complex tax detail. It is important to secure competent tax advice when designing the buy-sell agreement in order to take advantage of some of these tax choices.

The Sale of a Partnership Interest—Cross-Purchase. The tax treatment of buy-sell agreements differs depending on the approach used. First, we will discuss the cross-purchase approach since the taxation of that agreement is less complex.

Tax Treatment of the Deceased Partner's Estate. Generally speaking, the sale of a partnership interest pursuant to a cross-purchase buy-sell plan is taxable as a sale or exchange of property. As a capital transaction the sale of partnership property results in a taxable capital gain to the extent that the proceeds from the sale exceed the seller's basis in the property. If a partner sells the partnership interest during lifetime, there may be a substantial gain on the transaction if the partner's basis is relatively low. If, however, the buy-sell agreement takes effect at death, the basis of the partnership interest held by the estate is stepped up to its fair market value at the date of the partner's death. Thus the exercise of a buy-sell agreement at death will typically result in little or no taxable gain. If the valuation provision included in the buy-sell agreement was properly designed, the estate inclusion value will be equal to the purchase price for the partnership interest specified in the buy-sell agreement.

hot assets

Unfortunately the basis step-up available to the deceased partner's estate does not eliminate all income tax liability. A portion of the sale proceeds received by the estate may be attributable to *unrealized receivables* and *appreciated inventory* items, often called *hot assets*. The portion of the purchase price attributable to these assets will be treated as ordinary income to the estate, to which no step-up is available. Since this potential ordinary income tax treatment can have a substantial impact on the estate, it is important to note the definition for tax purposes of the terms *unrealized receivables* and *appreciated inventory items*.

Sale of Hot Assets

- Unrealized receivables—rights to income that has not already been included in the partnership's gross income for tax purposes
- Appreciated inventory items—all partnership assets that have appreciated in value except cash, capital assets, and Sec. 1231 assets

The amount of the purchase price attributable to "hot" assets is treated as ordinary income.

Unrealized receivables are rights to income that have not already been included in the partnership's gross income for tax purposes. In a cash basis partnership, for example, any bills that have been issued but are unpaid at the time of the partner's death will be considered unrealized receivables because a cash-basis business does not include receivables in income until payment is actually received. If the partnership has used the accrual method of accounting, unpaid bills do not constitute unrealized receivables because they are included in income as soon as they are billed.

Since most professional partnerships use the cash method of accounting, there may be substantial amounts of unrealized receivables at the time of any partner's death. The amount of ordinary income resulting from the sale of a professional partnership interest can be significant under these circumstances. This will result in an income tax liability to the estate despite the basis step-up available for the decedent's partnership interest.

Appreciated inventory items are certain partnership assets that have appreciated in value. For this purpose inventory items are not limited to the actual general inventory or stock in trade of the partnership. Inventory is defined for this purpose to include all partnership assets except cash, capital assets, and Sec. 1231 assets.

Tax rules provide that the amount of the purchase price attributable to the hot assets will be received as ordinary income. The remainder of the purchase price will be treated as a payment in exchange for the partnership interest. Any gain resulting from this portion of the payment will receive capital-gain tax treatment. As a result of the basis step-up available to the estate, the portion of the payment attributable to the partnership interest will result in little or no gain.

EXAMPLE

Jim, John, and Ted form an equal partnership law firm that uses the cash method of accounting for tax purposes. Business is thriving and the partnership is valued at $1,500,000. Jim, John, and Ted execute a cross-purchase buy-sell agreement under which the estate of any deceased partner will sell the decedent's $500,000 interest in the partnership equally to the two surviving partners. Each partner has a $100,000 basis for the partnership interest. Assume John dies on the first day of the partnership tax year, at which time the partnership has $300,000 in unpaid fees that have already been billed. Jim and Ted complete the cross-purchase arrangement by paying John's estate $250,000 each in exchange for his interest. John's share of the unrealized receivables is $100,000 ($300,000 x 1/3). This $100,000 is treated as income in respect of a decedent and is reported as ordinary income on John's estate income tax return. The remainder of the payment ($400,000) is treated as a payment in exchange for John's partnership interest. Tax law provides that the estate tax value of John's partnership interest is stepped up to the date-of-death value, except for the income in respect of a decedent. Therefore the estate tax value of John's partnership interest is $400,000 and no taxable gain results with respect to this portion of the purchase price.

The implications of this tax treatment are obvious. Businesses such as professional partnerships with substantial amounts of unrealized receivables will create a large income tax liability for the estate of the deceased partner whose interest is purchased under the buy-sell agreement. The IRS used to accept a provision in the partnership buy-sell agreement specifying the allocation of purchase price to specific assets, such as unrealized receivables. The current law mandates the allocation of purchase payments to partnership interest, goodwill, and hot assets according to a prescribed complex accounting formula. However, the partnership buy-sell agreement provides evidence of value and should specify a clear method for determining the amount of hot assets.

Tax Treatment of the Purchasing Surviving Partners. The purchasers of a decedent's partnership interest generally receive a basis for the purchased partnership interest equal to the purchase price for the interest. The surviving partners under the cross-purchase arrangement are treated as having purchased a capital asset—the deceased partner's interest in the partnership. This addition to basis is an important distinction between the cross-purchase and entity-type agreements.

Unfortunately the increase in basis received by the buyers under the cross-purchase agreement is not mirrored in the partnership's basis in the partnership assets. This means that the buyer's investment, while reflected in the buyer's basis, does not increase the basis of the partnership assets. An inequity may result since the payments made by a surviving partner in the cross-purchase agreement with respect to unrealized receivables do not increase the partnership's basis in the receivables. Consequently the receivables will result in full taxation when collected by the partnership. You should recall that the decedent's share of receivables was also fully taxed to the deceased partner's estate when payments were received by the estate with respect to the receivables. In other words, double taxation could eventually occur with respect to these unrealized receivables.

Sec. 754 election

Furthermore, suppose that part of the partnership interest purchased by the surviving partners is attributable to depreciable assets held by the partnership. If the partnership's basis in the depreciable assets does not increase when the interest is purchased from the estate, the partnership will lose depreciation deductions related to the foregone basis increase in the assets. Fortunately a provision of the Code known as the *Sec. 754 election* allows an adjustment in the basis in partnership assets for payments made by the surviving partners with respect to the purchase of the deceased partner's interest. The purchasing partners get the benefit of an increased basis in the partnership property reflecting their investment in the purchase of the deceased partner's interest.

The mechanics of the basis adjustment are extremely complex and will be discussed only in general terms here. In the example above a Sec. 754 election would generally have the effect of providing the unrealized receivables in the law firm with an increased basis of $100,000—the amount of the purchase price paid by Ted and Jim allocable to the unrealized receivables. The amount of the purchase price allocated to the unrealized receivables will be taxed only once—to John's estate.

Liquidation of the Deceased Partner's Interest—The Entity Approach. When an entity buy-sell is carried out, the deceased partner's interest is sold to the partnership. Although this sale seems similar to that in a cross-purchase buy-sell agreement, a different set of tax rules related to partnership-interest liquidations applies.

Tax Treatment of the Deceased Partner's Estate. The cash payments made by the partnership to the estate in exchange for the deceased partner's interest must be divided into two components. Part of the purchase price is allocated to the exchange of the partnership interest and receives sale or exchange (capital-gain) tax treatment. The rest is payment for items taxable as ordinary income, such as (1) distributive share of partnership income, (2) unrealized receivables, and (3) goodwill of the partnership except to the extent that the partnership agreement provides a payment with respect to goodwill. If a partnership buy-sell agreement provides a payment for goodwill, this amount will receive capital-gain tax treatment. It is to the advantage of the deceased partner's estate to maximize the amount allocated to the purchase of partnership interest. The estate receives a stepped-up basis for the partnership interest, and this portion of the liquidation payment will result in little or no taxable gain to the estate. If the partnership agreement does not allocate a portion of the purchase price to goodwill, the tax rules provide that payments related to goodwill will be treated as an ordinary income item. This indicates the significance of the careful allocation of the purchase price to specific partnership assets in the buy-sell agreement.

EXAMPLE

Suppose from the previous example that Jim, John, and Ted form the buy-sell agreement in the entity form. The partnership buy-sell agreement contains the following provision:

Purchase price. It is agreed that the value of the partnership property, including goodwill, is $1,200,000, and that the value of the partnership's accounts receivable, whether billed or unbilled, is $300,000. It is agreed that the purchase price for each partner's interest is as follows:

	Payment for partnership property (other than unrealized receivable), including goodwill	Payment for unrealized receivables
Jim	$400,000	$100,000
John	$400,000	$100,000
Ted	$400,000	$100,000

In this case the partnership payments of $500,000 to John's estate will result in $100,000 of ordinary income. The remainder of the purchase price will result in no taxable gain due to the step-up in basis for John's partnership interest to $400,000. If the partnership agreement had not specifically allocated part of the purchase payment to goodwill, the IRS might claim that part of the $400,000 is in fact an ordinary income distribution from the partnership. Allocations of the purchase price in the partnership agreement must abide by the procedures outlined by the IRS to avoid challenge.

Ordinary income payments received by the estate are considered income in respect of a decedent. As we have learned previously, these payments are included in both the estate income tax and estate tax return. The estate income tax return then receives a deduction for the amount of additional estate tax resulting from the inclusion of IRD in a gross estate.

Tax Treatment of the Surviving Partners and the Partnership. Under the entity approach payments made to the deceased partner's estate that are considered in exchange for the partnership interest do not affect partnership taxes unless the partnership recognized gain on the exchange. This is not likely since the distribution by the partnership is in exchange for a partnership interest of equal value. Distributions made to the estate in exchange for the partnership interest are not deductible by the partnership. However, payments made by the partnership for unrealized receivables are deductible by the partnership and, in turn, reduce the surviving partners' distributive share of taxable income from the partnership.

You will recall that the specific allocation of part of the purchase price to goodwill will result in sale-or-exchange treatment for the payments related to goodwill. These payments will not be deductible by the partnership and therefore will result in higher income tax liability to the surviving partners than if the payments were allocated to income items. Furthermore, payments allocated to goodwill will not be taxable to the estate as ordinary income. Under prior law this presented an interesting problem in designing the buy-sell since the partners in designing the partnership agreement had some flexibility regarding the allocation of purchase price to goodwill and other items. Currently the IRS has prescribed a series of complex regulations to be applied in allocating the purchase price to the various components of assets. These rules remove much of the flexibility in the allocation process when forming the partnership buy-sell agreement.

As in the cross-purchase situation when a partnership interest has been liquidated, the partnership can make a Sec. 754 election to adjust the partnership's basis for the assets.

Cross-Purchase Versus Entity Approach—The Effect of the Purchase on the Surviving Partners' Basis. Under a cross-purchase agreement the survivors who purchased the deceased partner's interest acquire a cost basis equal to the amount paid. This follows the general rule that a purchaser's basis for property is the cost of the property. In an entity buy-sell situation the surviving partners do not receive additional cost basis for the payment made by the partnership to liquidate the deceased partner's interest. The surviving partners are not deemed to be the direct purchaser of the decedent's interest. However, an insured entity approach will provide the survivors with some basis step-up due to partnership accounting rules.

Insured Cross-Purchase Agreement. The exact impact of the various types of buy-sell agreements on the partners' bases in the partnership interest depends on the funding mechanism used. If a cross-purchase agreement is insured, the agreement has no effect on a partner's basis for the partnership interest during all the partners' lifetimes because the insurance is owned by the partners personally and the premiums are paid by the partners. Since no funds are attributable to the partnership, there is no effect on partnership accounting. Under insured cross-purchase agreements the death proceeds from the insurance on the deceased partner's life will go directly to the surviving partners, who are presumably the policyowners. Again, there is no effect on partnership accounting. The insurance proceeds will then be used to purchase the deceased partner's interest, and each surviving partner will receive a basis in the interest purchased equal to his or her share of the purchase price.

Insured Entity Agreement. The effect of insurance funding on an entity buy-sell agreement is more complex. In this case the partnership makes the premium payments on the lives of the partners who are parties to the agreement. Partnership expenditures reduce the partners' bases in their partnership interests. Each time the partnership makes a premium payment, the partners' bases are reduced in accordance to their distributive share of the premium payment. The partners' distributive shares of income and expenditures are determined by the partnership agreement. If the policies used to fund the agreement have cash values, the reduction in basis is equal only to the net expenditures—that is, the premium expenditures less the corresponding increase in cash value. The cash value of the policy is an asset of the partnership. Therefore each premium payment lowers each partner's basis while additions to cash value increase each partner's basis.

Under the entity approach policy proceeds go directly to the partnership at the death of a partner. Even though the policy proceeds are received income tax free, these proceeds increase each partner's basis in the partnership interest in proportion to the partner's distributive share. In other words, for the purpose of basis the receipt of the policy proceeds is treated as any other partnership income. If cash value policies are involved, the basis increase is equal to the net proceeds in excess of the net premiums paid.

The basis increase from the proceeds received by the partnership is allocated to all partners according to the partnership agreement on distributive shares. This basis increase applies as well to the estate of the deceased partner but is unnecessary since the basis step-up already available to the estate at death eliminates all (or most) potential gain. Fortunately the partnership agreement can specifically allocate all insurance proceeds to the accounts of the surviving partners, to whom the basis increase will be more useful.

When the entity agreement is carried out by the partnership, the policy proceeds are transferred by the partnership to the deceased partner's estate for the partnership interest. This has no further effect on the surviving partners' bases in the partnership.

EXAMPLE

Jim, Jane, and Bob form a partnership to produce a financial planning newsletter. Each has a basis of $5,000 in the partnership, which is now worth $60,000. They decide to form a buy-sell agreement for the partnership to be funded with term life insurance. However, they are undecided about the type of agreement that should be used. Assume Jane dies first and the partnership agreement values her interest at $20,000. The following illustrations show the impact on basis of the two types of partnership buy-sell agreements. For simplicity the basis changes in the entity approach resulting from premium payments will be ignored.

- Cross-purchase agreement: partners' bases before Jane's death

Jim	$5,000
Jane	$5,000
Bob	$5,000

At Jane's death Jim and Bob receive the proceeds from the policies on Jane's life—$10,000 each. Jim and Bob each transfer the $10,000 to Jane's estate in exchange for her interest. Jim and Bob now have a basis of $15,000 each for their total partnership interest.

- Entity approach: partners' bases before Jane's death

Jim	$5,000
Jane	$5,000
Bob	$5,000

After Jane's death the partnership receives the $20,000 proceeds, and in the absence of a special allocation the proceeds increase the survivors' bases equally as follows:

Jim	$11,667 (5,000 + 20,000/3)
Bob	$11,667 (5,000 + 20,000/3)

Therefore the cross purchase gives the surviving partners a higher basis ($15,000 vis-à-vis $11,667) than the entity approach. If the partners agreed to allocate all insurance proceeds to the capital accounts of the survivors, the two approaches would achieve the same results.

The importance of these rules related to basis is the distinction they create between the entity approach and the cross-purchase plan with regard to the bases of the survivors after the buyout has been effected. This can be of great significance if any of the surviving partners decides to sell his or her partnership interest. Since the basis will affect the amount of taxable gain on the subsequent sale, the higher basis under the cross-purchase plan will result in a lower taxable gain. Thus if the surviving partners are likely to dispose of the partnership interest in the future, the higher basis available for their partnership interest under the cross-purchase buy-sell arrangement will be an important consideration.

FUNDING ALTERNATIVES FOR THE BUY-SELL AGREEMENT

The purposes of buy-sell agreements, which have been discussed at length in this and previous chapters, can be divided into two components—those that benefit the surviving owners and those that benefit the deceased owner's estate. The purchasers in the buy-sell agreement are current co-owners who survive the decedent or, in the case of proprietorship buy-sell agreement, new owners who intend to purchase the business. The benefit of the buy-sell agreement for the purchasers is the assurance that they will own the business without intrusion from outsiders.

For the decedent's estate the buy-sell agreement provides a guaranteed market for the business interest, resulting in enhanced liquidity for the estate. Furthermore, a buy-sell agreement with a properly designed valuation provision will peg the estate tax value of the business to the purchase price. These benefits currently provide the parties to the agreement with a more predictable estate for planning purposes.

It is clear that the parties to a buy-sell agreement must rely on the agreement to meet their goals. A high degree of certainty is required for the agreement to be a success. Without adequate funding the agreement is subject to the future economic uncertainties facing the parties and the business. An enforceable buy-sell agreement will be useless unless the purchasers are able to raise the necessary funds. Several possible methods for funding the buy-sell agreement will be discussed in this section. Some methods require the owners to fund the agreement while all the parties are still alive, while others involve financing the agreement following the death of an owner. These alternatives will be compared, giving careful consideration to the goals of certainty and low cost.

Methods to Fund Buy-Sell Agreement

- Savings program
- Installment payments
- Life insurance

Savings Fund

savings fund

One approach to funding the buy-sell agreement for an unincorporated business is the beginning of a program to create a *savings fund* to provide the purchase price. The identity of the saver depends on the type of agreement.

In the proprietorship buy-sell agreement the purchaser is known in advance. For example, a key employee of the proprietor is often recommended as the purchasing party to the buy-sell agreement. In this case the key employee would establish a savings fund that would ideally grow to the purchase price at the proprietor's death. A logical approach to meet this objective is to make annual deposits to a fund that will accumulate to the purchase price over the life expectancy of the proprietor.

The drawbacks to the savings fund approach are obvious. Neither objective for a buy-sell funding agreement is satisfied. First, this approach provides little certainty to the parties that a fund will be available at the proprietor's death, which could occur at any time after the agreement is formed. The sooner the actual death of the proprietor, the more inadequate the savings fund will be.

To provide more certainty to the savings fund approach, the proprietor's mortality risk will have to be assumed by the purchaser, which requires an extremely large fund to be accumulated in a short period of time in order to handle the early-death contingency. Of course, this approach fails the objective of low cost. Since the proprietor is likely to be much older and more affluent than the key employee, the cost of funding the individual mortality risk of the proprietor will be prohibitive to the purchasing employee.

Disadvantages of Savings Program to Fund Buy-Sell Agreement

- Little certainty that funds will be available at death of owner(s)
- High cost to fund mortality risk
- Funds subject to creditors' claims
- Deposits to fund not income tax deductible
- Earnings from fund taxable unless invested in tax-exempt instruments

The two types of partnership buy-sell agreements can also be funded by savings. The identity of the saver will again depend on the type of agreement chosen. In the cross-purchase agreement each partner must create a savings fund to purchase the interest of each of the other general partners. If an entity approach is adopted, the partnership should hold the savings fund to purchase the interest of a deceased partner. Regardless of the type of agreement chosen, the savings fund approach will generally be unsatisfactory for the same reasons as in the proprietorship-purchase agreement.

There are some additional considerations with the use of a savings fund approach regardless of the form of business enterprise. First, safety of principal of the fund is an important concern. The savings fund should be accumulated in a relatively low-risk investment vehicle. Assuming this is accomplished, there are other threats to the safety of principal. Since the fund is held by individuals or the business, it is subject to claims of creditors of the same individuals or entity. Furthermore, a liquid savings fund may provide a temptation to use the money for current needs. For example, the partners may decide to use the buy-sell savings funds for capital investment in the business.

Deposits to the savings fund are not deductible for income tax purposes regardless of the approach used. This forces the parties to fund the agreement with expensive after-tax dollars. The earnings on the savings fund will be taxable unless invested in tax-exempt investments.

The high cost and uncertainty associated with the savings fund approach make it the least appropriate of the funding alternatives. However, a hybrid of this and other funding approaches may be appropriate. For example, a savings fund can be combined with insurance so the protection available from the insurance can supplement the inadequate fund during the early accumulation years. As the fund increases, the amount of protection can be reduced as the ages of the parties and annual cost of the term insurance increase. This approach still does not solve the safety-of-principal problem for the savings fund. If the fund is depleted to satisfy business or personal needs, the amount of insurance protection needed to make up the deficiency in the savings fund will remain high and the insurance costs may increase dramatically in later years.

The savings fund approach will be indicated if one of the parties is uninsurable. The mortality risk will be a problem in this case and the savings fund will have to be supplemented in early years by another approach. Generally any deficiencies at the time of the buyout must be supplemented with some kind of installment payment or borrowing by the purchaser.

Installment Obligations

The buy-sell agreement can be completed without prefunding if the seller is willing to accept installment payments in lieu of cash for the business interest. If an installment buyout is the agreed-on purchase method, the buy-sell agreement should specify the details of the *installment obligation* (that is, the term of the installment, the principal amount, and a method for determining the interest rate). Unfortunately the installment method is often selected by default when prefunding is ignored or inadequate at the time of the buyout.

The installment purchase can be used in the proprietorship buy-sell agreement when the key employee-purchaser cannot afford to prefund the buyout through insurance or savings. Unfortunately the installment method has some disadvantages. The purchaser will receive the business interest at the death of the proprietor, but the future of the business is burdened by the need to make the installment payments. This will lower the income of the new owner while hampering the ability of the proprietorship to raise additional credit. On the other hand, the deceased proprietor's estate will not receive an immediate liquid fund for the proprietorship. The heirs must rely on the financial well-being of the purchaser if they are to receive full value for the business interest. This is contrary to the objective of providing certainty for the estate planning of the proprietor.

For the partnership buy-sell agreement an installment obligation can also be used to effect the sale. In the cross-purchase arrangement the surviving partners provide installment payments to the deceased partner's estate for the partnership interest. The partnership will issue the installment note to the estate if the entity approach is selected. In any event the installment obligation will not provide the desired level of certainty to the parties.

The installment purchase has an advantage over other funding methods in that there will be no current burden on the parties to the buy-sell agreement. This advantage is dubious if the success of the agreement is threatened by the future high-cost burden on the purchasing individual or entity. To examine the future cost of the installment purchase arrangement, it is necessary to look briefly at the tax treatment of the installment sale.

Tax Treatment of the Installment Payments

Proprietorship. The tax treatment of installment payments to purchase a proprietorship is firmly established in tax law. The installment payments received by the estate can be divided into two components. The first is the principal payment amounts received to cover the purchase price. Since the estate gets a stepped-up basis for the proprietorship assets (other than items of IRD), there should be little or no recognizable gain on the principal payments. A properly designed buy-sell agreement will fix the estate tax value at the date of death to the purchase price. Since the purchase is to be completed at the proprietor's death, there will be no gain to recognize on the principal payments.

The second component is interest payments on the remaining principal balance. These interest payments are ordinary income to the estate or the heirs.

The estate faces a potential liquidity problem because the sale of the business by the estate prevents the use of a Sec. 6166 election by the executor to pay the estate tax attributable to the business interest in installments. This means that the estate tax must be paid when the return is due, but the installment purchase delays the actual receipt of the total purchase price by the estate for several years. The parties should consider this estate liquidity problem in advance if the installment funding method is chosen.

Recent changes in the tax law limiting the interest-expense deductions could make the transaction more expensive to the buyer. This will generally not be a problem for the buyer of a proprietorship. Proprietorship assets are usually purchased for the business use of the buyer and the interest paid on the installments is fully deductible by the buyer as a business expense.

Partnership. In a cross-purchase partnership buy-sell agreement the tax treatment to the estate of a deceased partner is the same as in a proprietorship. If an entity approach is used, the installment payments from the partnership are treated as part liquidation payments for the decedent's interest and part distributive share. Again, the stepped-up basis of property held by the estate should shield the estate from recognizing gain on the liquidation payments. The payments for distributive share are treated as taxable income to the estate.

Disadvantages of Installment Obligation to Fund Buy-Sell Agreement

- Can create future high-cost burden for purchaser
- Seller's estate does not receive full purchase price at death
- Heirs' receipt of installments not guaranteed

The interest payments on the installment obligations issued by the surviving partners in a cross-purchase arrangement should be deductible by the purchasers as a business expense. Interest incurred to purchase an interest in a partnership or S corporation is a deductible business expense if

- assets represented by the interest are used solely in a trade or business
- the purchaser materially participates in the business

General partners are usually material participants in the partnership activities. Therefore interest incurred to purchase a partnership interest by a general partner would appear to qualify as a deductible business expense.

The interest on the installment obligations is not always considered a business expense. For example, the purchaser could be a passive investment partner. In this case the installment purchase could become quite expensive since the passive-activity rules would apply. The interest incurred in a passive activity is treated as a passive loss deductible only to the extent of the taxpayer's passive income. The interest paid by the partnership under the entity approach is a deductible business expense.

Table 6-1 Payment Schedule for a 10-Year Installment Buyout of a $500,000 Partnership Interest by a Surviving Partner*

Year	Principal Payment	Interest	Total Payment	Total Pretax Earnings Required
1	$50,000	$50,000	$100,000	$125,758
2	50,000	45,000	95.000	120,758
3	50,000	40,000	90,000	115,758
4	50,000	35,000	85,000	110,758
5	50,000	30,000	80,000	105,758
6	50,000	25,000	75,000	100,758
7	50,000	20,000	70,000	95,758
8	50,000	15,000	65,000	90,758
9	50,000	10,000	60,000	85,758
10	50,000	5,000	55,000	80,758
Totals	$500,000	$275,000	$775,000	$1,032,580

* Table 6-1 assumes a 34 percent combined state and federal income tax rate, 10 percent interest due on the remaining balance, and the treatment of interest paid on the installments as a deductible business expense.

The installment obligation method has some shortcomings for meeting the basic objectives of a buy-sell agreement. The seller's estate will not get the full purchase price at death; nor is receipt of installments by the heirs guaranteed. Furthermore, the purchasers also face a large financial burden in the future, as demonstrated in the table above.

Funding the Buy-Sell Agreement With Life Insurance

The usual method of funding the buy-sell agreement is life insurance purchased on the life (lives) of the owner(s). To meet the objectives of the buy-sell agreement, it is easy to demonstrate that life insurance is generally the appropriate choice.

Characteristics of Life Insurance Funding

Certainty in the Buy-Sell Agreement. Life insurance provides the maximum degree of certainty to the buy-sell agreement since life insurance is self-completing as a funding mechanism. The proceeds from the life insurance become available at the exact time they are needed to complete the transaction—the death of the owner. With proper insurance planning the insurance proceeds will be sufficient to fund the entire purchase price. The purchaser(s) will receive the unencumbered business interest, and the deceased owner's estate will receive the full payment for the business interest to provide for the estate costs and the heirs. No other funding alternative has this timing and certainty advantage.

Cost Considerations. Viewed prospectively, insurance funding creates a timing certainty to the buy-sell agreement. However, insurers will exact a price for assuming the timing risk. If term insurance is used, this is the premium for the life insurance policy. If ordinary life insurance is used, part of the premium is used to develop a savings fund in the policy that accumulates at competitive rates in most modern insurance policies. The remainder of the ordinary life policy premium is the annual cost of protection for the amount at risk in the policy. This is the amount charged by the insurer to assume the premature death risk. These protection costs are not paid if other funding mechanisms are used.

The actual cost of the insurance to fund the agreement is not known in advance since it depends on the timing of the owner's death. If the owner dies in the early years of the agreement, the cost of the funding is very low and represents a large windfall to the purchaser. Of course, the owner could also die in the distant future after many annual premiums have been paid. Compare this to the installment purchase situation in which no funds are paid out until after the death of the owner. The hypothetical costs of insurance funding and installment payments discounted to present value are shown in the tables above and below.

As the table below indicates, the present values of the premium costs are far below the actual purchase price. Furthermore, the time-value-of-money principles and the competitive-dividend scale on currently available ordinary life policies cause the net present cost of the buyout to increase slowly (and actually decrease in some cases) even if the premiums must be paid for many years. The table is based on a typical participating whole life policy, but similar projections can be made with nonparticipating policies, universal life, and other current life products.

Table 6-2 Net Present Value of Insurance Cost to Fund a $500,000 Business Buy-Sell at Death*

Age of Insured Owner	Death Occurs at Year 5	Death Occurs at Year 10	Death Occurs at Year 15	Death Occurs at Year 20	Actual Life Expectancy
35	$16,874	$24,414	$27,357	$27,546	$21,781
45	29,009	42,089	46,583	46,892	44,517
55	49,990	72,888	83,861	88,651	89,002

* Life insurance premium costs illustrated with dividends applied to reduce premiums. Discounted to present value at 9.5%.

Tax Considerations for Buy-Sell Agreements. The tax treatment of the insured buy-sell for an unincorporated business is fairly simple. The premiums for the insurance to fund the buy-sell agreement will not be deductible for federal income tax purposes. This makes the funding of the insured plan expensive currently from a tax standpoint. For example, if the party to an insured buy-sell agreement is in the current highest marginal individual income tax bracket (35 percent in 2011), $7,692 of income will have to be earned to make a $5,000 premium payment.

Fortunately the insurance funding mechanism has some tax advantages. For policies that have cash surrender values, there is no current tax on this inside buildup. When the full face amount is received at the death of an owner, these death proceeds are received income tax free. The income buildup on the policy will be taxable only if the policy is surrendered at a gain prior to the death of the insured. Therefore the insurance held to the death of the owner may provide considerable tax savings.

Generally speaking, the use of insurance to fund the buy-sell agreement will not result in adverse estate tax consequences for the deceased owner. If the ownership arrangements for the policies are properly designed (as discussed later), the insurance proceeds will not be included in the deceased owner's estate. Even if the proceeds are included in the deceased owner's estate, the tax law provides relief when the proceeds are designated as the purchase price for the decedent's business interest. Under these circumstances either the business interest or the insurance proceeds, but not both of them, will be included in the estate.

Advantages of Life Insurance to Fund Buy-Sell Agreement

- Produces the cash for the purchase exactly when it is needed, even if the insured dies early
- Is low in cost, even if the insured lives for many years after creation of the agreement
- Results in favorable income tax treatment of the inside buildup in the policy and receipt of the death benefits

Insured Proprietorship Buy-Sell Agreements

The design of the insured proprietorship buy-sell agreement is straightforward. Since the proprietor's death is the event that initiates the sale, the life insurance should be purchased on the life of the proprietor. Unless a trust is used as part of the agreement, the purchaser (for example, a key employee) is responsible for funding the agreement and should be the applicant, owner, and beneficiary of the policy. As the party responsible for funding the agreement, the key employee-purchaser should be the premium payor for the policy, at least in theory. The proceeds payable at the proprietor's death will be received by the key employee and transferred to the proprietor's estate in exchange for the proprietorship assets.

Use of a Trustee in Buy-Sell Agreements. It is generally recommended that an impartial trustee be used as part of an insured proprietorship buy-sell agreement. The trustee is made a party to the agreement and acts as custodian for the policy used to fund the agreement. The trustee may actually apply for and own the policy. The trust agreement may provide that the trustee collect the premiums from the key employee, or the key employee could pay the premiums directly to the insurance company. Generally, the trustee will be made beneficiary of the death proceeds.

The advantage of using a trustee to carry out the purchase agreement is that an impartial party is brought in to oversee the agreement. The trustee will be able to notify the parties if the key employee does not keep the funding up-to-date. This lends more certainty to the agreement since the proprietor might otherwise be unaware of a funding deficiency that could jeopardize the buyout. At the death of the proprietor the trustee collects the proceeds from the insurance and transfers them to the estate in exchange for the business assets.

The trustee will also determine the purchase price according to the valuation provision of the buy-sell agreement. A disinterested third party should perform this function, particularly if a formula price provision is included in the buy-sell agreement. Otherwise the buyer and the executor would have a conflict of interest at this time.

If the insurance proceeds are not adequate to fund the entire purchase price, the trustee can secure an installment note for the remainder from the purchasing employee. If a corporate trustee is selected, this adds the further advantage that the trustee will almost certainly be in existence through the entire course of the agreement.

Provisions for Termination of the Agreement. The proprietorship buy-sell agreement could terminate for several reasons. First, the purchasing party might terminate employment with the proprietor. Second, the purchaser could become bankrupt or disabled, or could predecease the proprietor. Finally, the proprietor may wish to sell the business during lifetime either to the purchasing employee or to a third party.

Regardless of the reason for termination, the terminated proprietorship buy-sell agreement will raise some questions. For example, what should be done with the insurance held by the purchasing party on the life of the proprietor? What should be done in lieu of this agreement to handle the business-continuation problems and to preserve the proprietor's estate? When insurance is used as the method to fund the buy-sell agreement, a provision for handling these questions should be added to the general provisions of the buy-sell agreement.

At the termination of the proprietorship buy-sell agreement the key employee will be holding insurance on the life of the proprietor. If the key employee has predeceased the proprietor, this insurance will be included in the key employee's gross estate. Generally speaking, this insurance should be purchased by the proprietor or by a life insurance trust created by the proprietor. Since the buy-sell agreement is terminated, the proprietor's estate tax problems caused by the lack of a continuation plan may arise. Additional insurance amounts on the proprietor can help solve some of these problems. If the insurance is transferred directly to the proprietor, the proceeds will be included in the proprietor's gross estate at death, perhaps increasing the tax burden. If the policy is transferred instead to a properly designed life insurance trust, the proceeds will pass to the trust beneficiaries without the estate tax shrinkage. This will also avoid some of the estate liquidity problems caused by the termination of the buy-sell agreement.

If the termination of the buy-sell agreement is caused by an event other than the lifetime sale by the proprietor, a replacement continuation plan should be adopted. One obvious solution is the formation of a new buy-sell agreement with another purchaser. In some instances another purchaser may be found quickly. For example, there may be other key employees of the proprietorship willing to become parties to the agreement. In such cases a new agreement could be formed and new life insurance could be taken out on the proprietor's life by the other party.

In general, the existing insurance held by the party terminating the current agreement should not be transferred to a new purchaser. The transfer-for-value rule provides that life insurance transferred for value to another individual will create income tax problems. This rule provides that the purchaser of the policy will be taxed on the amount of proceeds received that exceed (1) the amount paid for the policy plus (2) any additional premiums paid by this purchaser. It is recommended that the terminating party transfer this policy to the proprietor because an insured is always excepted from the transfer-for-value tax treatment. Any other individual who might become a party to the proprietorship buy-sell agreement would be taxed according to the transfer-for-value rule by purchasing the existing policy on the proprietor's life from the terminating party. The existing policy should be transferred to a new party only if the proprietor has become uninsurable since the existing policy was issued.

A proprietor's continuation plan should consider the contingency that the purchasing party may predecease the proprietor. If a key employee is the intended purchaser, insurance on the life of the key employee can be acquired by the proprietor. If the key employee predeceases the proprietor, the proceeds from this insurance can be used to enhance the liquidity position of the proprietor's estate, possibly easing the estate problems resulting from the loss of the continuation plan. It is particularly important to fund this contingency since an alternate buy-sell agreement may not always be practical after the initial agreement is terminated.

The Affordability Problem. While life insurance provides the most certain method of funding a buy-sell agreement, the insurance premiums may be an unaffordable burden since the intended purchaser (key employee) is generally much younger and has a lower income level than the proprietor. When the purchaser cannot afford the necessary insurance, two alternatives are available. First, the proprietor may be willing to help the employee fund the agreement since the proprietor is directly benefiting from the agreement. To assist the purchaser in funding the agreement, the proprietor could increase the salary payments to a key employee or assist in the actual premium payments by using a split-dollar life insurance arrangement.

In any event, this financial assistance to the key employee must, along with the employee's other compensation, represent reasonable compensation for the employee's services to be deductible by the proprietor as a business expense on Schedule C of the proprietor's income tax return.

Another alternative to the problem of affordability is for the employee to only partially fund the purchase commitment. An affordable level of insurance will be purchased by the employee and the remainder financed by other methods. For example, the agreement could provide that the proprietor's estate will accept an installment note from the employee for the unfunded amount. As mentioned earlier, this will provide less certainty to the proprietor's estate but has the advantage of not requiring the proprietor to contribute to the buyout funding.

Additional Considerations for Insured Buy-Sell Agreements. The insured buy-sell agreement will retain the advantage of certainty only if the insurance coverage is adequate to fund the purchase price. In general, the valuation provision of the buy-sell agreement will provide for regular increases in the purchase price either through periodic readjustment of the specified price or a formula that measures current value. For this reason the insurance purchased initially will generally not equal the purchase price at the death of the proprietor. An insured buy-sell agreement should contain a provision for adding, or substituting, policies in the agreement. This will allow the purchasing employee to acquire additional insurance on the proprietor as the agreed-on price increases. This provision will also allow the policyowner to increase the insurance amounts by electing any guaranteed insurability options if the proprietor has become uninsurable. Furthermore, this provision allows flexibility to replace current policies when appropriate.

If a formula price provision is used as the method of valuation in the buy-sell agreement, the insurance proceeds will seldom exactly equal the purchase price. A provision should be included in the agreement on how any discrepancy between the insurance proceeds and the purchase price will be handled. If the insurance proceeds exceed the purchase price, buy-sell agreements usually provide that the insurance proceeds will become the minimum purchase price. This provides certainty to the proprietor's estate plan, since the minimum purchase price will always be known in advance. If the purchase price exceeds the policy proceeds, the agreement should provide a method for the purchaser to make up the deficiency. The typical buy-sell agreement will provide that a proprietor's estate accept the installment obligation of the purchaser when the insurance proceeds are inadequate.

Insured Partnership Buy-Sell Agreements

The provisions of the insured partnership buy-sell agreement depend on the type of agreement adopted. Factors to consider in selecting the type of partnership agreement were covered earlier in the chapter. This section will discuss some additional considerations concerning the use of life insurance to fund each type of agreement.

Cross-Purchase Agreements. The cross-purchase arrangement provides that the surviving partners will each buy a prearranged share of a deceased partner's interest. The estate is bound to sell the interest to the other partners according to the agreement. The cross-purchase arrangement funded by life insurance requires that each partner purchase life insurance policies on the lives of the other partners with a face amount equal to the share of the business to be purchased. Unless a trustee is used, it is recommended that the partner purchasing the insurance be owner and beneficiary of each policy purchased on the lives of the other partners. At the death of a partner the other partners will receive the death proceeds from the policies, which will then be transferred to the deceased partner's estate in exchange for the share of the partnership interest.

The deceased partner's estate will include the value of the partnership interest and the value of the policies held by the decedent on the lives of the other partners. However, the death proceeds will not be included in the gross estate since the decedent had no incidents of ownership in the policies held by other partners on his or her life.

Use of a Trustee. The cross-purchase arrangement will be unwieldy as the number of partners increases. Each partner will be expected to buy a policy on the lives of each of the other partners. Using the formula presented earlier in the chapter, a six-partner business will require the purchase of 30 individual life insurance policies. When the cross purchase is selected, it is recommended that a trust be created to oversee the agreement and act as custodian of the individual policies. The trust arrangement will ease the operation of the transaction and monitor the premium payments by the individual partners. Furthermore, the trust arrangement can be designed to reduce the required number of policies to one per participating owner.

Disposition of Policies Held by the Deceased Partner. The insured cross-purchase agreement presents an interesting dilemma at the death of a partner. The estate of the deceased partner will be holding policies on the lives of the other partners subject to the agreement. The partnership agreement should specify in advance what is to be done with these policies. First, the executor might surrender these policies for their cash value to provide liquidity for the estate. More likely, the executor will be required to transfer these policies to the surviving partners for their replacement cost.[17] The policies could be transferred to the insured partners to supplement any personal insurance currently owned. The policies may also be transferred to the surviving partners, other than the insured, to fund a newly formed cross-purchase agreement among the surviving partners.

In either event transfer-for-value taxation will not occur since an exception to the rule provides that a policy may be transferred to an insured or to a partner of the insured without adverse tax consequences. Therefore neither alternative will result in taxable gain when the death proceeds become payable.

---

17. Replacement cost of a policy is its fair market value and is defined as the interpolated terminal reserve of the contract at the time of sale and the proportionate part of the last gross premium paid before the sale that is not yet earned. For example, suppose a policy with a $1,000 annual premium paid when due on January 1 of the current year is sold on July 1. If the terminal reserve was $10,000 on December 31 of the previous year and will be $12,000 at the end of this year, the interpolated terminal reserve is $11,000 on July 1. The unearned gross premium is $500 for the last 6 months of the current year. Therefore the replacement cost of this policy is $11,500 ($11,000 + $500).

Entity Agreements. The entity buy-sell approach provides that the partnership will liquidate the interest of a deceased partner at death. If insurance is used to fund the agreement, the partnership should own the policies and be the designated beneficiary. At a partner's death the proceeds will be received by the partnership and transferred to the estate in liquidation of the deceased partner's interest.

The entity approach is more practical if the firm has a large number of partners entering into the agreement. Fewer policies will be involved and the funding of the agreement will be more easily monitored since the partnership is obligated to pay the premiums. The entity approach is probably more practical when partners have a wide disparity in ages and ownership shares since there is a pooling approach to funding the buy-sell agreement. The life insurance costs will be absorbed by each partner through lower distributive shares. Therefore the older, higher-interest partners will be providing a subsidy to the other partners through this type of arrangement, but this may be the only practical method to keep the agreement fully funded.

Provisions for the Insured Buy-Sell Agreement

The provisions common to buy-sell agreements were discussed earlier in the chapter. If insurance is used as the funding mechanism, however, some additional clauses should be included in the agreement. These provisions specifically applicable to the insured buy-sell agreements include

- a provision specifying who will be the owner, beneficiary, and premium payer for each life insurance policy used to fund the agreement
- a provision to add new policies and replace existing policies as appropriate when the funding needs of the agreement change
- a provision indicating the procedure to follow if the insurance proceeds differ from the agreed-on purchase price at the death of the partner
- a provision indicating when and how the policies used in the agreement will be transferred. This will become important if the agreement is terminated for any reason (for example, the partnership is terminated during the lives of the partners or any partners' interests are liquidated or sold during their lifetimes). Furthermore, this provision will handle the disposition of policies on the lives of the surviving partners after the buyout of a deceased partner.

- a provision indicating the trustee's responsibilities if a trust is established to carry out the agreement

LLC BUY-SELL AGREEMENTS

The tax treatment of an LLC's buy-sell agreement should be analogous to a similar agreement for a partnership. That is, the agreement could be structured as an entity/liquidation or a cross-purchase buy-sell. We will not readdress the tax implications of these vehicles here. However, there are some unique issues concerning buy-sell agreements for LLCs that we must consider.

Impact of Buy-Sell Agreements on an LLC's Tax Classification

The goal of virtually every LLC was to achieve partnership pass-through taxation in a limited-liability form of entity. To achieve such tax status, LLC state laws often restricted the LLC's capability to hold certain corporate characteristics such as continuity of life and free transferability of interest. To the extent that state law permitted flexibility regarding these characteristics, individual LLC operating agreements were often formed to lack continuity of life or free transferability. Commentators have suggested that a binding buy-sell agreement could cause the LLC to hold either continuity of life[18] or free transferability of interest.[19] These factors are no longer important now that the check-the-box regulations have been made final. Many state laws have been amended and LLC operating agreements altered to remove the termination events. This will make buy-sell agreements more important for LLCs since a binding buy-sell agreement is the best guarantee for continuity for the business.

Impact of the Check-the-Box Regulations

With the check-the-box regulations now in final form, LLCs are able to select partnership taxation while holding otherwise corporate characteristics. Standard partnership entity purchase or cross-purchase buy-sell agreements can be formed, provided that state law permits such agreements. The

---

18. Burkhard, "LLC Business Continuation Agreements Can Create Continuity of Life," *Journal of Limited Liability Companies*, vol. 2, no. 4, spring 1996.
19. Friedman, "Buy-Sell Agreements and LLCs: Avoiding the Pitfalls," *Limited Liability Reporter*, July/August 1995.

structure to the funding and other contractual terms of such agreements should be identical to those of partnerships.

CHAPTER REVIEW

Key Terms and Concepts

specific performance	hot assets
income in respect of a decedent (IRD)	Sec. 754 election
cross-purchase agreement	savings fund
entity agreement	

Review Questions

The answers to the review questions are in the supplement. The self-test questions and the answers to them are also in the supplement and on The American College Online.

1. Explain what specific performance means and why it is significant in the context of the buy-sell agreement. [1]
2. Discuss the benefits of a buy-sell agreement. [1]
3. Identify the contents of the buy-sell agreement, and briefly discuss the purpose of each provision. [2]
4. Who are the potential purchasing parties in a proprietorship buy-sell agreement? [3]
5. Why is it important to enumerate the assets to be sold in a proprietorship buy-sell agreement? [3]
6. Why might a trustee be used to oversee a proprietorship buy-sell agreement? [3]
7. How are items of income in respect of a decedent (IRD) treated for tax purposes when received by the estate? [3]
8. There are two types of partnership buy-sell agreements-the cross-purchase type and the entity type. Describe the basic differences between these two types of agreements. [4]

9. Certain factors in a partnership relationship favor the use of an entity type of buy-sell agreement, whereas other factors favor a cross-purchase agreement. The buy-sell agreement will be insured. In each of the following sets of facts one type of agreement would be favored over the other. State which type would be favored in each case and explain why. [4]
   a. ABC is a partnership owned equally by 10 partners.
   b. X, Y, and Z contribute capital to form a partnership. Z is not a material participant and does not want to increase her interest in the future, while X and Y will operate the business.
   c. C, D, E, F, and G are in partnership. The ages and percentages of interest are as follows:

	Age	Percentage of Interest
C	60	50%
D	55	20
E	45	10
F	40	10
G	25	10

10. Explain why an entity buy-sell agreement should provide for consideration of the insurance funding in the valuation provision, and identify the alternatives for considering this funding. [4]

11. Discuss the tax treatment of the deceased partner's estate for sale proceeds received for unrealized receivables and inventory items. [5]

12. Do the surviving partners increase their bases in their partnership for the proceeds transferred to the estate in either the cross-purchase or entity agreements? Discuss. [5]

13. Identify the advantages and disadvantages of using a savings fund as the funding mechanism in a buy-sell agreement. [6]

14. Discuss whether the interest the buyer incurs in an installment purchase of a business interest will be deductible for a
    a. proprietorship
    b. partnership interest [6]

15. Identify the inherent advantage of life insurance over other funding alternatives for a buy-sell agreement. [7]

16. What factors make life insurance funding a relatively low-cost alternative? [7]

17. Describe the ownership, beneficiary, and premium-payment arrangements for a typical insured proprietorship buy-sell agreement. [8]

18. What adjustments are generally made if the insurance death proceeds do not equal the purchase price at the time of the owner's death? [8]

19. What possible alternatives may be considered if the purchaser cannot afford the cost of the insurance on the proprietor's life? [8]

20. If a cross-purchase agreement is used, the deceased partner's estate will be holding life insurance on the lives of the survivors. What dispositive alternatives does the estate have for these other policies? [8]

CORPORATE BUY-SELL AGREEMENTS 7

Learning Objectives

An understanding of the material in this chapter should enable the student to

1. Describe in general terms the contents of insured corporate buy-sell agreements, note how they are different from partnership agreements, and explain the reason for stamping stock certificates in a corporate buy-sell agreement.
2. Describe the cross-purchase and stock-redemption buy-sell arrangement, and analyze the factors that must be considered in selecting a form of agreement.
3. Discuss the mechanics of insured cross-purchase and stock-redemption plans.
4. Describe the federal income and estate tax treatments of insured cross-purchase and stock-redemption plans.
5. Discuss the special need for and the characteristics of buy-sell agreements for S corporations.

The death of a shareholder of a closely held corporation does not terminate the legal structure of the business. However, the actual business operations of the corporation may be dramatically affected. If the shareholder contributed significant services to the corporation, the surviving shareholders must find a way to replace the services of the decedent. Furthermore, the surviving shareholders and the deceased shareholder's executor must decide what to do with the stock held by the decedent's estate. Among the choices facing these individuals are the following:

- The surviving shareholders may buy the stock held by the decedent's estate.
- The surviving shareholders may accept the heirs of the decedent into the corporation.
- The heirs may continue to hold the decedent's stock as passive investors.

- The executor could sell the stock to outsiders who would then be accepted into the business.

These alternatives may not be the best solution for the parties involved. Generally speaking, the interests of the surviving shareholders will not coincide with those of the heirs. The surviving shareholders, who have the immediate problem of replacing the decedent's services to the business, will hope to increase their salaries and reinvest excess earnings to strengthen the future of the corporation. The heirs who are unable to contribute services to the business will want to receive dividends. Of course, the surviving shareholders will want to receive their share of corporate earnings in the form of deductible salaries and avoid the distribution of double-taxed dividends.

One solution might be to include the heirs as active employees of the corporation and provide the heirs with salary compensation instead of dividends. This alternative will generally be satisfactory only if the heirs have worked in the business for a period of time and possess the adequate skills and training necessary to replace the decedent's services. Usually the heirs will not possess the necessary skills and will be unwanted by the surviving shareholders. A final solution would be the sale of the decedent's stock by the executor to either the surviving shareholders or outside purchasers. However, the forced sale of stock by the executor will rarely yield adequate value for the decedent's stock. The executor and the heirs are unlikely to know the real value of the corporation, and the surviving shareholders have a personal interest in keeping the sale price low. Finding an outside buyer for the decedent's stock will generally fare no better than the sale of the stock to the surviving shareholders, particularly for a minority stock interest. Unless the surviving shareholders are willing to take the outside purchaser into the business, the stock held by this new purchaser will have dubious value. Furthermore, the outside purchaser in these circumstances is aware of the distressed nature of the sale and therefore has a bargaining advantage over the executor.

PURPOSE OF THE CORPORATE BUY-SELL AGREEMENT

A properly designed corporate buy-sell agreement will solve many of the business continuation problems for a closely held corporation. The actual design characteristics of the buy-sell agreement will depend on the goals of the parties forming the agreement. A corporate buy-sell agreement will typically serve some or all of the following purposes:

- A guaranteed market can be created for the stock of a deceased shareholder to provide a decedent's estate with a fair value for the business interest. The agreement can provide the same guaranteed market for the disability or retirement of the shareholder.
- A deceased shareholder's estate will be provided with cash to pay estate costs.
- The agreement can be designed to provide a purchase price that will fix the estate tax value of the decedent's stock.
- The agreement will assure the surviving shareholders that no unwanted or unexpected outsiders will buy into the corporation. It also keeps the executor and heirs from interfering in corporate affairs. This provides for the orderly continuation of the business during the transition to complete control by the surviving shareholders.
- The buy-sell agreement can prevent the termination of a corporation's subchapter S election by preventing the transfer of S corporation stock by the decedent's estate to disqualifying individuals or entities.
- A buy-sell agreement may provide the estate with funds from the corporation income tax free. This is particularly important in the family corporation.

The actual goals of the buy-sell agreement will depend on the circumstances existing in each corporation. The buy-sell agreement for corporations can provide for either (1) an option to buy or (2) the mandatory purchase of the deceased shareholder's stock. To serve the objectives above, a mandatory agreement will usually best suit the needs of the parties.

CONTENTS OF THE CORPORATE BUY-SELL AGREEMENT

The corporate buy-sell agreement can be designed as either a cross-purchase or a stock-redemption agreement. Each agreement will be covered in detail later, but the following provisions are generally included in both types of agreements:

- *parties to the agreement*. The parties to the corporate buy-sell agreement will usually be the corporation and the shareholders who will be subject to the agreement.

- *statement of purpose*. This provision will contain language that indicates the reasons for forming the agreement. Generally speaking, the parties will specify a corporate purpose for the agreement, such as the continuity of the business and its management. This provision can be a useful guide to the courts if some aspect of the agreement should become subject to dispute.
- *the commitment of the parties*. This provision obligates the parties to the agreement to carry out its terms. If the agreement is to operate at the death of a stockholder, this provision will bind the buyers to purchase the stock from the estate and the estate to sell the shares for the specified purchase price. This binding commitment will provide the parties with an enforceable contract. The unique nature of closely held business property will usually cause specific performance to be the appropriate remedy for a breach of the corporate buy-sell agreement. This remedy may be specifically provided for under this provision.
- *description of the stock subject to the agreement*. This provision will describe the number and classes of shares of stock subject to the agreement.
- *stock-transfer restrictions*. This provision sets forth any restrictions imposed on the shares of stock subject to the agreement. Generally speaking, the provision will contain a first-offer requirement preventing a shareholder from disposing of stock to a nonparty without first giving the other parties to the buy-sell agreement the option to purchase the shares at a specified price. The first-offer provision is important for the purpose of fixing the estate tax value of the stock at the purchase price set forth in the agreement.
- *endorsement of stock certificates*. This provision stipulates that all stock certificates subject to the agreement shall be endorsed with a statement indicating that the shares are subject to the buy-sell agreement. If the agreement is being formed for a corporation already in existence, this provision will direct the shareholders to surrender their shares to be so endorsed.
- *operative events of the agreement*. This provision specifies the occurrence(s) that will trigger the agreement. For the purposes of this chapter the purchase of shares will occur on the death of a shareholder. The agreement could also be drafted to operate at the disability, retirement, or termination of employment of a shareholder.
- *terms and conditions of purchase*. This provision specifies the details of the actual transfer of stock at the death of a shareholder. For example, the provision will specify the time and place that

the transfer will occur. Depending on the funding mechanism chosen, this provision will set up a procedure for the transfer of sale proceeds for shares of stock.

- *method for determining purchase price*. This provision states the method for determining the purchase price when the agreement becomes operable. This provision should be drafted with extreme care since the goals of a buy-sell agreement include providing the seller's estate with a fair purchase price and establishing a purchase price in the agreement that will be accepted by the IRS for estate tax purposes.
- *funding*. This provision specifies the means that the parties have selected to accumulate the purchase price for the agreement. Since an unfunded buy-sell agreement offers little certainty to the parties, this provision should be drafted carefully to ensure that the agreement will be carried out. For example, if life insurance is chosen as the funding mechanism, this provision should stipulate the amount of insurance, the applicant, the premium payer, and the beneficiary designation for all policies funding the agreement. If the buyout is to be completed with installment obligations, this provision should outline a method for determining the period of installment and the interest rate to be paid.
- *modification or termination of the agreement*. This provision gives flexibility for the agreement in the event that the original agreement becomes inappropriate. For example, the agreement should be drafted to consider any future issuance of stock by the corporation. In this case it will be necessary to make the new stock subject to the agreement or add new parties if the stock is issued to outsiders. This provision should outline a procedure for handling the bankruptcy of the corporation or any of the shareholders subject to the agreement. Furthermore, any future corporate reorganization should be considered.

Sample buy-sell agreements are often readily available, but the financial services professional should be aware that these agreements will not always contain every provision appropriate to a specific circumstance. In all cases the actual agreement should be drafted by an attorney who specializes in the business planning area.

TYPES OF CORPORATE BUY-SELL AGREEMENTS

The corporation is a distinct legal entity apart from its owners and theoretically has unlimited duration. Ownership in a corporation is evidenced by shares of stock. These corporate characteristics enable the corporate buy-sell agreement to take two general forms. The first is the *cross-purchase agreement*, which provides generally that the surviving shareholders will buy, and a deceased shareholder's estate will sell, the shares of stock held at the time of the deceased shareholder's death.

An alternative approach is known as a *stock-redemption agreement*. The stock-redemption agreement provides that the corporation will redeem the shares of stock held by a deceased shareholder at the time of death.

Corporate Cross-Purchase Buy-Sell Agreements

The corporate cross-purchase agreement is analogous to the partnership cross-purchase agreement. That is, each shareholder who becomes a party to the agreement agrees to purchase a specified percentage of the shares of stock held by a deceased coshareholder at the time of death. The shareholders entering into the agreement must also agree to bind their estates to sell their stock at death.

EXAMPLE

Wally, Theodore, and Lumpy form an incorporated closely held business known as WTL, Inc. Each receives 100 shares of stock in the new corporation at formation. The shareholders become concerned with the usual business-continuation problems that could be caused by the premature death of a shareholder and decide to form a binding buy-sell agreement. The surviving shareholders hope to continue the business in coequal ownership. A cross-purchase agreement will provide the following circumstances for Wally, Theodore, and Lumpy. All the shareholders form an agreement to bind their estates to sell their shares of stock to the surviving shareholders. Each shareholder agrees to purchase one-half of the shares of stock held by the estate of a deceased shareholder.

Suppose Theodore is the first to die. When the agreement is carried out, Wally and Lumpy each purchase 50 shares of stock in WTL from Theodore's estate. Theodore's estate is provided with liquid funds to meet expenses and distribution requirements. Wally and Lumpy will continue to operate WTL after the buyout. Each will hold 150 shares of stock out of the 300 shares of stock outstanding in WTL.

It is important that the shareholders rather than the corporation provide the funds for the cross-purchase buyout. If the corporation provides the funds, the purchasing shareholders will be deemed to have received a constructive dividend and will be subject to ordinary income tax on their share of the purchase price, even if the purchase price was provided by otherwise nontaxable life insurance.

EXAMPLE

Assume the facts from the example above. If the parties fund the agreement through life insurance purchased and owned by the corporation, the constructive dividend problem will result. When Theodore dies, the life insurance proceeds payable to WTL will be received tax free by the business. However, when the proceeds are distributed to Theodore's estate (or to Wally and Lumpy) to complete the cross purchase, Wally and Lumpy will be taxed as if they received a direct dividend distribution to the extent that WTL satisfies the obligations.

Stock-Redemption Agreements

stock-redemption arrangement

Under a *stock-redemption arrangement* the corporation is the "purchaser" of the stock at the death of a shareholder, subject to the agreement. The legal form of the transaction is that the corporation redeems or retires the stock of the decedent-shareholder. The agreement provides that the corporation will use its funds to buy the shares of stock from the decedent's estate, which are then held as Treasury stock.

EXAMPLE

Assume the same facts from the example above except that the buy-sell agreement will be carried out through a stock-redemption plan. Under these circumstances, Theodore's death obligates the corporation to purchase his stock at a prearranged price. Corporate funds are transferred to Theodore's estate in return for his 100 shares of stock. This stock is retired by the corporation, with the result that Wally and Lumpy now own 100 shares each of the 200 shares of stock outstanding in WTL.

Factors Affecting the Choice of Agreement

Selecting the form of buy-sell agreement to be used by a closely held corporation involves many of the factors presented in the previous chapter concerning the selection of partnership buy-sell agreements. In addition, complex provisions of state corporate law and federal corporate tax law should also be considered. The financial services professional should be aware that the selection of a corporate buy-sell agreement depends on the circumstances facing each individual closely held corporation and should be made with the assistance of the appropriate professionals.

Power of the Corporation to Purchase Its Own Stock

A stock-redemption agreement can be performed only if the corporation has the power to purchase its own stock. Under modern corporate law all states will permit a corporation to redeem its own stock under appropriate circumstances. A corporation can generally redeem stock provided that adequate surplus exists. Individual state statutes differ, but a typical statute provides that a stock redemption may not impair the capital or render the corporation insolvent. These determinations always require the examination of the individual state corporate statute and a careful examination of the corporate surplus accounts.

The stock-redemption agreement should be selected only when the corporation will have the ability to purchase its own stock. The financial services professional should be aware that a cross-purchase agreement might be appropriate when the corporate surplus accounts are expected to be inadequate at any time that the buy-sell agreement may become operative. This is also important if an installment obligation will be issued by the corporation when redeeming the stock. In this case the purchase price will be paid over several years and there must be adequate surplus each year to make the installment payment.

A solution to this problem is to provide a safeguard in the stock-redemption agreement. The agreement could include a provision requiring the surviving shareholders to purchase the deceased shareholder's stock if the buyout becomes effective when the corporation does not have the power to redeem.

Qualifying for Sale-or-Exchange Tax Treatment

sale-or-exchange treatment

The gains (or losses) from the sale of property are generally given separate *sale-or-exchange treatment* for federal income tax purposes. The key to sale-or-exchange (capital-gains) tax treatment is the tax-free recovery of the adjusted basis by the seller from the sale proceeds. If the seller's adjusted basis is substantial, there will be less gain subject to tax at the time of the sale. Long-term capital gains are currently taxed at a 15 percent rate. Thus there also is a significant tax rate advantage to sale-or-exchange treatment.

In a cross-purchase buy-sell agreement the seller will receive sale-or-exchange treatment on any gain resulting from the sale of stock. This is particularly advantageous if the buy-sell transaction occurs after the selling shareholder's death, since tax law permits an estate to adjust the basis in its assets to the fair market value at the time of death. If the fair market value for estate tax purposes is pegged to the purchase price in a buy-sell agreement, the sale proceeds will exactly equal the stepped-up basis in the stock held by the estate. Therefore no gain will be recognized by the estate on the sale of stock to the surviving shareholders.

The tax treatment of a stock-redemption agreement may be less advantageous. The stock-redemption arrangement requires the corporation to distribute the sale proceeds to the deceased shareholder's estate. Under the general rules of corporate taxation, distributions from a corporation to a shareholder are generally fully taxable to a shareholder as dividends unless special circumstances apply. If the stock-redemption proceeds are treated as a dividend, the entire amount will represent ordinary income (taxable at the rate applicable to long-term gains) to the estate. The basis step-up available to the estate will be wasted since the redemption proceeds will be taxed as dividend income to the extent of accumulated earnings and profits.

Fortunately complex provisions of the tax law provide exceptions where stock redemptions can be treated as a sale or exchange. These rules are provided in Secs. 302 and 303 of the Internal Revenue Code and are complex. However, it is important to note at this time that it is difficult to qualify the redemption of stock in a family corporation from one family member when other family members will continue to hold stock following the redemption. It is also difficult to qualify partial redemption of a shareholder's stock for sale-or-exchange treatment. If it is anticipated that a stock redemption will not qualify for sale-or-exchange treatment, it is recommended that the buy-sell agreement be designed in the cross-purchase fashion.

Number of Shareholders

The cross-purchase agreement will become burdensome as the number of shareholders entering into the agreement increases. The complexity of both the funding and the purchase transaction is far greater in a cross-purchase buy-sell agreement. As the number of shareholders increases, the cross-purchase agreement becomes prohibitive from an administrative standpoint.

The cross-purchase agreement requires each shareholder to purchase a portion of the deceased shareholder's stock. Furthermore, each shareholder must prepare for the contingency of any other shareholder's death by funding the buyout of every other shareholder. In other words, the number of individual funding arrangements needed for a cross-purchase agreement is

$$N\ (N - 1)$$

where N = number of shareholders

Therefore if a 10-shareholder closely held corporation is funding a cross-purchase buy-sell agreement with life insurance, 90 individual policies will have to be purchased.

Under a stock-redemption agreement, however, only one sale transaction will have to be performed at the death of a shareholder. Furthermore, only one life insurance policy on the life of each shareholder is necessary to fully fund the agreement. Therefore in a 10-shareholder closely held corporation only 10 (rather than 90) individual life insurance policies will be necessary. For this reason a stock-redemption agreement is recommended for a corporate buy-sell agreement including more than just a few shareholders.

Flexibility for Planning Corporate Control After the Buy-Sell Transaction

An important consideration in selecting the type of buy-sell agreement is the anticipated control of the corporation after the buyout is completed, particularly if the death of a controlling shareholder is anticipated to occur first. This is a common situation since the controlling shareholder is often older than the other parties to the agreement. When a controlling shareholder's stock is redeemed, control shifts to a new individual or group of individuals among the remaining shareholders. The ramifications of this action should be carefully considered in advance since the directors of a corporation, as fiduciaries, should not enter into a stock-redemption agreement that would shift control to an individual who might harm the interests of the corporation and the minority shareholders.

EXAMPLE

ABC Enterprises, a closely held corporation, has 500 shares of stock outstanding. The ABC stock is held as follows:

Owner	Number of Shares
Sage	350 shares
Plunder	100 shares
Unlucky	50 shares

The shareholders of ABC decided to form a buy-sell agreement. If the corporation adopts a stock-redemption plan, Sage's death will result in the control of ABC shifting to Plunder. If Plunder could be foreseen as using this control to prompt his own interest and waste corporate assets, the directors may have breached their fiduciary duty by adopting a stock-redemption plan.

A cross-purchase agreement is more flexible for planning the proportionate ownership of the surviving shareholders. Cross-purchase agreements between the shareholders can be designed to result in any post-buyout ownership percentages desired by the shareholders. This flexibility is useful for several reasons. First, some shareholders may desire to increase their involvement in the corporation, while others may want less participation in the future. Furthermore, the cross-purchase agreement will protect members of a controlling group of shareholders against any reduction of control that might occur from the normal stock-redemption agreement.

EXAMPLE

The TAC corporation has 100 shares of stock distributed in the following manner:

Owner	Number of Shares
Happy	40 shares
Snidely	35 shares
Happy, Jr.	15 shares
Snidely, Jr.	10 shares

Suppose Happy and Happy, Jr., combine to control the operations of TAC, Inc. Suppose further that Snidely and Snidely, Jr., form an opposition group to vote their shares. A normal stock-redemption agreement will not protect the control of Happy or Happy, Jr., should either of them be the first to die. In either case the control will shift to the opposition group. In this case it would be wise for Happy and Happy, Jr., to form a private cross-purchase agreement to protect their controlling interest should either die first.

Funding Corporate Buy-Sells With Installment Payments

The use of an installment obligation for some or all of the purchase price in a corporate cross-purchase buy-sell agreement has a major distinction from partnership buyouts with respective to the income tax treatment. The interest paid by a shareholder on debt incurred to purchase stock in a regular (C) corporation will be subject to the investment-interest-expense limitations. This interest will be deductible by the taxpayer only to the extent of the taxpayer's net investment income. Since a closely held corporation will rarely provide a shareholder with investment income, the purchaser will be able to deduct the interest on the installment obligation only if other investment income is earned.

The test for determining whether the investment-interest-expense limitation is applicable is whether the purchaser has a substantial investment motive in the purchase of stock. In deciding on this issue, the courts have usually found that a substantial investment motive exists in the purchase of corporate stock, and thus the investment-interest limitations are applicable. Therefore the use of installment obligations by a purchasing shareholder to fund the cross-purchase agreement will be expensive from a tax standpoint. For this reason the use of life insurance as a funding mechanism is even more favorable in the corporate buy-sell context.

Relative Financial Position. The relative financial position of the corporation and the individual shareholders should be compared when deciding the appropriate form of buy-sell agreement. A stock-redemption agreement requires the corporation to purchase the deceased shareholder's stock. In an unfunded agreement this purchase may generally be performed only if the corporation has adequate surplus, requirement for stock redemption. In a stock-redemption agreement funded with life insurance the premium dollars must be provided with corporate funds. If the shareholder-employees receive substantially all corporate earnings in the form of salaries, the corporation will not have the necessary cash to fund the stock-redemption agreement.

In the case of a cross-purchase agreement individual shareholders must provide the funds for the purchase of a decedent's stock. In many cases individual shareholders will not have the funds necessary for the purchase or even to pay the premiums for the life insurance necessary to fund the agreement. This is particularly true for younger minority-interest stockholders. Moreover, as the number of shareholders increases, the risk that some individual shareholders will not have adequate funds to participate in a cross-purchase agreement also increases. When the corporation has greater financial strength than some of the individual shareholders, a stock-redemption agreement will be favored.

Relative Tax Brackets. Income tax brackets of both the corporation and individual shareholders should be considered in choosing between a stock-redemption and a cross-purchase agreement. The funds to purchase the decedent's stock or to pay premiums on life insurance used to fund the agreement are not tax deductible. For this reason the cost of the buy-sell agreement will be higher if funded by the individual or entity in the higher bracket. Corporate tax rates have not changed since 1993.[20] Personal income tax rates have been reduced a result of the 2001, 2003, and 2011 tax law changes. The maximum bracket (35 percent) on corporate income is currently the same as that applicable to personal income.

EXAMPLE

Smith and Jones each own 50 of the 100 shares of the stock outstanding in Doe, Inc. Assume that each shareholder is in a 35 percent marginal tax bracket for the current year and that the life insurance premiums for the policies used to fund a buy-sell agreement for Doe, Inc., are $5,000 for each shareholder. If Doe has $50,000 of taxable income for the year, it is in a 15 percent marginal income tax bracket. If a cross-purchase agreement is selected, Smith and Jones would each have to earn $7,692 to pay an after-tax premium cost of $5,000. However, the buy-sell could be designed as a stock-redemption agreement to take advantage of the lower marginal rate imposed on Doe's earnings. In this case the corporation would require only $5,882.35 of earnings to provide the after-tax dollars necessary to fund each premium.

Exposure of the Funding Mechanism to Creditors. When a buy-sell agreement is funded in advance, funds must be accumulated in some form by either the corporation or individual shareholders. Since certainty is a major objective of a buy-sell agreement, the exposure of the funding mechanism to outside creditors presents a problem. If the cross-purchase agreement is selected, each shareholder will own policies on the lives of the other shareholders. Therefore the creditors of an individual shareholder can reach the cash values of the policies held by that shareholder to satisfy personal debts. This problem can be alleviated in the cross-purchase arrangement by forming a trust to hold the agreement, with the trustee as the owner of the policies.

If the stock-redemption agreement is chosen, the corporation holds the policies on the lives of the shareholders subject to the agreement. These policies become part of the general assets of the corporation and are subject to claims of corporate creditors. While the access to cash surrender values may be useful to the corporation, this benefit frustrates the goal of certainty

---

20. The deduction for qualified production activities income will lower the effective rate for income earned in domestic manufacturing by 9 percent in 2009 and beyond.

for the agreement. In any event the potential insolvency of the corporation or individual shareholders should be considered in designing the buy-sell agreement.

Fairness to the Participating Shareholders. The issue of fairness in funding a buy-sell agreement presents itself when the relative ages and ownership interests of the shareholders participating in the agreement are unequal. Under these circumstances the younger shareholders will generally hold fewer shares of stock. If a cross-purchase agreement is selected, these younger shareholders will have to purchase large amounts of life insurance on the older shareholders with higher percentages of ownership. This represents a fair allocation of costs. The younger shareholders benefit more from the agreement since they are more likely to survive and are purchasing a larger interest in the corporation. Due to the high funding costs facing these younger shareholders, however, they are often unable to afford the necessary premiums.

Under the stock-redemption agreement a corporation pays the premiums on all policies used to fund the agreement. This results in a pooling effect for the premiums since the expenditure of corporate funds reduces the income available to all their shareholders. However, this pooling effect is theoretically unfair to the older and higher-relative-interest shareholders since they would presumably be more seriously affected by a reduction in corporate income due to their larger shareholdings. In spite of this fact the older and higher-interest shareholders are often quite satisfied by the stock-redemption arrangement since it may be the only method that is practical and provides an inducement to the younger shareholders to enter into the agreement and remain with the corporation.

The Life Insurance "Ballooning" Problem. A stock-redemption agreement funded by life insurance presents a problem since the insurance inadvertently increases the value of the corporate stock subject to the agreement. First, the cash values of the life insurance policies held by the corporation increase its value. Second, the receipt of proceeds at the death of any shareholder inflates the value of the corporation prior to the buyout. Under the cross-purchase arrangement the life insurance policies are held by individual shareholders and therefore do not have an impact on the value of the corporation. Because this phenomenon was discussed in great detail in the last chapter in the section comparing partnership cross-purchase arrangements and entity buy-sell approaches, it will not be discussed further here. However, it is generally considered more equitable to consider the value of the life insurance in the purchase price if a stock-redemption agreement is chosen.

Cost Basis of the Surviving Shareholders. The cost basis of the surviving shareholders in the stock held following a buy-sell agreement will depend on the type of agreement chosen. This cost basis could become extremely important if the surviving shareholders sell their stock before death. At the time of any future sale the surviving shareholders will be taxed on the gain equal to the sale proceeds in excess of their adjusted basis. This will not be a problem if the surviving shareholders hold the stock until death and their estates receive the benefit of the basis step-up.

Under the stock-redemption agreement the corporation is providing the purchase price to the deceased shareholder's estate. This stock redemption increases the value of the shares held by the surviving shareholders. However, the purchase price paid by the corporation is not added to the survivors' cost basis. The ultimate impact of the stock-redemption agreement is that the surviving shareholders have an increased potential gain that must be recognized for federal income tax purposes if they later sell their stock.

The individual shareholders are the purchasers of a deceased shareholder's stock under the cross-purchase agreement. The purchase price provided by the individual shareholders becomes part of their investment or cost basis in the stock they hold in the corporation. Therefore the cost basis of the surviving shareholders increases by an amount equal to the increase in the total value of the stock they hold. As a result surviving shareholders will have a lower taxable gain to recognize if they subsequently sell their stock following a cross-purchase buyout of a deceased shareholder's stock. This should be an important consideration in designing the buy-sell agreement if some or all of the shareholders anticipate selling their stock prior to death.

EXAMPLE

The RRN Corporation has its 100 shares of stock held as follows:

	Ownership	Adjusted Basis
Reginald	60 shares	$180,000
Ralph	20 shares	60,000
Norton	20 shares	60,000

The price specified in the buy-sell agreement is $10,000 per share—the actual fair market value. Suppose Reginald is the first to die. The ownership after the buyout of Reginald is as follows:

Stock Redemption Approach

	Ownership	Adjusted Basis	Current Value
Ralph	20 shares	$60,000	$500,000
Norton	20 shares	60,000	500,000

Cross-Purchase Approach

	Ownership	Adjusted Basis	Current Value
Ralph	50 shares	$360,000	$500,000
Norton	50 shares	360,000	500,000

Assume Ralph decides to sell his stock in RRN one year later and that the fair market value hasn't changed. If the stock-redemption approach was used to buy out Reginald, Ralph's tax liability is $66,000 ($440,000 taxable gain at the current 15 percent rate). If the cross-purchase plan was adopted, Ralph owes only $21,000 tax on the gain ($140,000 gain at the current 15 percent rate).

The Transfer-for-Value Problem. The transfer-for-value tax rule provides that the death proceeds from a life insurance policy transferred for valuable consideration are taxable as ordinary income to the extent that the proceeds exceed the consideration paid by the transferee plus any net premiums paid by the transferee subsequent to the transfer. Fortunately there are exceptions to this general rule and in some cases death proceeds may be received income tax free. For example, the proceeds on insurance owned by the original applicant-owner until maturity are received federal income tax free. In addition, income taxation of proceeds will not occur if a transfer of a life insurance policy for valuable consideration is made to any of the following:

- the insured
- a partner of the insured
- a partnership in which the insured is also a partner
- a corporation in which the insured is a shareholder or officer

A potential transfer-for-value tax problem arises in the cross-purchase corporate buy-sell agreement. First, the shareholders initially entering into a cross-purchase agreement may decide to fund the agreement with existing insurance on their lives. Since the normal cross-purchase insured agreement requires the shareholders to hold policies on the lives of the other shareholders, the existing insurance would then be transferred from the insured to the other shareholders. This is a transfer for valuable consideration that will cause taxation of the proceeds when eventually received. What's more, the transfer-for-value rule is invoked even if the shareholders make like-kind exchanges of the policies on their lives. For this reason existing insurance should not be used to form a cross-purchase agreement. This raises the question of what should be done when existing insurance must be used because a shareholder has become uninsurable. In this case the agreement should be designed as a stock redemption since a transfer of a policy to a corporation in which the insured is a shareholder will not invoke transfer-for-value problems.

The death of a shareholder in a cross-purchase agreement presents another potential transfer-for-value situation. Since each shareholder in the cross-purchase agreement holds policies on the lives of the other shareholders, the estate of a deceased shareholder will hold policies on the lives of the surviving shareholders. These policies are of little use to the estate and the executor would typically like to dispose of them. A provision for the disposition of these policies should be included in the original buy-sell agreement. At first glance the most logical alternative would be to transfer the policies held by the estate for their cash value to the surviving shareholders other than the insured. This method will assist the surviving shareholders in the funding of a new cross-purchase agreement between the survivors.

Unfortunately the logical solution also presents the transfer-for-value problem. If the policies are transferred from the estate to shareholders other than the insured, the proceeds will be taxable to the extent they exceed the price paid for the policy plus any subsequent premiums paid by the shareholders who purchase the policy. To avoid a potential transfer-for-value problem, the estate should either (1) surrender the policies for their cash value or (2) transfer the policies to the insureds to supplement their personal insurance.

Accumulated-Earnings-Tax Penalty. The accumulated-earnings tax is imposed on the accumulated taxable income of a corporation. This amount is reduced by dividends paid by the corporation and the minimum credit, which is $250,000 for business corporations and $150,000 for personal-service corporations. Since premium payments for the life insurance used to fund a cross-purchase buy-sell agreement are not tax deductible, they reduce neither the corporation's taxable income nor its exposure to the accumulated-earnings tax. The insurance purchased in a cross-purchase agreement is outside the corporation and has no impact on the accumulated corporate earnings.

The accumulated-earnings tax may become a problem in the stock-redemption agreement when large policies are purchased on the lives of shareholders. The $150,000 credit for a professional corporation may be reached quite easily as the value of the business and the ages of the shareholders increase. Furthermore, the proceeds received by the corporation at the death of a shareholder may also become unreasonably accumulated earnings.

Fortunately there are reasons why the accumulation of earnings to fund a stock-redemption agreement is reasonable and will not subject the corporation to the accumulated-earnings-tax penalty. First, a corporation may accumulate earnings for the purposes of a Sec. 303 stock redemption (303 redemptions are covered in the next chapter). These accumulations are automatically exempt provided they take place in the year of the shareholder's death or later to fund the 303 redemption.

For accumulation of earnings before the year of the shareholder's death or for a redemption other than a 303 redemption, a business purpose must be established if accumulations above the minimum credit are to be deemed reasonable. The courts have decided both ways on this issue, depending on the circumstances of the individual case. It appears that accumulations to fund a stock redemption to (1) provide for the orderly continuation of a business, (2) keep the stock out of unfriendly hands, or (3) increase the equity interest of key employees will be deemed to suit the business purposes. Accumulations of earnings to fund stock-redemption agreements in most business-continuation-planning situations should meet these requirements. It is advisable to include a conspicuous statement indicating the business purpose of the buy-sell agreement to provide evidence of reasonable business needs.

The tax on unreasonably accumulated corporate earnings will apply primarily when the buy-sell agreement is solely designed to serve the private estate planning needs of the shareholders. For this reason the tax will typically be applicable when earnings are accumulated to fund a partial redemption (other than a 303 redemption) of a majority shareholder's stock. If a buy-sell agreement has questionable business purposes, the cross-purchase agreement should be favored to avoid the accumulated-earnings tax.

Cross-Purchase or Stock-Redemption: Factors to Consider

- Is the corporation allowed to buy its own stock?
- Can sale-or-exchange tax treatment of the transaction be obtained?
- How many shareholders are there?
- How is control of the corporation to be shared after a stockholder dies?
- Will installment obligations be used as a funding vehicle?
- What is the relative financial position of the corporation versus the owners?
- Who is in the lower tax bracket—the corporation or the owners?
- Will exposure of the funding mechanism to creditors' claims be a problem?
- Which approach will be fairer to the participating owners?
- Who, if anyone, will receive the benefit of life insurance "ballooning"?
- What will happen to the cost basis of the surviving owners?
- Will there be a transfer-for-value problem?
- Will there be exposure to a possible accumulated-earnings tax?
- Will there be an alternative minimum tax problem?

"Wait-and-See" Approach

To provide flexibility for the shareholders in planning the business-continuation agreement, an alternative approach to predetermining the form of agreement has been suggested.

wait-and-see buy-sell

The *wait-and-see buy-sell* agreement has the same purpose as other buy-sell arrangements except that the identity of the purchaser is not predetermined in the agreement. The agreement can be currently established and funded and will commit all parties to sell their stock at death. The purchaser, either the corporation or the surviving shareholders, will not be determined until the first death of a shareholder. The buy-sell agreement will first provide the corporation with an option to purchase the deceased shareholder's stock within a specified number of days after death. If the corporation does not exercise the option, the surviving shareholders are granted an option to purchase the stock. If the surviving shareholders refuse to exercise this option, the corporation is required by the agreement to purchase any remaining shares held by the deceased shareholder's estate.

The wait-and-see buy-sell agreement loses none of the guarantees provided by the traditional buy-sell agreement. The surviving shareholders know that the corporation will continue without intrusion from outsiders. The shareholders are certain that their estates will receive a specified purchase price for their stock at death. However, the wait-and-see approach allows the shareholders and corporation to postpone the decision to select the form of agreement until after the first death of a shareholder. This is particularly useful to a buy-sell agreement that will probably not be operative until far in the future. It allows the shareholders flexibility to adjust the percentages of ownership after the death of a shareholder in any manner they choose. Or the parties to the agreement will be able to wait until the death of a shareholder to determine whether a redemption will qualify for a sale-or-exchange treatment. This flexibility is extremely important since the ever-changing tax laws may be more or less favorable to one form of agreement or another in the future.

In the wait-and-see buy-sell situation it is generally recommended that the shareholders hold the insurance funding the agreement in a cross-purchase fashion. That is, each shareholder will own, pay the premiums on, and be beneficiary on policies insuring other shareholders. When a shareholder dies, surviving shareholders will receive proceeds from the policies they hold on the deceased shareholder's life. If a cross-purchase arrangement is most appropriate at this time, the corporation will allow its option to lapse, and the surviving shareholders will purchase the deceased shareholder's stock. If a stock redemption is more favorable, the surviving shareholders can contribute the death proceeds they receive to the corporation as a capital contribution. The corporation will then use the contributed amounts to redeem the stock. These contributions will increase the surviving shareholder's basis in their stock by the amount of the proceeds, thus removing one of the normal disadvantages of the stock-redemption agreement. As an alternative the shareholders can loan the death proceeds to the corporation at a normal rate of interest. This interest will then be deductible by the corporation when the surviving shareholders are repaid in installments.

The Wait-and-See Approach

- The corporation has the first option to buy the decedent's stock.
- The surviving owners have the next option to buy the decedent's stock.
- The corporation is required to buy any unpurchased shares of the decedent's stock.
- The option selected is based on financial and legal circumstances at the time of the purchase and sale.

PLANNING THE PROFESSIONAL CORPORATION BUY-SELL AGREEMENT

The nature of professional-corporation statutes makes business-continuation planning particularly important. Unlike ownership in a business corporation, professional-corporation ownership is restricted to licensed members of the profession. This means that the stock of a deceased professional-corporation shareholder must be transferred at death either to another licensed professional or to the corporation. Termination of employment may also require the sale of stock by a terminating shareholder.

The shareholders of a professional corporation will be able to pass the stock to members of the deceased shareholder's family only if those family members are licensed in the same profession. Furthermore, state law generally requires the estate of a deceased professional-corporation shareholder to transfer the stock within a reasonable period after death (for example, 60 days).

In the absence of a buy-sell agreement most state laws require the professional corporation to redeem the deceased professional's stock. State laws will vary on the terms of this redemption. Some laws provide that book value will be the redemption price for the shares, while others provide for fair market value.

In either case the results of the mandatory redemption are less favorable to the parties than a prearranged plan would be. First, book value is rarely an accurate measure of the actual value of the business. For example, goodwill is generally entered at zero value, and accounts receivable for a cash-basis taxpayer are not reflected on the books. Therefore a large part of the professional corporation's actual worth is excluded from the book value figure. And second, even if fair market value is specified as the required redemption price, the method for determining fair market value has not been chosen in advance and is subject to dispute between the corporation and the estate if not specified in a binding buy-sell agreement.

Without proper planning the professional corporation will usually not have the funds for a complete redemption of the decedent's stock. Some states require dissolution of the corporation if the redemption does not occur. From a business standpoint this may not be a problem to the surviving shareholders since they may continue the practice as partners or individual practitioners. However, the tax consequences of a liquidation may be burdensome and can be avoided by proper continuation planning.

Selecting the Purchaser

Cross Purchase Versus Stock Redemption

There are some distinctions created by a professional corporation that affect the choice of structure for a buy-sell agreement.

First, professionals tend to operate individual practices within the corporate structure. The deceased shareholder's estate may be transferring stock that in reality represents the client base of the individual professional. It often occurs that the other professionals in the corporation, particularly those at advanced ages, do not wish to expand their practice to include the clients of the deceased shareholder. In this case the shareholders could hire a new nonowner-professional to provide the services of the deceased shareholder, or the shareholders could form a buy-sell agreement during their lives with an outside professional who is willing to take over the decedent's practice.

If a stock-redemption agreement is selected, it is less likely that the accumulated-earnings-tax penalty will apply in a professional corporation than in a business corporation because the corporation is typically required under state law to redeem the stock of a deceased professional shareholder. It is unlikely that the IRS could successfully argue that accumulations to comply with state corporate law would serve no business purpose. However, the funding of a stock-redemption agreement specifying a purchase price far in excess of that required by state law may not suit a reasonable business need. It is important for the shareholders to carefully establish the business purpose for a stock-redemption agreement in the corporate minutes of the board meeting where the agreement is established. The business purpose should also be included in the actual stock-redemption agreement.

Sole-Shareholder Corporation

The sole-shareholder corporation, often called the incorporated proprietorship, may occur in both professional and business corporations. However, it is discussed only briefly here since the sole-practitioner professional corporation is quite common.

Business-continuation planning for the sole-shareholder corporation is similar to that for the proprietor. Without proper planning liquidation or a forced sale of the corporation by the estate will usually result. A sale planned during the lifetime of the professional will typically assure a more adequate purchase price. A sole shareholder should seek the appropriate purchaser for the corporation during his or her lifetime. Quite often sole shareholders employ young professionals just beginning their practice. They are the natural purchasers of the professional corporation since they will become familiar with the shareholder's practice. In this case a "one-way" buy-sell agreement is formed in which the employee agrees to purchase, and the shareholder binds his or her estate to sell, the stock held at the death of the shareholder.

Alternatively the sole-shareholder professional could seek another similarly situated professional and form a cross-purchase agreement. In this situation the two sole-shareholder professionals agree to purchase each other's corporation at an appropriate time—at the death of the professional.

FUNDING CORPORATE BUY-SELL AGREEMENTS WITH LIFE INSURANCE

Mechanics of the Insured Buy-Sell Agreement

Insurable Interest

insurable interest

A requirement of life insurance is that a valid *insurable interest* exists at the inception of the policy. All individuals have an insurable interest in their own lives. However, it is rarely appropriate in the classic buy-sell arrangements for the insured to own the policy on his or her own life.

Despite this fact the insurable-interest requirements will not present a problem if life insurance is used to fund a buy-sell agreement. An insurable interest is deemed to arise when the applicant has some pecuniary interest in the insured based on a business relationship—creditor, associate, and so forth. Pecuniary interests exist if the policyowner has a reasonable expectation of benefit from the continued life of the insured or will suffer a financial loss from the insured's death. The insurable-interest test is met in the buy-sell agreement since the policyowner is typically a business partner of the insured who relies on the insured coshareholder's continued service. The policyowner also suffers a loss since the buy-sell agreement requires the policyowner to purchase the deceased shareholder's interest.

Ownership and Beneficiary Designation

Cross-Purchase Agreement. The cross-purchase agreement requires each shareholder to purchase the stock of a deceased shareholder. In this case it is logical for the ultimate purchaser to hold the funds necessary to complete the transaction. In the classic cross-purchase arrangement each stockholder is the applicant of, owns, pays premiums for, and is the beneficiary of the life insurance proceeds on policies covering the lives of other shareholders.

EXAMPLE

Ted and Jim form TJ Enterprises, a closely held corporation. Each contributes capital to the corporation in exchange for 100 shares of common stock. Ted and Jim plan to remain as equal co-owners and form a classic cross-purchase agreement to be funded with life insurance. The agreed purchase price is $1,000 per share. To fund this agreement, Ted takes out a life insurance policy on Jim's life in the amount of $100,000 and names himself as beneficiary. Jim funds his half of the agreement by purchasing $100,000 of insurance on Ted's life and names himself as beneficiary. At Ted's death Jim receives the $100,000 of life insurance proceeds and transfers this amount to Ted's estate in exchange for 100 shares of stock in accordance with the agreement.

Stock-Redemption Agreement. The corporation will provide the funds necessary to complete the purchase of a deceased shareholder's stock in a stock-redemption agreement. Therefore the corporation should be the owner, premium payer, and beneficiary of a policy on the lives of all shareholders subject to the stock-redemption plan. The amount of insurance purchased on the life of each shareholder depends on the purchase amount required to redeem the shares of that individual shareholder.

Shareholders who are parties to the stock-redemption agreement will often desire their estates or selected heirs to be the direct beneficiary of the life insurance proceeds held by the corporation. Apparently these clients feel more secure that the purchase price will be received by their estate with this type of beneficiary designation. However, the designation of the insured's estate might cause some problems. For instance, both the proceeds of the policy and the decedent's stock are held by the executor. It is generally accepted that either the insurance proceeds or the stock, but not both, will be includible in the gross estate for estate tax purposes. However, the mere fact that the executor is holding both amounts creates some difficulties. First, the corporation and other shareholders may have to resort to litigation to force the executor to specifically perform under the terms of the agreement. Second, the insurance amount becomes subject to the claims of estate creditors.

Insurance Funding Alternatives

Term or Permanent Insurance. Selecting the life insurance used to fund the buy-sell agreement presents the age-old question of term versus permanent insurance. Of course there is no general answer applicable to all cases. The financial services professional should look at all the facts and circumstances surrounding the individual business-continuation planning case and select the appropriate funding vehicle. The main objective is to see that the buy-sell agreement is substantially funded. This goal can be reached by insuring the full purchase price specified in the agreement, which will be easy if the agreement provides for a fixed price. If a formula valuation approach is used, an estimate will have to be made to determine the purchase price.

The life insurance chosen to fund the agreement will depend on several factors in the business planning situation. The first is the expected duration of the agreement. If the buy-sell agreement is expected to continue beyond the shareholder's 65th birthday, term insurance may be inappropriate. This is also true if the buy-sell agreement will operate at the disability or retirement of the shareholders. Pure term insurance will typically be renewable only to age 65 or 70 and will become quite expensive at advanced ages. Furthermore, term insurance will not build up cash values within the policy, and this lack of an internal fund will make the policy inappropriate to fund a buyout at the time of a shareholder's disability or retirement. On the other hand, ordinary life insurance will provide level annual premiums (or decreasing premiums if participating policies are used) that will not result in high premiums in later years. In addition, the internal buildup on the life insurance policy provides a source of cash that may accumulate to assist in funding a disability or retirement buy-sell agreement.

Naturally the consideration of cost and the ability of the shareholders or corporations to pay the premiums is an overriding concern. Term insurance will provide lower annual premiums in the early years of the buy-sell agreement and may be the most cost-effective way for young shareholders of a new expanding corporation to fund the buy-sell agreement. The term insurance can be replaced with permanent life insurance after the shareholders or corporation has increased their financial strength. Furthermore, term insurance riders can be used to supplement permanent insurance if some, but not the full amount, of the purchase price can be affordably funded with permanent insurance. In any event the selection of the type of insurance should first meet the primary need—substantial funding for the buy-sell agreement.

Permanent insurance owned by the corporation to fund a stock-redemption agreement also provides some benefits secondary to the buy-sell purpose. The cash surrender value building up inside the policy provides the corporation with liquidity and a source of collateral for corporate borrowing.

Should the Buy-Sell Agreement Be Funded by Term Insurance?

- Term insurance may be appropriate if
  - the buy-sell agreement is expected to end by age 65 or 70
  - low annual premiums in the early years are important
- Term insurance may be inappropriate if
  - the purchase and sale are triggered by an owner's disability or retirement
  - level or decreasing annual premiums are important
  - the insurance is needed as a source of liquidity or collateral for the corporation

Use of a Trustee

A trustee may be a useful addition to a corporate cross-purchase buy-sell agreement. The trustee is an independent third party who can handle the details of the buy-sell transaction in a fair and swift manner. The use of a trustee adds certainty to the agreement because it lowers the risk that a dispute will arise between the surviving shareholders and the deceased shareholder's estate in carrying out the terms of the agreement. Furthermore, the trustee monitors the funding of the agreement and relieves the surviving shareholders of the details of carrying out the purchase of the decedent's stock when the survivors' efforts should be focused on continuation of the corporation.

The use of a trust in the cross-purchase agreement changes some of the standard insurance arrangements we discussed earlier. First, the trustee, not the individual shareholders, is named beneficiary of the policies funding the agreement. The trustee will hold the policies and the stock certificates subject to the agreement. Normal ownership rights, such as the right to receive dividends from the life insurance policy and to vote the shares of stock, are retained by the individual shareholders.

Either the shareholders or the trustee will have the responsibility of paying the premiums. If the trustee is selected to pay the premiums, the individual shareholders must contribute the necessary funds to the trust. This adds certainty to the buy-sell agreement since the trustee can carefully monitor the insurance funding.

At the death of a shareholder the trustee collects the proceeds from the insurance company. The trustee then determines, or selects an independent professional appraiser to determine, the value of the stock in accordance with the provisions of the buy-sell agreement. The trustee transfers this purchase price to the decedent's estate and endorses the decedent's stock certificates over to the appropriate surviving shareholders. The trustee must also dispose of the policies held by the decedent on the lives of the survivors in accordance with the terms of the buy-sell agreement. These remaining policies will usually be transferred to the surviving insureds for their replacement costs. The use of a trust agreement is far less frequent if the buy-sell agreement is carried out through a stock redemption.

TAXATION OF THE INSURED CORPORATE CROSS-PURCHASE BUY-SELL AGREEMENT

Federal Income Tax

Premium Payments

The classic cross-purchase agreement requires the individual shareholders to pay the premiums on the insurance funding the agreement. These payments are a nondeductible expense to the individual shareholders and may be directly or indirectly provided by the corporation. First, the corporation could provide the shareholder with additional income necessary to pay the premiums in the form of a dividend or additional salary. Obviously a dividend distribution to provide the funds to pay these premiums would not be a wise choice. The dividends would be a nondeductible expense to the corporation and taxable as income to the shareholder.

If the corporation provides the funds necessary to pay the premiums as additional salary to the shareholder, this salary expense is deductible to the corporation and will be received as ordinary income by the shareholder. The corporation should not directly pay the premium on behalf of the shareholder in a cross-purchase agreement. Direct payment by the corporation would be a constructive dividend to the shareholder and represent both a nondeductible distribution by the corporation and taxable income to the shareholder.

Receipt of Death Proceeds

The receipt of life insurance proceeds by a surviving shareholder on the life of the deceased shareholder will not usually result in federal income tax liability. However, the proceeds could be taxable to some extent if the transfer-for-value rule discussed earlier applies. For this reason a shareholder should avoid purchasing an existing policy from another individual to fund a cross-purchase agreement.

Transfer of Stock

The transfer of stock by the estate to the purchasing surviving shareholder will be treated as a sale or exchange. This means that the estate will recognize a taxable gain to the extent that the sale proceeds exceed the estate's adjusted basis in the stock. Fortunately the estate receives a basis step-up to fair market value for all property that is held by the decedent at the time of death. A properly drawn buy-sell agreement will peg the estate tax value of the stock to the purchase price specified in the purchase agreement. This means that the sale proceeds will typically be equal to the stepped-up basis of the estate in the stock and no gain will be recognized. For buy-sell agreements occurring at times other than at the death of a shareholder, the usual tax rules related to the sale of corporate stock apply.

The surviving shareholders are responsible for purchasing the deceased shareholder's stock in a cross-purchase agreement. If the corporation assumes the shareholders' obligation to purchase the decedent's stock, the purchase price will be treated as a constructive dividend to the purchasing shareholders subject to ordinary income tax. However, if the surviving shareholders make the payment to purchase the decedent’s stock, they will receive a basis in the shares of stock they purchase equal to the purchase price.

Estate Tax Considerations

In a properly designed cross-purchase agreement the deceased shareholder's estate will include the value of the stock as specified in the valuation provision of the buy-sell agreement. Court cases have dealt with the situation in which a cross-purchase agreement is designed with the insured shareholder's estate as the beneficiary of the insurance proceeds. Presumably this beneficiary designation was selected by the shareholders to ensure that their estates would receive the insurance proceeds as the purchase price.

This arrangement will normally not result in adverse estate tax consequences if the insurance proceeds are received pursuant to a plan that binds the estate to transfer the stock to the purchasing shareholders. The cases have held that the maximum of either (1) the value of the stock or (2) the insurance proceeds, but not both, will be included in the decedent's gross estate. However, this arrangement is not advised since it may expose both proceeds and the stock to claims of estate creditors.

TAXATION OF THE INSURED STOCK-REDEMPTION PLAN

Income Tax

Premium Payments

Premium payments by a corporation for the purchase of life insurance covering the life of a shareholder are nondeductible if the corporation is either a direct or an indirect beneficiary of the policy. In a properly designed stock-redemption agreement the corporation will be the beneficiary of the policy. If any other entity or individual is the beneficiary of the policy and uses the proceeds to fulfill the corporation's obligation to purchase the stock, the corporation is indirectly benefiting from the policy and the premium will be nondeductible. This situation might occur if the stock-redemption agreement is transacted through a trust arrangement.

Payment of premiums by the corporation on the life of a shareholder to fund the stock-redemption agreement will not result in taxable income to the shareholder. This is true even if the shareholder's estate is named as the policy beneficiary, provided the agreement binds the shareholder's estate to transfer the stock to the corporation on receipt of the proceeds.

Receipt of Death Proceeds

The receipt of death proceeds by the corporation from a policy used to fund the stock redemption is income tax free even if the policy was transferred to the corporation for valuable consideration by a shareholder. You should recall that an exception to the transfer-for-value rule is provided when the transfer is made to the corporation in which the insured is a shareholder.

The amount of death proceeds in excess of the premiums paid by the corporation will increase the corporation's earnings and profits, which (1) allows the corporation to distribute additional dividends or (2) may increase the corporation's exposure to the accumulated-earnings tax.

Transfer of Stock

The corporation will usually not have a tax liability when the insured redemption is performed. There is no gain to recognize since the sale proceeds should be equivalent to the value of the stock redeemed. However, if appreciated property is distributed to the estate in lieu of the insurance proceeds, the corporation will have to recognize a taxable gain in the amount of the excess of the fair market value over the adjusted basis of the property distributed. If the corporation instead distributes property with an adjusted basis in excess of its fair market value in redemption of the deceased shareholder's stock, the loss inherent in the property will not be recognized for tax purposes. For these reasons the corporation should not distribute property when redeeming stock.

The deceased shareholder's estate hopes to receive sale-or-exchange treatment on the stock redemption. Since the estate will receive a stepped-up basis in the stock, this tax treatment will result in no taxable gain to the estate. However, stock redemptions are treated as dividend distributions if certain complex tax rules are not satisfied. Obviously the stock redemption should be planned to avoid this dividend treatment.

Alternative Minimum Tax

The alternative minimum tax (AMT) imposed on larger corporations may have an impact on the insured stock-redemption plan because a properly structured arrangement will include corporate-owned life insurance. The tax is equal to 20 percent of the alternative minimum taxable income (AMTI) base of the corporation. The AMTI is determined by adding a list of tax-preference items to the regular taxable income of the corporation. The corporation will have to pay this tax if it exceeds the corporation's regular tax income liability for its tax year. Among the preferences added to the AMTI is current adjusted earnings providing for an increase in the regular taxable income base by an amount equal to 75 percent of the current adjusted earnings over AMTI (including all preferences except this current adjusted earnings amount). Corporate-owned life insurance has the following impact on current adjusted earnings:

- Current adjusted earnings is increased by the excess of the annual increase in cash surrender value over the annual premium for the policy.
- Current adjusted earnings is increased by the amount of death proceeds over the policy's cash surrender value.
- There is *not* a decrease in adjusted current earnings if the policy premium exceeds the annual increase in cash surrender value.

The earnings preference specified above resulting from corporate ownership of life insurance might cause an insured stock-redemption agreement to expose the closely held corporation to an alternative minimum tax liability. However, there is an exemption for smaller corporations (generally, those corporations with average annual gross receipts of $7.5 million or less over the previous 3 years).

Estate Tax

Since the corporation is both the owner and the beneficiary of the policy used to fund the stock-redemption agreement, the insurance proceeds are excluded from the gross estate of the deceased shareholder. However, theincidents of ownership in a life insurance policy held by a corporation on the life of a controlling shareholder may be attributed to the controlling shareholder's estate. Court cases and IRS regulations provide that these incidents will not be attributed to the controlling shareholder's estate if the death proceeds are payable to the benefit of the corporation. The IRS takes the position that the proceeds of a policy payable to a corporation to fund the redemption of a controlling shareholder's stock are not includible in the deceased shareholder's estate. In this situation the corporation is the irrevocable beneficiary and owner of the policy. However, the policy proceeds must be considered in determining the value of the stock in the majority shareholder's gross estate.

In the case of a minority shareholder the proceeds payable to the corporation to fund the redemption of the minority shareholder's stock will not be included in the minority shareholder's estate. Furthermore, the proceeds will not be considered in the valuation of the minority shareholder's stock unless the buy-sell agreement's valuation provision includes consideration of the insurance proceeds in the purchase price.

BUY-SELL AGREEMENTS FOR S CORPORATIONS

S corporations have become extremely popular for owners of closely held corporations for many reasons. First, there may be state income tax advantages for S corporations. Second, S corporations will avoid gain recognition at the corporate level for appreciated property acquired and held while the corporation operated under the S election. Third, S corporation rules permit significantly more flexibility in structuring the ownership of an S corporation. Finally, many business owners will not revoke the S election since they will want to avoid the expense of professional advisers to evaluate the decision. The financial services professional must be aware of the continuing importance of S corporations and the special factors to be considered for continuation planning.

Preserving the Election Through Buy-Sell Agreements

S corporations create a special need for a binding shareholder agreement concerning the disposition of stock. Only certain small business corporations are eligible for the subchapter S election. A corporation is ineligible for the election if it has

- more than 100 shareholders (members of the same family are treated as only one shareholder for this purpose)
- shareholders who are corporations, partnerships, nonresident aliens, or ineligible trusts
- a class of stock other than voting and nonvoting common stock

Actions that cause the S corporation to fail to meet the requirements of S status will cause termination of the S election. Furthermore, this termination might prevent a future S election by the disqualified corporation for 5 years. Recent tax changes give the IRS more flexibility to waive inadvertent terminations and permit reelection of S status. However, since the S election was presumably made in an effort to save taxes, actions that disqualify the corporation can result in unnecessary taxes and should be avoided.

A corporation making or contemplating the S election should take steps through a shareholder agreement to prevent unexpected terminations. The shareholder agreement should be designed to prevent the disposition of S corporation stock to an ineligible shareholder. The binding buy-sell agreement with a lifetime first-offer provision should be formed for this purpose.

Generally a shareholder agreement can prevent a disqualifying disposition by including a provision such as the following:

> Each shareholder warrants and represents to the S corporation and to the other shareholders that he or she shall not, without the consent of the other shareholders, take any action, or dispose of his or her shares of stock in the S corporation, that will result in the termination of the S election.

The mandatory buy-sell agreement operative on the death of a shareholder can prevent any transfers to ineligible shareholders. Obviously the standard stock-redemption or cross-purchase arrangements would cause the deceased S corporation shareholder's stock to be retired by the corporation or transferred to individuals who already own stock in the S corporation. Along with the usual benefits of a buy-sell agreement preventing outsiders from owning stock in the corporation, the classic buy-sell arrangement will prevent termination of the S election. As always, these restrictions on stock transfers must be reasonable to be legally enforceable and should be clearly indicated by endorsement on the stock certificate.

As an additional safeguard to prevent disqualifying transfers of stock by a shareholder, the S corporation might use a trustee to monitor the agreement. The trustee will hold the shares of stock for the S corporation shareholders and ensure that the stock is disposed of only in accordance with the conditions of the buy-sell agreement.

The trustee can also be vested with the power to vote the share of stock since a voting trust is not a disqualifying shareholder. The voting trust can be a useful arrangement if the shareholders of a regular corporation contemplate the possibility of an S election in the future. If this decision is made, the trustee of the voting trust will file all the necessary consents for the election as authorized under the provisions of the shareholder's agreement. This voting trust can be a useful ongoing device to provide consistent management to the S corporation, preventing interference from individual shareholders.

The Taxation of Buy-Sell Agreements for the S Corporation

The basic structure of the corporate buy-sell agreement is unchanged by an S election—that is, the usual choices of the cross-purchase arrangement or the stock-redemption plan are available. However, S corporations are taxed differently from regular (C) corporations. Therefore the financial services professional should be aware of the special tax aspects since the S status is widely employed for small businesses.

Cross-Purchase Agreements

The S corporation cross-purchase agreement is taxed similarly to the cross-purchase agreement between shareholders of a C corporation. That is, the agreement is treated as a sale or exchange of stock between the purchasing surviving shareholders and the decedent's estate.

If the agreement is funded by life insurance, the shareholders will pay for the premiums with expensive after-tax dollars. Of course, the proceeds from the insurance will be received tax free, and the purchase price will result in an increase in the purchasing shareholders' basis in their stock by the amount of the purchase price.

One significant difference does exist between the tax treatment of cross-purchase agreements in S corporations and the tax treatment in C corporations. The IRS has taken the position that interest on a debt incurred to purchase S corporation stock by a material participant will be treated as a trade or business expense and will be fully deductible if the assets of the corporation are used solely in the conduct of a trade or business. This means that a shareholder-employee of an S corporation may deduct the interest incurred in the installment buyout of a coshareholder.

If the purchaser is a passive investor, the interest deduction is subject to restrictive limits. You will recall that the interest paid on a debt that is incurred to purchase C corporation stock is typically treated as investment interest and is subject to limitations. Therefore an S corporation cross-purchase agreement is more likely to be funded by an installment obligation than is a C corporation buy-sell agreement.

Stock-Redemption Agreements

Since an S corporation cannot deduct premiums paid on insurance to fund a stock-redemption agreement, the funds used to pay the premiums will be treated as undistributed net income of the corporation and consequently will be included in the shareholders' taxable incomes. These nondeductible premium expenditures also serve to reduce the basis of the shareholders in proportion to their ownership interests, resulting in the same subsidy effect that occurred with the C corporation stock-redemption plan. That is, the older and higher-interest shareholders will be assisting in the funding of their own buyout.

EXAMPLE

Sage and Brush are coshareholders of Sagebrush, Inc., an S corporation. The facts related to the stock-redemption buy-sell agreement are as follows:

	Sage	Brush
Age	65	35
Ownership	90 shares	10 shares
Basis in stock	$50,000	$20,000
Annual premiums required to fund redemption	$19,000	$1,000

The total annual premiums required to fund the agreement ($20,000) must be paid out of the profits of Sagebrush but are not a deductible expense. Therefore, Sage and Brush have taxable income from these amounts related to their percentage of ownership. Sage must report $18,000 (90 percent of $20,000) of taxable income related to the profits used to purchase the insurance, while Brush must report $2,000 (10 percent of $20,000) of taxable income. When the premiums are paid as a nondeductible expense, the shareholders will lower their basis in Sagebrush stock, again in relation to their percentage of ownership. That is, Sage's basis is reduced to $32,000 ($50,000 – $18,000), while Brush reduces his basis to $18,000 ($20,000 – $2,000). As you can see, Sage is effectively funding the majority of the buy-sell agreement, which will probably operate in favor of Brush.

The treatment of the redemption for tax purposes will depend first on whether the redemption qualifies for sale-or-exchange (capital-gains) treatment. If the redemption does qualify, the distribution to the estate to redeem a deceased shareholder's stock will result in no taxable gain to the estate. Of course, this is due to the step-up in basis available to the estate for property held at the date of death. The rules covering qualification of a redemption as a sale or exchange are the subject of the next chapter.

earnings and profits (E & P)

The income tax treatment of a redemption not qualifying for sale-or-exchange treatment will depend on the circumstances existing in the S corporation. The principal question is whether the S corporation has accumulated *earnings and profits (E & P)*. If no E & P exists, a redemption is taxed as a capital gain regardless of whether the redemption qualifies for sale-or-exchange treatment. That is, the redeemed shareholder must pay capital-gains tax on the excess of the redemption proceeds over the shareholder's adjusted basis in the stock. This treatment is logical since the S corporation shareholder has already paid ordinary income tax on the corporation's income if no E & P exists. An S corporation will not have E & P under two circumstances. First, a corporation electing S status at its inception will not have E & P since all income has already passed through to the shareholders for tax purposes. Second, an existing C corporation may have no E & P at the time the shareholders decide to make the S election. In either case a redemption will not have to qualify for sale-or-exchange treatment to receive favorable capital-gains treatment. Of course this means that a redemption of a deceased shareholder's stock will result in no taxable gain due to the favorable basis step-up available to the estate.

When a redemption occurs in an S corporation with accumulated E & P, the qualification for sale-or-exchange treatment becomes significant. If the redemption qualifies, the estate will recognize no taxable gain due to the basis step-up. However, if the redemption does not qualify, the distribution may result in ordinary taxable income (taxable at the rate applicable to dividends—currently 15 percent) to the estate. The actual amount of the distribution that will be treated as ordinary income depends on complex S corporation accounting rules that are beyond the scope of this text. In general terms redemption proceeds in excess of undistributed S corporation earnings will be taxed as ordinary income to the seller to the extent of accumulated E & P.

Since many corporations have made the S corporation election, the financial services professional should be aware that a stock-redemption plan in these corporations must qualify as a sale or exchange or adverse tax consequences might occur.

You should recall that stock redemption by a C corporation funded by life insurance will not result in an increase in basis to the surviving shareholders. This will cause greater capital gain to the surviving shareholders who subsequently sell their stock than if the shareholders form the buy-sell agreement in a cross-purchase fashion. Fortunately the S corporation stock redemption can be designed to avoid this problem.

Since the corporation owns and is beneficiary of the life insurance policies funding the stock-redemption agreement, the S corporation receives the proceeds tax free when a shareholder dies. The receipt of the proceeds by the S corporation increases the basis of the shareholders in their stock in proportion to their ownership interest. If the receipt of the insurance proceeds and redemption occurs in the same tax year, all the shareholders, including the deceased shareholder, get a proportionate share of this basis increase.

EXAMPLE

Manny and Jack each own 50 percent of the stock in Esco, an S corporation. The corporation has an insured stock-redemption plan that provides that the corporation will redeem a deceased shareholder's stock from his estate for $200,000. At Manny's death the $200,000 of insurance proceeds is received by Esco, increasing each shareholder's basis by $100,000.

The basis increase demonstrated in the above example is helpful to the surviving shareholder if the shareholder will subsequently sell his or her stock. However, the basis increase in the deceased shareholder's stock is wasted since the estate already qualifies for the automatic step-up in basis to the fair market value of the stock at the date of death.

CHAPTER REVIEW

Key Terms and Concepts

- stock-redemption arrangement
- sale-or-exchange treatment
- wait-and-see buy-sell
- insurable interest
- earnings and profits (E & P)

Review Questions

The answers to the review questions are in the supplement. The self-test questions and the answers to them are also in the supplement and on The American College Online.

1. Many of the basic provisions of a partnership buy-sell agreement are also found in a corporate buy-sell agreement. List the basic provisions that are common to both partnership and corporate buy-sell agreements. [1]

2. For each of the following clauses in a typical corporate buy-sell agreement, state the basic content of the clause and its purpose:
   a. the first-offer commitment
   b. the provision for stamping the stock certificates
   c. the provisions governing the life insurance policies purchased to fund the agreement
   d. the provision modifying or terminating the agreement [1]

3. There are two types of corporation agreements-cross-purchase and stock-redemption (entity). Explain how each of the following factors and desired results would favor the adoption by a corporation's stockholders of one type of agreement over the other: [2]
   a. convenience and practicality
   b. equity of results
   c. desired ratio of stockholdings among survivors
   d. relative top income tax rates of the stockholders and the corporation

4. Anne and Barbara, equal stockholders in the AB Corporation, have decided to enter into a funded buy-sell agreement. How would each of the following factors tend to affect their decision, if at all, regarding the adoption of a cross-purchase plan or a stock-redemption plan? Explain. [2]
   a. They plan to use the existing policies that each owns on her life.
   b. The surviving stockholder would probably not sell her interest in the business during her lifetime.

5. Special corporate tax rules come into play if insurance policies are owned by the corporation in a stock-redemption agreement. Describe the impact of the following tax provisions: [3]
   a. accumulated-earnings tax
   b. alternative minimum tax

6. [3]
   a. Discuss the structure of a wait-and-see buy-sell agreement.
   b. Summarize the benefits of using this flexible arrangement.

7. What solution does state law provide at the death of a professional-corporation shareholder in the absence of a prearranged agreement? [3]

8. Who are the potential purchasing parties for a sole-shareholder professional-corporation buy-sell agreement? [3]

9. Discuss whether the insurable-interest concept is a barrier to the insured corporate cross-purchase agreement. [3]

10. Identify the recommended ownership premium payment and beneficiary-designation provision of the insured corporate buy-sell agreement. [3]

11. How does the use of a trustee in a cross-purchase agreement change the mechanics of the usual insurance funding arrangement? [3]

12. Discuss how the use of a trustee facilitates the actual purchase under a trusteed buy-sell agreement. [3]

13. Reed, Sterling, and Tucker are stockholders in the Rust Corporation. You have been invited to attend a meeting of the three stockholders at which you are told that they would like to arrange a cross-purchase agreement between the shareholders. Sterling suggests the following plan: The corporation should be applicant, owner, and premium payer for life insurance on the life of each owner to fund the agreement, but the beneficiary should be the survivors. When a stockholder dies the insurance proceeds will be paid to the survivors, and the estate will turn the deceased's stock over after receiving the proceeds from the survivors. Discuss the income tax treatment of (i) premiums and (ii) death proceeds to the corporation and the stockholders. [4]

14. Will inappropriate beneficiary designations typically result in inclusion of both the stock and death proceeds in the gross estate of a deceased shareholder in an insured buy-sell agreement? Discuss. [4]

15. Why is a buy-sell agreement particularly important for an S corporation? [5]

16. Under what circumstances might a redemption of S corporation stock from a deceased shareholder's estate result in adverse income tax consequences? [5]

PLANNING FOR STOCK REDEMPTIONS 8

Learning Objectives

An understanding of the material in this chapter should enable the student to

1. Identify the primary tax objective for a corporate stock-redemption agreement, describe the general rule for corporate distributions for federal income tax purposes, and explain the exception granted for certain stock redemptions.
2. List and describe the four types of stock redemptions that will receive capital-gain treatment under Sec. 302.
3. Explain how the attribution rules may prevent a stock redemption from qualifying for capital-gain treatment, identify the potential persons or entities from whom stock may be attributed, and describe how the family attribution rule can be waived in a complete redemption.
4. Describe the problems facing a decedent's estate that may be solved through a stock redemption under Sec. 303.
5. Give the rules for qualifying for a Sec. 303 stock redemption, and describe the amount of stock that can be redeemed under a Sec. 303 redemption.
6. Discuss the planning applications of Sec. 303 redemptions.

Many problems in financial and estate planning for shareholders in closely held corporations can be solved through redemptions of some or all of their stock. The Internal Revenue Code defines a redemption of stock as an acquisition by a corporation of its own stock from a shareholder "in exchange for property, whether or not stock so acquired is canceled, retired, or held as Treasury stock."

In many states local law provides that a corporation cannot purchase its own stock without adequate surplus funds or if the corporation would be rendered insolvent as a result of the redemption. For this reason the financial planner should be aware of local corporation law, including how it determines the amount of a corporation's surplus, whenever a redemption of stock is considered.

For tax-planning purposes the primary objective in arranging a stock redemption is to achieve capital-gain treatment as opposed to dividend treatment on the exchange of stock for money or other property. If the transaction is treated as a dividend distribution rather than as a capital transaction, the redemption proceeds will be taxable as ordinary income.

Capital transactions are subject to tax treatment that is more favorable than the treatment that applies to dividends. First, an individual's capital losses are deductible in full against capital gains for any given year. On the other hand, net capital losses are deductible against ordinary income only to the extent of $3,000 per year. Capital losses, therefore, can "shelter" capital gains fully.

Second, in a capital transition a taxpayer receives back his or her basis as a tax-free return of capital when property is sold. This can be very important, for example, if a shareholder's basis in redeemed stock is high. Of course, return of basis is much less significant if the redeemed shareholder's basis in the shares is very low. In addition there is a lower maximum tax rate on long-term capital gains than on ordinary income—15 percent vis-a-vis 35 percent (until 2013). This would further increase the benefit of treating a corporation distribution as a capital transaction.

It is important to note in this context that an estate receives a stepped-up basis in a decedent's stock that is generally equal to the value of the stock at the date of the decedent's death. Therefore the qualification of a redemption from an estate as a capital transaction is very important. Stock redemptions from estates that qualify as capital transactions will usually provide little or no income tax liability because the redemption price will be approximately equal to the estate's basis in the decedent's stock. (Note, however, that the corporate AMT may apply to the corporate-owned life insurance used to fund the stock redemption.)

On the other hand, if a stock redemption from a decedent's estate is treated as a dividend, the estate's stepped-up basis in the stock is ignored, and the full amount of the redemption proceeds will be taxed as a dividend to the extent of the corporation's earnings and profits. Hence, qualification as a sale-or-exchange is extremely important when planning a stock redemption.

GENERAL RULES FOR TAXATION OF CORPORATE DISTRIBUTIONS

Unless the Internal Revenue Code provides otherwise, a distribution of property from a corporation to a shareholder is treated as a dividend to the extent of the corporation's current and accumulated earnings and profits. "Earnings and profits" are computed according to tax accounting principles. It may be said that the earnings and profits of a corporation for a given taxable year are determined by reference to the corporation's income; with some positive and negative adjustments.

However, if a distribution that would otherwise be taxable as a dividend is in excess of the corporation's earnings and profits, the amount distributed by the corporation in excess of its earnings and profits is treated as a capital transaction. That is, the amount of excess is treated as a return of capital to the extent of the shareholder's basis in the stock. The balance, if any, will be treated as capital gain. In addition, there will be a capital-gains tax at the corporate level if appreciated corporate property is distributed in the redemption.

EXAMPLE

Mark is the sole shareholder in the Commonwealth Corporation, which has $40,000 in current and accumulated earnings and profits. Mark's basis in his Commonwealth stock is $6,000. The corporation distributes to Mark $50,000, which is not compensation for his services. Of this amount Mark must treat $40,000 as a dividend, taxable as ordinary income. The next $6,000 of the distribution is treated as a return of Mark's capital investment in the Commonwealth stock. His basis in the stock is thereby reduced to zero. The remaining $4,000 of the distribution will be treated as capital gain.

Taxation of Corporate Distributions

- In general, a distribution to a shareholder is treated as a dividend to the extent of the corporation's current and accumulated earnings and profits; therefore, it is taxed as ordinary income.
- A distribution in excess of the above is treated as a capital transaction; therefore, it is treated first as a return of capital, then taxed as a capital gain.

REDEMPTIONS THAT ARE TREATED AS CAPITAL TRANSACTIONS

As already stated, the general rule provides that dividend treatment is applied to the proceeds of a redemption to the extent of the corporation's current and accumulated earnings and profits. However, the tax law provides exceptions to the general rule. These exceptions apply to certain types of redemptions in which the redeemed shareholder's percentage of ownership of the corporation is materially affected by the redemption. These types of redemptions are treated as capital transactions rather than as dividend distributions.

One type of redemption treated under the general rule is a pro rata redemption. A redemption that is pro rata among shareholders does not change the percentages of ownership, so the redeemed shareholder's percentage of ownership is not affected.

EXAMPLE

Two shareholders each own a 50 percent interest in a corporation, and the corporation redeems half of each shareholder's stock. After the redemption both shareholders still have the same proportionate interest in the corporation that they had before the redemption. The ownership of the corporation has not been materially affected by the transaction. Therefore the proceeds will be treated as a dividend distribution to the extent of current and accumulated earnings and profits.

The Internal Revenue Code contains specific provisions describing certain types of redemptions that materially affect a shareholder's percentage of ownership. If a given redemption qualifies under one of these provisions, the transaction will be treated as a capital transaction for tax purposes.

Sec. 302 allows such treatment for the following four types of redemptions:

- a redemption that is not essentially equivalent to a dividend
- a substantially disproportionate redemption
- a complete redemption
- a distribution to a noncorporate shareholder in partial liquidation of the distributing corporation

Redemptions Not Essentially Equivalent to a Dividend

not essentially equivalent to a dividend

A redemption that is *not essentially equivalent to a dividend* involves questions of fact. Each redemption for which a taxpayer seeks treatment under this provision must be evaluated according to its particular facts if the IRS challenges capital-gain treatment claimed by the redeemed shareholder. There are several revenue rulings in which the IRS has conceded that certain redemptions resulted in a "meaningful reduction" in a shareholder's interest in a corporation. A meaningful reduction is required for a redemption to be considered not essentially equivalent to a dividend. This is not a mathematical test, but a subjective one.

The wisest course of action for a planner is to enlist the aid of a competent tax attorney to obtain a private ruling from the IRS for any redemption that must be evaluated under this subjective test.

Substantially Disproportionate Redemptions

substantially disproportionate redemption

The second category under Sec. 302 is that of a *substantially disproportionate redemption.* Sec. 302 provides for automatic qualification of a substantially disproportionate redemption as a capital transaction if a mathematical safe-harbor test is met. The test defines a substantially disproportionate redemption as follows:

- After the redemption the shareholder must own less than 50 percent of the total voting power of the corporation.
- The shareholder's percentage ownership of voting stock of the corporation after the redemption must be less than 80 percent of the shareholder's preredemption percentage ownership of voting stock.
- The shareholder's percentage ownership of common stock of the corporation after the redemption must also be less than 80 percent of his or her percentage ownership of common stock before the redemption.

EXAMPLE

Sobel and Sherman (unrelated individuals) each own 400 of the 800 outstanding voting common shares of Thor Industries, Inc. Thor has no other classes of stock outstanding. A proposal is made to redeem 300 of Sobel's shares. Under the test for substantially disproportionate redemptions, the following results:

- After the redemption Sobel will own 100 of the 500 outstanding Thor shares. This is less than 50 percent, so the first test is met.
- Before the redemption, Sobel's interest was 50 percent of Thor. Eighty percent of 50 percent is 40 percent. After the redemption, Sobel's interest will be 20 percent of Thor (100 of the 500 outstanding voting common shares). Because this is less than 40 percent, the 80 percent test is met for both voting and common stock, since only one class of stock is outstanding.

The redemption will thus qualify as substantially disproportionate.

It is important to note that for purposes of the 80 percent test, the shareholder's proportionate percentage of ownership is the ratio of his or her shares owned to the total shares outstanding. Therefore both parts of the ratio will change after the redemption. The postredemption ratio must reflect the reduction in the total number of shares outstanding. The planner should multiply the preredemption ratio of ownership by 80 percent. Any postredemption ratio that is less than 80 percent of the preredemption ratio is an acceptable reduction of percentage ownership under the 80 percent test.

Complete Redemptions

complete redemption

A *complete redemption* of the shareholder's interest in the corporation is the third category under Sec. 302. To qualify for capital treatment under this category, the corporation must redeem all the stock the shareholder owns. If the redemption is a complete redemption, it will be treated in its entirety as a capital transaction.

Redemptions That Avoid Dividend Treatment

- Not essentially equivalent to a dividend
- Substantially disproportionate
  - 50 percent test
  - 80 percent test
- Complete termination of ownership

Partial Liquidations

partial liquidation

The fourth category under Sec. 302 is that of a distribution in which there is *partial liquidation* of the distributing corporation. In determining whether a redemption qualifies under this category, the nature of the distribution must be examined at the corporate level, rather than from the point of view of the shareholder receiving proceeds.

ATTRIBUTION OF STOCK OWNERSHIP

attribution

Attribution of ownership means that stock owned by one individual or entity is considered to be owned by another individual or entity for the purpose of determining how a particular transaction is taxed.

In evaluating a redemption under each of the first three categories described above, the rules for attribution of stock ownership must be considered. Attribution may adversely affect the tax treatment of a redemption. Also referred to as constructive ownership, attribution can cause a redemption that would otherwise be taxable as a capital transaction to be treated as a dividend distribution to the extent of the corporation's current and accumulated earnings and profits, since attribution changes a shareholder's percentage of ownership for purposes of determining the tax effects of a redemption.

The rationale for attribution of ownership is that a shareholder may effectively control the operation of a corporation through shares owned by related individuals and entities as well as through shares he or she actually owns. Although this may not in fact be true in many instances, redemptions should always be structured to comply with the attribution rules when these rules are applicable.

Any redemption involving stock of a corporation owned by related parties should be evaluated with these rules in mind. An understanding of the basic elements of constructive ownership is particularly important for planners who deal with transactions involving changes in stock ownership in corporations owned by family members.

Attribution of Stock Ownership

- Stock owned by the stockholder's parents, spouse, children, and grandchildren
- Stock owned by a partnership in which the stockholder is a partner
- Stock owned by an estate in which the shareholder has a direct present beneficial interest
- Stock owned by a trust of which the shareholder is a beneficiary
- Stock owned by a corporation in which the shareholder is at least a 50 percent owner of the outstanding stock

Family Attribution

Stock owned by an individual shareholder's parents, spouse, children, and grandchildren will be attributed to the shareholder for purposes of determining the tax treatment of a redemption. Stock owned by the shareholder's grandparents or siblings will not be attributed. There is a rationale for these distinctions. In most instances dealings between siblings are more likely to be at arm's length than are dealings between parent and child or between spouses. In addition, it is a more natural situation for stock of a grandparent to pass to a grandchild and remain effectively controlled by the grandparent than for a grandchild to attempt to effectively exercise rights of ownership in stock owned by a grandparent.

Attribution From an Entity

In general, ownership of stock is attributed to a shareholder from an entity in proportion to the shareholder's interest in the entity. However, partnerships, estates, trusts, and corporations are all treated somewhat differently in the application of this general rule.

Attribution From Partnerships

If a partnership owns stock in a corporation, a partner is deemed to own that amount of stock owned by the partnership that is in proportion to the partner's interest in the partnership.

EXAMPLE

The Hamilton partnership owns 100 shares in Commonwealth Realty Corporation. Harold is a 50 percent partner in Hamilton and owns 100 shares in Commonwealth Realty, which redeems 25 of Harold's shares. For purposes of determining the tax treatment of Harold's redemption, Harold is also deemed to own 50 of the 100 shares in Commonwealth Realty owned by the Hamilton partnership.

Attribution From Estates

The general rule that ownership of stock is attributed to a shareholder from an entity in proportion to the shareholder's interest in the entity applies to attribution from an estate to a beneficiary of the estate. However, the beneficiary must have a direct present interest in the estate for attribution to occur. An individual holding a remainder interest in an estate would not have ownership of stock attributed from the estate. Also after an estate has completed its distribution of property to a beneficiary, any stock still owned by the estate will generally no longer be attributed to the beneficiary.

Attribution From Trusts

To determine whether stock owned by a trust is attributable to a trust beneficiary, another variation of the general rule is applied. An actuarial computation of a beneficiary's interest in a trust is made to determine the percentage of stock owned by the trust that will be attributed to the beneficiary. Therefore a beneficiary having only a remainder interest in a trust is subject to attribution of ownership from the trust, even though a remainder interest in an estate would not result in attribution to the beneficiary from the estate.

Attribution From Corporations

The general rule also applies in attributing ownership of stock from a corporation to a shareholder of the corporation, with one important modification. Stock ownership will be attributed from a corporation to a shareholder only if the shareholder is a 50-percent-or-greater owner of the value of all the outstanding stock of the corporation that owns the stock to be attributed.

EXAMPLE

Suppose Kevin is a 60 percent owner of the Building Corporation and also owns stock in the Hammer and Nail Corporation. The Building Corporation is also a shareholder in the Hammer and Nail Corporation. When the Hammer and Nail Corporation redeems a portion of Kevin's shares, 60 percent of the stock in Hammer and Nail that is owned by the Building Corporation will be attributed to Kevin for purposes of determining the tax treatment of Kevin's redemption. However, if Kevin were only a 49 percent owner of the Building Corporation, the stock in Hammer and Nail owned by Building would not be attributed to Kevin when Hammer and Nail redeems a portion of Kevin's shares.

Special Rule for S Corporations

It is important to note that the stock attribution rules treat an S corporation as if it were a partnership. Therefore to determine the attribution of stock ownership both to an S corporation and from an S corporation, the rules that apply to partnerships must be used.

Attribution to an Entity

When a corporation redeems shares owned by a partnership, estate, trust, or another corporation, the attribution rules must be examined to determine the tax treatment of the entity receiving proceeds of the redemption.

In general, all the stock owned by a partner, a beneficiary of an estate or trust, or a controlling shareholder in a corporation will be attributed to the partnership, estate, trust, or corporation.

EXAMPLE

The Horseshoe Corporation redeems stock owned by the Trail partnership. Marjorie, a partner in Trail, also owns stock in the Horseshoe Corporation. For purposes of determining the tax treatment of the redemption of Trail's stock in Horseshoe, Trail is deemed to own the stock in Horseshoe owned by Marjorie

There are modifications to this general rule that apply to trusts and to corporations.

Stock owned by a contingent beneficiary of a trust will not be attributed to a trust if, considering the trustee's discretionary powers under the trust instrument, the beneficiary's largest potential interest in the value of the trust property, determined actuarially, is 5 percent or less of the value of the trust property.

Stock in one corporation owned by a shareholder who also owns stock in a second corporation will not be attributed to the second corporation unless the shareholder owns 50 percent or more of the value of the second corporation that is receiving proceeds of a redemption by the first corporation.

EXAMPLE

Paul is a 40 percent owner of Landscape Corporation. Both Paul and Landscape Corporation own stock in the Tractor Corporation. Tractor redeems the Tractor stock owned by Landscape. To determine the tax treatment to Landscape in this transaction, stock in Tractor owned by Paul is not considered to be owned by Landscape since Paul owns less than 50 percent of Landscape.

Note how attribution to a corporation is not the same as attribution from a corporation. A corporation is deemed to own all the stock in another corporation owned by one of its shareholders if attribution applies. However, attribution of stock from a corporation to a shareholder receiving proceeds of a redemption by another corporation applies only to the extent of the shareholder's percentage interest in the corporation from which ownership is attributed.

EXAMPLE

Suppose Paul in the above example is a 50 percent owner of Landscape Corporation. Paul and Landscape each own 100 shares of the Tractor Corporation. If Tractor redeems Landscape's stock in Tractor, Landscape will be considered to own all 100 shares in Tractor owned by Paul. However, if Tractor redeems Paul's stock in Tractor, Paul will be considered to own only 50 of the shares in Tractor owned by Landscape.

Reattribution

The term *reattribution* refers to situations in which constructive ownership rules are combined to attribute ownership from one shareholder to another shareholder not directly related under the rules.

EXAMPLE 1

A father will be considered to own the stock owned by a trust of which his son is the sole beneficiary.

EXAMPLE 2

A corporation will be considered to own 50 percent of the stock owned by a partnership in which the corporation's sole shareholder is a 50 percent partner.

There are two important types of situations in which the Internal Revenue Code prohibits reattribution. First, the family ownership rules cannot be applied two times in succession.

EXAMPLE

A father will be considered to own stock that is owned by his son. Likewise, a daughter will be considered to own stock that is owned by her father. However, family attribution rules cannot be applied twice in succession to attribute ownership of the son's stock to the daughter. If this type of constructive ownership applied, it would result in sibling attribution.

The second situation in which reattribution is prohibited under the Internal Revenue Code is referred to as "sidewise" or "in-out" attribution. The effect of this exception is that there is no attribution between parties having an interest in the same entity.

EXAMPLE

Barbara and Maria are both partners in the Consultant Associates partnership. They both also own stock in the Employee Corporation. If the Consultant Associates partnership owns stock in Employee Corporation and receives proceeds of redemption from the corporation, it will be considered to own both Barbara's and Maria's stock in the corporation. However, if the Employee Corporation redeems Maria's stock, Maria will not be considered to own Barbara's stock in the Employee Corporation. Barbara's stock may be attributed into the Consultant Associates partnership, but it cannot be reattributed to Maria out of the partnership.

Waiver of Family Attribution in Complete Redemptions

waiver of family attribution

If a shareholder has all the stock he or she owns in a corporation redeemed, it is possible to avoid the application of the family attribution rules. In order to qualify for a *waiver of family attribution* in a complete redemption, a shareholder must comply with a number of requirements imposed by the Internal Revenue Code.

These requirements include the following:

- The redeemed shareholder may retain no interest in the corporation after the redemption. For these purposes "interest" includes the status of officer, director, or employee of the corporation. It is permissible for the redeemed shareholder to remain a creditor of the corporation.
- The redeemed shareholder must not acquire any prohibited interest in the corporation for a period of 10 years beginning on the date of the distribution of the redemption proceeds. However, if the redeemed shareholder receives stock in the corporation by bequest or inheritance, this provision is not violated.
- The redeemed shareholder must file an agreement with the IRS to notify it if any acquisition of a prohibited interest takes place within the 10-year period. The redeemed shareholder must retain the necessary records to comply with this requirement.

- The redeemed shareholder must not have acquired any portion of the stock redeemed during a 10-year period prior to the date of the redemption from a person whose stock would be attributable to the redeemed shareholder.
- The redeemed shareholder must not have transferred any stock in the redeeming corporation to any person whose stock would be attributed to the redeemed shareholder within a 10-year period before the date of distribution of the redemption proceeds. This requirement will not apply if the corporation also redeems such stock of the person to whom it was transferred by the redeemed shareholder.

The last two requirements above may not apply if the redeemed shareholder can show that the transfer or acquisition that is in question did not have the avoidance of federal income tax as one of its principal purposes. The waiver of attribution is available only in the case of a complete redemption.

The difficulty in waiving entity attribution is a significant roadblock to using a stock-redemption plan in the buy-sell agreement of a family corporation. The stock held by the beneficiaries of an estate will be attributed to the estate. This means that complete redemption of the stock held by the estate generally would be impossible since the waiver of attribution to an estate is difficult to effect. This will generally be a problem in a family corporation since heirs will often hold stock prior to the death of the senior family member.

It is possible to safely redeem the stock from the estate if prior to the redemption the heirs who hold stock receive complete distribution of their inheritances and waive further rights to the assets of the estate. After terminating the children's interest in the estate, the executor can cause the redemption of the stock since the entity attribution of the children's stock to the estate will no longer exist.

EXAMPLE

The ownership of the Connecticut Corporation is divided as follows:

Dad	90%
Daughter	5%
Son	5%

A stock-redemption agreement is in place between Dad and Connecticut. Dad's will provides an outright marital bequest of the stock and the residuary estate to Mom and a bequest of investment real estate to Daughter and Son. At Dad's death the redemption of the shares held by the estate prior to the satisfaction of any bequests will not qualify as a complete termination since Daughter's and Son's stock will be attributed to the estate due to the entity attribution rules. After the redemption the stock in Connecticut held by the children will be 100 percent of the outstanding shares of Connecticut. Their ownership will be attributed to the estate; thus the redemption of Dad's shares will not result in a complete redemption (nor will it be substantially disproportionate or not essentially equivalent to a dividend). The entire distribution, to the extent of Connecticut's E & P, will be received as a dividend. If the real estate is distributed to the children prior to the redemption, the children will no longer be beneficiaries of the estate at the time of the redemption and a complete termination redemption will be possible.

It is important to note that it is difficult in practice to terminate the beneficial status of the family heirs. This is particularly true if substantial distributions are required prior to the redemption since the estates of family corporation shareholders will generally not have the necessary liquidity until the redemption proceeds are received.

PLANNING OPPORTUNITIES WITH REDEMPTIONS

Shifting of Control

Redemptions are sometimes overlooked as a means of transferring a controlling interest in a corporation. In the case of a corporation whose stock is owned by unrelated individuals, a substantially disproportionate redemption can be used to shift percentages of ownership by means of a transaction financed with corporate funds. If the shareholder who is to acquire a controlling interest in the corporation by means of the redemption does not have sufficient assets to finance an acquisition, a redemption may be the best solution for all concerned.

EXAMPLE

Ted owns 60 of the 100 outstanding shares in Life Style Corporation, and Jeff, an unrelated individual, owns the other 40 shares. Ted and Jeff have agreed that a controlling interest in Life Style is to be shifted to Jeff. Life Style Corporation has enough cash to fund a redemption, but Jeff does not have sufficient personal assets to finance the acquisition of a controlling interest.

In this situation, a redemption of at least 24 of Ted's 60 shares in Life Style will be sufficient to meet the test for a substantially disproportionate redemption and to shift the controlling interest to Jeff. In this way control of Life Style Corporation can be shifted to Jeff with no out-of-pocket expense for him.

Since Life Style has a substantial amount of cash, the corporation is in a better position to finance a transfer of the controlling interest. Ted's receipt of the redemption proceeds will be taxed as a capital transaction; that is, the amount of proceeds in excess of his basis in the Life Style shares that are redeemed will be treated as capital gain.

Termination of Interest

In a family corporation a complete termination type of redemption can be used to achieve capital-gain treatment for a controlling shareholder's redemption, as long as the controlling shareholder complies with the requirements for waiver of family attribution. It is often difficult for a withdrawing shareholder to sever his or her relations with the corporation just to comply with the waiver requirements. However, if the shareholder who is to acquire control of the corporation does not have the funds to purchase the controlling owner's shares, a termination-of-interest redemption with a waiver of family attribution may be the only viable alternative.

A termination-of-interest redemption with a waiver of family attribution is particularly appropriate for converting shares of a nonemployee-shareholder into cash.

EXAMPLE

The nonemployee-spouse of Cruise Corporation's controlling shareholder also owns shares in Cruise. Cruise redeems the spouse's shares. The spouse may comply with the waiver of attribution rules without terminating an established employee relationship.

Transactions Involving Family Members

The planner should also keep in mind the exceptions to the family attribution rules. In some situations it may be appropriate to transfer stock to one's grandparents in order to qualify a subsequent redemption from the transferor as a capital transaction. If the transferor-shareholder then inherits the stock back from the grandparents, no violation of the redemption or attribution rules has occurred.

It is also important to remember that if stock in a corporation is owned among brothers and/or sisters, family attribution does not apply, and capital-gain treatment can be achieved by means of a substantially disproportionate redemption.

The planner should remember that family attribution can be waived only in the case of a complete termination of interest type of redemption. There is no waiver of family attribution available to qualify a redemption as a substantially disproportionate redemption.

Use of Notes in Sec. 303 Redemption

Although the planner may find that a redemption is the most appropriate means of transferring a controlling interest in a corporation, the corporation may lack sufficient surplus to finance the redemption. This problem may sometimes be overcome by having the corporation issue installment obligations in exchange for the redeemed stock. As long as the installment obligation of the corporation is drafted properly and does not have any earmarks of an equity interest in the corporation, capital-gain treatment will not be jeopardized.

SEC. 303 REDEMPTIONS

The Internal Revenue Code contains a relief provision, Sec. 303, that applies to estates in which stock of a closely held corporation constitutes a substantial portion of total estate assets. The purpose of this section is to provide liquidity for such estates in order to avoid forced sales of the closely held stock to meet tax obligations and administration expenses.

Sec. 303 redemption

A *Sec. 303 redemption* allows distributions in redemption of such stock to be treated as made in exchange for a capital asset and therefore eligible for capital-gains treatment, subject to certain requirements and limitations. Sec. 303 is totally independent of the other Code provisions describing the tax treatment of redemptions of stock. Therefore neither the rules under Sec. 302 nor the constructive ownership rules need to be considered in determining whether favorable tax treatment is available under Sec. 303. As long as Sec. 303's own requirements are met, favorable tax treatment can be achieved.

What Estates May Qualify Under Sec. 303?

In order for an estate to be eligible for a Sec. 303 redemption, the value of corporate stock includible in the gross estate for federal estate tax purposes must be more than 35 percent of the value of the adjusted gross estate. The adjusted gross estate is defined for this purpose as the gross estate less deductions for funeral and administration expenses, debts, and deductible losses of the estate. To determine whether the corporate stock meets the percentage test, all classes of stock in the corporation owned by the estate are counted; that is, preferred is counted as well as common.

For estates that own stock in two or more corporations there is a variation of the 35 percent test. If the stock in the two or more corporations owned by the estate represents 20 percent or more of the outstanding value of all the stock in each corporation, the stock in the two or more corporations may be combined and treated as stock in one corporation for purposes of the 35 percent test. If the test is met by combining stock in two or more corporations, a Sec. 303 redemption may be made with shares of any of the two or more corporations.

EXAMPLE

Richard's estate needs liquidity to meet its tax obligations and administration expenses. The estate owns 100 shares in the Jersey Video Corporation. These shares represent 25 percent of the value of Richard's adjusted gross estate and 33 percent of the value of Jersey Video, Inc. The estate also owns 100 shares in Philly Stereo, Inc. These shares represent 15 percent of the value of Richard's adjusted gross estate and 25 percent of the value of Philly Video, Inc. Because the stock in each corporation owned by the estate represents 20 percent or more of the value of the stock in each corporation, and because the stock in the two corporations has a total value in excess of 35 percent of Richard's adjusted gross estate, Richard's estate will qualify for a Sec. 303 redemption.

There is one further wrinkle that applies only to the special rule for stock in two or more corporations. For purposes of the 20 percent requirement 100 percent of the value of stock the decedent held with his or her surviving spouse as community property or in joint tenancy, tenancy by the entirety, or tenancy in common is treated as having been included in the decedent's gross estate. This wrinkle applies only when the rule for stock in two or more corporations is applied and not to the 35 percent test in general.

How Much Stock May Be Redeemed Under Sec. 303?

There is a limitation on the dollar amount of proceeds received for redeemed stock that will qualify for favorable treatment under Sec. 303. Redemption proceeds eligible for favorable tax treatment may not exceed the sum of the estate, inheritance, legacy, and succession taxes for which the estate is liable (including interest, if any) and the amount of funeral and administration expenses that are allowable as deductions to the estate under the Internal Revenue Code.

The amount of proceeds qualifying for treatment under Sec. 303 will be further limited if the redeemed shareholder (usually the estate) is not legally liable for the full amount of the taxes and expenses. Only that portion of the taxes and expenses that the redeemed shareholder is legally obligated to pay is considered in determining the maximum amount of proceeds allowable under Sec. 303.

EXAMPLE

A trust owns stock in the Texas Corporation that is included in Alvin's gross estate. The trust instrument does not require the trust to pay a portion of the taxes or administration expenses of Alvin's estate. However, Fergus, the trustee, uses proceeds of a redemption of the trust's stock in Texas to pay a portion of Alvin's estate taxes. In this situation the trust may not treat the redemption under Sec. 303.

Who May Receive Favorable Tax Treatment Under Sec. 303?

If the requirements of Sec. 303 are met, any shareholder owning stock included in determining a decedent's gross estate is eligible for a Sec. 303 redemption. Generally the eligible shareholder will be either the decedent's estate itself or a beneficiary of the estate. However, in this context it is important to remember that unless a beneficiary of the estate has an obligation to pay death taxes or administration expenses, the beneficiary will not be eligible for Sec. 303 treatment.

When Must a Sec. 303 Redemption Be Made?

Sec. 303 treatment is available for distributions in redemption of stock made after the decedent's death and within 3 years and 90 days after the filing of the estate's federal estate tax return. If the estate has filed a petition in the

Tax Court concerning an estate tax dispute, the time limitation is extended until 60 days after the decision of the Tax Court becomes final.

Furthermore, if the estate has elected to pay its estate tax in installments under Sec. 6166 of the Internal Revenue Code, redemption distributions may receive the benefit of Sec. 303 if they are made within the time period of the installment payments.

Under any of these rules if redemption proceeds are paid more than 4 years after the death of the decedent, distributions eligible to be treated under Sec. 303 cannot exceed the lesser of the taxes and administration expenses remaining unpaid or the amount of such expenses that are paid within one year after the redemption.

Planning Considerations Under Sec. 303

Minimal Taxable Gain

Because of its fiduciary duties to its other shareholders, a corporation will generally redeem the stock of a decedent-shareholder at a price equal to the stock's current fair market value. For income tax purposes an estate or its beneficiary receives a "stepped-up" basis in a decedent's assets that is generally equal to the value of the assets as of the date of the decedent's death.

Therefore if a redemption is made under Sec. 303 within a short time after the decedent's death, the redemption price should be equal to or very close to the basis in the stock held by the estate or the beneficiary. Since proceeds in a Sec. 303 redemption are treated as received in the sale or exchange of a capital asset, and not as a dividend, there will generally be little or no taxable gain realized by the redeemed shareholder.

If the stock has increased in value between the time of the decedent's death and the time of the stock redemption, any amount that is in excess of the estate's or beneficiary's basis in the stock will be taxed as long-term capital gain. Therefore unless there has been a significant change in the corporation's fortunes during that time, the amount of taxable gain will probably not be significant.

Redemption of More Than One Shareholder

In some situations both the estate itself and a beneficiary of the estate may wish to take advantage of a Sec. 303 redemption. In such cases it is important to remember that the total amount of distributions that are allowable under Sec. 303 will be reduced by the first shareholder whose stock is redeemed.

EXAMPLE
Both an estate and its sole beneficiary are liable for the death taxes and administrative expenses of the estate. If part of the estate's stock is redeemed under Sec. 303 first, and the estate receives an amount equal to the full amount of death taxes and administrative expenses of the estate, the beneficiary receiving any remaining stock from the estate will not be able to treat proceeds of a later redemption under Sec. 303.

Redemptions in a Series

If the requirements under Sec. 303 are met, qualifying redemptions can be made in a series. As long as the estate or beneficiary receives the proceeds of the redemptions within the prescribed time limitations, more than one redemption can be made. This may be useful when the redeeming corporation needs some time to marshal enough assets to fund the full amount of the contemplated redemption proceeds.

Use of Notes

The redeeming corporation can issue notes in payment of its obligation in the redemption. Use of notes by the corporation will not jeopardize Sec. 303 treatment unless the IRS can show that the notes are not truly debt instruments but represent an equity interest in the corporation. The use of notes affords the corporation more time to fund the redemption since the installment payment dates for the notes may extend beyond the time limitations prescribed for Sec. 303 redemptions. The availability of the installment payment technique provides additional flexibility for both the corporation and the estate.

Use of Sec. 303 in a Liquid Estate

Proceeds in a redemption under Sec. 303 are limited by the amount of the estate's death taxes and administration expenses. However, there is no requirement that funds distributed in a Sec. 303 redemption must actually be used for those purposes. In other words, even an estate with sufficient liquidity to pay the qualifying expenses can take advantage of Sec. 303 as long as the percentage and time requirements of the section are met.

This allows an estate or beneficiary the opportunity to get funds out of the corporation with favorable tax treatment.

Accumulated-Earnings Tax

One problem that may arise in planning for the corporation to fund a Sec. 303 redemption is the accumulated-earnings tax. The Internal Revenue Code states specifically that corporate accumulations may be made to fund a Sec. 303 redemption without being subject to the accumulated-earnings tax. However, such accumulations are specifically exempt only when made in the taxable year of the corporation in which the decedent died or any taxable year thereafter. Therefore accumulations prior to the year of the decedent's death to meet an anticipated funding need for a redemption may present the corporation with an accumulated-earnings-tax problem. This problem is amplified by the requirement mentioned earlier that in some states a redemption may be effected only if the corporation has adequate surplus to fund the redemption.

If the IRS can show that the funding objective was not for a corporate purpose, but only for the benefit of the shareholder or the shareholder's estate, the accumulated-earnings tax may become a problem. It may be difficult to convince the IRS that a Sec. 303 redemption serves a business purpose of the corporation. Therefore as a practical matter the use of life insurance owned by the corporation may be the most appropriate method of funding a Sec. 303 redemption. Even though the accumulation of earnings to meet premium obligations for such insurance may be subject to the accumulated-earnings tax, the dollar amount needed for premiums will be substantially less than the dollar amount needed for cash funding. As a result, any possible exposure to the accumulated-earnings tax is minimized. The proper life insurance funding will also provide any surplus required to permit the redemption.

Sequence of Redemptions

The planner should also bear in mind that all redemptions qualifying under Sec. 303 reduce the dollar amount of the allowable limits applicable to Sec. 303 redemptions, even if the redemptions are also eligible for capital treatment under Sec. 302. If a proposed redemption will qualify as a sale or exchange under both Sec. 302 and Sec. 303 and the estate also wishes to use the maximum amount allowable under Sec. 303, careful planning is required. One possible approach is to make all redemptions qualifying only under Sec. 303 first. After the Sec. 303 dollar amount limitation has been reached, the state or beneficiary can then take advantage of Sec. 302 if favorable treatment is available under that section. This may avoid "wasting" potential Sec. 302 redemptions that would qualify for capital treatment even if Sec. 303 was not available.

CHAPTER REVIEW

Key Terms and Concepts

not essentially equivalent to a dividend
substantially disproportionate redemption
complete redemption
partial liquidation
attribution
waiver of family attribution
Sec. 303 redemption

Review Questions

The answers to the review questions are in the supplement. The self-test questions and the answers to them are also in the supplement and on The American College Online.

1. Explain why the qualification of an exchange for capital-gain tax treatment is extremely important in the context of stock redemptions. [1]

2. In general, how is a corporate distribution of cash or property treated for federal income tax purposes? [1]

3. Identify the types of redemptions that qualify as exceptions to the general rule for corporate distributions. [2]

4. What is the basic requirement for a redemption to be considered "not essentially equivalent to a dividend"? [2]

5. Will a redemption of nonvoting preferred stock be able to qualify as substantially disproportionate? Explain. [2]

6. Alice and Bertha are sisters and the sole owners of the AB Corporation. Alice owns 80 shares of the 100 shares outstanding and Bertha owns 20 shares. There is only one class of stock outstanding. Alice has decided to become less active in the business and wishes to have a portion of her shares redeemed in order to invest in another business. She does not wish to effect the redemption if the transaction will result in ordinary income tax treatment on the entire distribution. [2]
   a. If Alice were to have 50 shares redeemed, would such a redemption qualify as a substantially disproportionate redemption? Explain.
   b. Suppose she were to have 70 shares redeemed. Would this redemption qualify as a substantially disproportionate redemption? Explain.

7. If an individual shareholder's entire stock is redeemed (a complete redemption), the redemption is considered to be a capital transaction. Explain briefly how each of the following may prevent such a redemption from being considered a complete redemption: [3]
   a. stock ownership by certain members of the shareholder's family
   b. stock ownership by estates of which the shareholder is the beneficiary
   c. stock ownership by partnerships in which the shareholder is a partner
   d. stock ownership by trusts of which the shareholder is a beneficiary
   e. stock ownership by corporations owned by the shareholder

8. What family relationships will result in attribution of stock ownership to the individual whose stock is redeemed? [3]

9. Dad's stock is attributed to Junior under the family attribution rules. Briefly describe the circumstances under which stock owned by other persons or entities related to Dad could also be attributed to Junior. [3]

10. Where an estate is to be redeemed, rather than an individual, what is the principal attribution problem that is likely to be encountered in a family corporation? [3]

11. Matt and his sister, Nan, founded the MN Corporation a number of years ago. Of the 1,000 shares of stock outstanding Matt owns 750 and his sister owns 250. Matt died recently, and under the terms of his will he left Nan one of his two automobiles and bequeathed the remainder of his estate to his wife, Wilma. The MN Corporation is extremely liquid. The executor has agreed with Nan that the corporation will redeem the 750 shares of stock owned by Matt's estate before the estate is settled. [3]
   a. Would Nan's stock ownership be attributed to Matt's estate under the circumstances? Explain.
   b. Would Nan's stock ownership be attributed to Matt's estate if the redemption occurs after the executor has distributed the automobile to Nan? Explain.

12. Farley founded the FS Corporation 25 years ago and was the sole stockholder until 15 years ago when he gave his daughter, Sarah, 50 percent of the common stock, the only class of stock outstanding. Farley wants to retire from the business and proposes to have all his stock redeemed so that he can make other investments. [3]
   a. Explain why the proposed redemption will not be treated as a complete redemption (and therefore will be taxed as ordinary income) unless Farley takes certain specific steps.
   b. What conditions must Farley satisfy in order to avoid the effect of the family attribution rules and have the redemption treated as a complete termination of interest?

13. Sec. 303 gives the executor of the estate of a sole stockholder or a stockholder in a family business the opportunity to redeem stock of the corporation on a favorable income tax basis. Describe the income tax treatment of a stock redemption under Sec. 303. [4]

14. Miles is president of the MNO Corporation, which has a fair market value of $6 million. He owns 60 percent of the stock, and his long-time associate, Norm, owns the remaining 40 percent. Both Miles and Norm have sons who are active in the business and are taking more and more responsibility while Miles and Norm are devoting less time to the business. Both fathers want their stock to remain in the family after they die and want their sons to take over the management of the company. Miles's attorney estimates that his gross estate will be $9 million, including his stock in the MNO Corporation. He also estimates that Miles's executor will have the following needs for liquidity at Miles's death:

Personal debts	$ 25,000
Funeral expenses	10,000
Administration expenses	300,000
Federal estate tax	1,282,750

a. Assuming that Miles's executor decides to use a Sec. 303 redemption to provide liquidity in the estate, calculate whether or not such a redemption can be made without the redemption being treated as the equivalent of a taxable dividend. Show your figures.
b. What is the maximum amount of stock that can be redeemed under Sec. 303? Show your calculations.
c. Miles has expressed a desire that his family retain a controlling interest in the business after his death. Will a maximum Sec. 303 redemption affect the family's control? Explain. [5]

15. A decedent, Lazarus, owned stock in a closely held corporation. The executor can qualify the stock for a Sec. 303 redemption. There are, however, sufficient liquid assets in the estate to pay death taxes, administration costs, and burial expenses.
a. May the executor still make a Sec. 303 redemption? Explain.
b. If the stock passes to Mrs. Lazarus, can she have it redeemed under Sec. 303 after the death taxes, administration, and funeral expenses have been paid by the estate? Explain. [5]

16. The corporation can make Sec. 303 redemptions in a series. Describe how this might be a useful planning device if Sec. 6166 installment payment of estate tax is elected by the executor. [6]

17. Discuss the issues that must be considered if a corporation distributes interest-bearing notes instead of cash in a Sec. 303 redemption. [6]

18. Is life insurance that is purchased and owned by a corporation in order to fund a Sec. 303 redemption likely to cause the imposition of the accumulated-earnings tax? Explain. [6]

THE LIFETIME DISPOSITION OF A BUSINESS INTEREST 9

Learning Objectives

An understanding of the material in this chapter should enable the student to

1. Describe some situations in which the disposition of a business interest during the owner's lifetime may be an appropriate financial or estate plan.
2. Describe the general tax treatment of a corporate liquidation, discuss how an S corporation is taxed at liquidation and whether the election causes tax savings for a corporation considering liquidation, and describe some special considerations involved in liquidating a professional-service corporation.
3. Describe the differences between a taxable sale of corporate stock and a taxable sale of assets.
4. Describe the general rules for installment sales and private annuities.

Some owners of closely held businesses will retain their business interest until death, but there are often situations in which a sale or other disposition of the business represents good financial planning. For example, the owner may wish to retire from active involvement in the business and withdraw his or her investment rather than relying on successor managers to preserve the value of that investment. Or the owner many simply be tired of the business and wish to withdraw the investment for use in another business venture. Business reasons may also be determining factors. The business may be going downhill and the owner senses it is time to get out while something can still be salvaged. Or the business may be growing and continued expansion requires an infusion of capital that the owner does not wish to provide, so he or she would prefer to sell out to a larger organization that has the available capital.

For most owners of closely held businesses the value of the business is a large portion of their total assets. Withdrawing those assets through a disposition of the business interest is a transaction that can be complex and must be done carefully. Tax considerations are significant; improper design can produce bad tax results, including double taxation of the transaction—taxation at both corporate and individual levels—or taxation of proceeds as a dividend rather than taxation of the capital-gain element only.

Planning a successful business disposition often requires the services of specialized lawyers, accountants, and valuation consultants. This chapter is not intended to provide a detailed treatment of these dispositions. Instead it will describe the basic issues in the disposition of a closely held business interest, so that the financial services professional is aware of the planning options available.

WHEN A DISPOSITION MAY BE APPROPRIATE

Obviously the decision by a business owner to dispose of a business interest is not one that should be taken lightly. In fact, many planners will advise that a disposition should be considered only as a last resort. A badly planned disposition could result in serious tax and financial problems for the owner. Furthermore, there are emotional aspects to a decision of this type that cannot be ignored. The decision to dispose of the business, therefore, will often be more difficult than choosing among options that allow the owner to retain an interest in the business.

The need to investigate a change in ownership of the business usually occurs when the owner reaches his or her mid-fifties, begins to develop health problems, or wishes to devote more time to other, perhaps more profitable, business. When this decision-making time is reached, the owner must think about the future of the business.

If the owner is to retain a connection with the business interest until death, the owner's financial security rests on the continued viability of the business. This will depend on the continued management quality of the business, which is often based on key employees. Perhaps even more important, it will depend on how the business is able to deal with external factors in the future—for example, how it will be affected by foreseeable economic conditions, such as the effect of foreign competition, technological change, and the need for financing in tight capital markets over the next few years. If it is unlikely that the business in its present form will be able to deal with these problems effectively, it might be better to find a new owner for it sooner rather than later. In addition, tax considerations may dictate a lifetime sale.

A decision must also be made regarding how the business interest is to be handled at death. If a buyout by co-owners or key employees or a transfer of the business to family members at death is not likely to be satisfactory, it may be appropriate to consider disposing of the business before death.

TYPES OF DISPOSITIONS

While the planning of a disposition is a complex matter in many cases, the financial services professional should be aware of the basic options available to the owner in disposing of a business and of what the tax and other consequences of these options are. The following are methods for disposing of a corporation:

- *liquidation*. In a corporateliquidation the corporation's properties are simply distributed to shareholders and the corporate stock is cancelled. In general, as discussed below, liquidation has unfavorable tax consequences and should be considered only in certain situations or as a last resort.
- *tax-free exchange of stock or assets*. Under appropriate conditions the stock or assets of a corporation can be exchanged tax free for stock of an acquiring corporation. If the stock of the acquiring corporation is a liquid asset—say, the stock of a publicly held company—then this type of tax-free exchange is almost as favorable to the owner as a sale for cash, and the tax-free nature of the exchange may make it quite attractive. Of course, the seller will be taxed on the gain if the stock in the acquiring corporation received in the sale is subsequently sold. However, the gain on the sale may avoid tax altogether if the seller holds this stock until death. In general, since tax-free reorganizations are complex, this chapter will only describe some of the basic rules. Of course, to plan a tax-free exchange, it is necessary to have an appropriate acquiring corporation.
- *taxable sale*. The sale of a business can be accomplished with taxation only of the capital gain, and in some circumstances the recognized gain may be spread over several tax years. This chapter will discuss some of the consequences of a taxable sale and some of the forms by which the sale may be carried out, such as through an installment sale or a private annuity transaction. The latter two types of taxable sale may be useful as estate planning devices for transferring the business from an owner to a successor family member.

Corporate Liquidation

corporate liquidation

The tax treatment of a *corporate liquidation* is unfavorable in most cases. To understand why a liquidation is usually inappropriate for planning purposes, some background in this tax treatment is necessary.

Tax Treatment of a Corporate Liquidation

- The corporation pays tax on its capital gain when it sells assets or distributes assets to shareholders.
- Shareholders are taxed on the gain equal to the difference between the fair market value of what they receive from the corporation and their basis in their stock.

Under current law a corporate liquidation can result in tax at both the corporate level and the individual shareholder level. If a corporation distributes assets to shareholders, the corporation must recognize any gain or loss on the assets that are distributed. Or if the corporation sells assets to third parties for cash, it also must recognize gain or loss on the sale. Then when the corporate assets or cash is distributed to shareholders, the shareholders must recognize capital gain to the extent that the fair market value of the property received exceeds the basis of their stock. The tax paid by the corporation will reduce the amount of assets available to distribute in the liquidation.

EXAMPLE

Wizz purchased all the stock of the American Flamer Corporation for $50,000 in 1980. Flamer now owns property with a net fair market value of $400,000 plus (to simplify the example) an amount of cash that is just enough to pay its corporate tax. Flamer's basis for this property is $300,000. Wizz decides to liquidate Flamer. The $400,000 worth of Flamer's property is transferred to Wizz personally, Flamer pays its taxes with the cash remaining, and Wizz cancels his Flamer Corporation stock. (The transaction will most likely be treated as a liquidation for federal tax purposes even if the corporation is not legally dissolved under state law.) Flamer must recognize and pay tax on the capital gain of the $100,000 that it (Flamer) realizes as a result of distributing appreciated property in liquidation. In addition, Wizz is treated as having exchanged his Flamer stock with a $50,000 basis for property worth $400,000. Wizz therefore realizes and recognizes a capital gain of $350,000. Thus, there is a tax on $100,000 of income at the corporate level and a tax on the long-term capital gain of $350,000 at the individual level as a result of this transaction.

S Corporations

Corporations that have always been S corporations avoid double taxation on liquidation because of the pass-through of corporate income to shareholders and the basis rules for S corporation stock. An example will explain this best:

EXAMPLE

G. Wozz made an S election at the time of organizing the Slammer Corporation in 1986. He made an initial capital contribution of $50,000, which formed his initial basis for the Slammer stock; this basis has been adjusted upward each year to reflect income earned by the corporation and downward to reflect corporate losses or distributions to shareholders. At the beginning of this year, G. Wozz's basis in Slammer stock is $100,000. Slammer owns property with a net fair market value of $400,000 and a basis to Slammer of $300,000. Wozz decides to liquidate Slammer. All of Slammer's property is transferred to Wozz personally and Wozz cancels his Slammer stock. Slammer recognizes a gain on the distribution of appreciated property of $100,000—the fair market value of the property less Slammer's basis of $300,000. This gain of $100,000 realized by Slammer is passed through to Wozz, since Slammer is an S corporation. Wozz pays tax on the gain and also adjusts his basis in the Slammer shares upward by $100,000 (the gain realized).

Upon receipt of the Slammer properties worth $400,000, Wozz reports a long-term capital gain of $200,000 ($400,000 less his adjusted basis of $200,000). Thus for an S corporation there is only an individual tax on the liquidation transaction. Tax at the corporate level is avoided.

It looks as if the double tax on liquidation could be avoided even for a regular or C corporation simply by making an S election in the year of liquidation, since then the corporate-level gain would be passed on to shareholders. However, the Code provides that an S corporation is taxed at liquidation on the recognition of any gain "built in" at the time an S election is first made. Thus the usefulness of making an S election in the year of liquidation is very limited.

A partial liquidation is generally treated the same as a complete liquidation. If a corporation distributes appreciated property to shareholders in partial liquidation, there is a corporate-level tax on the difference between the property's fair market value and the cooperation's basis. In addition, there is a tax to the shareholders on the difference between the property distributed and the basis in their stock that is cancelled in the partial liquidation. A partial liquidation generally requires some actual contraction of the business activity. If a corporation simply distributes property to shareholders without this contraction, the transaction will probably be treated as a dividend to the shareholders, which will result in taxation to the shareholders of the entire fair market value of the property distributed, without any deduction for their stock basis.

Liquidation of a Professional-Service Corporation

The liquidation of a professional-service corporation is often required for business reasons, and such a liquidation particularly emphasizes certain problems inherent in liquidations.

One such problem is the potential distribution of goodwill. For example, suppose a business is liquidated and tangible assets worth $400,000 are distributed to shareholders in liquidation. If the shareholder's basis is $50,000, a capital gain of $350,000 will result. However, it is possible that in certain situations the IRS might assert that the liquidation involves a distribution of goodwill in addition to the tangible assets. If in this example the IRS values the goodwill at $100,000, the shareholders will have to pay tax on $450,000 of gain. The possibility that goodwill could actually be distributed to shareholders in liquidation exists only in specific situations, but it is potentially an argument when a professional-service corporation is liquidated and the shareholder/professional plans to continue practicing the profession using goodwill that was built up in the incorporated professional business.

Another problem in liquidating a corporation may arise if the corporation uses the cash method of accounting and distributes substantial accounts receivable to the shareholder in liquidation. This is a particular problem for professional corporations, since their major tangible asset may be accounts receivable. The shareholder's basis in property distributed in liquidation is generally the fair market value of that property as of the date of liquidation. This usually gives the shareholder a stepped-up basis for the property received in liquidation. Since the accounts receivable that are distributed to the shareholder in liquidation get a stepped-up basis, the amount of income reportable when the receivables are collected by the former shareholder will be minimal. However, the corporation must pay tax on the value of the receivables at the time of the liquidation, creating a substantial additional cash requirement at the time of liquidation.

Both these potential problems underscore the careful planning that must go into decisions about the form of business organization. In some cases the bad tax consequences of corporation liquidation may be a factor in a decision not to incorporate.

Sale of Business

stock sale

asset sale

A liquidation that results in the distribution of corporate assets directly to the business owners is often an inappropriate way to dispose of the business. If the owners wish to get out of the business altogether, they will usually attempt to find an outside buyer. Normally a *stock sale* results in a capital gain to the business's selling shareholders that is equal to the difference between the selling price and their basis. Alternatively the corporate assets can be sold. An *asset sale* will usually result in taxable gain to the corporation if the selling price exceeds the corporation's basis, and the shareholders will also be taxed on the capital gain when the proceeds from the sale are distributed to them in liquidation. The choice between a taxable stock or asset sale involves a number of factors.

As an alternative to a taxable sale of a business, the Code includes a number of provisions by which a business can be transferred to a new corporate owner tax free in return for stock of the acquiring corporation. In some cases this has the same practical effect as a cash sale. For example, the acquiring corporation might be a publicly held corporation whose stock is tradable on an established exchange and is virtually as good as cash to the seller. However, if such an acquiring corporation cannot be found, a tax-free sale (generally referred to as a tax-free reorganization) may not be available as an alternative to a taxable sale. Furthermore, a tax-free reorganization involves very complex rules.

Taxable Sale: Asset Sale Versus Stock Sale

The choice between a stock sale and an asset sale may be based on both tax and nontax factors. In addition, the interests of both buyer and seller must be considered. Some factors affect the interest of one or the other disproportionately, and the negotiations will reflect this imbalance.

One significant difference is that in purchasing the stock of a corporation, the buyer acquires the whole corporation with all its assets and liabilities, both known and unknown. In an asset sale, on the other hand, it is possible for the buyer to pick and choose only those assets that are appropriate. Thus the asset sale may pose less risk of picking up unwanted liabilities for the buyer.

However, in certain circumstances courts have held that in an asset sale the buyer may become *personally* responsible for paying liabilities of the corporation. In a stock sale the existence of the corporation acts as a screen that prevents the buyers from incurring direct liability for the corporation's debts. In summary, both methods of sale involve possible risk for the buyer that results from unknown or undisclosed liabilities or debts, but this risk takes various forms and therefore may dictate different results in different situations.

A second important nontax factor is the paperwork and other mechanical problems involved in making the transfer. A stock sale is usually simpler than an asset sale. First, shares of stock are more easily transferable than physical assets (again, one of the advantages of the corporate form). Furthermore, shareholder approval is not usually required under state corporate law for the sale of stock. Each selling shareholder in a stock sale is theoretically acting individually. By comparison, an asset sale may require shareholder action under state law, such as a majority (or super majority) vote by the shareholders of the selling corporation. Those shareholders who do not approve may have the right to bring an action in court (appraisal rights) to force their stock to be bought out at a fair price determined by the court. On the other hand, one possible complication of a stock sale is that not all shareholders may agree to sell their stock. This refusal leaves the buyer with the problem of dealing with these remaining minority shareholders in the future.

A tax factor that is significantly different in the two types of sales involves the basis of corporate assets to the purchaser. In a stock sale the purchaser receives stock that has a basis in the hands of the purchaser equal to the purchase price. However, the sale of stock does not affect the basis of the corporation's assets. This means that the sale does not automatically result in any increased depreciation basis or cost of goods sold for inventory. An asset sale, on the other hand, results in the purchaser's gaining a new cost basis for the assets. In addition, state and local taxes may have an impact on the choice. For example, significant real estate transfer taxes may apply to an asset sale.

EXAMPLE

Wizz is negotiating for the sale of his business, the American Flamer Corporation. The assets and the stock both have a fair market value of $400,000. Flamer's basis for its assets is $100,000.

Asset sale: If Flamer's assets are sold to Octopus Oil Company for $400,000, Octopus will have a basis of $400,000 for these assets. A portion of this basis will be allocated to depreciable property, which may result in a higher depreciation basis for the assets in the hands of Octopus than they had when held by Flamer. Other portions of the increased basis may be allocated to inventory, and a higher basis for inventory will result in a smaller amount of taxable income to Octopus when the inventory is sold.

Stock sale: If Flamer's stock is sold to Octopus, Octopus will have a basis for the stock of $400,000. However, Flamer Corporation will continue to exist and its basis for the assets will remain at $100,000.

Another tax factor distinguishing an asset sale from a stock sale is the problem of double taxation. When corporate assets are sold, there is potentially a tax at the corporate level and then another tax at the shareholder level when the "shell" of the selling corporation is liquidated.

These tax differences will dictate different sale prices or other terms for the sale of a given business depending on whether it is a stock or asset sale:

- The price for the assets will be increased (compared with the price for stock) to reflect the fact that the buyer's depreciable basis in the assets will be higher.
- The price for the assets will be increased (compared with the price for stock) to reflect the tax cost to the seller for selling assets and liquidating the corporation.

These two tax factors do not necessarily dominate in all cases; thus in a given situation an asset price could be lower than the stock price.

Tax-free Dispositions

tax-free reorganization

The vast majority of sales of businesses, particularly small or closely held businesses, are the taxable type because of the obvious difficulty in finding an appropriate buyer in a *tax-free reorganization.* However, when there is an opportunity for a tax-free reorganization, it provides unique benefits to the seller. Like a taxable sale a tax-free reorganization can be carried out either as a sale of assets or as a sale of stock. In addition, tax-free treatment is available for what is known as a "statutory mergers," a procedure under state law by which two or more corporations combine to form a single corporation and one of the old corporations ceases to exist.

Tax-Free Dispositions

- Asset sale will qualify if substantially all of the seller's net assets are sold only for voting stock in the buyer.
- Stock sale will qualify if at least 80 percent of the voting power and at least 80 percent of the other stock in the seller are sold only for voting stock in the buyer.

The tax-free reorganization provisions of the Internal Revenue Code involve many complicated requirements and qualifications. Some significant requirements can be mentioned here. For a tax-free asset sale—sometimes referred to as a "C" reorganization since it is described in Code Sec. 368(a)(1)(C)—"substantially all of the properties" of the selling corporation must be transferred to the acquiring organization in exchange for voting stock. There is no statutory definition for "substantially all," but the selling corporation should typically not retain more assets than necessary to meet existing liabilities. The IRS will issue a favorable advance ruling for a C reorganization if at least 90 percent of the fair market value of net assets (gross assets less liabilities) of the acquired corporation are exchanged in the transaction. The selling corporation must then liquidate, and its shareholders will then directly own the stock in the acquiring corporation received in the reorganization.

For a tax-free stock sale (a "B" reorganization described in Code Sec. 368(a)(1)(B)), it is not necessary to sell all the stock of the corporation. However, a "controlling" interest must be sold. For this purpose control means the ownership of stock that has at least 80 percent of the total voting power of the voting stock and the ownership of at least 80 percent of the total number of shares of other types of stock.

For both types of sales—stock or assets—the sale must be made "solely for voting stock" of the buying corporation to receive tax-free treatment.

The primary tax consequences of a tax-free sale are that

- there is no tax to the seller or to the selling corporation at the time of the transaction
- the seller receives stock in the acquiring corporation at a basis equal to the seller's basis in the property sold—that is, a carryover basis

EXAMPLE

To summarize the facts of a previous example, G. Wizz acquired his stock in American Flamer Corporation in 1980 for $50,000, and therefore has a cost basis for this stock of $50,000. American Flamer's properties, for which it has a basis of $100,000, are now valued at $400,000. Octopus Oil Company has indicated an interest in purchasing American Flamer's stock or assets for $400,000. Octopus Oil is a Fortune 500 company trading on the Big Board.

Tax-free stock sale (B reorganization): Octopus Oil transfers Octopus stock worth $400,000 to G. Wizz in return for all his American Flamer Corporation stock. American Flamer now becomes a wholly owned subsidiary of Octopus Oil Company. Wizz's basis for his Octopus Oil Company stock is $50,000, the same as his basis for the American Flamer Corporation stock he has given up. Wizz pays no current taxes. However, if he subsequently sells any Octopus Oil Company stock, he will have to recognize any resulting capital gain. If he holds on to the Octopus stock until death, his basis will be stepped up to its date-of-death value, and the gain on the sale of American Flamer Corporation will escape taxation altogether. (Note that for simplicity all the American Flamer stock was sold in this example, although only 80 percent of it has to be transferred to achieve a tax-free reorganization.)

Tax-free asset sale (C reorganization): If this alternative is chosen, American Flamer Corporation must sell "substantially all of its properties." Suppose that it sells all its assets to Octopus Oil Company in return for $400,000 worth of Octopus Oil Company stock. Octopus Oil now directly owns the former assets of American Flamer Corporation, which in turn owns $400,000 worth of Octopus Oil Company stock. Flamer is then liquidated as part of the plan of reorganization. The Octopus stock ends up in Wizz's hands, with a basis equal to Wizz's former basis of $50,000. Neither Wizz nor Flamer is subject to income taxes on these transactions. However, if Wizz sells any of the Octopus Oil Company stock, he must pay tax on any capital gain that results.

PLANNING THE TAXABLE SALE

Most sales of businesses will be taxable sales. In that case the primary planning issues are the amount of the payment and the form of payment. Determining the amount of the payment involves a valuation of the business, both objectively by valuation consultants and subjectively from the owners' point of view, because the owners will not sell unless the selling price is personally acceptable to them. The form of the sale (stock or assets) can affect the price because of the differing tax treatment. In addition, a stock sale usually involves the whole business while an asset sale may involve only selected assets.

The selling price for the business may not be a fixed amount but rather an amount that depends on the future performance of the business. A formula based on the future performance of the business over a selected future period is sometimes called an "earnout" formula. For example, an earnout formula might determine a selling price that is equal to 20 percent of the net profits of the business over the next 5 years.

Another issue in planning the sale is the *form of payment*. The basic types of payment the buyer could make include cash, notes, property (such as stock of another corporation), or stock of the buying corporation. (If the transaction is not solely for voting stock of the buying corporation, but includes cash and notes, it may not qualify as a tax-free reorganization.) The stock used in payment by the buyer can be preferred, common, a new class of stock, or whatever combination the parties may deem appropriate.

Installment Sales

installment sale

Businesses are often sold in return for an installment note. The *installment sale* has some significant advantages:

- From the seller's standpoint it allows any gain on the sale to be spread over a period of years. Basically the installment-sale rules in the Internal Revenue Code allow the taxpayer to spread taxable gain recognition on an installment sale over the time period during which payments are made unless an election is made to have all the gain recognized in the year of sale.
- From the buyer's standpoint the installment sale will often make it easier to carry out the transaction because the buyer will not have to come up with the cash immediately. Of course, this advantage to the buyer carries a corresponding disadvantage to the seller because the seller cannot be sure that the full purchase price will actually be received. However, the seller can retain a security interest in the business property (stock or assets) in an installment sale. The security provision allows the property to revert to the seller if the installments are not forthcoming under the circumstances specified in the sale agreement. This security interest is a double-edged sword, since the reversion of property to the seller upon the buyer's default will cause immediate recognition of all taxable gain on the transaction.

The installment-sale provisions of the Code are flexible, and the sale can be arranged with almost any type of deferred-payment schedule. For example, the agreement of sale might provide that half the purchase price be paid in the year of sale and the remaining amount be paid over a 5-year period. Or it might provide that the second installment be in the form of a "balloon" that is not due until several years after the first payment. The sale agreement might even specify that no payment is due in the year of sale. This type of moratorium on the initial payment may be helpful in consummating the deal because the buyer will then have more opportunity to establish the business so that enough cash can be generated to carry out the purchase.

In addition, the "earnout" formula can be used in an installment sale. All that is required to receive installment reporting for income tax purposes is that at least one principal payment be received by the seller in a tax year later than the year of the sale.

Installment sales are also flexible regarding the amount and schedule of interest payments. However, there are minimum interest requirements imposed by tax law.

The buyer can make part of the payment by assuming liabilities of the corporation or of the selling shareholders. For example, if the property to be sold in an asset sale is subject to a mortgage, the buyer might agree to assume the mortgage and therefore relieve the corporation of having to pay the mortgage note. Generally speaking, for tax purposes the seller treats the assumption of liabilities the same as if cash was received equal to the amount of the liability assumed.

The Mechanics of Installment Sales

The simplest way to explain the mechanics of an installment sale is to use an example. Suppose that G. Wizz sells the stock of American Flamer Corporation (with a basis of $50,000) for $400,000 to Octopus Oil Company. The terms of the sale call for Octopus to make a principal payment of $100,000 this year and $100,000 in each of the next 3 years. The contract also calls for interest payments. Under the installment-sale rules the capital gain is recognized ratably over the period during which installments are paid.

The amount of capital gain recognized in any specific year is given as follows:

$$\text{Capital gain} = \text{payment received during year} \times \frac{\text{gross profit}}{\text{total contract price}}$$

In this sale the gross profit to Wizz is $350,000 (the total price less Wizz's basis of $50,000). The total contract price is $400,000. Wizz will recognize and report capital gain as follows:

$$\text{This year : } \$\,100,000 \times \frac{\$\,350,000}{400,000} = \$\,87,500$$

$$\text{Next year and successive years : } \$\,100,000 \times \frac{\$\,350,000}{400,000} = \$\,87,500$$

Wizz will report the interest payments as ordinary income as he receives them and Octopus can deduct the interest payments as they are made, subject to the investment interest limitation discussed below.

As this example shows, there are three elements to each installment payment: capital gain (taxed at the 15 percent long-term capital-gain rate), return of basis (recoverable free of income taxes), and interest income (taxable at ordinary income tax rates).

Taxation of Installment Sale

- Seller's gain can be spread ratably over the period during which installment payments are made.
- Buyer's interest payments are deductible (within limits) when made and taxable to the seller when received.

Interest on an Installment Note

The rate and time for payment of interest might be a consideration in the sale negotiations. Under the special long-term gains tax rate, the seller will generally prefer to receive taxable gain rather than interest. The buyer, however, might wish to maximize the interest element because interest could be a deductible expense, and principal payments are nondeductible, except to the extent that they provide a higher basis for future depreciation deductions.

imputed interest

The Code provides for a minimum rate of interest on installment obligations under the *imputed interest* (Code Sec. 483) and original issue discount (OID) rules (Code Sec. 1274). These rules will be summarized here in general terms, but be aware that many exceptions and complexities apply. For sales of property with a principal amount of $2,800,000 or less, an interest rate up to a maximum of 9 percent can be applied. For sales of property greater than $2,800,000, the minimum rate of interest is the applicable federal rate (Code Sec. 1274(d)—the applicable rate is published monthly by the Treasury). Exceptions include the sale of land to a related person if the purchase price is not greater than

$500,000. In this instance, the interest rate cannot exceed 6 percent. In addition, the OID rules do not apply to the sale of a farm by an individual, estate, testamentary trust, partnership, or small business corporation if the purchase price is $1 million or less.[21]

Unless an exception applies, the stream of scheduled payments is discounted to present value at the appropriate rate of interest—either (1) a maximum of 9 percent or (2) the applicable federal rate, depending on the size of the sale price. The present value of the payment stream is compared to the stated principal amount (purchase price). If the stated principal amount is greater, the excess amount is imputed interest. This imputed interest or OID is taxed over the installment period by a complex set of rules. In sum, the sale cannot be planned to avoid the tax on interest to the seller by understating the interest at artificially low rates.

Investment Interest Limitation

If the buyer in an installment sale is a corporation, there is no limit on the amount of interest it can deduct. However, if the buyer of a business is an individual, there may be limitations on deduction of interest paid on the installment note.

- If the business purchased is a C corporation, the interest on the note will generally be considered investment interest, which is deductible only to the extent of the buyer's net investment income each year.
- If the business purchased is a partnership or S corporation, and its assets are used solely in the conduct of a trade or business in which the taxpayer materially participates, it appears that the interest will be considered business interest, which is not subject to limitation.
- If the business purchased is a partnership or S corporation and the taxpayer does not materially participate in the trade or business, the business will be considered a passive activity of the taxpayer, and interest will be subject to a limitation effectively similar to that for investment interest—deductions of a passive activity are allowable only to the extent of income from the passive activity.

Installment Sales for Estate Planning

An installment sale is a useful device in family financial and estate planning, particularly when a controlling family member wishes to pass on the business

---

21. Defined by Sec. 1244(c)(3).

to a successor in the family. This can lead to estate tax savings in the seller's estate and some income tax advantages for the buyer. An installment sale for estate planning purposes is one of the methods of "freezing" the seller's estate and shifting the growth in the value of a family business to a new generation without payment of transfer taxes on the growth element.

Private Annuity

The private annuity is a variation on the installment sale as an estate planning technique. However, the rules and tax advantages are different. A private annuity is a sale of property, such as a business, in exchange for the buyer's agreement to make periodic payments of a specified sum to the seller for the remainder of the seller's life. The amount of the payments is based on actuarial factors.

EXAMPLE

G. Wizz is aged 65. If he decides to sell the American Flamer Corporation to Chip in return for a private annuity worth $400,000, Chip's annual payment, based on the valuation rules and an assumed discount rate of 5 percent, will be $37,918. When Wizz dies, the annuity payments stop, even if Wizz had not yet reached his life expectancy as determined when annuity payments began. On the other hand, if Wizz lives longer than his life expectancy, annuity payments will continue for the rest of his life.

From Wizz's point of view the income tax treatment is significantly different than an installment sale. The value of the annuity received by Wizz is treated as if it was cash—that is, the capital gain on the sale is taxable immediately even though the annuity payments are spread over time.[22]

However, a private annuity might offer estate tax advantages, assuming the income tax consequences are manageable. In a regular installment sale some amount will be included in the seller's estate if the seller dies holding the installment note, since the remaining payments are still an enforceable obligation and therefore a valuable asset to the estate. However, in a private annuity no further payments are due when the seller dies. Therefore there may be nothing to include in the estate of a seller who dies holding a private annuity agreement. Of course, any annuity payments received by the seller before death become part of the gross estate to the extent that the payments have not been consumed or gifted by the seller.

22. This tax treatment generally applies to private annuity transactions where the sale occurs after April 18, 2007. For private annuity transactions that occurred before that date, the gain on the sale is spread over the seller's life expectancy.

Private Annuity

- Payments are made for the remainder of seller's life.
- Gain on the sale is recognized at the time the annuity is received to the extent the value of the annuity exceeds the seller's basis.

CHAPTER REVIEW

Key Terms and Concepts

corporate liquidation
stock sale
asset sale
tax-free reorganization
installment sale
imputed interest

Review Questions

The answers to the review questions are in the supplement. The self-test questions and the answers to them are also in the supplement and on The American College Online.

1. List some factors that indicate when a lifetime disposition of the business may be an appropriate course of action for a business owner. [1]
2. In general, how is a corporate liquidation treated for tax purposes? [2]
3. [2]
   a. What is the general tax rule for liquidation of an S corporation?
   b. How is the general rule changed if the S corporation makes its election after operating as a C corporation?
4. Briefly describe several problems that can occur in liquidating a professional-service corporation with regard to
   a. goodwill
   b. accounts receivable of a cash-method corporation [2]
5. Why are most sales of businesses carried out as taxable transactions rather than tax-free transactions? [3]
6. Describe some of the nontax and tax factors involved in the choice between a taxable asset sale and a taxable stock sale. [3]
7. List some of the important requirements for a transaction to qualify as a
   a. tax-free asset sale (C reorganization)
   b. tax-free stock sale (B reorganization) [3]

8. In planning a taxable sale discuss the planning considerations involving
   a. amount of payment
   b. form of payment [3]
9. Briefly discuss the advantages of an installment sale from the point of view of the
   a. seller
   b. buyer [4]
10. Describe in general how the Internal Revenue Code treats an installment sale. [4]
11. Why would a buyer want to use an interest rate on an installment note that is not the going market rate of interest? [4]
12. Describe the rules limiting flexibility in the interest stated on an installment note. [4]
13. Discuss briefly whether the interest incurred by the buyer in an installment purchase of a business will be deductible. [4]
14. What are some of the differences between an installment sale and a private annuity? [4]

KEEPING THE FAMILY BUSINESS 10

Learning Objectives

An understanding of the material in this chapter should enable the student to

1. Describe the objectives of the family business owner during his or her career life cycles.
2. Describe how a family business interest can be transferred to successors in exchange for an installment note or private annuity.
3. Identify the possible uses of restructuring a family corporation or partnership for the purpose of transferring a family business.
4. Describe how a grantor-retained annuity trust (GRAT) may be used to transfer a family business.
5. Identify the advantages and disadvantages of using a buy-sell agreement between family members to transfer a family business.
6. Describe how IRC Secs. 6166 and 303 can be used to provide estate liquidity if parents leave a family business through their wills.
7. Describe how a life insurance trust can facilitate the transfer of a family business.

The transfer of a family business presents many unique problems. First, a successor for the primary owner must be found within the family unless the business is to be terminated or transferred outside the family. Second, the family group who will replace the current owner generally does not include all of the business owner's heirs. Since the business interest is likely to represent the largest asset held by the business owner, it may be difficult to provide significant inheritance to heirs who will not inherit the business.

The tax laws provide some special problems that must be addressed before a business may be transferred within the family without adverse tax consequences. One such problem is the family attribution rules applicable to the redemption of stock in a family corporation. A new more difficult problem is the anti-estate-freeze provisions of Secs. 2701–2704.

Finally, there are some intangibles that create problems for the transfer of the family business. Quite often the parents procrastinate their planning. They cannot see themselves without control of the business and fail to take the steps necessary to educate their successors as to the significance of the business to the family. The parents' estate and business plans are made in a piecemeal fashion and are not explained to the children or other family successors. The potential additional estate costs brought about by incomplete or incoherent plans are certainly a hindrance. This problem is amplified by the conflict between successors who were kept in the dark about their parents' plans. These individuals might have found their fate more palatable if the parents had explained their reasoning behind the plan.

In any event fewer than 35 percent of family businesses are successfully transferred to the next generation. The financial services professional is uniquely situated to assist the family business owner in planning this transfer. This chapter discusses some advanced planning techniques that facilitate the transfer of an interest in a family business to younger generation family members.

OBJECTIVES OF THE FAMILY BUSINESS OWNER

Prior to Retirement

A family business owner generally relies on the business as the primary source of income for his or her family. Therefore prior to retirement the business must provide the owner with a substantial stream of income. The current income demands of the owner must be balanced with several other goals. First, substantial assets must often be reinvested in the business to provide for future growth and competitiveness. Second, the compensation of key employees, including family successors, must be sufficiently attractive to retain these individuals. Finally, current federal income tax burdens may force the deferral of some current income through various types of tax-deferred retirement arrangements. Since most business owners will wish to maintain a high standard of living, the owner will probably desire a steadily increasing income flow until retirement.

Transition to the Owner's Retirement

At some point most individuals will decide to terminate their full-time working careers. Although the owners of family businesses tend to work longer than other employed individuals, they still must face the transition to retirement.

Since the family business owner is the most significant contributor to the success of the business, some long-range planning should be done to ease this transition. First, logical successors among the owner's children must be selected. Since children will quite often show little or no interest in taking an active role in the family business at first, a parent may need a significant period of time to convince the appropriate children that it is in their best interest to work for the family business. Once the junior family members are employed by the business, their development into mature and capable successors may take a number of years. It may be necessary to find executives from the outside to smooth the transition if the family successors are not prepared to take over when their parent(s) retires. An outside board of directors is often recommended for this purpose. The process of grooming the appropriate successors should begin as early as possible and certainly long before the owner is approaching retirement.

Assuming the appropriate family members become employed by the business, steps should be taken to prevent these individuals from becoming dissatisfied and thus leaving the business. Providing a substantial salary to the family successors may meet with the parents' other tax-planning needs. You will recall that income taxes can be saved if the business income is divided among several family members. If the reasonable-compensation tests are met, salaries paid to the owner's children and taxed at their lower income tax brackets are deductible by the business. These funds flowing from the business to the employed children can in some circumstances be used by the children for expenditures that would normally have been provided by the parents. Furthermore, if the business is incorporated, the payment of substantial salaries to family members is an effective method for removing cash from the corporation and reducing exposure to the accumulated-earnings tax.

Once the intended successors have worked for the business for a period of time, they will probably also demand an increased role in the decision-making process of the business. These individuals should be afforded this opportunity since their eventual roles will require creativity and decisiveness. It may also be necessary and advisable to begin providing these individuals with equity interests in the business. These steps are consistent with the phaseout of the senior family member's contributions to the business as his or her retirement grows near and may also be consistent with the estate planning goals.

Problems in Transition of the Family Business

- Selecting (convincing) the appropriate junior family members to assume active roles in the business
- Developing the selected junior family members into capable successors
- Compensating both the business owner and the selected junior family members
- Giving the selected junior family members a gradually increasing role in business decision making
- Providing liquid assets for the nonparticipating family members

Other issues must be faced before the business owner transfers the business to his or her successors. It must be determined when and how the senior family member will pass the actual control of the ownership interest to the successors. Alternate choices for transferring the family business to successor family members include

- the sale of a controlling interest in the business to the successors at retirement
- lifetime gifts of the business interest to the successors
- the sale of the business interest at death through a buy-sell agreement
- the testamentary bequest of the business interest to successors

Another consideration that should be planned in advance is how the business owner and his or her spouse will be provided for during retirement. The owner will probably expect the business to provide his or her continuing family needs during retirement. If the expected standard of living is high, a substantial flow of income may be required. The choices for providing this postretirement income include

- benefits from qualified and/or nonqualified retirement plans adopted by the family business
- payments for the continued services of the senior family member (for example, consulting fees, director fees, or a part-time salary)
- proceeds from the sale of the business to the successor family members (such as installment or private annuity payments)
- the business owner's other accumulated wealth

It is likely that none of these choices will be adequate unless the necessary funding is made in advance. This funding should be carefully planned since the owner's other wealth accumulation and estate planning objectives must be handled in a consistent fashion.

Another concern of family business owners is how to leave their estates to heirs. Some of the family business owner's children will probably not become actively involved in the business. Providing these individuals with significant ownership interests is generally not recommended, because it is difficult to compensate the passive owners adequately for their interests. For example, if the business is incorporated, these passive owners must be compensated as shareholders through nondeductible dividend payments. However, the active family members holding stock must also take these dividends. This is costly and usually inappropriate. Even if the business will be run as a partnership or an S corporation, the family members providing substantial services to the business must be adequately compensated before any business income can be paid to the passive owners. Unfortunately the division of ownership in the family business between active and passive family members often creates disputes over their relative shares that may cause an irreconcilable division between family members.

Most individuals hope to provide for their children equitably from their accumulated wealth. If all the children will not become involved in the business, the owner faces a troublesome dilemma. Since the family business is likely to represent a substantial portion of the owner's wealth, it may be difficult or impossible to transfer the business to the family successors while also providing assets of similar size to inactive heirs. This problem often leads to procrastination by the family business client. However, financial services professionals generally have adequate products and tools to handle the problem if is recognized. Potential resolutions to the dilemma of providing for all the family business owner's heirs include the following:

- An irrevocable life insurance trust can be used to substantially enhance the estate of the business owner without adding to the estate tax burden. Beneficiaries of the trust generally include the inactive heirs and/or the surviving spouse of the family business owner because the active heirs will benefit from the growth in the business.
- The lifetime or postmortem sale of the business can be made to the successor family members. Since the successor will pay full value for the business interest, adequate liquidity should be available to the estate so that the other family members can be provided a fair share.

- A substantial investment fund can be accumulated by the client outside the business to provide for the inactive heirs. This fund can be partially invested in life insurance covering the life of the business owner to ensure the liquidity of the estate and adequacy of the nonbusiness wealth accumulations.

Finally, if no family members are appropriate successors, the business will either terminate at the death or retirement of the owner, or a sale to individuals outside the family will be transacted. If a sale of the business is preferable to liquidation, the best results occur if the owner plans well in advance.

Estate Planning

As the senior family member of a family business prepares to turn over the reins to successors, several estate planning objectives should be considered. These objectives include

- transferring control and future appreciation of the business to the appropriate family successor
- reducing the amount of the business owner's assets includible in his or her gross estate
- retaining assets (business or otherwise) that provide adequate retirement income while minimizing the size of the taxable estate
- planning adequate liquidity for the estate
- arranging for an orderly and equitable disposition of the business owner's other assets to meet his or her dispositive objectives

Since the ownership interest in a family business is likely to represent the most significant asset held by the owner, it is appropriate for estate planning to focus on this asset. At first, many of these estate planning objectives appear to be incongruent or even mutually exclusive. How does a business owner give up his or her business interest while retaining a substantial income flow? How does a business owner retain sufficient income while also reducing the size of his or taxable estate? How can liquidity be provided to the estate if illiquid assets, such as a business interest, might be included? There are no universal answers to these questions. Furthermore, provisions of the tax law applicable to family businesses are adverse to, and increase the complexity of, meeting these objectives. The facts and circumstances of each particular case require careful consideration before an appropriate estate and business plan can be devised.

Role of the Financial Services Professional

The failure of a family business to continue successfully into a second generation is quite often the result of an inadequate estate plan for the business owner. The business owner is unlikely to arrive at the appropriate estate planning solution without professional assistance. Most entrepreneurs have a difficult time facing up to their own mortality. They see their very existence commingled with the business and cannot imagine one without the other. This procrastination leads to several of the following problems, which will generally prevent the successful transfer of the business to the next generation:

- The business transfer plan will either be inadequate or not communicated to the family successors.
- Any planning that has been done will not be coordinated. For example, the wills and trusts executed in conjunction with the estate planning attorney will no longer be appropriate for the transfer of the growing business asset. The entrepreneur's life insurance policies will have inappropriate ownership and beneficiary designations. The estate and family financial planning of the family successors will not work in conjunction with the senior family member's plan. (For example, successors with ownership interests in the family business will often expose these ownership interests to unwanted claims through their own wills if they predecease the business owner or through equitable distribution if they become divorced.)
- The appropriate successors will not be sufficiently trained to step into the entrepreneur's shoes at his or her death.
- The successors will become dissatisfied with the business since the dominant senior family member will control their actions in the business and stifle their creativity.
- The family successors will become disillusioned since their future roles with the business are unclear.
- The business itself will stagnate due to the phenomenon of "harvesting." This occurs when the aging entrepreneur becomes less ambitious and puts less energy into the future growth of the business. The entrepreneur may begin to siphon off substantial funds from the business to reap the benefits of his or her earlier sacrifices.

A major problem leading to procrastination is the inability of the entrepreneur to face the fact that difficult and sometimes unpopular decisions will have to be communicated to his or her successors. The entrepreneur is concerned that hard feelings will develop between his or her heirs regardless of how the wealth is divided. If the business becomes enormously successful, inactive family members will harbor resentment if their share of the estate—the nonbusiness assets—grow at a slower rate. On the other hand, the successors to the business may feel that their share of the estate was earned as a result of their loyal service and may resent the fact that inactive heirs will receive investment interests in the business or more liquid gifts or bequests from the entrepreneur or his or her estate.

An additional potential conflict exists within the select group of heirs who are the chosen successors to the entrepreneur's control of the business. For practical purposes not all successors are born equal. Some of these individuals are more suitable than others for significant roles in the family enterprise. The more creative and industrious successors should be rewarded with control of the enterprise. It would be a serious mistake for the entrepreneur to cloud his or her objectivity with concern over the feelings of the family successors who must accept a lower rung on the ladder. Nothing will make the failure of the closely held business more certain than placing the wrong individuals at the helm. Unfortunately the entrepreneur often finds that the most convenient solution to the problem is to ignore it. There is no benefit to the entrepreneur or the successors in delaying this decision. The entrepreneur is less likely to have a smooth transition to retirement, and the likelihood that the business will be successfully transferred to the successors decreases as the planning of this transfer is delayed. The hard feelings and disappointment that might develop in the family successors is enhanced by the period of time that they are kept in the dark about the entrepreneur's future plans.

All too often the entrepreneur's professional advisers are unsuccessful in dealing with this problem. This results more from a lack of focus than a lack of ability to meet these needs. Often the adviser defines his or her role narrowly with respect to the entrepreneur. The attorney who works on the estate plan often limits his or her role to the preparation of the documents, such as wills and trusts, to handle the orderly transfer of the entrepreneur's estate at death with minimum adverse estate tax consequences. The attorney for the business is primarily concerned with business contracts and is often unfamiliar with the transfer taxes associated with the estate of a closely held business owner. The accountant that works with the business is concerned with maximizing the business's current net income and market value. The life underwriter is concerned with providing the necessary death and disability protection for the entrepreneur and providing liquidity for his or her estate. Finally, the investment adviser is primarily concerned with the performance of the entrepreneur's investment portfolio. Each of these professionals may be highly competent and perform their individual tasks superbly without addressing the overall problem.

The financial services professional is in a position to assist the entrepreneur. What is needed more than anything else in this process is focus; an adviser who gains the client's confidence as the center of influence should be able to get the task done. If each of the other advisers is satisfied with his or her role in the process, the team will be capable of handling the orderly succession of the family business.

To succeed in this role the financial services professional must become acquainted with (and gain the trust of) the entrepreneur's family and key employees. This individual may come from any part of the financial planning team.

The necessary familiarity may come from several months or even years of regular visits with the entrepreneur and the business. It will soon become clear to the family members and employees that the financial services professional is the entrepreneur's key adviser. The personal knowledge that the financial services professional gains through contact with the entrepreneur's family members and key employees will prove invaluable when the succession plan must be explained to these individuals. The adviser might pick up signals from these individuals that will reveal who will or will not be happy with the entrepreneur's plan. These insights may indicate who might be best at persuading individual members of the family and key employee group that the entrepreneur's plan is in fact best for all concerned. The entrepreneur's spouse is often a key figure in this counseling process.

The entrepreneur might want the financial services professional to communicate the plan to members of the family and key employee group. If these individuals have learned to place their trusts in this primary adviser, the plan may be more widely accepted. In many ways this communication process is the most difficult and important step in the succession plan. The inability to face individuals who may be receiving unpopular news is often a stumbling block. It may be necessary to bring in outside professionals such as counselors and psychologists to handle the personal concerns of the family members. The actual implementation of the plan will be a smoother process if the senior family member's intentions for the future of the business are understood by all parties.

Once the plan has been described to the appropriate individuals, the plan must be implemented. At this point it is necessary for members of the financial planning team to perform their individual steps—legal documents must be prepared by the business owner's attorney; the CPA might have to value the family business; the life underwriter will have to secure the necessary coverage to fund the various aspects of the agreement. The key adviser must make sure that these necessary steps are taken. The adviser must be satisfied that the individual steps fit together properly to meet the overall goal. When the advisers are satisfied that all tasks have been completed appropriately, the plan can be executed.

After the plan is in place, the role of the key adviser is not finished. It is probable that future events will cause the need for the plan to be updated or even substantially altered. For example, more insurance funding may be needed if the family business grows. Changes in the status of family members and key employees may necessitate modification of the plan. Finally, changes in the tax laws and business marketplace may lead to further updating. In any event it is the responsibility of the financial services professional to remain on top of the situation.

Other members of the client's team should be more than willing to cooperate since the updating of the plan will result in additional commissions or fees for their part of the process. The financial services professional who performs his or her role properly will create a situation where everyone wins. The entrepreneur and his or her family members and key employees will have a plan for the business that has the highest possible probability for success. The individual advisers of the employee will be well compensated for their services and have a greater degree of satisfaction that they have performed their tasks thoroughly.

However, the low success rate of the succession of a family business indicates that this opportunity is too often forsaken by the entrepreneur and his or her advisers.

SPECIAL FEDERAL TAX PROVISIONS APPLICABLE TO THE TRANSFER OF THE FAMILY BUSINESS

Congress has recognized the special problems associated with family ownership of a business and has enacted tax statutes designed to preserve the family business. For example, provisions of the law discussed earlier, such as special-use valuation (Sec. 2032A), Sec. 303 redemptions, and installment payment of estate taxes (Sec. 6166), will help prevent forced liquidation if the business is included in the decedent-owner's estate. However, Congress has also anticipated abuses to the estate tax system if the ownership of a family business is divided between several family members and imposed rules to prevent schemes to reduce the gift or estate tax value of family business transfers.

Valuation Rules for Family Transfers

Tax rules have been created to reduce the estate planning advantages of traditional estate-freeze transactions. These rules, codified in Secs. 2701-2704.

estate freeze

The anti-estate-freeze law provisions are aimed at perceived "loopholes" in the estate and gift tax laws. Congress enacted the statute to prevent senior family members from avoiding the estate and gift tax systems through estate-freeze transfers to family successors. An *estate freeze* is a transaction in which a senior family member transfers property with substantial appreciation potential (for example, common stock in a family corporation) to a younger family member at a reduced transfer tax cost. Of course, the senior family member usually wishes to retain some rights to the transferred property, such as the right to income from the property. The estate freeze refers to the fact that the retained interest is designed to be "frozen" in value at the time the growing "unfrozen" interest is transferred. Examples of frozen interests include preferred stock or limited partnership interests.

The law restricts estate freezes through the gift tax law provisions rather than delaying the estate-freeze penalty provisions until the estate tax return is due. The law focuses on the appropriate gift tax valuation of the initial transfer to junior family members in the freeze transaction.

Under these provisions, the senior family member will be treated as if he or she transferred the entire value of property gifted to junior family members for gift tax purposes even if rights are retained by the senior family member. For the freeze transaction to result in any gift or estate tax savings, the transferor must retain rights that have *value*. The provisions of Secs. 2701-2704 deal with the appropriate valuation of the retained rights.

Anti-Estate-Freeze Provisions

- Rules focus on a more realistic measurement of what value is actually transferred (and therefore what value is actually retained).
- Unless the transferor's retained rights have value, the senior family member will be treated as if transferring the entire value of the gifted property to the junior family member for gift tax purposes.
- Planning mistakes will incur immediate gift tax rather than future estate tax.

The practical goal of most estate freezes is for the senior family member to retain some interest in the property. Additional gift tax is incurred if the retained interest fails to provide the appropriate rights to the transferor any time after the transfer. Therefore transfer planning mistakes (intentional or not) will have immediate gift tax consequences rather than future estate tax consequences. However, because many gifts are not reported on gift tax returns, the imposition of the taxes and penalties may not occur until a transferor dies and the estate tax return is examined.

Stock Redemptions and the Family Attribution Problem

Under the family attribution rules, a shareholder is deemed to own shares of stock held by certain family members and certain entities for the purpose of determining whether a redemption of such shareholder's stock results in sale-or-exchange treatment under Sec. 302. (The failure to qualify generally results in dividend tax treatment.) Under certain circumstances the family attribution rules can be waived. To qualify for a waiver the redeemed shareholder must completely terminate his or her interest in the corporation. A redeemed shareholder terminates his or her interest in the corporation by having a complete redemption of his or her stock and by agreeing not to become an officer, director, or employee of the corporation for 10 years.

The transfer of a family corporation through a complete stock redemption of the senior family member's stock is often inappropriate. First, the corporation will need huge amounts of surplus to redeem a large controlling interest in the corporation. Second, it is unlikely that the senior family member will wish to break all ties with the corporation. He or she will probably want to retain some stock and/or a continuing employment relationship with the corporation. If any of these interests is retained, the amount of the redemption proceeds would usually be treated as a dividend—fully taxed to the extent of the corporation's earnings and profits (E & P).

The parent may wish to hold the family corporation's stock until death. The stock could be left to the appropriate children through the provisions of the decedent's will. This method of transferring the family business would require the estate to contain substantial liquid assets. As discussed previously the decedent will probably need substantial assets to provide for those heirs who will not receive stock in the family corporation. In addition, the stock may cause a large estate tax burden that would generally have to be paid either out of the estate's liquid assets or from distributions from the corporation.

Suppose the business was transferred through a stock redemption at the death of the parent. If the successor family members already own stock in the business, the complete redemption of the parent's stock would probably result in the successors obtaining control of the corporation. However, the attribution problems associated with this transaction might be difficult to solve because there is no waiver for entity attribution. Thus if the family members for whom attribution applies are otherwise beneficiaries of the estate, the estate will be deemed to own the shares of stock held by those family members. If a redemption of the estate's stock is attempted, the estate will be deemed to own the stock held by these beneficiaries and the redemption will likely fail to qualify as a sale or exchange. It is possible to qualify the redemption as a complete termination if all beneficiaries who own stock receive their distributions from the estate and sign a release terminating their beneficial interest in the estate. If this can be accomplished, they will no longer be beneficiaries and their stock will not be attributed to the estate. Thus a complete termination redemption of the estate's stock will be possible. In practice, however, it is difficult to terminate the beneficiaries' interest in the estate, and this method is hard to plan.

The risk of dividend treatment of the redemption proceeds is an unnecessarily high price to pay since a redemption that *does* qualify as a sale or exchange will probably be nontaxable due to the basis step-up available to the estate. In any event the redemption of stock in a family corporation is quite complex and should be planned carefully if this is the method selected to transfer the family corporation.

DESIGNING AN EFFECTIVE TRANSFER OF THE FAMILY BUSINESS

The business owner's objectives associated with passing the family business to his or her children were outlined above. The tax laws concerning family business make these objectives even more difficult to reach. In some cases it may be too costly or otherwise inappropriate to retain the businesses in the family. Under these circumstances the business could be liquidated or sold to outsiders. Fortunately certain planning techniques and tax opportunities permit the family business owner to pass the business to his or her heirs while meeting some, if not all, of his or her objectives.

The methods for transferring the family business can be grouped into four basic categories. The business can be transferred gratuitously or sold to family successors, and the transfer can take place while the owner is alive or after his or her death. All potential techniques have advantages and shortcomings, and the specific circumstances of each case must be carefully examined to make an optimal choice. We will first discuss lifetime (inter vivos) transfers of the family business.

INTER VIVOS TRANSFERS TO FAMILY SUCCESSORS

There are several reasons why the senior family member may wish to transfer the family business prior to his or her death. The entrepreneur may wish to retire from the business and make a clean break from all responsibilities as owner. The family successors may pressure the senior family member into such a transfer through their desire to gain freedom and control. Even if the senior family member retires from active participation, his or her retention of a controlling interest in the business until death may cause conflict between the family members. The retired entrepreneur may feel obligated to provide guidance to the family successors. The family successors, on the other hand, may feel obligated to continue to "clear" major decisions with the retired owner. In any event, the scenario where the senior generation hands over the reins to the family business with no further involvement is rare.

Installment Sales of the Family Enterprise to Family Successors

An installment sale is a useful device in family financial and estate planning, particularly when a controlling family member wishes to pass on the business to a successor in the family. This type of transfer can lead to estate tax savings in the seller's estate along with income tax advantages. An installment sale for estate planning purposes is one of the methods of freezing the seller's estate and shifting the growth in the value of a family business to the next generation without payment of transfer taxes on the growth element.

EXAMPLE

Suppose Eddie Entrepreneur decides to transfer his family corporation, Familyco, Inc., to his son, Ernie. Eddie sells the Familyco stock to Ernie for its fair market value of $1 million. (Eddie's basis for the stock is $100,000.) Ernie executes an installment note providing for annual payments of $100,000 to Eddie over a 10-year period. (For simplicity this example ignores the interest complications.)

This sale can result in significant estate tax savings to Eddie. The installment sale will remove the Familyco stock from Eddie's estate. His estate, however, will include any of the cash received from the installment payments (or property purchased by the cash payments) unless Eddie gives away that cash or consumes it before death. In addition, if the installment payments are not fully paid at Eddie's death, the present value of the installments then unpaid is included in Eddie's estate. It is possible that the full $1 million value at the time of sale could be included in Eddie's estate, and no basis step-up will be available to the estate for the installment obligation. However, there is a significant potential estate tax advantage to the sale. If the property (in this case, the business) is appreciating in value, the installment sale will remove any growth in the value of the property occurring after the date of the installment sale from Eddie's estate. Consequently, the estate tax value of the business is "frozen" at $1 million. In addition, if Eddie survives the term of the installment sale and consumes (or gifts) the payments received, the estate tax savings will be far greater. Therefore the installment sale can solve what is often a significant estate planning problem.

Self-Canceling Installment Notes (SCINs)

The installment note can be designed with a cancellation-at-death provision (self-canceling provision). Briefly, this provision causes the note to be canceled automatically at the seller's death. If properly designed, this provision removes the value of the note from the gross estate even if the seller dies before the installment terms ends. Care should be taken in designing the SCIN. The terms of the cancellation provision should be bargained for and reflected in the purchase price and/or the interest rate imposed. If the seller instead merely cancels or forgives the remaining indebtedness through his or her will, the remaining payments will be treated as a testamentary transfer and included in the estate.

Self-Canceling Installment Notes (SCINs)

- Remaining unpaid installment obligations are canceled at seller's death, so no remaining value of the business is in the estate.
- To achieve this, the terms of the cancellation provision must be bargained for and reflected in a higher purchase price and/or interest rate.

EXAMPLE

Suppose Eddie Entrepreneur decides to transfer his family corporation, Familyco, Inc., to his son, Ernie. Eddie hopes to sell the Familyco stock (fair market value is $1 million) to Ernie. Eddie could sell Familyco to Ernie for an installment note that was self-canceling at his death. Since the mortality risk is borne by Eddie, he should receive more than the $1 million purchase price or receive a higher rate of interest on the principal amount. The increased purchase price will reflect the fact that the seller might not receive all the installment payments. The IRS will be successful in claiming that a gift was made by Eddie to Ernie unless the purchase price or interest rate is increased to reflect the mortality risk borne by Eddie.

Regardless of the form of installment note chosen, the installment sale of a business is a useful estate planning technique if the seller wishes to pass on the business, along with any future appreciation in the business value, to a family member. The installment payments provide cash to the seller for retirement income or for building a diversified investment portfolio without the anxieties of direct involvement in the business. The tax burden of the installment payments is minimized by spreading them out over a period of years. The business itself may generate enough cash for the buyer to make the installment payments. It is important, however, to avoid payments that are so large that they burden the business and make it difficult for the successor to operate it at a profit. Finally, any postsale appreciation in the value of the business accrues to the transferee family member and is out of the seller's estate.

Private Annuity

The private annuity is a variation on the installment sale as an estate planning technique. However, the rules and tax implications are somewhat different. A private annuity is a sale of property, such as a family business, in exchange for the buyer's agreement to make periodic payments of a specified sum to the seller for the remainder of the seller's life. The amount of the payments is based on actuarial factors. For example, suppose that Eddie is aged 65. If he decides to sell Familyco to Ernie in return for a private annuity worth $1 million, Ernie's annual payment, based on IRS valuation methods, will be $94,796 (assuming a discount rate of 5 percent and life expectancy of 85). When Eddie dies, the annuity payments stop, even if he has not yet reached his life expectancy. If Eddie lives longer than his life expectancy, the annuity payments will continue for the rest of his life.

A major advantage of the private annuity is its estate tax treatment. In a regular installment sale some amount will be included in the seller's estate if the seller dies holding the installment note, since the remaining payments are still an enforceable obligation and therefore property of the estate. However, in a private annuity no further payments are due when the seller dies. Therefore it is well established that there is nothing to include in the estate of a seller who dies holding a private annuity agreement. Of course, any annuity payments received by the seller before death become part of the gross estate to the extent that the payments have not been consumed or gifted by the seller. A private annuity is particularly suitable for the transfer of a family business to successors. The guaranteed annuity amount will provide a retirement annuity for the seller, presumably funded by income from the business. Even if the seller does not live to life expectancy (and the sale becomes a bargain for the buyer), the benefit accrues to the family heir. As with a self-canceling installment note (SCIN), the IRS valuation rules must be used to determine the annuity amount. If the value of the annuity is less than the fair market value of the business, the IRS will claim a taxable gift was made to the family successor.

Lifetime Gifts of the Family Business to Successors

Quite often the parent would prefer the gratuitous transfer of the business interest to his or her children. This might be accomplished by the gradual transfer of the business through annual-exclusion gifts to the successors. Outright gifts of family business interests to successors of up to $13,000 annually (in 2011) per donee qualify for the gift tax annual exclusion. If the business owner's spouse elects to split all gifts during the year, the annual gift tax exclusion is increased to $26,000 per donee. Because of the limits of the annual exclusion, gifts of a substantial business interest to limited numbers of successors will generally result in taxable gifts and cause the donor to use unified credit or incur gift taxes. To minimize (or avoid) current gift tax liability, gifts of family business interests are often designed through sophisticated trust arrangements or *recapitalization* of the enterprise. Recapitalization is essentially a rearrangement of a corporation's capital structure that involves exchanging all or part of a shareholder's stock for newly issued stock.

Regardless of the form of the transfer, the senior family member who currently owns the business will have to address the following concerns if a lifetime disposition occurs:

- The donor might need to retain a significant portion of the business interest to provide for his or her needs during retirement.
- The donor must have other substantial assets if inactive heirs are to be treated equally.
- Valuations of the business interest must be performed (at least informally) to determine if the annual exclusion has been exceeded (and, if so, the amount of any taxable gift).

Use of Multiple Classes of Stock in the Family Corporation

The use of preferred stock received in either recapitalization stock or dividends to assist in transferring a family business was substantially curtailed by the new valuation rules. However, business reorganization techniques can still be used to solve some of the family business transfer problems if the statute can be complied with. They must be carefully drafted and fully explained to the business owner before they can be implemented.

Common Versus Preferred Stock

Preferred stock is a separate class of the corporation's stock that provides certain preferences or priorities over the corporation's common stock. Such preferences are generally provided for in the corporation's articles of incorporation or amendments thereof. In general, state corporation laws do not substantially restrict corporations in designing the terms and preferences of preferred stock. However, these state laws must be consulted before designing the terms of any proposed issue of preferred stock. For federal tax purposes it is important to note that an S corporation *cannot* issue preferred stock.

The preferences or priorities that holders of preferred stock receive include the following:

- *dividend rate*. Holders of preferred stock are generally entitled to a dividend rate based on a fixed percentage of the preferred's par value. Such dividends must be paid before any dividends are paid on the corporation's common stock. The terms of the preferred may provide that the dividends are "cumulative." The right to receive cumulative dividends continues so that all dividends unpaid in prior years on the preferred must be paid before the common shareholders can receive dividends.

- *liquidation preference*. A second basic feature of preferred stock is the preferential right of the preferred shareholders over common shareholders. In the event of a liquidation or bankruptcy of the corporation the preferred shareholders will receive payment equal to the par value of their stock to the extent of available funds before any payments are made to common shareholders. However, unless the preferred stock is participating preferred, payment to the preferred shareholders is limited to the par value of the stock and provides no opportunity for preferred shareholders to participate in the growth of the business.

The dividend and liquidation preferences are the two hallmarks of preferred stock. However, a preferred stock issue can also contain a variety of other terms and conditions that are tailored to suit the needs of a particular client and these items will affect the value assigned to the preferred stock.

The Impact of the Special Valuation Rules on the Recapitalization of a Family Business

The special valuation rules of Sec. 2701 hinder the plans to transfer a family business through recapitalization of the enterprise. The rules limit the ability to freeze the senior family member's estate through recapitalization. The example below illustrates how a plan of recapitalization combined with family gifts might be used to transfer a family corporation at a reduced transfer tax cost.

EXAMPLE

Suppose Eddie Entrepreneur owns all 100 shares of common stock in Familyco, Inc. The common stock is worth $10,000 per share. Familyco's board of directors, controlled by Eddie, passes a resolution to recapitalize. Familyco exchanges $990,000 of par value preferred stock that has an 8 percent cumulative dividend percentage with Eddie for 99 shares of his common stock. Eddie subsequently gifts the remaining common stock to his son, Ernie, who is a key employee of Familyco and is Eddie's natural successor to Familyco. Eddie shelters the entire gift with the annual gift tax exclusion ($13,000 in 2011). After the transfer Eddie will receive only the dividends when declared by the board, which is now controlled by Ernie. The preferred stock should have a frozen value and will not appreciate prior to Eddie's death or his disposition of the preferred. This transaction is called an estate freeze since the entire transfer tax cost is the estate or gift tax cost of transferring the preferred retained. The subsequent growth in Familyco accrues to the common stock held by Ernie and is not subject to transfer tax.

The Valuation of Retained Rights in a Family Corporation or Partnership. The classic estate-freeze transaction involves the transfer of growth interests (common stock or general partnership interests) in a family business by a senior family member who retains other rights (preferred stock or limited partnership interests). Sec. 2701 focuses on proper valuation of assets at the time of the transfer of growth interests if the senior family member retains other interests in the family business.

For purposes of determining the gift tax value of an interest in a corporation or partnership *controlled* by the transferor and transferred to (or for the benefit of, such as through a trust) a *member of the transferor's family*, the value of rights retained by the transferor or an *applicable family member* immediately after the transfer is generally deemed to be zero. In other words, no valuation credit is generally given for the frozen interest retained by the senior family member. Therefore, unless the statute is complied with, the gift tax value of the growth interest transferred will be equal to the entire value of the business interest held by the senior family member. The result will be *immediate* gift taxation of the entire interest held by the senior family member (even of the interest retained by such senior family member).

EXAMPLE
Suppose Eddie Entrepreneur owns all 100 shares of common stock in Familyco, Inc. The common stock is worth $10,000 per share. Familyco's board of directors, controlled by Eddie, passes a resolution to recapitalize. Familyco exchanges $990,000 of par value preferred stock that has an 8 percent cumulative dividend percentage with Eddie for 99 shares of his common stock. Eddie subsequently gifts the remaining common stock to his son, Ernie, who is a key employee of Familyco and is Eddie's natural successor to Familyco. Eddie shelters the entire gift with the annual gift tax exclusion ($13,000 in 2011). After the transfer Eddie will receive only the dividends when declared by the board, which is now controlled by Ernie. The preferred stock should have a frozen value and will not appreciate prior to Eddie's death or his disposition of the preferred. This transaction is called an estate freeze since the entire transfer tax cost is the estate or gift tax cost of transferring the common stock to Ernie. The subsequent growth in Familyco accrues to the common stock held by Ernie and is not subject to transfer tax. However, the rules of Sec. 2701 provide that the current gift tax value of the common stock transferred to Ernie will be $1 million instead of $10,000, and the value of the retained preferred stock will be zero.

Fortunately, there are exceptions to these extreme rules, which have planning implications that will be discussed below.

For the purposes of applying Sec. 2701, the following definitions apply:

- *controlled entity*. A controlled corporation is a corporation in which the transferor owns at least 50 percent of the stock of the corporation; a controlled partnership is a partnership in which the transferor holds at least 50 percent of the capital or profits interest.
- *member of the transferor's family*. A member of the transferor's family is (1) the transferor's spouse, (2) the transferor's lineal descendants, and (3) the spouse of any such descendants.
- *applicable family member*. An applicable family member is (1) the transferor's spouse, (2) an ancestor of the transferor or such transferor's spouse, and (3) the spouse of such ancestor.

Meeting Family Corporation Transfer Objectives Through Recapitalization

qualified payments

Preferred Stock Recapitalization Providing Qualified Payments. When enacting Sec. 2701, Congress did recognize that real retained rights (preferred stock or limited partnership interests) should be credited with some value that can be used to offset the gift tax cost of the transferred common stock or general partnership interests. Retained rights to qualified payments are valued under normal valuation principles. *Qualified payments* are dividends payable on a periodic basis on cumulative preferred stock or comparable payments under a partnership interest to the extent that such dividend or comparable partnership payment is determined at a fixed rate. A payment is treated as having a fixed rate if it is determined at a rate that bears a fixed relationship to a specified market interest rate.

In addition to the distribution rights, the statute provides that a positive value be given to liquidation, put, call, and conversion rights held by the retained preferred stock or limited partnership interest. However, the law provides that such rights be valued as if exercised in a manner resulting in the lowest possible value.

The new rules provide for an additional restriction on the recapitalization technique. The total common stock of the corporation may not be valued at less than 10 percent of the sum of the total value of all stock interests in the corporation and the total indebtedness of the corporation to the transferor or an applicable family member following the recapitalization. A similar minimum-value rule applies in the partnership context. In our example, the recapitalization will not qualify since the value of the common stock was one percent of Familyco following the recapitalization. If the recapitalization of Familyco was performed in a manner that resulted in a value of $100,000 for common stock, the plan would qualify.

To ensure that no disguised gifts escaped the new rules, Congress provided one additional catch in the case of transfers in which the transferor or applicable family member retains rights to qualified payments. If the qualified payments are not in fact made at the times and in the amounts used in valuing the retained right to the qualified payments, the transferor (or the transferor's estate, if appropriate) will incur a taxable gift for the amount of the undeclared dividend payments. There is a grace period of 4 years during which the distribution can be made and treated as timely. If the dividends are not declared on the qualified payment preferred stock at this time, the amount of undeclared qualified dividend payments is an additional taxable transfer. The amount of the taxable gift includes not only the amount of the undeclared dividend payments, but also compound interest from the date the dividends were not declared.

EXAMPLE

Suppose Eddie Entrepreneur owns all 100 shares of common stock in Familyco, Inc. The common stock is worth $10,000 per share. Familyco's board of directors, controlled by Eddie, passes a resolution to recapitalize. Familyco exchanges $990,000 of par value preferred stock that has an 8 percent cumulative dividend percentage with Eddie for 99 shares of his common stock. Eddie subsequently gifts the remaining common stock to his son, Ernie, who is a key employee of Familyco and is Eddie's natural successor to Familyco. Eddie shelters the entire gift with the annual gift tax exclusion ($13,000 in 2011). After the transfer Eddie will receive only the dividends when declared by the board, which is now controlled by Ernie. The preferred stock should have a frozen value and will not appreciate prior to Eddie's death or his disposition of the preferred. This transaction is called an estate freeze since the entire transfer tax cost is the estate or gift tax cost of transferring the preferred retained. The subsequent growth in Familyco accrues to the common stock held by Ernie and is not subject to transfer tax. However, the rules of Sec. 2701 provide that the current gift tax value of the common stock transferred to Ernie will be $1 million instead of $10,000, and the value of the retained preferred stock will be zero.

Applying the requirements of Sec. 2701, it appears that the recapitalization would be effective if 8 percent cumulative preferred Familyco stock was retained by Eddie. Normal valuation rules would apply since the retained preferred provide qualified payments. In addition, the common stock of Familyco should be revalued to at least $100,000 to meet the 10 percent minimum rule. After these adjustments are made to the recapitalization, dividends must in fact be declared and distributed to Eddie or he will be treated as making additional taxable gifts to the other common shareholders; in this instance to his son Ernie. This reduces the value of the preferred stock estate freeze for a senior family member. If the qualified payments are declared and distributed to Eddie, these payments enhance his estate (and increase the transfer tax ultimately paid) unless they can be consumed or gifted prior to his death. The dividend distributions also reduce the growth of the corporation and reduce the appreciation potential for Familyco that would otherwise accrue gift/estate tax free to his son, Ernie. If the qualified payments are not declared, Eddie will incur a gift tax that increases the cost of transferring Familyco to Ernie.

An additional consideration must be discussed with respect to the preferred stock recapitalization of a family corporation. The statute and regulations issued thereunder provide little guidance as to the actual valuation of the preferred. The qualified payments are required to be fixed or set to a specified market rate. But what rate must the preferred pay? To value the preferred stock, the stream of qualified payments must be discounted by a capitalization rate. What discount rate must be used? As a result of these types of issues, a recapitalization of a family corporation passing muster under Sec. 2701 is a rare event.

Other Exceptions to the New Valuation Rules. There are five classes of exceptions to these rules in addition to the retention of preferred stock with qualified payments. In the following family business transfers with retained interests, the senior family member will not be considered to have retained a zero-value interest if transfers are made to family members:

- *publicly traded stock exception.* The stock or other interest retained, given away, or sold is publicly traded when market quotations are available.
- *same type transfers.* The retained interest is of the same class as the transferred interest. For example, a client makes a gift or sale of common stock but retains rights in the same class of common stock, or a client makes a gift of a partnership interest but all the income, losses, and so forth are shared equally by all partners.
- *nonvoting stock transfers.* The retained interest would be of the same class as the transferred interest—except for nonlapsing differences in voting power. For example, a client gives away or sells nonvoting common stock in a corporation but retains voting common stock of the same class.
- *proportional transfers.* The rights in the retained interest are proportionately the same as all the rights in the transferred interest. For example, assume that a client gives away or sells one class of stock and keeps another class of stock. Both the class of stock that was given away and the class of stock that was retained share equally in all distributions, liquidations, and other rights.
- *convertible preferred retained interests.* The retained interest can be converted into a fixed number or percentage of the shares of the same class as the transferred stock.

Gifts of Nonvoting Common to Family Successors. Nonvoting common stock is another means of using two classes of stock to meet a family business owner's transfer and estate planning needs. Suppose that instead of creating a new class of preferred stock, a recapitalization bifurcates the ownership of the corporation into two classes of common stock—voting and nonvoting. Of course, the senior family member desires voting control over the family corporation. However, he or she could begin transferring ownership of a family corporation to children by gifting nonvoting common stock. The parent would then retain the voting common stock as long as he or she desires, even until death. Gifts of the shares of the nonvoting common can be made to children tax free if limited in amount to $13,000 (in 2011; $26,000 if split with a spouse) annually. Over a period of years the parent can use this method to shift substantial quantities of the ownership interest in the family corporation to children, and consequently reduce his or her gross estate.

If the voting and nonvoting common are valued appropriately, the nonvoting stock should be discounted significantly as a minority interest. However, the appreciation potential should be the same, and the transfer would not be subject to the new valuation rules.

EXAMPLE

Eddie Entrepreneur owns all 100 shares of Familyco, Inc., a closely held corporation valued at $1 million. Eddie has a son, Ernie, who is a key employee. Suppose Familyco is recapitalized into 50 shares each of voting and nonvoting common. The voting common is valued at $600,000 and the nonvoting common at $400,000. Eddie, whose wife elects to split all gifts, decides to give 3.25 shares of nonvoting common to his son each year. In year one the gift qualifies for the annual gift tax exclusion ($26,000 of stock gifted to Ernie since Eddie's wife elects to split gifts). As the corporation increases in value (and the value of the gifts increases), Eddie will have to decrease the number of shares gifted or use unified credit to shelter such gifts. Suppose Eddie dies 10 years after beginning the transfer. At this time he has given away 65 percent of the nonvoting common (3.25 shares per year for 10 years). Assume the corporation doubles in value. Eddie will have successfully transferred $520,000 in value of Familyco without transfer tax simply by using the annual exclusion and unified credit. A buy-sell agreement with Ernie for the voting common stock and the remaining nonvoting common held by Eddie is more feasible as a result. In any event significant estate tax savings have been realized, and the likelihood of a successful transfer of Familyco has increased.

Gifts of Family Limited Partnership (FLP) Interests

What Is an FLP. Another type of freeze involves the transfer of family business and/or other property to an FLP. The FLP is a partnership structured specifically to provide a substantial discount for the limited partnership interests. To accomplish estate and gift tax goals, the senior-generation family members create an FLP and transfer their business and/or other income-producing property to the partnership. The property transferred into the FLP has specific and unfrozen value. The senior generation retains small (for example, one percent) general partnership interests. These general partnership interests control the management of the partnership and hold liquidation power over the partnership.

The remainder of the ownership interests are limited partnership interests. The limited partnership interests do not hold any management rights or the right to liquidate. In fact, the partnership agreement generally guarantees little or nothing to the limited partners in the form of distributions. All such distributions will be controlled by the general partners in their sole discretion.

Thus, the limited partners have no right to demand distribution or to get at the underlying assets of the partnership.

Discounted Gifts of FLP Interests. The value of these limited partnership interests can be significantly discounted for gift or estate tax purposes as minority interests (the inability of the limited partners to control the business) and for lack of marketability (the lack of available buyers for such dubious rights). Discounts of 25 percent–65 percent (from the value of the partnership property) have been applied to the limited partnership interests in an FLP.

The senior generation will transfer limited interests in the FLP to junior-generation family members through lifetime gifts. Such gifts can be sheltered by the donor's annual exclusion or exemption amount (currently $5 million) for taxable gifts.

IRS Attacks on FLPs. The use of the FLP has garnered a great deal of attention from the IRS. Discounted gifts and estate transfers will attract scrutiny when the transferor's estate tax return is examined.

The IRS has several approaches to attack the problem. First, the argument could be made that a partnership consisting solely of investments and not active business property is not a valid partnership for tax purposes. This would be a difficult argument to make since state law determines the legitimacy of the partnership. Second, the argument could be made that the partnership restrictions on the limited partners could be ignored for valuation purposes and that the total proportionate value (without minority or marketability discounts) of the underlying assets is the true value of the transfer for transfer tax purposes. Under special valuation rule Sec. 2704, restrictions on the limited partner's interest can be ignored for valuation purposes if such restrictions go beyond those of state law. This argument has been used recently in several private rulings involving partnerships established just before the transferor's death in which substantial discounts were taken on the gift/estate tax returns. Third, the IRS has denied the annual exclusion for gifts of limited interests in FLPs due to the limited partners' lack of a present interest.[23] Fourth, the IRS has attempted to argue that a gift occurs on formation of the FLP if the senior generation contributes property and takes back limited partnership interests that are valued less

---

23. This argument was upheld by the Tax Court in a family LLC case (*Hackl v. Commissioner*, 92 AFTR 2d 2003-5254 (335) F3d 664).

than the property contributed. Finally, the IRS might argue that the senior generation has a retained life estate in the contributed property if the partner continues to control and benefit from the property as if the property had never been gifted. Sec. 2036(a) of the Code would cause the inclusion of the full value of the underlying property in the contributor's gross estate for federal estate tax purposes if this argument is successful.

Case law has sometimes resulted resoundingly in taxpayer victories in appropriately structured and administered FLPs.[24] However, the IRS was successful in raising the Sec. 2036(a) argument in the estate of some founders of FLPs.[25] In each instance, the senior-generation family member who created the FLP continued to control and commingle the underlying property with his or her own personal holdings. The donee junior-generation partners operated under the implied understanding that the FLP property remained the property of the founding partner. It is clear from the current series of cases that the founder of the FLP should have at least one legitimate nontax reason for forming the FLP. In addition, there should be no express or implied understanding that the founder has retained the right to enjoy or control the property held by the FLP, outside of the normal rights of ownership in a properly structured and administered business partnership. Another message seems to be that the founder should retain adequate assets outside of the FLP for personal support and maintenance. The net result of a successful challenge by the IRS under of Sec. 2036 is that the underlying property returns to the donor's estate without the FLP discounts.

One principle is clear: The valuation discount for the limited partnership interests should be substantiated by a complete independent appraisal, and

---

24. See, for example, *Kerr v. Comm'r*, 113 TC No. 30; *Church v. United States*, 2001 USTC Para. 60,369; *Estate of Weinberg v. Comm'r*, TC Memo, 2001-51; *Knight v. Comm'r*, 115 TC N. 36; *Estate of Strangi v. Comm'r*, 115 TC No. 35; *Estate of Jones v. Comm'r*, 116 TC No. 121; Kimbell v. United States, No. 03-10529 (5th Cir. May 20, 2004) where one or more of the IRS arguments against FLPs were rejected by the courts. The allowable discounts varied significantly in these cases, however. On the other hand, see *Shepherd v. Comm'r* and 115 TC. No. 376 and Senda v. Comm'r, T.C. Memo 2004-160 where the court held that a gift of the underlying property, rather than the FLP interests, was made when the transfers of property preceded the formation of the partnership.
25. See, for example, *Schauerhamer v. Comm'r*, TC Memo 1997-242; *Reichardt v. Comm'r*, 114 T.C. No. 9; and *Turner v. Commissioner*, 94 AFTR 2d 2004-5764; where the partnership property was included in the FLP founder's gross estate because of the retained control over the property transferred to the partnership. These cases indicate the need to follow the normal state law requirements and operating formalities for a partnership if the taxpayer wants to achieve the desired valuation discounts.

the appraisal should justify the value based on the specific circumstances of the FLP being valued. The recent court cases, although generally taxpayer victories, focused not only on the discounts taken for gift or estate tax purposes, but also on the valuation methods employed for the underlying FLP property.

Gifts of Business Interests in Trust

The valuation rules, codified in Sec. 2702, have a direct impact on an estate-freeze transaction through a family trust. For the purposes of determining whether a transfer in trust to or for the benefit of a member of the family of the transferor is a gift and determining the value of such gift, the value of any interest in the trust retained by the transferor or any applicable family member is generally treated as zero. Therefore, if a senior family member creates a trust benefiting a member of his or her family while retaining current beneficial rights, the senior family member is deemed to have retained none of the beneficial rights to the trust and is treated as if he or she had given away the entire trust corpus for gift tax purposes. This is analogous to the new rules for estate freezes through preferred stock recapitalization.

A similar rule is provided for term interests if a parent retains a term or life estate interest in property and gifts the remainder to a family member. The value of the gift will be the current fair market value of the interest with no discount for the value of the retained term. A split purchase will be treated for this purpose as a transfer of the remainder with a retained term by the parent.

EXAMPLE

Eddie Entrepreneur owns 100 percent of Familyco, Inc., valued at $1 million. Eddie creates an irrevocable trust funded with all of his Familyco stock and retains all income from the trust for 10 years. The remainder interest in the trust is gifted to his son, Ernie, who is his natural successor to Familyco. This arrangement will cause Eddie to incur an immediate $1 million taxable future-interest gift to Ernie. Eddie's retained interest is valued at zero, despite the fact that he could receive substantial income from Familyco through his beneficial interest in the trust for the next 10 years.

Fortunately there is an exception to these harsh valuation rules. A retained *qualified interest* in the trust (or the property subject to a term interest) by the transferor or applicable family member will be valued at its full value as determined by normal estate and gift tax rules. These value rules are determined pursuant to the complex methods mandated by Sec. 7520. Such interests are valued based on the monthly federal interest rates and current IRS mortality tables.

grantor-retained annuity trust (GRAT)

A qualified interest is either

- a right to receive fixed amounts payable at least annually, which is a *grantor-retained annuity trust (GRAT)* interest

grantor-retained unitrust (GRUT)

- a right to receive amounts payable at least annually that are a *fixed percentage* of the trust's asset determined annually, which is a *grantor-retained unitrust (GRUT)* interest
- any noncontingent remainder interest if all other interests in the trust are GRATs or GRUTs

The normal valuation rules also apply when

- the property is a property to be used as the personal residence of the person holding a *term interest* in the trust or
- the exercise or nonexercise by the holder of a *term interest* in tangible property would not affect the valuation of the remainder interests in such property (The value of the term interest in the property is the amount the transferor can show could be obtained on its sale to an unrelated third person.)

Transfer of a Family Business to Grantor-Retained Annuity Trusts or Grantor-Retained Unitrust Interests

Two tax-favored trust structures of the anti-estate freeze law are GRATs and GRUTs. To meet the requirements for the safe harbor as a qualified retained interest for Sec. 2702, the GRAT (or GRUT) must provide the grantor with a qualified interest. The GRAT provides that the grantor must retain the right to a fixed amount annually from the trust for the retained term. The GRUT provides that the grantor must retain an amount each year of a fixed percentage of the fair market value of the corpus (which is determined annually). The GRUT is virtually never used. The remaining discussion will focus on GRATs

The GRAT is generally a grantor trust, and all income tax consequences are passed through to the grantor during the retained interest term. This results from the fact that the grantor could have his or her retained interest in the trust satisfied by corpus distributions. Therefore these techniques are useful only for estate planning purposes. They are not useful for current income-shifting purposes. However, the status of the grantor trust is important for business-planning purposes since a grantor trust is an eligible shareholder for S corporation stock.

The irrevocable transfer of the remainder interest in the GRAT is a current gift for gift tax purposes. Since the gift provides a future interest to the donees, the gift does not qualify for the annual exclusion. However, the gift is discounted from the full fair market value of the corpus by subtracting the value of the grantor's retained interest term valued under the Sec. 7520 rules. This discounted gift can be sheltered by the grantor's exemption amount. Any retained trust interest other than a GRAT will be valued at zero for gift tax purposes, and the grantor will be treated as having gifted the entire remainder with no discounting.

The rules do require the actual payment of the fixed amount in a GRAT, which may limit the ability to transfer a closely held business in trust. The business must have the cash and surplus to make such payments to the trust. Otherwise, the trustee will have to liquidate some of the business interest to make the required payments. The failure to make such payments will result in additional gift tax liability for the grantor when he or she does not receive qualified payments from the retained interest. However, if the problems can be resolved, this technique can be useful because the grantor will (a) be able to shift the growth in the business property to his or her heirs at a fraction of its total value and (b) still retain current income rights to the business.

If the grantor survives the retained interest term of a qualified GRAT, the corpus, including any post-transfer appreciation, is excluded from the estate of the grantor. Therefore a significant growing property interest can be transferred to family heirs for a greatly discounted transfer tax cost.

If the grantor fails to survive the term, some portion of the trust corpus (but less than the full corpus) is returned to his or her estate. The amount returned to the estate depends upon the Sec. 7520 valuation rate at the time of death and inclusion fraction for the GRAT. In any event, the maximum estate freezing potential for a GRAT will only be realized if the grantor survives the retained interest term.

EXAMPLE

Eddie Entrepreneur, aged 65, wants to transfer $1 million in closely held Familyco, Inc., stock to a GRAT for the benefit of his son, Ernie, who is his successor to Familyco. If Eddie retains a 10-year term in the trust with a $70,000 per year annuity payable to Eddie during this term, the retained interest will be treated as providing qualified payments. Since Eddie has retained a qualified interest, the value of the gift of the remainder interest is determined by subtracting the full value of Eddie's retained interest from the total value of the corpus at the time of the GRAT's creation. If Eddie survives the 10-year term, the financial benefits of the gift are as follows:

Trust term	10 years
Value of stock	$1,000,000
Assumed valuation rate	5%
End-of-year payment	$70,000
Value of retained income interest	$540,519
Taxable gift (value of remainder interest)	$459,481
Assumed growth rate of Familyco stock	9%
Value of property at termination	$1,303,858

TRANSFERRING THE FAMILY BUSINESS TO SUCCESSORS AT DEATH

Insured Buy-Sell Agreements Between Family Members

The family or nonfamily successors to the ownership of a closely held business are generally employed by the business for a period of time prior to taking over ownership. A buy-sell agreement effective at death between the current controlling owner(s) and the family successors is one method of reaching some of the business owner's estate planning objectives. To avoid any potential impact of the special valuation rules, additional consideration must be given to buy-sell agreements between family members.

One distinct advantage of transferring a business interest through a buy-sell agreement is the ability to use the purchase price terms of the agreement to establish (or be persuasive evidence of) the estate tax value of the business interest. This facilitates the estate planning for the owner since a reliable estimate of the estate settlement costs can be made if the date-of-death value of the business interest is known in advance. The ability to establish the value of a business interest serves to quantify the liquidity needs of the estate and make tax- and cash-needs planning predictable. In addition, the establishment of the estate tax value through a buy-sell agreement could eliminate the need for the executor to hire a business appraiser to perform an often costly (and always uncertain) valuation appraisal for the business interest.

Under prior law, a binding buy-sell agreement fixed (or was highly persuasive evidence for determining) the value of closely held business interests for estate tax purposes. The agreement had to require the estate to sell and the business or other persons to buy the closely held business interest.

The agreement had to meet the following tests:

- It must have had a bona fide business purpose and be binding on the deceased owner's estate.
- It must not have been a device for transferring the business to members of the business owner's family for less than full consideration.
- It must have had a provision for determining the price of the business that was fair when the agreement was signed.
- It must have contained lifetime restrictions that placed a ceiling on the amount the business owner could sell his or her interest for while alive equal to the price contained in the agreement for sales effective at death.

The committee reports explaining the special valuation rules and regulations issued by the IRS indicate that the traditional rules continue to apply to buy-sell agreements involving unrelated parties. Therefore an agreement meeting the tests above will be effective in establishing the estate tax value of a business interest of a decedent if his or her co-owners are not family members.

For family businesses, a higher standard of valuation rules applies. Unless more stringent tests are met, the value of a business interest (or any other property) is determined without regard to any option, agreement, or other right to acquire or use the property at a price less than the fair market value. The fair market value will be determined without giving any consideration to such agreement, or right, or any restriction on the right to sell or use the property. The family business buy-sell agreement is, of course, the type of right or restriction affected by the new valuation rules.

For this purpose, the affected rights or restrictions could be contained in a formal buy-sell agreement or similar restrictions contained in the businesses' articles of incorporation, bylaws, partnership agreements, and those created implicitly in the capital structure of the enterprise.

The Special Valuation Rules Create an Exception

Fortunately, there is an exception to the valuation provisions for family buy-sell agreements. The following three requirements must be met for the IRS to recognize the price provision in a family buy-sell agreement for establishing the estate or gift tax value of a business interest subject to the agreement:

- The agreement must be part of a bona fide business arrangement.
- The agreement must not be a "device" to transfer the property to members of a decedent's family for less than full and adequate consideration in money or money's worth.
- The terms of the agreement must be comparable to similar arrangements entered into by persons in an arm's-length transaction.

If the family buy-sell price provisions are not recognized for gift, estate, or generation-skipping tax purposes, more likely than not the estate will find itself in a valuation dispute with the IRS and a liquidity shortfall could result. Therefore planning must be aimed at either meeting the exception so that the buy-sell price is accepted by the IRS for estate tax purposes or obtaining greater life insurance to fund the additional liquidity needs.

The regulations indicate that the tests be applied independently, and all three parts must be met. Generally, an agreement that preserves the continuity of the management and provides for a smooth transition to the family successors serves a bona fide business purpose. However, the executor must carefully document facts that indicate the arrangement was not a device to pass the property to members of a decedent's family at a bargain price. The IRS has traditionally been suspicious that family buy-sell prices are undervalued and serve as mere "will substitutes."

The new requirement that the family buy-sell agreement be comparable to arm's-length agreements will likely prove to be difficult. In order to establish the estate tax value of the family business interest, there must be an indication that the terms in the family buy-sell agreement could have been obtained in an arm's-length transaction.

Factors to be taken into account include (a) the expected term of the agreement, (b) the present value of the property, (c) its expected value at the time of exercise, and (d) the consideration, if any, offered for the agreement.

It is likely that a fixed price based on the value at the time the agreement was entered into will be challenged by the IRS unless the price has been updated to result in fair market value at the time of death. This implies that the use of formulas or independent appraisal to determine value must be used as the valuation provisions in a family buy-sell agreement. Certain formulas, such as those based solely on book or adjusted book value, may not be viewed as the kind of arrangement that would be reached in an arm's-length agreement. If the agreement uses a formula, the funding of such an agreement must keep pace with the formula. The regulations indicate that it is permissible to limit the purchase price provision to the use of one valuation method, even where appraisers would generally use a combination of several methods. This seems to be consistent with the IRS's feeling that the purpose of buy-sell agreements is to avoid unnecessary appraisal costs. Of course, the valuation method selected must meet the standard for comparable businesses in generally accepted business valuation practice.

The regulations indicate that comparable agreements for the *same* business negotiated by unrelated parties, to the extent they exist, must first be used to determine the validity of the valuation provision used in a family buy-sell agreement. If all parties included in the family business are related, comparable valuation provisions from agreements formed by similar businesses must be used. Meeting the requirement of comparability will obviously increase the cost and time involved in negotiating and executing a family buy-sell agreement. It is clear that it will be very difficult to transfer the business interest at a "discounted" cost to a family member through a buy-sell agreement. These rules give increased importance to full (or substantial) funding of any family buy-sell agreement with life insurance.

Handling "Grandfathered" Buy-Sell Agreements

The new requirements do not apply to family buy-sell agreements or options entered into before October 9, 1990, unless there is a *substantial modification* after October 8, 1990. Presumably, any family buy-sell agreement entered into before such date would be subject to the less stringent standards of prior law. Careful thought should be given to amending existing agreements since the grandfather status of such agreements is lost if the agreement is substantially modified.

The law does not define a substantial modification, but the regulations provide some guidance on this issue. Any discretionary modifications (whether authorized in the initial agreement or not) resulting in a substantive change to the quality, value, or timing of the restriction are treated as substantial modifications. Specific examples of substantial modification given by the regulations are

- failure to update a price provision if the agreement requires periodic update (an oversight that often occurs)
- the addition of a new family member to the agreement unless the original agreement required such addition

The regulations indicate that the following modifications will be permitted to an existing buy-sell agreement without the loss of grandfather status:

- modifications required by the agreement
- a change in the capitalization rate used in the valuation provision if it is modified in a manner that bears a fixed relationship to a specified market interest rate
- a modification that results in a price that more closely approximates fair market value
- a discretionary modification that does not change the restrictive agreement

In evaluating an existing family buy-sell agreement, it is important to remember that an inherently unfair agreement or unrealistic price could have been challenged successfully by the IRS under prior law. Under these circumstances, the grandfather provision might not be that important and should be ignored (and the family buy-sell agreement modified) if there is a business reason to do so.

The following are advantages of using a binding buy-sell to transfer the family business to heirs:

- The business interest is sold only to heirs who will provide services to the family business.
- The parent retains his or her interest (and the income associated with the ownership interest) until death.
- The insurance proceeds used to fund the agreement will provide the estate with liquid proceeds in lieu of an otherwise unmarketable business interest.
- The liquid sale proceeds received by the estate can be used to provide an equitable share to other inactive heirs.

- The business can help the family successors fund the cross-purchase buy-sell through split-dollar or Sec. 162 bonus plans.

Disadvantages of the buy-sell effective at death include the following:

- The parent may be involved in the business for a period of time longer than he or she desires since ownership may continue beyond retirement.
- The premiums on the insurance used to fund the agreement may be more than the family successors are able to afford. (This problem can be alleviated by (1) making split-dollar arrangements with the parents or (2) increasing the salary of the family successor so he or she can make the payments.)
- The gross estate of the parent will include the full date-of-death value of his or her share of business interest.
- The buy-sell will occur at the owner's death, and income payments from the business to the owner's inactive survivors cease at that time.
- Because of the family attribution problem a cross-purchase might be the only viable alternative for a family corporation buy-sell.
- The new valuation rules may result in an estate tax value of the business interest that is in excess of the buy-sell price unless the safe harbor is met.

Leaving the Family Business Through Will Provisions

The parent may decide to transfer the family business to the successor children through his or her will rather than through a buy-sell arrangement. First, the parent may prefer the *gratuitous* bequest of the business. Second, the owner may wish to delay the transfer of control of the business until his or her death (or the later death of his or her surviving spouse). This delay would protect the surviving spouse because income would be provided from the business until the surviving spouse's death. The usual will of a wealthy business owner will provide this result. The business interest will probably be placed in a marital and/or family trust to benefit the surviving spouse while he or she is alive.

Some additional planning must take place to ensure the success of a testamentary transfer. First, the problem of estate liquidity must be addressed. Since a potentially unmarketable business interest will be included in the gross estate of the business owner and, perhaps, the estate of the surviving spouse, other liquid assets will be needed to pay the death taxes whenever they are incurred.

Second, the heirs of the business owner who do not inherit the business interest must be considered. If the business represents a major portion of the owner's gross estate, an equitable distribution to all heirs may be difficult.

Finally, the family successors must gain the ability to control the business and receive adequate compensation when they take over. This may cause conflicts between the active successors and the surviving spouse, inactive heirs, and the executor. The actual controlling interest in the business may not be received by the active heirs until the subsequent death of the surviving spouse. Fortunately with appropriate planning these difficulties can be minimized by the family business owner.

Installment Payments of Estate Taxes—Sec. 6166

The Sec. 6166 installment payment of estate tax was put in place by Congress to permit an estate that contains closely held business interests to pay estate taxes caused by the business interest in periodic installments. This provision was enacted by Congress to preserve the closely held business. A closely held business would often otherwise have to be liquidated to pay estate taxes if the taxes were due immediately.

Advantages of electing the Sec. 6166 installment payment of estate tax include the following:

- The decedent can leave the business interest directly to the successor family members through his or her will provisions, and his or her estate will receive the benefit of Sec. 6166. The unlimited marital deduction permits the entrepreneur to leave a controlling portion of the business interest in trust for his or her surviving spouse to provide the surviving spouse with substantial income until his or her death while deferring the impact of estate taxes until the second death. The installment plan of Sec. 6166 can also be elected at the second death.
- The estate tax associated with the inclusion of the business interest can be delayed until the death of the second spouse and then deferred in part for an additional 15 years.
- A favorable 2 percent interest rate is applicable to a portion of the deferred estate taxes.
- It is possible for Sec. 6166 relief to be used with any form of closely held business entity.

- The tax liability that is associated with the business interest can be passed to the heirs inheriting the business and might be withdrawn from the business as deductible salary payments in the case of a corporation.
- Sec. 303 redemptions can be made to pay the deferred amount as it becomes due in the case of a corporation.
- Life insurance proceeds with flexible settlement options can be used to provide the installments.

Disadvantages of electing the Sec. 6166 installment payments of estate taxes are as follows:

- A buy-sell agreement cannot be used with this arrangement since the business interest must be included in the gross estate for the purposes of electing Sec. 6166.
- Providing for the decedent's other heirs may be difficult if the business interest is ultimately left to only the active successors.
- Installment payments will put a substantial cash drain on the business for many years.
- There is no income tax deduction for the interest incurred on the deferred taxes.
- The estate must be left open for a much longer period of time while the taxes are deferred.
- There is a false sense of security that the taxes will be easily manageable in the deferred form.

Use of Sec. 303 Redemptions

Avoiding Family Attribution Troubles. Sec. 303 stock redemptions provided special estate and income tax relief to estates that hold stock in a closely held corporation. This section provides that a corporation may redeem stock from an estate that holds stock in the closely held corporation valued in excess of 35 percent of the adjusted gross estate. The redemption will be limited to the amount of death taxes and funeral and administrative expenses that are allowable as deductions to the estate. Sec. 303 is useful because the family corporation actually provides liquidity of the deceased shareholder's estate by making distributions in the form of the redemption proceeds. This technique is particularly favorable for the family corporation since family attribution is not applied and a Sec. 303 redemption is treated as a sale or exchange. Thus the estate will generally recognize no taxable gain on the redemption due to the available basis step-up.

The Sec. 303 redemption is appropriate if the family corporation stock will be held by the parent until death. The Sec. 303 redemption might be available to both spouses' estates if the stock is passed to the surviving spouse. Even if no estate tax will be due at the first spouse's death, Sec. 303 redemptions can be used to provide funds to pay other death costs such as state death taxes and funeral and administration expenses. Furthermore, these redemptions can occur even if Sec. 6166 installment payments are elected. A Sec. 303 redemptions distribution in the amount of the installment due under Sec. 6166 may be made by the corporation each year as the installment becomes due.

Postredemption Control. Whenever a stock redemption is performed, one question that must be answered is, What is the impact of the stock redemption on the control of the corporation? The question of control will generally not be a problem if the family corporation includes as shareholders only the parents and lineal descendants. When the stock is redeemed from either parent's gross estate, the control will shift to the other shareholders who in this case are the intended long-run recipients of the ownership of the corporation.

EXAMPLE

Mr. and Mrs. Jones operate Jones, Inc., a closely held family corporation. Each owns 40 percent of the voting stock with the remaining 20 percent divided equally between their daughters, Martha and Sheila, the intended successors in the business. Assume Mr. and Mrs. Jones each has a will leaving his or her property to the other spouse.

At the first death of Mr. and Mrs. Jones, no federal estate tax will be due because of the marital deduction. The surviving spouse will inherit the stock held by the decedent-spouse and will hold 80 percent control in the corporation. A Sec. 303 redemption at the first death will cover any state death taxes and funeral and administration expenses payable. The redemption will only slightly reduce the control of the surviving spouse.

At the second death the Sec. 303 redemption that is available will be sizable if there are substantial federal estate taxes that must be paid. When the redemption is effected, the control of the corporation will shift in equal shares to Martha and Sheila—the intended successors.

When Nonfamily Members Are Also Shareholders. The problem of control following a Sec. 303 redemption might be significant if nonfamily members (or more remote family members) hold stock in the corporation. For example, suppose two unrelated individuals are 50 percent shareholders in a corporation. If each shareholder plans to leave stock in the corporation to his or her children, a Sec. 303 redemption effected by the estate of the first shareholder to die will cause the surviving shareholder to hold more than 50 percent control in the corporation. This result will probably be troublesome to the shareholders since each expects his or her heirs to receive a 50 percent interest in the corporation. If this unintended result occurs, the survivor is placed in a position to control the corporation, possibly to the detriment of the decedent's heirs.

Does this mean that a Sec. 303 redemption should not be used under these circumstances? Fortunately the answer is "no." A recent ruling by the IRS helps shareholders solve this problem. Quite simply, the shareholders can recapitalize the family corporation by having each shareholder exchange some of his or her voting common stock for newly issued nonvoting common or preferred stock. If a Sec. 303 redemption will occur at the death of either shareholder (or at the death of their spouses if they inherit stock), *nonvoting* stock can be redeemed by the corporation without affecting voting control.

The recapitalization that creates the new nonvoting class of stock could even occur after the death of the shareholder and still qualify for a redemption under Sec. 303. If the corporation is an S corporation, there is a requirement that only one class of stock exists. However, nonvoting common stock is *not* treated as a separate class of stock, and an S corporation can safely recapitalize to create nonvoting common stock for this purpose. The process of adding new classes of stock through a recapitalization or a stock dividend will be discussed later in this textbook.

EXAMPLE

Jane and Audrey are equal and unrelated co-owners of Tours, Inc., a travel agency. Each shareholder has a son who works for the travel agency and is the intended successor at his mother's death.

Assume Audrey dies this year and leaves a substantial estate. Audrey's stock could be redeemed by Tours to pay death taxes and funeral and administration expenses. If this plan is followed, Audrey's son will inherit less than 50 percent of the stock of Tours since some of the estate's stock will be redeemed to pay those costs. Suppose instead that Tours declared a stock dividend that provides one share of nonvoting common stock for each share of voting common held by the shareholders. Following the dividend, the nonvoting common stock can be redeemed from Audrey's estate under Sec. 303 without affecting voting control because her son will inherit 50 percent of the *voting* common stock.

Advantages of using a Sec. 303 redemption include the following:

- The family corporation shareholder can retain the corporation until death (or his or her surviving spouse's death) and leave the business to the appropriate successors.
- The family corporation will pay the deceased shareholder's death taxes and funeral and administration expenses.
- The family corporation reduces E & P in the redemption distribution and lowers both its exposure to the accumulated-earnings tax and the surviving shareholder's exposure to future dividends.
- The family attribution rules are inapplicable, and the redemption automatically gets sale-or-exchange treatment.
- The redemption will generally be tax free due to the estate's basis step-up.
- The redemption can still be made even if the estate has adequate liquidity.
- The redemption may occur over the period of Sec. 6166 installments.
- Nonvoting stock can be redeemed without reducing the estate's voting power.
- The redemptions can be funded in advance with life insurance.
- The redemption provides flexibility to the estate plan and does not have to be preplanned through a binding agreement.

Disadvantages of Sec. 303 redemptions include the following:

- The redemptions are limited to death costs and will not solve all dispositive and liquidity needs.
- The redemption can only be made if surplus exists under the typical state corporate law.
- The provision only applies to corporations and cannot be used by other family businesses.
- The redemption must be timely and is limited after 3 years and 90 days after the estate tax return is due.
- The estate of some deceased shareholders may not meet the 35 percent threshold. This might create doubt over the applicability of Sec. 303 until postdeath valuations are completed.
- The death costs must actually be allocated by will or state tax apportionment rules to the redeeming shareholder. Inconsistent will provisions or intestacy may render this provision ineffective.

Use of Life Insurance in a Family Business Transfer Process

Life insurance is more valuable than ever before in the process of transferring the family business. The new valuation rules have reduced the estate planning value of many estate freezing arrangements. These rules do not affect the use of life insurance in the transfer process. For example, life insurance is often used as the funding vehicle for a family buy-sell agreement. The family enterprise can be used to help fund the buyout of the senior family member by providing certain benefits to the family successors. For example, the business could split dollar the policy funding the buy-sell agreement with the intended buyers. Or the business could provide the additional premium dollars to the buyers through reasonable-compensation bonuses to these individuals.

Outside the business setting the *irrevocable life insurance trust (ILIT)* is extremely important in the estate plan of the family business owner. This life insurance trust can be designed to provide substantial appreciation in the form of death benefits to the survivors of the business owner. These death benefits could be used to provide liquidity to the estate. The life insurance trust could be set up for the benefit of the family business successors. The trust would receive the proceeds, which in turn could be used to buy the business interest from the estate. The trust would then administer the business interest for the benefit of the business successors. The estate, on the other hand, would receive cash in exchange for the business interest so adequate liquidity will be available and substantial bequests to the inactive heirs could be funded. As with all parts of the business transfer plan, the life insurance covering the life of the senior family member should be designed to coexist with the rest of his or her business and estate plan.

CHAPTER REVIEW

Key Terms and Concepts

estate freeze	grantor-retained annuity trust (GRAT)
qualified payments	grantor-retained unitrust (GRUT)

Review Questions

The answers to the review questions are in the supplement. The self-test questions and the answers to them are also in the supplement and on The American College Online.

1. What are the problems that must be addressed if family successors are employed by the family business? [1]
2. How might the owner of a family business provide for inactive heirs? [1]
3. Identify the typical estate planning objectives of the family business owner. [1]
4. Describe how the financial services professional might communicate the transfer plan for the family business to affected family members and employees. [1]
5. Describe the structure of the following types of sales proceeds received in the sale of a family business:
   a. installment note
   b. self-canceling installment note (SCIN)
   c. private annuity [2]
6. Why are outright lifetime gifts of a family business often impractical for transferring a family business to successors? [2]
7. Identify the preferences that shareholders of preferred stock typically hold. [3]
8. Suppose a parent (P) would like to recapitalize her controlled corporation and receive preferred stock. As part of the transaction, P will gift the remaining common to her children. Describe the gift tax consequences of the transaction if
   a. P retains preferred stock providing qualified payments
   b. P retains noncumulative preferred [3]
9. How might gifts of nonvoting common stock to family members be used to reduce the gross estate of a shareholder while avoiding Sec. 2701? [3]
10. Describe the restrictions on the limited partnership interests in a family limited partnership that create the minority interests and lack of marketability discounts. [3]
11. Describe the requirements for a grantor-retained annuity trust (GRAT). [4]

12. How is the use of a GRAT to transfer a family corporation in trust affected by the following:
    a. federal gift taxes
    b. federal estate taxes
    c. cash distributions from the business to the GRAT [4]

13. Describe the requirements that a buy-sell agreement must meet for the purchase price provision to establish the estate tax value of the underlying business interest. [5]

14. Identify the advantages and disadvantages to forming buy-sell agreements between family members to transfer a family business. [5]

15. Describe the usefulness of the installment payment of estate taxes under Sec. 6166 to the family business owner. [6]

16. Ralph and Ed are unrelated, and each owns 50 of the 100 shares of common stock outstanding in Honeymoon, Inc., a closely held corporation. Each shareholder has a daughter employed by the business who represents the natural successor to her father in the business. Suppose Ralph dies this year, and his executor would like to use a Sec. 303 redemption to provide estate liquidity. Devise a plan that meets these objectives and prevents the shift of corporate control to Ed following a Sec. 303 redemption. [6]

17. Explain how a life insurance trust can be used to help a family business owner reach his or her dispositive objectives. [7]

THE VALUATION OF A CLOSELY HELD BUSINESS 11

Learning Objectives

An understanding of the material in this chapter should enable the student to

1. Identify the situations in which business valuation may be necessary, and define fair market value for estate tax value purposes.
2. Describe the basic principles of the adjusted-book-value method of valuation, and explain the problems in obtaining the data necessary to use this method in practical situations.
3. Describe the basic principles of the capitalization-of-earnings and discounted-future-earnings (DFE) methods of valuation, and explain the data problems associated with using these methods.
4. Identify some of the factors, in addition to the use of valuation techniques or formulas, that must be considered in any practical business valuation.
5. Describe the additional considerations apart from the value of the underlying business that must be used in valuing corporate stock and some of the factors that must be considered in valuing preferred stock.
6. Discuss the issues that must be considered in valuation of a business for buy-sell purposes.
7. Explain the issues associated with employing an appraiser for tax purposes.

Business valuation is an extremely complex topic. Valuation consultants receive large fees for formal valuation studies often consisting of hundreds of pages. Because practical business valuation methodology includes characteristics of both art and science, it is common for skilled appraisers to differ on the value of a business. Consequently business valuation disputes often result in costly litigation. Although this course cannot include a detailed treatment of business valuation, every financial services professional should have a thorough understanding of the basic principles.

THE PURPOSES OF BUSINESS VALUATION

A person who advises a business owner or professional typically faces the issues concerning valuation when it becomes necessary to determine the fair market value of a closely held business. Such situations might include the following:

- A business owner is planning to sell to an outsider and needs to know an appropriate asking price (or if someone is looking to purchase a business, an appropriate offering price).
- A corporation is facing a merger and dissenting shareholders demand statutory appraisal rights. The fair price for the dissenting shareholders' stock must be determined.
- A stockholder in a closely held corporation or a partner in a partnership dies and the stock or partnership interest is a major asset of the estate. What is its value for tax purposes? If beneficiaries are to receive equal shares of the estate, what is the value of the business for this purpose? How much life insurance will be needed to plan for these problems?
- The owners of a business have executed a buy-sell agreement to dispose of the business at death. What purchase price should be included in the agreement and how much life insurance funding is needed? Should the purchase price be modified over time and if so, how?
- A closely held business has decided to adopt an employee stock ownership plan (ESOP) or stock bonus plan to increase the motivation of employees. What value should be assigned to the shares of stock?
- A corporation plans a stock redemption to provide cash to a stockholder. What value should be paid for each share of the corporation's stock?
- A senior family member may wish to gift interests in the family business to successor family members. A valuation may be required to determine the qualification of the gift for the annual gift tax exclusion or, if the gift is taxable, the amount of the gift for tax purposes.
- The new valuation rules add new importance to the valuation of family enterprises. Valuations are critical for the family buy-sell agreement since the valuation provision must satisfy Sec. 2703 to avoid adverse estate tax consequences.
- The estate and income tax advantages of donating business interests to charity may appeal to a business owner. The valuation

of these interests by a qualified appraiser would be required for donations of appreciated closely held stock valued in excess of $10,000.

liquidation rights

The value that an owner derives from a closely held business interest comes from one or more of three sources. First, there are the rights that an owner holds in the business assets. Recall that a sole proprietor owns any property used by the business. The owners of a partnership or corporation have no direct individual rights to specific business property but have a legal interest known as *liquidation rights* against business property should the business be dissolved. Another source of value to the business owner is the right to receive income from business operations. This right will usually be significant only if the business is being valued as a going concern. Finally, the right to control the business by the majority owner, or majority group, is a source of value. Therefore ownership units representing controlling blocks can be worth relatively more than ownership units that are in the minority group.

The valuation technique selected by the financial services professional depends on the purpose for the valuation. The valuation technique chosen will differ depending on whether the business is being valued for liquidation purposes or for sale as a going concern. Furthermore, a valuation being performed for tax purposes must fall within the acceptable guidelines of the IRS.

IRS BUSINESS VALUATION GUIDELINES

fair market value

The tax laws do not specify the business valuation technique to be used for each circumstance, but the estate and gift tax regulations make it clear that fair market value is the standard. For this purpose the IRS has issued many advisory rulings stating the appropriate factors to consider in ascertaining fair market value. The regulations define the *fair market value* as "the net amount at which a willing purchaser would pay a willing seller, neither being under any compulsion to buy and sell and both having reasonable knowledge of all relevant facts." Important factors to consider for this purpose include the value of all business assets, including goodwill, and the earning capacity of the business.

Fair Market Value

- The net amount a willing buyer would pay to a willing seller
- No compulsion on either side
- Reasonable knowledge by both sides of all relevant facts

Recognizing the difficulties in applying such vague standards to the valuation of a closely held business interest, the IRS issued a landmark ruling enumerating the factors to be considered in such a valuation.[26] The ruling states that no one basic valuation formula (popular valuation formulas will be discussed later) is sufficient to establish an audit-proof valuation of a business. Rather the valuation methodology must take into account all relevant facts and circumstances of the business. The factors listed in the ruling are

- the nature of the business and the history of the enterprise from its inception
- economic outlook in general, and the condition and outlook of the specific industry in particular
- the book value of the stock and the financial condition of the business
- the earning capacity of the company
- the dividend-paying capacity
- determination of whether the enterprise has goodwill or other intangible value
- sales of the stock and the size of the block of stock to be valued
- the market price of actively traded stocks of corporations engaged in the same or a similar line of business

Although these factors must all be considered in determining fair market value, the weights accorded to each factor will depend on the circumstances of the specific business. Generally speaking, the earning capacity of the company is primary. Other factors will be weighted depending on the circumstances of the business being valued and the purposes for which the valuation is being performed. For example, goodwill may be an important intangible asset for a business operating as a going concern. However, the goodwill value of a business may be attributable to the skills and services of

26. Rev. Rul. 59-60, 1959-1 C.B. 237.

its owner. If the business is being valued for liquidation purposes or at the death of the owner, goodwill may no longer be significant.

VALUATION METHODS—FOCUS ON THE BUSINESS ASSETS

Business valuation methods can be divided into two basic categories: (1) those focusing on assets and (2) those focusing on earning power. In the previous section we noted some factors established by the IRS for valuing a business. Among these factors were the book value and the goodwill of the business. In this section we will discuss some techniques that can be used to determine the value of a firm's assets.

Book Value

Valuing the assets of a business starts with an analysis of the balance sheet. A simple balance sheet for Hypo Enterprises is displayed in the following table.

book value

Hypo's balance sheet reveals one type of business value, *book value*, which is equal to the excess of assets over liabilities. Book value is generally indicated on the balance sheet under the entry "owners' equity" for a proprietorship or "capital account" for a partnership or corporation. The table shows the book value of Hypo to be $343,000.

Table 11-1 Hypo Enterprises Balance Sheet

Assets		Liabilities	
Real property	$440,000	Mortgages	$357,000
Equipment and fixtures	50,000	Current indebtedness	50,000
Inventory	140,000	Accounts payable	25,000
Accounts receivable	150,000	Other	30,000
Cash	25,000	Owners' equity (or capital account)	343,000
	$805,000		$805,000

In valuing closely held corporate stock, book value per share is the total book value divided by the number of shares outstanding at the end of the accounting period. The value of a block of stock is simply the number of shares in the block multiplied by book value per share.

Is the book value the "real" value of the corporation, that is, the fair market value? For a number of reasons it generally is not. The value of the assets on the books is usually not their fair market value. Rather, book value of an asset is usually equal to its initial cost less accumulated depreciation. The fair market value of any asset may be more or less than its book value. Some assets, such as real estate, eventually appreciate over time and have a fair market value that is considerably higher than their book value. On the other hand, there may be assets whose values on the books are in excess of their actual fair market value. For example, some accounts receivable are typically uncollectible. If no adjustment is made on the books for these accounts, book value will be in excess of actual value. Furthermore, obsolescent equipment may be on the books, and its depreciated cost figure will be higher than its market value.

The values of liabilities as shown on the books are likely to be more realistic. It is unlikely that a liability will decline in value because the obligation to pay will generally remain legally enforceable as long as the debtor and the liability continue to exist.

Book Value

- Book value equals total balance sheet assets minus total balance sheet liabilities.
- Assets are usually valued on the balance sheet at cost, perhaps less accumulated depreciation.
- Book value may be much more or much less than fair market value.

Adjusted Book Value

Although the courts have long recognized that book value should not be the primary factor in valuation disputes, it is nevertheless one of eight factors on the IRS's enumerated list for valuation of a closely held business. The valuation appraiser should always consider book value, particularly if it yields results consistent with other methods.

One way to obtain a more realistic book-value figure is to recast the balance sheet and adjust each asset so that its value is closer to its fair market value. This of course requires the valuation of each asset, which can be difficult. However, it is sometimes easier to arrive at a separate value for each asset than to attempt to value the entire business. In adjusting the book value of individual assets it is generally easier to adjust the value of investment-type assets held by the business to current market value. Because the true value of operating assets is more difficult to determine, firms consisting primarily of operating assets should be valued by other techniques. Adjustments to Hypo's balance are incorporated in the following table, revealing a more realistic book value.

Table 11-2 Hypo Enterprises Adjusted Book Value (not including intangibles)

Assets		Liabilities	
Cash	$ 25,000	Accounts payable	$ 25,000
Accounts receivable	125,000	Current indebtedness	50,000
Inventory	110,000	Other	30,000
Equipment and fixtures	40,000	Mortgages	357,000
Real property	600,000		
	$900,000		$462,000
Assets as adjusted: $900,000			
Less total liabilities: $462,000			
Adjusted book value (not including intangibles): $438,000			

Valuing Goodwill

Is this adjusted-book-value figure any closer to Hypo's fair market value? Note that the adjusted book value was determined "not including intangibles." This means that the value of a business may differ from the sum of all the tangible assets less liabilities. A business may have customer relationships that can be transferred to the remaining owners or to a new owner. In addition, the business may have developed "know-how" in producing its product or service that will also carry over to the new owner. Furthermore, the business may have a perfect location that is particularly good for its type of product or service, but the location is not necessarily reflected in the market value of the real property.

intangible assets

adjusted book value

None of these characteristics normally appear as an asset on the unadjusted balance sheet, but these *intangible assets* will increase the fair market value of the business. Therefore in order to arrive at an *adjusted book value* that approximates fair market value it may be necessary to add a value for goodwill to the value of the firm's tangible assets.

goodwill

One problem that exists in the process of adjusting book value for intangibles is the difficulty in valuing goodwill. The IRS has changed its opinion over the years and currently allows a formula valuation of goodwill only when better evidence of its value is unavailable. Theoretically *goodwill* represents the earning power of a business in excess of a fair return on its tangible assets. A formula technique may be used to estimate this theoretical value.

EXAMPLE

Assume Hypo's earnings have averaged $100,000 annually over the previous 5 years. If a fair rate of return on tangible assets in Hypo's industry is 10 percent and Hypo is considered an average risk, Hypo could expect to earn $90,000 per year based on its tangible assets (10 percent of $900,000). The additional $10,000 of annual income ($100,000 less $90,000) may be attributed to goodwill. The annual earnings attributable to goodwill are capitalized, as discussed in the section "Capitalization of Earnings," to reach the total value of goodwill.

Although the IRS has taken the position that formula valuation of goodwill should be used only as a last resort, it is often used by appraisers and generally accepted by the courts.

Some other facts about goodwill should be mentioned. First, goodwill can often be attributed to identifiable factors such as effective management. If these factors will not be present in the future, then the value of the goodwill should be reduced or eliminated. Second, goodwill can generally be claimed as an element of value only when the business is sold as a unit. If a business is sold in a piecemeal fashion, the value of goodwill is usually lost. It may be possible to sell know-how or the license to use a particular trade name, or in some cases it may be possible to recoup the value of a certain location for a particular business. Usually, however, the full amount of goodwill can be obtained only if the business is sold as a unit.

VALUATION METHODS—FOCUS ON EARNINGS

So far the discussion has concentrated on valuation techniques for estimating a fair market value of the assets of a business. Income has not been the focus. However, business income is one of the bases of the theoretical concept of value that owners derive from a business. Furthermore, note that the earning capacity of the firm is a prominent factor among those enumerated by the IRS. Fundamental in determining the value of a business derived from its earnings capacity is the capitalization-of-earnings concept.

The capitalization-of-earnings concept is based on the premise that business property has value only to produce profits. When we speak of the fair market value of a going concern, we are talking about a market that is composed of buyers interested only in the income-earning potential of the property. Thus the value of a business property is equal to the present value of the income stream that the property will produce in the future.

For example, if a property will never produce any income and has no liquidation value, its fair market value is obviously zero. Assume a certain property will produce an income of $10 per year indefinitely. If the expected average rate of return on capital is 10 percent over this indefinite period, then an income stream of $10 per year will correspond to a capital investment of $100. Consequently the fair market value of the property will be $100.

Capitalization of Earnings

capitalization of earnings

The concept that the value of property is the value of the earnings stream it produces leads to one of the most common methods of valuing a closely held business—*capitalization of earnings*—often used for valuing the stock of a closely held business for buy-sell agreements. This method is particularly appropriate in determining the value of a going concern that is not intended to be liquidated in the foreseeable future. This technique will be more likely than any other to give an appropriate valuation where there are substantial earnings from a business with relatively low book value.

The starting point in the capitalization-of-earnings method is the determination of normal earnings for the business. The simplest method is to begin with an examination of the recent after-tax earnings as a means of estimating *future* earnings. Based on its rulings, the Internal Revenue Service would generally recommend at least a 5-year period for a representative sample.

The earnings for the period selected will often have to be adjusted to eliminate nonrecurring or nonrepresentative events such as extraordinary capital gains or losses, unusual retirement payments, or any extraordinary income or expense items. Likewise, earnings should be adjusted to eliminate the effect of any changes in the accounting method used during the period. In a closely held business it is also important to examine the salaries paid to stockholder-employees to see whether they are reasonable. That is, would nonowner-employees receive the same compensation as the stockholder-employees performing the same services? If a portion of the stockholder-employees' salaries is in reality a disguised dividend, then the net income shown on the income statement is understated because salary is deductible from gross income while dividends are not. On the other hand, it may be that a stockholder-employee is taking an artificially low salary to provide funds for additional capital investment in the business. In such situations it would be appropriate to reduce stated earnings to arrive at an accurate earnings figure for the valuation process.

If loans are made to shareholders, stated earnings may also have to be adjusted. Loans to shareholders from closely held corporations are typically interest free or bear a very low rate of interest. This deprives the business of interest income that could ordinarily be earned on the funds loaned to shareholders. Stated earnings should be adjusted upward by the amount of this lost income to produce a more representative figure. Note that if a large part of the business's capital is loaned to shareholders, it may be difficult to value the business because so much of this capital is not actually used in the business itself.

weighted-average earnings

The next step is deciding how to make use of the adjusted earnings figure. The simplest approach would be to use the average of all years examined. However, if there is a strong trend in the earnings or earnings have been erratic, a simple average will not be indicative of current value. For example, if the earnings trend is consistently increasing or decreasing and the trend is expected to continue, a simple average would be misleading. One solution would simply be to use a single year, namely the latest year. Another approach would be to use *weighted-average earnings* in which the most recent year is given the greatest weight and the preceding years progressively less weight, as illustrated below.

Table 11-3 Hypo Enterprises Adjusted Earnings

2006				$ 80,000
2007				85,000
2008				90,000
2009				95,000
2010				100,000
		Total earnings		$450,000
Average earnings (unweighted): $90,000 ($450,000 5 years)				
Most recent year's earnings: $100,000				
Weighted-average earnings				
2010	$100,000	x	5 =	$ 500,000
2009	95,000	x	4 =	380,000
2008	90,000	x	3 =	270,000
2007	85,000	x	2 =	170,000
2006	80,000	x	1 =	80,000
			15	$1,400,000
	$1,400,000	÷	15 =	$ 93,333

Other techniques may be used to determine the most representative earnings figure. For example, it may be permissible to throw out the earnings figure for a given year if it can be shown that the year was unrepresentative for some reason (for example, the business was wiped out by a flood, or the earnings were influenced by a national economic catastrophe).

After an appropriate earnings figure has been determined, the next step is the calculation of an appropriate rate of return for the capitalization procedure. The question that must be answered here is, What rate of return is appropriate for capital invested in this particular business? As a starting point it is permissible to look at capital market factors such as interest rates on long-term bonds, but this will not give the final answer.

For a given business the rate of return will depend not only on the current capital market rates, but also on the amount of risk in the particular business (note again that risk is implicit in several of the IRS's enumerated factors). A high-risk business would dictate a higher required rate of return than would a stable, less risky business.

capitalization factor

In recent years the IRS has tended to use a rate of 10 percent for a medium-risk business, so this is often used as a standard. However, because current interest rates may be different, it might be appropriate to substitute another rate as a point of reference. In any event after the rate of return has been selected, the inverse of this rate (100 divided by the percentage capitalization rate) is the *capitalization factor.*

EXAMPLE

An investor in a business similar to that of Hypo Enterprises would expect a 15 percent return on investment. Thus the capitalization factor for Hypo Enterprises would be 6.67 (100 ÷ 15). To determine the value of Hypo Enterprises using the capitalization-of-earnings method, the weighted-average earnings figure determined from Table 11-3 is multiplied by the capitalization factor:

$93,333 x 6.67 = $622,531

This figure of $622,531 is the value of the business as determined by the capitalization-of-earnings method.

Capitalization-of-Earnings Method of Valuation

- Determine normal annual earnings by reviewing past results.
- Eliminate effect of nonrecurring or nonrepresentative events.
- Adjust for unusually high or low salaries of owners.
- Adjust for loans to owners.
- Compute unweighted or weighted average annual earnings.
- Decide on an appropriate rate of return.
- Multiply the adjusted earnings figure by (100 ÷ rate of return).

Discounted Future Earnings

discounted future earnings (DFE)

Another method of valuation, *discounted future earnings (DFE)*, is a somewhat sophisticated variation of the capitalization-of-earnings method but is based on the same underlying principles. One problem with the capitalization-of-earnings method is its dependence on historical data, whereas in theory the value of a business is equal to the present value of the *future* earnings flow. The DFE method is therefore based on projected future earnings.

The first step in the DFE method is to forecast future earnings. This is more speculative than simply taking past earnings and weighting them as in the capitalization-of-earnings method discussed above. There are a number of sophisticated mathematical techniques for projecting future earnings that are based on earnings data from the past. Regardless of the technique used in the forecast, however, any projection is inherently speculative. The basic rule of mathematical modeling should be kept in mind: garbage in, garbage out. That is, a projection can never be any better than the factual data on which it is based. Furthermore, a projection becomes increasingly unreliable as it reaches farther into the future. It is traditional to project for only a few years, even though the DFE valuation could theoretically be based on a projection into the indefinite future. A 5-year income projection will be used here for illustration, with the income leveling off for all future years. Theoretically the projection should continue indefinitely, but in reality it does not change the result significantly if the earnings forecast is leveled off after a few years because of the impact of discounting for the time value of money. A typical earnings projection for Hypo is illustrated below.

Table 11-4 Projected Future Earnings for Hypo Enterprises

Year	Projected Earnings
1	$100,000
2	120,000
3	130,000
4	140,000
5	150,000
6 and subsequent years	150,000

After forecasting future earnings, the next step in applying the DFE method is to discount the projected earnings stream to determine its present value since the value of earnings to be received in the future is less than if the same earnings were available today. The *discount factor* is a percentage representing the time value of the money deferred. The *discount rate* should be the rate of return that the investor would expect from the next best alternative investment opportunity with comparable risk. This discount rate is known as the investor's opportunity cost for investing funds in the business venture. The *opportunity cost* is the profit rate that an investor would expect to receive on an investment as an incentive to make that investment, also referred to as the *return on common equity*. The long-term average rate of return that is earned by investors in common stocks listed on the New York

Stock Exchange is about 10 percent. However, these are large companies and are relatively low-risk investments, so 10 percent might be taken as the lowest appropriate discount rate for a closely held business.

After the appropriate discount rate is determined, the stream of future payments is discounted using the selected rate for each future year in the forecast. The sum of the discounted future earnings is the current value of the firm for valuation purposes.

EXAMPLE

Suppose it is determined that the appropriate discount rate for Hypo Enterprises is 15 percent. Applying this rate to the projected earnings displayed above yields the results below.

In the example above the same discount rate (15 percent) was applied to all years in the forecast, but this may not always be appropriate. The prediction for next year's earnings is likely to be more accurate than that for the 5th year, so it may be better to give a higher weight to the earlier years in order to improve the accuracy of the method.

Table 11-5 Discounted-Future-Earnings Value of Hypo Enterprises

Year	Projected Earnings	Discount Factor (15%)	Present Value
1	$100,000	0.870	$ 87,000
2	120,000	0.756	90,720
3	130,000	0.658	85,540
4	140,000	0.572	80,080
5	150,000	0.497	74,550
6 and subsequent years	1,000,000*	0.497†	497,000
Current value			$914,890

* This is the value of a constant annual income stream of $150,000 at 15% (that is, $150,000 multiplied by the capitalization factor 6.67).

† $1,000,000 is the value of the income stream of $150,000 per year at the end of the 5th year, so a discount factor is used for 5 years.

There are several ways of doing this, including the simple use of numerical multipliers such as those that were applied in the example earlier in this chapter for the capitalization-of-earnings method. Another weighting approach uses a higher discount rate (up to 30 percent, for example) for earnings that are projected far into the future. Using the higher discount rate reflects the fact that estimated future income streams become more uncertain as the projection reaches farther into the future.

Discounted-Future-Earnings Method of Valuation

- Forecast future annual earnings for a specified number of years.
- Select an appropriate discount rate.
- Give greater importance to early years than later years.
  - Assign weights or
  - Apply different discount rates.
- Compute present value of each year's earnings.
- Total the results.

Years' Purchase

One simple capitalization formula is the *years' purchase* technique. Quite simply, the purchaser picks a prescribed payback period and multiplies this period by the forecasted annual earnings of the target business. For example, a 5-years' purchase price for a firm with projected after-tax annual income of $100,000 would be $500,000. This technique is primarily used as a quick rule-of-thumb by would-be purchasers of a business and should not be the sole method of valuation for tax purposes.

Validity of Capitalization Approaches

The capitalization-of-earnings and DFE methods of valuation are theoretically attractive, but it is not easy to apply them practically. First, the valuation appraiser can never be certain that the earnings figure used in the capitalization procedure (or the projected earnings used in the DFE method) is actually representative of the earnings potential of the business. Second, the capitalization (or discount) rate chosen is subject to speculation, and even small changes in the rate can produce dramatically different valuations.

It is worth repeating that the IRS looks with disfavor on valuations determined solely by a fixed formula. Wherever possible, the valuation reached by formula should be supported by other factors, but capitalization formulas are generally acceptable as some evidence of value.

MISCELLANEOUS VALUATION METHODS

Hybrid Valuation Formulas

Because of the inherent difficulties in applying either a capitalization method or the adjusted-book-value method, various valuation formulas have been devised as shortcut methods. Some of these formulas have been approved in various court decisions and consequently are often used with the hope that if the valuation is litigated for tax or other purposes, consideration will be given to prior judicial approval.

For example, one formula determines a value based on capitalization and another based on adjusted book value and then combines the two using weighting factors. Suppose that a capitalization method produced a value of $500,000 and the adjusted book value of $400,000. If the valuation consultant found court cases that had applied this type of formula to a similar business and had given a weight of 60 percent to the capitalization result and 40 percent to the adjusted-book-value result, the valuation would then be

60 percent of $500,000	$300,000
40 percent of $400,000	160,000
Total	$460,000

Another type of formula is demonstrated below using a capitalization approach to determine the value of the goodwill and an adjusted-book-value method for the other assets. The two values are added together to produce the final valuation. Under this method the adjusted book value is first determined, sometimes by using the average book value for a period of years, and then the average earnings are determined. At a given nominal capitalization rate the average earnings may exceed the expected return on the adjusted book value. This excess return, attributable to goodwill, is then capitalized at a higher rate, usually reflecting the fact that the return on goodwill is riskier or more speculative. The value that is attributable to goodwill is then added to the adjusted book value.

Table 11-6 Hybrid Valuation of Hypo Enterprises		
Adjusted book value (average)		$300,000
5-year average earnings	$60,000	
12 percent return on adjusted book value	36,000	
Excess attributable to goodwill	$24,000	
$24,000 capitalized at 20 percent rate		120,000
Total value of corporation		$420,000

As with other methods the results from hybrid valuation formulas are only as good as the data and the validity of the assumptions used in making the computations. The advantage of the hybrid methods is that they have the ability to show more clearly the impact of various factors (such as the effect of goodwill, the comparison of adjusted book value with capitalized earnings), and they therefore may be of some assistance in determining whether the assumptions and data are valid.

Valuation by Comparison

One method the IRS often employs to check the validity of an appraiser's evaluation is comparative analysis. The goal of comparative analysis is to determine the current fair market value of a business by comparing it to comparable businesses of known value. This involves the comparison of various ratios of the business being valued with the ratios of comparable businesses with established values.

A business with an established value, either a company listed on a national exchange or a company whose price has been recently determined, must be selected as a benchmark. The company that is selected should be similar in (1) line of business, (2) size, (3) growth potential, and (4) degree of risk to the closely held business that is being valued.

The appraiser may find a comparable company by searching lists that are published by Dow Jones or Standard & Poor's. Once the appraiser has selected a comparable company, the next step is to compare various ratios of the benchmark to the business that is being currently valued to arrive at an estimate of the price.

Price-Earnings Ratio

The price-earnings (P/E) ratio is used quite often by private valuation appraisers and the IRS. It is determined by dividing the average price for the comparable company over a selected period by its average earnings over that period. This factor is then multiplied by the earnings of the business interest being valued to arrive at an estimate of current fair market value. To achieve the most accurate estimate of value, it may be best to use a P/E ratio that is the average of several comparable firms in the industry. It may also be wise to find an average of the P/E ratio over years for each comparison firm.

EXAMPLE

Suppose a company comparable to Hypo had the price and earnings data for the last 3 years as shown above. If the earnings for Hypo over the past year were $150,000, the current value of Hypo would be $342,000 ($150,000 x 2.28).

Table 11-7 Price and Earnings Data for Company Comparable to Hypo

Year	Earnings	Average Price	P/E
Year 1	$250,000	$550,000	2.20
Year 2	300,000	750,000	2.50
Year 3	325,000	700,000	2.15
			Average P/E 2.28

Price Book-Value Ratio

The price book-value (P/BV) ratio is determined by dividing the average price of a comparable company for the year by its average book value for the year. Again, the P/BV factor is multiplied by the book value of the closely held business interest being valued. For example, if the comparable firm has an average price for the year of $750,000 and an average book value for the year of $500,000, the P/BV ratio is 150 percent. Therefore the current market value of the closely held business being tested should be 150 percent of its book value, using this method.

Valuation by Ratios

- Determine the P/E ratio and/or P/BV ratio for a comparable company.
- Apply the ratio(s) to the earnings and/or book value of the company to be valued.

The variations on these basic types of comparative analysis can become extremely complex. This discussion was included at this point to give the reader an introduction to the terminology and techniques of comparative analysis. Additional ratios could be utilized and complex adjustments could be made to the data to increase the accuracy of the valuation. Since the IRS often uses this type of analysis, it is advisable for the valuation appraiser to perform a basic comparative computation.

ADJUSTMENTS TO BUSINESS VALUE

Applicable Discounts

It is often justifiable and necessary to discount the value of a business interest determined by one of the above-mentioned valuation techniques. These discounts are appropriate when the value determined by one of the methods is greater than the actual current market value. Reasons for the disparity between actual value and the value of the business interest reached by established techniques are that (1) the interest being valued represents a minority interest, (2) the interest being valued suffers from a lack of marketability, (3) the property is held in individual fractional ownership, (4) the interest being valued has built-in capital-gains tax or other liabilities, and (5) the interest is being liquidated on a distressed basis.

The Minority Discount

minority discount

We mentioned earlier that one basis of value of a business interest is control power. A *minority discount* interest stems from the inability to control the business. The owner or controlling group of owners of a business possesses benefits that translate into market value. The benefits derived from this control are the ability to

- direct the management of the business (that is, elect and sit on the board of directors)
- hire and terminate employees
- establish compensation structure
- determine the goals and operations of the business
- acquire and dispose of business property
- make distributions to partners or pay dividends to shareholders
- terminate the business

The appropriate size of a minority discount depends on the degree to which these control powers are lacking. Many of the control powers are often not an either/or situation for the majority and minority owners. There are many instances in which some degree of control is retained by even a minority interest holder. For example, cumulative voting allows minority shareholders to elect a minimum number of directors. State corporation statutes or individual corporate charters may also require a super majority of shareholders to approve extraordinary corporate actions. In these cases it is not appropriate to fully discount the minority interest. The appropriate degree of minority discount depends on the individual circumstances within the business since the number of owners and the relative sizes of the interests held by the majority and minority groups have an impact on the degree of control possessed by each.

EXAMPLE

LIFO, Inc., has two owners. The majority owner holds 90 percent of the stock outstanding and the minority owner the remainder. The degree of control lost by the minority owner is substantial, and the minority interest is worth far less than 10 percent of the total value of LIFO. Now suppose FIFO, Inc., has four equal shareholders. Each shareholder owns a minority interest, but no discount for lack of control is probably appropriate under these circumstances.

The IRS has accepted the validity of minority interest discounts in many cases, especially in valuing minority interests held by estates for estate tax purposes. As always, minority interests should be valued for this purpose at fair market value (including applicable discounts). Suppose the business is worth $1 million and the decedent's interest is 10 percent. It is highly unlikely that the decedent could have sold the interest for $100,000 on the date of death because this interest did not possess the benefits of control. In this case it would be unfair to assess federal estate taxes as if the value of the interest was really 10 percent of the value of the business.

Both the IRS and the courts have allowed discounts for minority interests, but the facts and circumstances surrounding the valuation are generally closely scrutinized to make sure the discount is appropriate. Some recent studies have revealed that the average discount is approximately 30 percent and can be much higher in appropriate circumstances.

The methods for valuing minority interests are analogous to the methods used to value the entire business. For example, the normal capitalization-of-income methods can be used to determine the value of the business. The value of the minority interest is then determined by reducing the total value to the pro rata share held by the minority owner and applying a discount factor appropriate for the minority interest.

Another technique would be to employ comparative analysis and look for the actual discounts received in transactions involving sales of minority interests in similar situations. In either event the amount of the discount to be applied is highly speculative and should be well documented by relevant evidence if used for tax purposes.

The IRS published a ruling that further solidifies the minority discount in the valuation of a family business.[27] The ruling indicates that each transaction will be valued independently for tax purposes without aggregating the interests held by the taxpayer's family. Thus, each gift of a business interest to a family member will be valued with a minority discount unless a controlling interest is transferred. Therefore, a gift or sale of stock in a closely held corporation that transfers 50 percent or less of the shares in the company can be valued with an appropriate minority discount, even if the transferee's family controls the corporation. Likewise, the transfer of limited partnership interests or nonmanaging membership interests in an LLC can be valued with a minority discount for a family limited partnership or LLC.

Discount for Lack of Marketability

marketability discount

It is generally accepted that a *marketability discount* is appropriate for a lack of an existing market for a closely held business interest. If the business interest cannot be quickly converted to cash, its fair market value may be less than the value determined by one of the conventional valuation methods. The lack of marketability for a closely held business interest may stem from several factors.

First, there may be little or no market for a minority interest. Second, a closely held business interest is not traded on a public exchange and a ready buyer may not be found on a timely basis. Finally, interests in closely held businesses are often subject to transfer restrictions that further limit the ability to convert the businesses into cash. The typical discount for the lack of marketability ranges from 10 to 35 percent, but cases have been reported in which the appropriate discount was as high as 90 percent.

---

27. Rev. Rul. 93-12, 1993-1 C.B. 202.

blockage discount

Publicly traded corporate stock is also valued as if closely held in some instances. The IRS will allow a so-called *blockage discount* when a large block of corporate stock is valued for estate tax purposes. This discount reflects the suppressed market that would exist if a large block of stock was sold in a short time span. The IRS regulations provide that the large block may be discounted to a price below market quotations to reflect true fair market value in these circumstances.

Fractional-Interest Discount

Cases have established that fractional undivided interests (joint tenancies) may create a valuation discount. The discount is based on the built-in costs of partitioning the property if one joint owner chooses to transfer his or her interest, and it is, essentially, a marketability discount.[28] The cases have held that the fractional-interest discount could incorporate evidence of the historical difficulty of selling the interest and an owner's lack of control. The fractional-interest discount would ordinarily apply to jointly titled real estate. This is certainly important for closely held businesses because business real estate is often held outside the business by the owners or, perhaps, in separate entities such as partnerships or LLCs. It appears from case law that the fractional-interest discount would be 10 to 20 percent and is viable even if the joint interest was transferred just prior to the owner's death.

Discount for Built-in Tax Liability

The question has arisen in several cases about whether built-in capital gains in a C corporation should give a discount for the potential corporate-level tax liability when valuing stock in a corporation for gift or estate tax purposes. The position of the IRS and the Tax Court has been that the likelihood of the event that would cause the taxation to occur must be considered. (That is, would a willing buyer sell or liquidate the property?) However circuit courts have disagreed. The landmark cases allowed a discount for the built-in corporate-level capital gains.[29] The court noted that it would be impossible for the transferee to avoid this tax upon disposition, whenever such disposition occurs. The IRS acquiesced (AOD CC-1999-001) in the decision only to

---

28. For example, in *Brocato v. Commissioner*, TCM 1999-424.

29. *Eisenberg v. Commissioner*, 155 F.3d 50 (2d Cir. 1998), *Estate of Davis v. Commissioner*, 110 TC 530. Note that this discount was disallowed in an FLP case since the Sec. 754 election could be made in a partnership to step up the inside basis of the assets with built-in gain at the time of the transfer (*Jones v. Commissioner*, 116 TC 121).

the extent that there is no legal prohibition for the discount. The question has also recently arisen about whether the built-in gains tax might apply in pass-through entities when underlying property with potential gain is valued. Be aware that the courts have not been consistent in evaluating the potential discount for built-in capital gains and the associated tax liability.

Discounts to the Calculated Value

Discounts are applicable if the interest being valued

- is a minority interest
- lacks marketability
- has built-in capital-gains tax or other liabilities
- is held in fractional undivided ownership

Liquidation Discount

Most people are aware that a forced sale of property generally produces a lower price than a sale that is carried out at a time when the seller is ready and willing to sell. A liquidation or forced sale of business assets on a piecemeal basis will generally produce no recovery of the goodwill inherent in the value of the going business.

In addition, a forced sale may produce a price that is below the total fair market value of all the tangible assets less liabilities. A fair market value assumes a ready-and-willing buyer and seller. When the seller is compelled to liquidate, business assets will often sell for less than for market value. In this sense a liquidation discount represents the ultimate discount for lack of marketability.

Some assets suffer more than others in a forced sale. As a result of experience some rough estimates can be given for the values that are recoverable in a forced sale:

- *real property*. The forced-sale value of real property can depend on many factors, including the location, type of structures, adaptability for various purposes, and other circumstances. Forced-sale values may vary from 50 percent to 90 percent of the fair market value of the property, less real estate commissions, legal fees, and other transfer costs.
- *equipment and fixtures*. The forced-sale value of fixtures and equipment generally varies from 10 percent to 25 percent of the fair market value of these items. Such items are normally purchased

by buyers to meet specific needs, and it is rare that such buyers will be found at the time of a forced sale.

- *inventory*. The forced-sale value of inventory is usually less than 50 percent. Again, the reason for this is that it is rare to find a buyer who needs exactly the inventory items stocked by the business at the time of its forced sale.
- *accounts receivable*. The forced-sale value of accounts receivable generally varies from 25 percent to 75 percent of their face amount, especially if the business is sold following the death of an owner.

The effect of a forced sale on the expected proceeds can be devastating. Compare the result in the table above of a forced sale of Hypo Enterprises with the proceeds that could be realized if all Hypo's assets were sold at their fair market value.

Table 11-8 Hypo Enterprises

Assets	Fair Market Value	Forced-Sale Value
Real property	$600,000	$540,000
Equipment and fixtures	40,000	10,000
Inventory	110,000	55,000
Accounts receivable	125,000	93,750
Cash	25,000	25,000
	$900,000	$723,750
Less liabilities	(462,000)	(462,000)
	$438,000	$261,750

Control Premium

The ability (or inability) to control a business is a component of value. Quite often, tender offers are made for corporate stock far in excess of its market value. This reflects the desire of the purchaser to possess the control value inherent in a business—the ability to direct management and policy.

The control "premium" represents the additional increment of value for control beyond the asset and earning-capacity values of a business. This amount can be determined by comparing sale prices for controlling interests in similar business entities with the theoretical values for the same interests determined by an appropriate valuation method. The control premium has been used by the IRS in valuation disputes to offset the taxpayer's argument for a marketability discount.

SELECTING THE VALUATION METHOD

The approaches to business valuation focus on the value of the firm's assets or the earning capacity of the firm or in some cases represent a hybrid between the two approaches. In theory investors with complete information applying any of the techniques should reach the same estimates for the value of a business. In practice one method may be more appropriate and easier to apply to a given set of circumstances. Valuation methods that focus on the earnings of a business (capitalization of earnings, DFE, P/E, and the like) are most appropriate in situations in which earnings can be accurately determined and the production of income is the primary purpose of the business assets. For example, capitalization methods can be used to value a firm whose earnings have been relatively stable and present a predictable trend. In addition, there should be no substantial assets held solely for investment as typically occurs in a personal holding company. Finally, the firm's earnings should be regularly distributed to the owners rather than reinvested in the firm. For this reason service-oriented businesses are usually valued by techniques that focus on the firm's earning capacity.

Some methods of business valuation that focus on the fair market value of the assets held by the business. These methods, such as the adjusted book value or P/BV ratio, are appropriate when the business holds substantial assets for investment purposes or has a highly fluctuating earnings history that does not lend itself to a reliable earnings forecast. An example of such a business is a holding company used primarily as a vehicle for maintaining investment assets such as stocks, bonds, and royalty interests. Capitalization of the earnings of this type of firm will not accurately reflect the value of the underlying assets. The market value of these assets is readily ascertainable, and the sum of these values representing the value of the entire business is likely to represent an accurate measure of the actual market value of the company.

A valuation method focusing on business assets might also be appropriate in situations in which earnings do not accurately represent the business's fair market value. For example, a closely held business with few owners typically (1) reinvests earnings or (2) pays the majority of earnings out as salaries to the owners. In this case it might be difficult to get an accurate picture of the actual earnings capacity of the business, and a method such as adjusted book value might yield more appropriate results. A business in the process of liquidation should also be valued by some technique focusing on the value of the assets since future earning capacity is an insignificant factor.

Which Method to Use?

- Use earning-based methods if earnings are readily measurable or predictable and if income production is the main purpose of the assets, with no major assets held for investment purposes.
- Use asset-based methods if earnings are volatile and difficult to forecast or if substantial assets are held for investment purposes.

In many cases a hybrid between the two major types of valuation procedures is necessary to reach an accurate figure. For example, comparative analysis involves the use of ratios that take into account both earnings and asset values. Regardless of the method chosen for valuing the entire business, goodwill can generally be valued accurately only by a method focusing on the earnings related to the goodwill value. In any event a valuation performed for tax purposes must take into account all the factors provided by the IRS guidelines.

VALUATION OF PREFERRED STOCK

The valuation of different classes of stock presents another problem. Preferred stock generally has rights and restrictions different from those of common stock. Although preferred stock typically has a priority right to income and liquidation proceeds, these rights are limited to a fixed amount and preferred shareholders generally have no opportunity to share in the growth of the firm. Preferred stock may also be callable (returnable to the corporation at the corporation's option) for a fixed price. These factors tend to put a ceiling on the value of preferred stock. In addition, preferred stock may or may not have voting rights. Since we learned in chapter 10 that preferred stock dividends and recapitalizations may play an important role in the closely held corporation, it is worth mentioning a few words about the valuation of preferred stock.

The IRS has issued rulings specifically applicable to the valuation of preferred stock.[30] In general, the application of these rulings will often cause the fair market value of preferred stock to be below its par value. The rulings provide the following special factors to consider in the valuation of preferred stock:

- yield of the preferred stock
- dividend coverage
- liquidation preference of the preferred
- question of whether the preferred is voting or nonvoting
- any restrictive provisions on the preferred stock that could affect value

dividend coverage

The IRS instructs the valuation appraiser to compare the yield, dividend coverage, and liquidation preference of the corporation being valued with the values of these factors for high-grade publicly traded preferred stock. *Dividend coverage* is determined by the ratio of the sum of pretax and pre-interest earnings to the sum of the total interest to be paid and the pretax earnings necessary to pay the after-tax dividends. If some of the factors are below the benchmark levels, the preferred stock must be valued at less than par.

Other considerations in valuing preferred stock are the provisions included in the stock. For example, voting stock should be valued higher than nonvoting stock. Any restrictions on transferability limit the current market value of the stock, while benefits such as redemption privileges should increase the valuation of the preferred stock. These recent rulings by the IRS are an indication that the valuation of preferred stock received through dividends and recapitalization will be closely scrutinized and discounts from par value will probably be appropriate.

VALUATION FOR BUY-SELL PURPOSES

For several reasons it is imperative that the method for determining the buyout price be established at the time the buy-sell agreement is formed. First, the buy-sell itself may be jeopardized if the valuation must be agreed on after the death of one of the owners when the buyers and the estate have unequal bargaining power and incongruent goals. That is, the surviving owner(s) will want a low purchase price and the estate will want a high

---

30. Rev. Rul. 83-119, 1983-2 C.B. 57; and Rev. Rul. 83-120, 1983-2 C.B. 170.

purchase price. Such a dispute may be impossible to settle unless the method of resolution is included in the original buy-sell agreement.

Second, a prearranged valuation agreement allows the parties to the agreement to plan their estates in an orderly fashion. Advance knowledge of the buyout price will allow the parties to determine the property that can be distributed to the heirs and estimate the eventual expenses of the estate.

Finally, a buy-sell agreement with a prearranged method for determining the business value will provide considerable, and maybe conclusive, evidence of the value of the business interest for estate tax purposes. The price determined by the buy-sell agreement will establish the estate tax value of the business interest if the following conditions are satisfied.

- *If the buy-sell agreement involves family members:* If the agreement involves the transfer of a business between family members, the purchase price provision must satisfy the following rules to be accepted by the IRS as evidence of the business value for transfer tax purposes:
  - "Bona Fide Business Arrangement" Rule: The agreement must be part of a bona fide business arrangement.
  - "Device" Rule: The agreement must not be a device to transfer the property to members of a decedent's family for less than full and adequate consideration in money or money's worth.
  - "Comparability" Rule: The terms of the agreement must be comparable to similar arrangements entered into by persons in an arm's-length transaction.
- *If the buy-sell agreement involves unrelated parties:* Less scrutiny will be applicable to buy-sell agreements involving business transfers between unrelated parties. The traditional view of such agreements indicates that the purchase price provision will be acceptable in establishing the estate and gift tax value of the business interest if the price is binding on the deceased business owner's estate and the price provision was reached as a result of arm's-length bargaining (generally presumed if the parties are unrelated).

Alternative Buy-Sell Valuation Approaches

There are three basic approaches used by valuation consultants to structure the provision for valuing the business in a buy-sell agreement. Experts differ on the best of the approaches, each of which probably has merit in specific circumstances. The following are the three types of approaches:

- agreed value—At the time the agreement is executed, the parties agree on the purchase price that will apply at the time the buy-sell is carried out. Typically a provision is included for periodic revaluation of the business at specific intervals. This approach should be avoided in buy-sell agreements for family businesses.
- independent appraisal—The parties agree that the valuation will be performed at the time the buy-sell is transacted by an independent appraiser, or appraisers, selected by a procedure specified in the agreement. It is common to either (1) name one independent appraiser in the agreement to perform the valuation or (2) provide for independent appraisers to be selected by each party, with a provision for arbitration if the two appraisers cannot reach an agreement. This approach can be used with family buy-sell agreements if the independent appraisal can be expected to arrive at fair market value.
- formula valuation—The agreement provides a specific valuation method that will be employed at the time the sale is transacted. Any one or a combination of the valuation methods discussed earlier in the chapter can be designed in the agreement. The IRS generally takes a more favorable view of a formula valuation when the formula is set in advance in a buy-sell agreement. The formula approach will work in a family buy-sell only if the formula is the type used in comparable agreements entered into at arm's length.

Common Errors in Buy-Sell Valuation Approaches

The primary purpose of a buy-sell agreement is facilitating the orderly transition of an ongoing business at the death of one of the owners. Quite simply, the surviving owners want to continue the business without interference. The estate of the decedent wants to receive cash in lieu of the business interest on a timely basis. These goals will not be achieved if the valuation provision in the buy-sell agreement is perceived as unfair by one of the parties and costly disputes and/or litigation follow.

Common errors in the valuation provision of the buy-sell agreement include the following:

- failure to update an agreed-on amount provision on a periodic basis
- failure to consider the life insurance funding as part of the overall business values

- failure to include goodwill in the valuation
- failure to discount fairly for lack of marketability and minority interests

USE OF THE APPRAISER

The task of valuing a closely held business interest involves gathering voluminous, sometimes subjective data about the business. The appropriate valuation method(s) must then be selected for the specific task. The entire procedure is extremely complex and should virtually always be handled by a qualified valuation appraiser.

For tax purposes valuation disputes that end in litigation usually find the parties with valuation estimates at opposite ends of the spectrum of reasonable choices. That is, the IRS will use a valuation approach that results in a high estate tax value for the closely held business interest. The executor will tend to select the valuation methodology resulting in the lowest possible tax liability. The courts have tended to adopt a compromise opinion somewhere between the estimates of the two parties. However, some recent cases have indicated a willingness of the courts to accept the valuation deemed more accurate to discourage the parties' adoption of grossly inaccurate valuations for bargaining purposes. Since litigation creates unwanted risk, an important goal for the taxpayer is to avoid review of the valuation by the IRS. As a general rule a thorough, well-documented valuation appraisal performed by a highly qualified independent appraiser will reduce the likelihood of audit by the IRS.

Appraisal for ESOP Purposes

Employee stock ownership plans (ESOPs) maintained by closely held businesses were sometimes criticized in the past for overstating the value of their stock in order to maximize the employer's tax deduction and perhaps mislead employees about the value of the ESOP as an employee benefit. To minimize abuses in this area, current law requires ESOPs to use an independent appraiser to value stock unless the stock is traded on an established securities market. The appraiser must meet requirements prescribed by the IRS.

Selecting an Appraiser

Congress recently chose to define a qualified appraiser for tax purposes in the area of charitable contributions. It is likely that this definition will apply as well to other types of tax appraisals. The statute requires the qualified appraiser to have two characteristics—ability and independence. That is, the qualified appraiser should be (1) capable of making appraisals for the specific type of property being valued and (2) disinterested in the transaction. To ensure the appraiser's independence, the appraisal fee typically should not be contingent on the size or success of the valuation. Finally in light of the statutory penalties discussed below, the appraiser should also be qualified to present evidence in cases against the IRS.

Statutory Sanctions

Tax law provides severe sanctions for understated valuations for estate and gift tax purposes. An incorrect valuation resulting in an understatement of taxes by at least $5,000 results in additional tax penalties. If the valuation of the business interest is between 50 percent or less of the correct valuation, a penalty tax equal to 20 percent of any tax deficiency is imposed. The penalty tax increases to 40 percent if the valuation claimed is 25 percent or less of the actual fair market value. These severe penalties make it imperative that a qualified independent appraiser be selected for business valuations for tax purposes.

A potentially more severe trap exists in the statutory sanctions against appraisers. The appraiser may be fined for assisting in the preparation of an appraisal for tax purposes that results in an understatement of tax. This sanction applies to the appraiser and not the taxpayer and is not important for our purposes. However, an appraiser penalized under these provisions may be barred in the future from presenting evidence in cases against the IRS. Once barred, the appraiser cannot present expert testimony in any case against the IRS, even if the testimony is unrelated to the case for which the penalty was imposed. This leaves the taxpayer in a highly unprotected situation. That is, the taxpayer using the business valuation expert is in jeopardy of losing the appraiser as an expert witness at any time following the appraisal for reasons beyond the taxpayer's control. Therefore the list of disqualified appraisers published by the IRS should be checked by the financial services professional before retaining an independent appraiser. However, this provides no protection if the appraiser should become disqualified subsequent to the appraisal.

Penalties for Undervaluation

- Taxpayer may incur a tax penalty of up to 40 percent of any resulting tax deficiency.
- Appraiser may be fined and barred from presenting evidence in future cases against the IRS.

CHAPTER REVIEW

Key Terms and Concepts

liquidation rights
fair market value
book value
intangible assets
adjusted book value
goodwill
capitalization of earnings
weighted-average earnings
capitalization factor
discounted future earnings (DFE)
minority discount
marketability discount
blockage discount
dividend coverage

Review Questions

The answers to the review questions are in the supplement. The self-test questions and the answers to them are also in the supplement and on The American College Online.

1. What is meant by the fair market value of a business? [1]
2. Identify the factors prescribed by the IRS for valuing a closely held business interest. [1]
3. Describe the book value of a business, and explain why it is generally not the same as the fair market value. [2]
4. What is an intangible asset? The value of the goodwill of a business is generally excluded from its book value.
   a. Describe how an estimate of the value of goodwill might be reached.
   b. Why is the value of goodwill irrelevant for a piecemeal, forced sale of the business? [2]
5. What is the basis for the capitalization-of-earnings concept of business value? [3]
6. Briefly describe the capitalization-of-earnings technique of valuation, focusing on the two factors used in the calculation. [3]

7. Zilch Industries is considering a sale of its stock to Octopus Industries, Inc., and is trying to arrive at a fair asking price for the stock by using the capitalization-of-earnings method. Explain the relevance, if any, of the following factors in applying the capitalization-of-earnings method.
   a. Zilch Industries is engaged in supplying materials to the toy industry, a volatile and fad-ridden business.
   b. The two chief officers of the company are Bill and Angelo Zilch who together hold 80 percent of Zilch's stock.
   c. Zilch's best year in its 60-year history was a year in which it supplied an essential material for the manufacture of hula hoops.
   d. Zilch's worst year occurred several years ago when its upstate New York facility was swept into the Niagara River during a hurricane. [3]

8. Explain how the discounted-future-earnings (DFE) method differs from the basic capitalization technique. [3]

9. Describe some problems in forecasting future earnings, and explain the necessity of weighing the forecast. [3]

10. Describe some considerations in choosing the appropriate discount rate for the DFE method. [3]

11. Explain why valuation by comparison of ratios is sometimes used, and give examples of such methods. [4]

12. The value of Aardvark Industries has recently been determined by a prestigious consulting firm to be $1 million. There are 1,000 shares of Aardvark's stock of all classes outstanding (950 common and 50 preferred). Explain why the value of the following blocks of stock might not be determined simply by computing the ratio of shares held by the shareholder to the total shares of Aardvark stock outstanding and multiplying that by $1 million.
    a. a 400-share common-stock interest held by the estate of the late Morris Aardvark
    b. a 550-share common-stock interest held by Bertha Aardvark, Morris's sister
    c. a 50-share preferred-stock interest held by Frank Slick, the Aardvarks' attorney [5]

13. Note in the example in the chapter that the value for Hypo Enterprises determined by the DFE method was $914,890. Refer to the adjusted balance sheet (not including intangibles) for Hypo Enterprises of the text. What value for intangibles would be suggested by this result from the DFE method? Explain. [5]

14. Explain the relationship, if any, between the unadjusted book value of assets and the proceeds that might be received from these assets in a forced sale pursuant to a liquidation. [4]

15. Discuss the methods typically used to determine the value of a business interest pursuant to the valuation provision of a buy-sell agreement. [6]

16. Certain methods of valuation may be more appropriate in one situation than another. Give some situations in which the following would be preferable or would work better:
    a. the adjusted-book-value method
    b. the capitalization-of-earnings method [2, 3, 4, 5]

17. Discuss the possible sanctions that may be imposed on the following for an inaccurate valuation of property for tax purposes:
    a. a taxpayer
    b. an appraiser [7]

PLANNING FOR THE DISABILITY OF A BUSINESS OWNER OR PROFESSIONAL 12

Learning Objectives

An understanding of the material in this chapter should enable the student to

1. Describe some of the business problems resulting from the long-term disability of an owner-employee in a closely held business.
2. Describe the principal features of and funding alternatives for a disability buy-sell agreement and explain how the funding for the "deathtime" buy-sell agreement can be integrated with the disability buy-sell agreement.
3. Describe the principal features of a salary continuation plan, explain alternative designs that a disability salary continuation plan may take, and describe the tax consequences of various salary continuation plans.
4. Explain the factors that should be considered in the selection of individual disability income protection by a business owner or professional.
5. Describe the operation of business-overhead-expense insurance.

No discussion of planning for business owners and professionals should ignore the contingency of disability. This risk, although manageable through planning, presents a variety of complex issues that will be the subject of this chapter.

The owners of a closely held business are placed in a difficult situation if one or more of them should become disabled. First, the healthy owners must find a way to replace the disabled owner's services. Second, the disabled owner and his or her family must be provided for, or discord will result between the disabled and the healthy owners. Generally the disabled owner's income must be continued for a period of time, and if the disability becomes permanent, the disabled owner's share of the business will have to be sold either to the healthy owners or to outsiders. As always this process will be smoother and provide more certainty to the owners if prearranged in a binding agreement.

A business owner or professional practitioner typically derives a substantial portion of his or her income from the business or practice. Similarly the financial success of the closely held business or professional practice often depends on the contribution of a specific individual. It is unlikely that the business will be able to provide payments out of current income to this individual during a lengthy disability. To prepare for this situation, there are a number of options available to the business and its owners. First, the business can purchase disability income protection insurance to fund a formal salary continuation plan. Second, the business and/or its owners might enter into a disability buy-sell agreement to provide substantial payments to a disabled owner to purchase his or her business interest. If the disabled owner will not be provided for by the business, individually purchased disability insurance is certainly a viable alternative.

Income replacement protection will not be enough to handle all the contingencies of disability. For example, many disabilities are of a short-term nature. The small-business owner or professional operating a solo practice is likely to lose many customers or clients if all operations are terminated during a period of disability. If this occurs, the individual will have to reestablish the business or practice after recovery. To avoid such an unattractive possibility, the business owner or professional can plan ahead to provide for continued operations during a period of disability.

DISABILITY—THE MAGNITUDE OF THE RISK

The problems associated with the premature death of a business owner were discussed at length earlier. Fortunately many business owners and professionals recognize and plan for the contingency of premature death. The disability risk, however, is often ignored, as shown in the following table. As the table demonstrates, individuals and employers insure against the risk of death more frequently than against the risk of disability. Of course, life insurance can be purchased by virtually any individual, while disability income protection is available only to individuals with earned income. Even when focusing the attention solely on employed individuals, the penetration rate for disability protection is surprisingly low. And often, the risk insured is not the most significant problem—that is, a significant amount of the coverage is short-term disability.[31] The financial services professional should

---

31. Twenty-three percent of all disability coverage is short term—typically 24 months of benefit. *Life Insurance Fact Book 2000,* American Council of Life Insurance.

be aware that most individuals do not have formal disability income protection and should advise business and professional clients of the possible options available.

Table 12-1 Individuals With Protection for Life and Disability Income Risks in the United States (2001 Data)			
	Number of Individuals Covered By		
Type of Risk	Individual Policies	Group Policies	Total
Disability	6,041,000	44,106,000	50,147,000
Life	214,047,000*	163,081,000	377,128,000
* Includes credit life insurance. Source: American Council of Life Insurance—www.acli.com			

Since the risk of disability is less frequently considered than the life insurance risk, it would be comforting to know that the disability risk was less significant. Unfortunately this is not the case. First, a working individual is far more likely to sustain a disability of significant duration than to die prematurely. Second, the problems created for the disabled person and his or her family are often greater than those created by an individual's death. Finally, the continuation problems facing a business following the disability of an owner are more difficult to handle and require more complex planning than the continuation planning for an owner's death.

Frequency of Disability

The frequency of disability in the U.S. population is staggering. For example, recent annual statistics reveal that almost 10 percent of the civilian noninstitutional U.S. population have sustained a disability that imposed limitations, at least temporarily, on their major activity.[32] This large number is a particular concern since the majority of the workforce has no protection against the risk.

Most disabilities are short-term in nature and are not a significant financial burden. For example, the average work time lost per occurrence is less than 5 days. Generally speaking, both the disabled worker and the employing business should be able to manage the short-term loss. In the case of the closely held business it will be assumed that the business and

32. *Sourcebook of Health Insurance Data,* Health Insurance Association of America.

owner-employee can provide for a disability of less than 3 months. For this reason we will focus our attention on the contingency that a business owner or professional will be disabled for a period longer than 3 months. Even if disabilities longer than 3 months are focused on, the following table reveals the greater likelihood of a long-term disability than of death of a business owner during the working years.

Table 12-2 Likelihood of Long-term Disabilities Compared With Likelihood of Deaths

			Long-term Disabilities per 1,000 Workers					
Deaths per 1,000 Lives			Male			Female		
Age	Male	Female	3 Months	1 Year	2 Years	3 Months	1 Year	2 Years
37	2.40	1.89	16.52	4.84	2.67	30.06	5.05	2.29
47	5.32	4.05	21.70	7.27	4.66	37.96	6.05	3.31
57	12.49	8.03	34.35	12.66	9.32	41.43	10.62	6.57
67	30.44	17.43	43.32	21.71	19.80	48.95	15.76	12.37

The statistics reveal that the likelihood of a disability of at least 3 months far exceeds the chance of death at all relevant ages. The disparity between the frequency of these risks has been increasing in recent years and will continue to increase with improvements in life expectancy. Despite the increasing relative importance of the long-term disability risk, the percentage of the population insured for this risk has declined slightly in recent years.

The frequency of long-term disability is a problem that should not be ignored by the closely held business owner. Recent statistics reveal that a firm established by two 35-year-old co-owners faces a 75 percent probability that at least one owner will sustain a long-term disability prior to age 65. If the firm was formed by six or more co-owners, it is almost a certainty that at least one long-term disability will have to be faced before the owners reach age 65. Since the average disability lasting at least 3 months will continue for more than 5 years, even one such occurrence could have a devastating impact on the closely held business.

Impact on the Disabled Owner

The typical closely held business owner or professional receives a substantial portion of total income from the closely held business or professional practice.

Furthermore, the ownership interest in the closely held business is likely to be the most substantial asset held by the owner. Consequently the disability of a closely held business owner or professional creates two problems. First, the owner will lose a major source of income unless his or her salary is continued in some manner. Second, the owner will be holding a substantial asset that may not be readily convertible into cash.

The owners of a closely held business usually have a close relationship and will probably harbor the best intentions to maintain a co-owner's salary during a period of disability. However, a conflict is almost certain to occur if the business does not have provisions for funding the continuation of an owner-employee's salary during disability. The healthy owners face the strain of continuing their services to the firm along with picking up all the responsibilities of the disabled owner. Furthermore, the income of the business may drop as a result of the loss of the disabled owner's services. For example, the disabled owner may have been particularly skilled at marketing and the other owners may have relied on the disabled owner to retain most of the good business prospects.

Under most circumstances the closely held business will be unable to indefinitely meet the continued income payments to the nonproductive disabled owner. If the salary continuation payments are terminated by the healthy co-owners, the disabled owner and his or her family will have to rely on other sources of income to maintain their standard of living. These other sources could be unearned income, a spouse's income, or payments from personal disability income insurance. If the disabled owner has not prepared for this contingency, it is unlikely that his or her family will be able to maintain its previous standard of living.

When a disabled owner begins to feel financial strain as a result of the loss of earned income from the business, an obvious solution is to sell the business interest. This solution will provide satisfactory results for all the parties involved if planned for in advance. However, this continuation problem receives considerably less attention than does the problem of the death of an owner. In the absence of a prearranged binding agreement the disabled owner is likely to be dissatisfied with the sale proceeds. First, it may be difficult to dispose of a closely held business interest to an outsider, particularly if the disabled owner possesses a minority interest in the business. The potential marketability problems for a minority interest were well documented in the last chapter.

If the disabled owner and the healthy co-owners can reach an agreement, the disabled owner's interest can be transferred to the remaining owners, preventing any unwanted outsiders from entering the business. Unfortunately the disabled owner is in a precarious bargaining position because if he or she has a minority interest, the healthy owners can terminate income payments to the disabled owner at their whim. Under these circumstances the disabled owner is likely to be compelled to accept a purchase price that is far below the fair value of the interest.

The disabled owner may be in the position to force the liquidation of the business in some circumstances, as in a partnership where any general partner can force liquidation, or in a corporation where the disabled shareholder holds a majority interest. The forced liquidation of the business is unlikely to make any of the parties satisfied with the results. As we learned in the last chapter, a liquidation results in business assets being disposed of quickly and generally below fair market value. The business may lose goodwill and the healthy owners will temporarily lose their livelihood. In any event the forced liquidation of the business by the disabled owner will not result in the receipt of adequate proceeds for his or her interest.

The Impact of an Owner's Disability on the Closely Held Business

The disability of an owner-employee of a closely held business can have varying ramifications. In some cases the disabled owner can threaten the very continuation of the business by forcing liquidation, as discussed above. Even if the disabled owner does not have the ability to force dissolution of the business, continuation may be impractical for other reasons. For example, a small business whose income is related to the personal services and goodwill generated by the owners is likely to suffer reduced earnings if a participating owner is unable to contribute because of a disability. If the reduction in earnings is substantial, practical considerations will dictate the termination of the business by the owners.

Some closely held businesses rely on productive capital for their income rather than on the owner's personal services. In this case the disability of an individual owner may not have an immediate effect on the firm's revenues. However, the typical closely held business owner expects his or her earnings to be maintained during a period of disability. Co-owners of closely held businesses tend to have close personal relationships solidified by the common goal of success for their common business venture. Under these circumstances the healthy owners feel a strong personal, as well as business, obligation to continue income or salary payments to the disabled co-owner. In a small business these payments to a nonproductive disabled owner can generally be continued only for a short period of time unless prefunded. Assuming no prior planning was done, the expectation that these payments will continue for an indefinite period is unrealistic. Eventually the continued payments will place a strain on the financial capacity of the business and the personal relationship of the co-owners.

A closely held business must find a way to replace the disabled owner's services to the firm if all owners materially participate in the business. This will place the financial burden on the business for hiring and compensating a replacement while continuing the nonproductive disabled owner's share. The most likely scenario is that the disabled owner cannot be replaced on short notice for the same level of compensation. Replacement employees are not likely to possess the experience necessary to immediately perform all the services of the disabled owner. Therefore the healthy owners will most likely increase their workload to pick up the slack.

Impact of Business Owner's Disability

- The disabled owner loses his or her major source of income, or the other owners have to continue that income.
- The disabled owner holds an important but illiquid asset.
- The healthy owners have to take on added responsibilities or hire a replacement for the disabled owner.
- The income of the business may decline.
- If the disabled owner is able to sell to outsiders, the other owners' careers may be disrupted.

This creates obvious tension between the healthy and the disabled owners, since the productive owners will have to work harder and perhaps accept reduced income to keep the business afloat while continuing the disabled owner's salary payments. Before long, the working owners will become dissatisfied with the situation and attempt to reduce or discontinue payments to the disabled owner. Of course, the disabled owner will feel that the others have turned their backs on him or her and will want to sell his or her business interest. This presents the situation discussed before in which the remaining owners must face (1) the possibility of intrusion by outside purchasers into the firm or (2) an uncomfortable adversarial purchase and sale with the disabled owner.

Obviously the problems created by the disability of a closely held business owner should be considered when continuation planning is done for the business. The financial services professional should make clients aware of the ramifications, both to the individual owners and to the business itself, of a co-owner's long-term disability, particularly because the probability of an owner's long-term disability is greater than the probability of his or her premature death.

DISABILITY BUY-SELL AGREEMENTS

An obvious solution to the problems created by the long-term disability of a business owner is the purchase-and-sale agreement between the business and its owners. Since the continuation problems created by an owner's death are similar to those created by disability, it is natural to incorporate a provision in the "deathtime" buy-sell agreement to consider the contingency of an owner's disability. The financial services professional should advise business clients of the hazard of disability and make them aware of the possibilities of incorporating disability provisions into a new or existing "deathtime" buy-sell agreement.

Design of the Agreement

Forms of Disability Buy-Sell Agreements

Buy-sell agreements that become operative upon the disability of a closely held business owner are structured in the same basic forms as "deathtime" purchase agreements. That is, either the business entity or the co-owners can be the intended purchasers. In a partnership a cross-purchase agreement involves an agreement between partners to purchase the partnership interest held by a disabled partner when the agreement becomes operative. In an entity buy-sell agreement the partnership is a party to the agreement and is the designated purchaser of a disabled partner's interest.

Corporate disability buy-sell agreements are designed as either cross-purchase or stock-redemption plans. Again, in the cross-purchase agreement each shareholder agrees to purchase a designated portion of a disabled coshareholder's stock when a disability triggers the agreement. Each coshareholder entering the cross-purchase agreement is similarly bound to sell his or her stock upon disability. The stock-redemption disability buy-sell agreement binds the corporation to redeem a disabled shareholder's stock. Again, each shareholder entering the agreement must agree to be redeemed when disabled, according to the terms of the agreement.

The disability buy-sell agreement could be designed in a mandatory fashion as described above, or the owners could be provided with an option to buy a disabled owner's stock. The optional agreement provides flexibility to the parties by delaying the actual decision to purchase the disabled owner's interest until the circumstances are known. However, the basic purpose of a disability buy-sell agreement dictates the use of a mandatory agreement. Such an agreement ensures that a disabled owner will have a guaranteed market for his or her business interest and will receive fair proceeds that can be used to provide for the owner and his or her family during the period of disability. The healthy owners have the satisfaction of the assurances that a binding agreement provides. That is, the healthy owners will not have to deal indefinitely with a potentially disgruntled disabled co-owner who might sell to outsiders or force liquidation of the business.

Provisions of a Disability Buy-Sell Agreement

Typically the disability buy-sell agreement provisions will be incorporated in one agreement providing for all the contingencies stipulated by the owners to trigger a buy-sell agreement—death, disability, retirement, and the like. The inclusion of disability as a triggering event for a buy-sell agreement creates the need for the following provisions:

elimination period

trigger date

- *elimination period.* The elimination period in a disability buy-sell agreement is the amount of time that must elapse following the onset of an owner's disability before the purchase must occur. The date the buy-sell agreement becomes operative is also referred to as the *trigger date.* An elimination period is also included in any disability income or buyout insurance policy that might be used to fund the agreement. Although it is generally recommended, these elimination periods do not necessarily have to be the same length, but the elimination period used in the agreement should not be shorter than the elimination period of the disability policy. If this were to occur, the buyout would be mandated before the insurance funding was providing benefits.

- *definition of disability.* This provision specifies the degree of disability that an owner must face before a purchase becomes mandatory. This provision should also specify who will determine an owner's disability. Since the degree of disability is often the subject of dispute, it is generally recommended that an independent party make a determination of disability. In an insured agreement the definition of disability should be the same as that contained in the policy, and the determination of disability is typically left to the insurer.
- *salary continuation payments.* This provision will indicate the salary continuation payments to be provided during an owner's disability. These payments will usually be provided during the elimination period and may or may not be credited against the purchase price. Salary continuation payments are often made on an informal basis by the business entity, but disputes can be avoided if the provision for payments is spelled out in the agreement.
- *recovery of a disabled owner.* The possibility exists that a disabled owner will recover sufficiently to provide the usual services to the business. This recovery could occur either during or after the elimination period. If recovery occurs during the elimination period, it is commonly provided that a new elimination period will have to be satisfied if the disabled owner returns to work for a reasonable length of time. If recovery occurs after the buyout has become mandatory, this provision can provide for modification of the agreement if the owner is to be allowed to reenter the business. Again, this provision should be designed to consider the insurance funding the buy-sell agreement. Some disability buyout policies provide for continued benefit payments even after a disabled insured recovers.
- *funding.* A disability buy-sell agreement provides more certainty to the agreement if it is funded in advance. Disability income protection insurance or special disability buyout insurance policies can be used to fund a disability buy-sell agreement. If the agreement is to be insured, this provision will provide all the specifics related to insurance funding. The purchaser, the premium payer, and the beneficiary of each policy will be specified in this provision.
- *disposition of policies held by the seller after a buyout has become effective.* If a disability buy-sell agreement is insured, there will be one or perhaps several policies covering each owner. Furthermore, each owner may be covered by life insurance if the disability provisions are included in the "deathtime" buyout agreement. This

provision will specify the method of disposition of any unnecessary insurance policies after a buyout occurs following the death or disability of an owner. The actual design of this provision will depend on the type of agreement selected and the circumstances of the individual business.

- *premature death during the period of disability buyout.* Disability buy-sell agreements are often carried out through installment obligations. Of course, it is possible for the disabled owner to die before all the installment payments are made. It is usually recommended that the life insurance covering each owner under the "deathtime" buy-sell agreement be continued until the disability installment payments are completed. This provision might stipulate that the death of a disabled owner will accelerate the installment obligation and the balance will be due in one lump sum. The purchasers can then use the proceeds of the life insurance policies to complete the buyout.

Triggering the Buyout

Definition of Disability. Because a disability buy-sell agreement or salary continuation program is triggered by the total disability of an owner, the definition of total disability for purposes of the agreement is of critical importance. The definition used in the agreement must depend on a number of circumstances. First, the degree of disability that would prevent a business owner from contributing productively to his or her business or profession must be determined. The definition used in the agreement should reflect this degree of disability; otherwise the buyout will not become effective in circumstances when an owner can no longer be productive.

A closely held business owner or professional performs services that often consist of one or more specialized skills. The definition of disability in this case should provide for total disability when the owner or professional is unable to perform these specialized skills. For example, a group surgical practice should provide for the buyout of one of their members when a disability renders a physician unable to perform surgery. Typically the definition of total disability should include the business owner or professional who is unable to perform his or her normal services on a full-time basis.

An important additional consideration is the insurer's definition of total disability if the agreement is to be funded in some manner by disability insurance. The definition of disability in an insured agreement should never be more liberal than the definition used in the disability insurance contract.

Otherwise, the parties could become bound to a mandatory buyout at a time when no benefits are forthcoming from the funding insurance contract. For this reason it is typically recommended by financial services professionals that the insured disability buy-sell agreement contain the definition of total disability used in the insurance contract. This places the burden on the insurer to determine when the benefits will be paid and thus when the buyout will occur. The use of the insurer's definition removes the potential for a dispute among the parties to the agreement. Furthermore, it provides that benefits will be forthcoming when the agreement becomes effective. Insurers currently offer policies with varying definitions of disability to suit the needs of specific business and professional clients.

Note that the high frequency of disability claims has caused insurers to become wary of narrow disability definitions, particularly in some occupational categories, such as physicians. Please be aware that the most liberal definition (that is, "own occupation," explained below) may not be available to all classes of occupations, particularly for disability income insurance. To the extent "own occupation" is available, it may be available only for a limited period of time (for example, 2 years) or cause a reduction in the maximum monthly coverage amounts.

Own Occupation. The most liberal definition of disability contained in a disability insurance contract is the *own-occupation definition of disability.* This definition will probably be the most appropriate for a disability buy-sell situation. Generally speaking, the closely held business owner or professional possesses special skills necessary to make the business or professional practice succeed. If the business owner or professional loses the ability to perform these specific tasks, he or she will no longer be a productive member of the business. Unless there is another function that the disabled owner or professional can perform for the business, the buyout should occur when the individual is unable to perform his or her usual functions. A typical own-occupation definition of disability reads as follows:

> Total disability shall mean the continuous inability of the insured to engage in his or her regular occupation or profession due to illness or injury.

Traditionally most disability policies containing an own-occupation definition provide this coverage only for a temporary period of time, after which the definition of disability is shifted to a more restrictive definition, such as those discussed below. For example, a policy might provide own-occupation coverage for a period of 2 years and then shift to an "any-occupation" requirement thereafter. This type of hybrid definition would be unsuitable for the typical disability buy-sell agreement since the parties wish to permanently terminate the involvement of an owner or professional who is unable to perform the usual duties of the specific business. Disability policies designed for buy-sell funding purposes will provide own-occupation disability coverage to age 65 and beyond for specific skills or professions. The own-occupation guarantee will be provided for in the actual contract, or in some cases insurers will provide the insured with a "specialty letter" that guarantees benefits if the insured is unable to perform the usual duties of the occupation or professional specialty.

Any Occupation for Which the Insured Is Reasonably Suited. This definition of disability requires the insured to be unable to perform the duties of any occupation for which the insured is reasonably suited by education, training, or experience before benefits will be received. This definition is not a particularly good one for a closely held business or professional disability buy-sell agreement. No benefits will be received if the insured is unable to perform the normal duties of the closely held business or profession but is able to perform some occupation commensurate with the insured's background. Therefore the funding for the buy-sell agreement will not be available even though the insured owner or professional is unable to contribute productively to the closely held business or professional practice.

EXAMPLE

Kingsly and Norwood are partners in a law firm that specializes in criminal defense litigation. The partners form a binding insured cross-purchase, disability buy-sell agreement triggered by a disability satisfying the insurer's definition of total disability. Unfortunately Kingsly, Norwood, and their advisers were not careful in selecting the disability policies and secured protection that provides benefits only when the insured satisfies the "any-occupation-for-which-the-insured-is-reasonably-suited" requirement.

When the high-pressure nature of the work overcomes Kingsly and extreme hypertension results, several doctors advise him that he will no longer be able to handle the stress of being a trial lawyer. However, the physicians see no reason why Kingsly cannot engage in basic legal research or perhaps teach at a law school. The insurer views these other tasks as occupations for which Kingsly is reasonably suited by his education and training, and it will provide no benefits under the policy. Because the buy-sell agreement was not triggered since the insurer's definition of disability was not satisfied, Norwood is not required to purchase Kingsly's interest. A conflict will probably arise since Kingsly will want continued income payments while Norwood will soon be dissatisfied with carrying the case load of both partners. This problem could have been avoided if the partners had secured an own-occupation disability contract or a specialty-coverage letter from the insurer.

Some disability buyout insurance policies provide a hybrid definition specially applicable to the closely held business buy-sell situation. This definition will provide benefits if the insured is unable to perform the duties of the insured's regular occupation and any other occupation within the business organization for which the insured is reasonably suited in consideration of education, training, and experience. Under these circumstances the buyout will be completed and the benefits will be paid when the disabled owner or professional is unable to contribute productively to his or her specific business or professional practice.

Other Disability Definitions. There are definitions of disability found in some disability income policies that are less appropriate for the purposes of a disability buy-sell agreement. The financial services professional should be aware of these definitions and advise business and professional clients against the use of these disability income policies for funding buy-sell agreements.

Some Definitions of Disability

- Own occupation: very appropriate for a buy-sell agreement
- Any occupation for which reasonably suited within the business: may be appropriate for a buy-sell agreement
- Any occupation for which reasonably suited: not appropriate for a buy-sell agreement
- Any occupation for which reasonably suited: not appropriate for a buy-sell agreement
- Any occupation: definitely inappropriate for a buy-sell agreement

First, the any-occupation disability definition literally prevents the insured from receiving benefits until the insured is unable to substantially perform in any occupation. This is similar to the definition used in the Social Security disability program. Although the courts have generally interpreted this provision in favor of the insured, a definition this restrictive is obviously inappropriate for a buy-sell agreement.

presumptive-disability provision

Disability policies often include a *presumptive-disability provision* that provides benefits automatically when an insured has sustained the loss of certain functions. For example, the complete loss of eyesight and the loss of the use of two limbs are typical presumptive disabilities. Since this provision is typically in addition to the policy's normal definition of disability, it creates no problem if the policy is used in conjunction with a disability buy-sell agreement.

Some disability policies include other provisions in the definition of disability. For example, some policies provide that benefits will not be paid unless the insured is under a physician's care for the disability. Policies may also restrict the insured from working in any occupation if benefits are to be received. The financial services professional should avoid these restrictive provisions when using insurance to fund a disability buy-sell agreement. The parties will want to receive benefits and complete the buy-sell agreement if the insured is no longer able to contribute to the business. It could be devastating to the agreement if benefits were terminated because the disabled owner returned to work in another occupation.

Disability Buy-Sell Agreements Funded Without Disability Insurance. Special care should be taken when drafting the definition of disability if the agreement is funded without disability insurance since the third-party insurer will not be making the determination of disability. The definition should be drafted to make the buyout mandatory when an owner is restricted by a disability to such a degree that he or she is expected to be indefinitely unable to perform the regular functions of the job.

To prevent conflict between the business owners, it is also essential to include a method by which a binding determination of disability can be made. For example, the agreement could provide that a designated medical professional or team of medical professionals will make the ultimate determination of disability. This provision can also be included as a backup in an insured agreement in the event that the disability policies funding the agreement lapse. The parties to the agreement should never retain the burden of determining when a disability occurs, or an unresolvable conflict may follow.

Elimination Period. The elimination period is the time interval for which a party must be disabled before the buyout will occur. If disability insurance is used to fund the agreement, the policy will also contain an elimination period that must be satisfied before benefits will be paid. It is generally recommended that the elimination period contained in the buyout agreement coincide with that of the funding insurance.

The elimination period used in the agreement should be selected carefully since an inappropriate choice will cause problems after a disability occurs. If the elimination period is short, the probability is high that a disabled owner will recover and be capable of returning to work after the buyout has occurred. This will create an unnecessary expense to the parties since the buyout could be avoided with a longer elimination period. Furthermore, the disabled owner will become disgruntled if he or she would prefer to return to the business after a recovery but is unable to do so because the purchase is mandated by the terms of the agreement.

The choice of elimination period depends on many factors. First, it should be determined how long the business can afford the burden of the continued salary payments to the disabled owner since such a situation cannot continue for an indefinite period of time. If the income to the disabled owner is to be provided for by personal disability income insurance or a funded sick-pay plan, the burden will be lighter and a longer elimination period will be possible.

Second, the owners must decide how long the business can operate before a disabled owner must be replaced. This depends on the type of services provided by the specific owners. The sooner a disabled owner must be replaced, the shorter the elimination period that should be incorporated.

A third factor in selecting the elimination period is the method of funding the agreement. If insurance is to be used, the elimination period will depend on the insurance contract. Disability income protection insurance typically has elimination periods of 30, 60, or 90 days. Other elimination periods can usually be selected by the client. These typical elimination periods are too short for the buyout situation, since the odds of recovery are too high at 90 days to make a mandatory buyout practical at this time. Of course, if benefits are paid prior to the trigger date of the buyout, these payments can be used to continue the disabled owner's salary or provide for a replacement.

Insurers have developed special disability buyout policies to fund disability buy-sell agreements. These policies have more appropriate elimination periods for this purpose, the typical period in these policies being 24 months. Some of these policies provide optional elimination periods with higher benefit amounts available for longer elimination periods.

Finally, the age of the owners should be considered in determining the elimination period. Statistics reveal that the odds of recovery from a disability of significant length decrease with age. Furthermore, the unnecessary buyout of a disabled owner is less damaging to an older individual. Presumably the older individual has fewer productive years remaining until retirement and would be less concerned about returning to the business after recovery. Younger owners, on the other hand, will probably want to return to their previous career after recovering from a disability. Generally speaking, the elimination period should be longer if the owners of the business are relatively young.

Financial services professionals should carefully consider all these factors when assisting a business or professional client in the selection of the elimination period. This will require extensive investigation into the circumstances of the business and its owners. For example, the existence of any formal or informal salary continuation agreements, disability insurance owned personally by the owners, and the relative skills and functions of each individual owner will have to be ascertained. For most purposes an elimination period of between one and two years is appropriate.

Factors to Consider in Choosing the Elimination Period

- How long can the business afford to continue the disabled owner's salary?
- How long can the business operate before having to replace the disabled owner?
- What elimination periods are available in disability income insurance contracts?
- How old are the owners?

Other Considerations. Additional problems to be considered in triggering a buy-sell agreement are the issues of recurring disabilities and recovery of a disabled owner. Failure to consider these possibilities when designing the agreement may cause the dissatisfaction of the parties and the failure of the agreement to meet its objectives.

Successive Disabilities. Disability insurance contracts often provide for the possibility of recurring disabilities. This problem is handled by allowing short time gaps to exist between periods of a recurring disability without requiring a new elimination period to be satisfied. The typical contract provides that the recovered insured must return to work for at least 6 months before insurers will require the satisfaction of a new elimination period. This is only true, however, if the second disability is a recurrence of the first condition. By employing this provision, insurers provide an incentive for the insured to rehabilitate and attempt to return to work.

Because recurring disability is often ignored in the sample forms available for drafting disability buy-sell agreements, the financial services professional should make the parties aware of this problem and recommend appropriate drafting of such a provision. If insurance is used to fund the agreement, it is logical to incorporate the insurer's provision for recurrent disabilities in the buy-sell agreement.

EXAMPLE

Louis and Clark form the Exploration Corporation as 50 percent shareholders. The corporation forms a stock-redemption agreement with the shareholders providing for a mandatory buyout in the event that a shareholder becomes disabled and is unable to perform his normal services for the corporation for a continuous period of 12 months. The agreement is silent on the issue of successive disabilities. It is to be funded by a disability buyout policy that provides benefits to the corporation if an insured is disabled for a period of 12 consecutive months. However, the disability policy provides that an insured may recover and return to work for a period of up to 6 months before a new elimination period must be satisfied. Louis suffers a disabling injury and is continuously disabled for 7 months, after which his physician believes that he may be able to return to work and perform most of his usual functions. Louis returns to work for a period of 2 months, aggravating the earlier injury. Disability recurs and is expected to continue indefinitely. Under the terms of the insurance contract the corporation will receive benefits at the end of the original 12-month elimination period. However, the buyout of Louis's stock is not mandatory under the terms of the redemption agreement until his subsequent disability has lasted an additional 12 months.

The problems with the above example are obvious. A party to this agreement will be concerned that a temporary recovery period will delay the stock redemption. A disabled party will be discouraged from taking rehabilitative measures under these circumstances. This problem could be avoided by matching the disability definition provisions in the buy-sell agreement with the funding insurance contract.

Post-Buyout Recovery. The parties should consider the possibility of recovery once the buyout has become mandatory. There are several options available to deal with this contingency. First, the agreement can provide that the recovered former owner will be allowed to repurchase and return to the business. Second, the agreement may specifically provide the buyers with an option to terminate the buyout and allow the recovered owner to return. Finally, the agreement could provide that the buyout, once initiated, is binding, and the recovered owner is prevented from reentering the business.

It is usually not recommended that the parties be bound to allow a recovered owner to reenter the business after the buyout is completed. A properly selected elimination period should be the maximum amount of time that should elapse before a disabled owner's interest is terminated. After this time the disabled owner will have to be replaced by a new employee, and the possibility that the disabled owner might return could hinder the recruitment of a worthy replacement. Furthermore, an owner disabled for a long time may be of little value to the business upon subsequent recovery. The disabled owner might have lost some skills or find that business contacts have dried up during this period of inactivity.

The funding of the agreement has an effect on how this problem is treated. The benefits from disability income protection insurance will terminate when the insured recovers. If the buyout must continue despite the lack of benefits, a large potential financial burden could be placed on the business and its remaining owners. The agreement might provide for an extended installment period for the balance of the purchase price if receipt of benefits ceases.

Many disability buyout policies are designed more appropriately for the buy-sell situation. These policies provide that benefits will be paid once the elimination period has been satisfied even if the insured subsequently recovers. Therefore a mandatory buyout will be completed without a funding problem even if the seller recovers. Some of these policies require the purchase of a "presumptive-disability rider" for benefits to continue if a disabled insured recovers.

There may be instances where all parties to the agreement would prefer that a recovered former owner be allowed to return to the business. In this case the parties should be able to reach an ad hoc agreement permitting the recovered owner to repurchase his or her interest at a fair price. The advantage of an ad hoc arrangement is its voluntary nature. If the circumstances indicate that it is in the best interest of all parties for the owner to return to the business, it will happen. If the agreement instead binds the parties to permit an owner to return after recovery, a potentially unproductive owner may be forced upon unhappy remaining owners.

Form of Purchase Payments

The purchase price for a disabled owner's interest will be in the form of either a lump-sum or an installment obligation. Lump-sum purchases have traditionally been impractical to fund in the case of a disability buy-sell agreement because the funding of the lump-sum buyout is difficult. Saving for a disability buyout is impractical since the parties do not know in advance when the purchase will occur. If a disability occurs soon after the agreement is formed, saving for a substantial purchase price is not feasible. Even if such a saving fund was possible, a large accumulation in a corporation to fund a stock redemption at the disability of an owner may create an accumulated-earnings tax problem.

Most traditional disability insurance policies are unsuitable for funding a lump-sum buyout. Since disability income protection policies provide a stream of payments during the benefit period, it will be difficult for the purchaser to provide the lump-sum amount when benefit payments will be spread over many years.

Several companies provide special disability buyout insurance plans. Some, but not all, of these contracts provide a lump-sum benefit when the elimination period has been satisfied. The maximum benefit available under these contracts, however, is limited to a specific percentage (for example, 80 percent) of the value of the insured's ownership interest. Therefore even if a disability buyout contract is purchased, there may be a gap between the amount of proceeds and the lump-sum purchase price required.

Under most circumstances the only practical method of completing the buyout is an installment obligation. The installment payments can be made out of the business earnings in an uninsured agreement. This allows the owners to spread the payments into the future, thus preventing an immediate financial drain on the business and on the healthy owners. Installment payments can also be coordinated with the benefits received from an insurance company if the agreement is funded with disability insurance. Disability income protection or buyout insurance contracts are both adaptable to an installment purchase. The benefits will be collected by the buyer-beneficiary and transferred at the appropriate time to the seller to meet the scheduled payments of the installment obligation.

To make the installment approach satisfactory to the seller, the agreement can be designed to provide annual installments to the seller sufficient to satisfy his or her financial needs. Furthermore, there is no step-up in basis of the seller's interest as in the buy-sell at death. The disabled seller may have to recognize a substantial taxable gain on the sale. As discussed in chapter 10, the use of an installment sale can relieve this tax burden by spreading the tax liability over the period of the installment.

Valuation of the Disabled Owner's Interest

There are some special valuation issues related to the disability buy-sell situation must be addressed. The valuation methods are one of the most important components of any buy-sell agreement.

Date of Valuation. The valuation date will be a key consideration in determining the purchase price of a disabled owner's interest. The value of the business most likely will change from the time the seller first becomes disabled to the time the buyout actually occurs. If the seller was a key contributor to the business, the disability may cause a reduction in the fair market value of the business during the elimination period. The agreement should be clear on the valuation date to determine if the disabled owner's sale proceeds will reflect this reduction in value.

Treatment of Salary Continuation Payments

The closely held business will often provide a disabled owner-employee with salary continuation payments during a period of disability. These payments may be pursuant to a formal plan or be provided as a result of an informal understanding between the owners. The salary continuation payments will generally be provided until the buyout occurs.

The valuation provision in the buy-sell agreement should specify whether salary continuation payments made by the business will be credited against the purchase price. The allocation of the proceeds received in the buy-sell agreement between salary continuation amounts and purchase payments may have a significant impact on the tax status of the payments. Salary continuation payments are received as ordinary income by the recipient, while purchase payments often qualify for capital-gain treatment.

Impact of Funding on Valuation. The type of funding chosen by the parties can have an impact on the valuation provision included in the agreement. Disability buyout policies provide periodic or lump-sum payments with limits based on the actual fair market value of the business. The insurer must know the purchase price in advance to establish the coverage amounts. A fixed price provision, providing for periodic readjustment of the stated price and the insurance funding, must be used in this case.

The use of a disability buyout policy prevents the funding of the full purchase price. These policies typically have participation limits and will only cover a portion of the purchase price. Insurers providing these policies will also underwrite strictly and will not provide coverage for an excessive purchase price; the parties to the buy-sell agreement do not have to use the value determined by the insurer as the purchase price. Company practices vary, but insurers providing this type of coverage will require financial statements from the business before insuring the buy-sell agreement. The insurer uses the financial data to establish the fair market value of the business based on some reliable formula-valuation technique. However, a purchase price in excess of the insurer's value will result in an underfunding problem.

Funding the Disability Buy-Sell Agreement

The business-continuation risk associated with an owner's disability has often been ignored because of the lack of an appropriate funding mechanism. Accumulation of business earnings to fund a disability buy-sell agreement is impractical, since a disability may occur soon after the agreement is formed. While life insurance presents a suitable funding alternative for a buy-sell agreement at death, traditional disability insurance has been inadequate to meet the funding needs of a disability buyout. When disability buy-sell agreements are formed, they usually provide for an installment purchase. The installment payments have typically been financed by any combination of current earnings, disability income insurance, and cash values from the life insurance contracts funding the "deathtime" buy-sell agreement. Fortunately several insurers currently offer specialized disability buyout policies more appropriate to the disability buy-sell situation.

Disability Insurance

Disability Income Replacement Protection. *Disability income protection insurance* can be used to contribute to the funding of the disability buy-sell agreement. The purchaser, premium payer, and beneficiary of each policy used to fund the agreement will be the designated purchaser under the buy-sell agreement. That is, if the cross-purchase approach is used, the individual owners will purchase disability income insurance covering the other owners who must be bought out. If the entity or stock-redemption approach is used, the business will be the purchaser, premium payer, and beneficiary of the disability income policies covering the owners who are parties to the buy-sell agreement.

A shortcoming associated with the use of disability income protection insurance is the mismatch of the benefits available with the intended purpose of the agreement. The agreement is designed to provide a disabled seller with purchase payments for his or her business interest. A lump-sum purchase would require a large amount of proceeds at the time of the buyout. Even installment obligations involve ample principal and interest payments over a limited period of time. Disability income protection is designed to replace a disabled insured's income during a period of disability. These benefits will be inadequate for the purpose of funding either a lump-sum or an installment buyout of a substantial interest.

The monthly benefit payments available from disability income policies are subject to participation limits established by each insurer. Insurers limit the amount of protection available to an insured individual to a specified percentage of earned income, generally 40 to 70 percent. Some insurers apply these limits on a cumulative basis to all disability protection covering a specific insured. Therefore an insurer might not issue additional coverage to an insured whose protection under other policies has already reached the participation limits. On the other hand, some insurers will provide full coverage on an insured for both business buyout and personal income protection.

The cumulative application of participation limits by some insurers might cause a problem if the insured must be covered for both disability income and buyout purposes. If disability income protection is used in the business buy-sell agreement, the amount of personal disability protection available to the owner or professional may be reduced. Under these circumstances it is important to ensure that the buyout payments are adequate to meet the disabled owner's income requirements, since individual disability coverage may be unavailable because of the participation limits. The practices of individual insurers differ on the cumulation of participation limits. The financial services professional should be cognizant of the underwriting practices of any insurers through which the client is or will be insured.

The maximum monthly benefits available from disability income protection have traditionally been inadequate to fund a buy-sell agreement. Insurers currently have monthly benefit limits of up to $35,000 per month. Disability policies may be available with even higher limits on a specialty underwriting basis. These limits may facilitate the funding of disability purchase agreements with traditional policies. However, be aware that the maximum monthly limits will vary based on the type of occupational class and, perhaps, the definition of disability. For example, some companies now provide for lower monthly limits for physicians.

Since the monthly benefit amounts vary with the insured's income, additional disability income protection can be secured when the insured owners' incomes increase. Presumably the valuation provision in the buy-sell agreement will provide periodic upward adjustments as the value of the business increases. Additional insurance amounts should be purchased, where participation limits allow, to keep pace with these funding requirements. Many disability income policies have cost-of-living riders that may also be considered.

In spite of the potentially high benefits available, payments from disability income insurance will generally be insufficient to meet all the funding requirements of both a wage continuation plan and a buy-sell agreement. If disability income protection is used to fund the buy-sell agreement, some supplementary method of funding must be considered.

Disability Buyout Insurance. Several insurers underwrite specialty policies designed to handle the disability business-continuation risk. These plans vary a great deal from insurer to insurer and are rapidly evolving. Since the disability risk has been largely ignored in the business-planning situation, insurers believe that this is a fertile market for product growth and that new products will be available in the future. The financial services professional should be aware of these product innovations to assist business and professional clients in planning for the disability risk.

Benefits Available. The general rule for these disability buyout policies is that the coverage limits are carefully underwritten. Insurers will issue buyout protection with benefit limits up to a specified percentage of the purchase price. The percentage participation limits vary from 80 to 100 percent, but virtually every carrier reduces its participation after the insured business owner reaches age 59. Aggregate limitations also exist for this type of policy, which may also be somewhat restrictive. Currently the regular policy limitations on these policies range from $500,000 to $1.5 million depending on the carrier. Again, the coverage available will vary with the type of occupational class for the business. Larger policies may also be negotiated with specialty underwriters with at least one advertising benefits up to $100 million.

The benefits available under these special disability buyout policies are often related to the elimination period. Higher limits are available as the elimination period increases. Elimination periods on the buyout period are typically longer than those found in disability income policies. For example, elimination periods of 24, 36, or even 60 months are available with these policies.

Some of these plans provide for lump-sum benefits. Since the benefits are limited to a percentage (for example, 80 percent) of the actual purchase price, even a lump-sum benefit will be insufficient to provide the entire purchase price. Therefore some form of installment buyout is almost always used in a disability buy-sell agreement regardless of the choice of funding.

One advantage of these special buyout policies is that they often provide the full benefit even if the insured recovers after the elimination period. This particular policy provision should be examined carefully since it is generally recommended that the buy-sell agreement provide for the buyout to continue even if the disabled owner recovers. Failure to secure the appropriate insurance for this type of agreement will cause a funding problem if benefits cease at the recovery of the seller.

Disability buyout policies may instead provide substantial benefits on a periodic basis, facilitating the use of an installment sale. Higher aggregate limits are available if the periodic alternative is selected. With this type of plan high monthly benefit amounts are paid for a limited period of years (generally 60 months) until the policy limit is reached.

Some innovative disability policies provide for a combination of periodic benefits followed by a lump sum. Presumably the monthly installment benefits will be used to (1) continue salary payments to the disabled owner, (2) begin installment purchase payments to the disabled owner, or (3) provide an accumulation fund to enable the purchasers to provide a lump-sum purchase price when the periodic benefits terminate. When the periodic benefits cease, the insurer will provide a lump-sum benefit that may coincide with the elimination period used in the buy-sell agreement and provide a portion of the purchase price at this time. These policies have both monthly and overall policy benefit limits.

Financial Underwriting of the Disability Buyout Policy. Insurers carefully underwrite the disability buyout risks. As discussed earlier, insurers will provide protection for only a specified percentage of the actual purchase price. It is usually required that the purchase price be fixed in the agreement with provisions for annual review. Insurers will require financial data from the closely held business to determine that the purchase price is not excessive. The insurers apply some type of formula valuation method to the data to arrive at an estimate of fair market value.

As an additional restriction, insurers will not provide disability buyout protection for a purchase price that exceeds the price specified in the "deathtime" buy-sell agreement. The valuation provision included in the "deathtime" and disability buy-sell agreements must be given careful consideration if a disability buyout policy is used. The buyout policies often require specific valuation methods, which must be complied with.

Form of Agreement Permitted. Insurers traditionally required either a trustee or a business entity to be the beneficiary of a disability buyout policy. Policies now offer more flexibility, and one insurer even offers buyout benefits without a written buy-sell agreement.

Other Sources of Funding

The noninsurance methods of funding discussed in the chapters covering "deathtime" buy-sell agreements are also applicable to disability buy-sell agreements. For example, the agreement could be funded by savings, current earnings, or borrowing. Although the use of these methods leaves the buy-sell agreement lacking in certainty, these methods can nevertheless be used to supplement insurance funding, since the entire purchase price cannot typically be insured with disability coverage.

Waiver of Premiums. Most disability buy-sell agreements are incorporated as provisions in the "deathtime" buy-sell agreement. If insurance is used to fund both agreements, premiums on these policies can be waived if an insured becomes disabled. This waiver is available at no extra charge in disability policies and may be added for a small additional premium in a life insurance policy. Such waivers make a substantial amount of funds available when an insured owner becomes disabled. These waived premium amounts are no longer paid to the insurer and can presumably be used to contribute to the purchase payments. Obviously the amounts freed up by the waivers will be insufficient to fund the entire purchase price and may be logically applied only to an installment sale.

EXAMPLE

Ed and Ralph, both aged 45, are each 50 percent shareholders in Acme, Inc., a small manufacturing firm. Acme has an insured stock-redemption agreement providing for the redemption of Ed's or Ralph's stock at death or total disability. The life and disability policies funding the agreement total $15,000 in annual premiums for each shareholder; each policy contains a waiver of premium. Assume Ed becomes totally disabled and his stock must be redeemed by Acme. The waivers of premium free up $15,000 annually that Acme would otherwise have spent on Ed's premiums. These amounts can be used to assist Acme in making the redemption payments.

Coordination With the "Deathtime" Buy-Sell Agreement

Disability buy-sell agreements have traditionally been funded through elaborate schemes involving the life insurance funding for the "deathtime" buy-sell agreement. First, the waiver-of-premium amounts from the life insurance policies, discussed above, can be applied annually to help fund the purchase price at an owner's disability. Second, cash values and dividends available in the life insurance policies funding the agreement are also available to fund the disability buyout. These funds have typically been combined with the firm's current earnings to provide installment-sale payments to the disabled owner. Because the installment purchase of a disabled owner's business interest may continue for many years, the life insurance in the "deathtime" buy-sell agreement should remain in effect until the purchase payments have been completed. If the disabled seller dies before the buyout is completed, the death proceeds can be applied to the balance due.

The full funding of disability and "deathtime" buy-sell agreements can be prohibitively expensive to some closely held businesses. However, some funding methods have been developed that can meet the needs of the parties while holding funding costs down to a reasonable level.[33]

---

33. Milton H. Stern, *Inside the Family-Held Business,* Law & Business Inc., 1986.

Sources of Funding the Disability Buyout

- Disability income insurance
- Disability buyout insurance
- Life insurance waiver-of-premium provision
- Life insurance cash values
- Life insurance dividends
- Life insurance death proceeds (if death occurs before the buyout is completed)

EXAMPLE

Flash, Dale, and Zarkov are equal shareholders in Space, Inc. The shareholders form an insured stock- redemption plan to take effect at their death or disability. The owners decide that they cannot afford three disability buyout policies. The proposed purchase price is $500,000, and a life insurance policy (including waiver of premium) with this face amount is purchased by Space on each of the shareholders. At an owner's disability the stock is to be redeemed; however, no principal payments will be made until the death of the owner. Suppose Zarkov becomes totally disabled in this year and is redeemed by the corporation. Assuming a 9 percent interest rate on the unpaid balance of the purchase price, Zarkov will receive $45,000 interest annually from Space until his death. At this time the corporation will receive the death benefit, which may be transferred to Zarkov's estate to satisfy the unpaid balance. The $45,000 annual interest payment will provide for Zarkov and his family during his life. These interest payments can be supplied partially by the premium amounts freed up by the waiver-of-premium provision. The remainder of the interest payments can be provided for by current earnings. If the interest payments are insufficient to satisfy Zarkov's support needs, he should purchase personal disability income protection insurance.

Tax Considerations

The tax rules applicable to the lifetime sale, liquidation, or redemption of an owner's business interest discussed in previous chapters are applicable to the disability buy-sell situation. The tax specifics of the disability buy-sell agreement are summarized below.

Table 12-3 Taxation of an Insured Disability Buy-Sell Agreement

	Partnership	**Corporation**
Cross-purchase Agreement	Premiums paid by partners are nondeductible. Disability benefits are received tax free by partners. Sale proceeds received by disabled partner are • ordinary income to the seller to the extent they represent unrealized receivables, appreciated inventory, and depreciation recapture • capital gain to the extent they are received for the partnership interest including goodwill (no basis step-up available)	Premiums paid by shareholders are nondeductible. Disability benefits are received tax free by shareholders. Sale proceeds received by the disabled shareholder are capital gain to the seller (no basis step-up available)
Entity (Stock-redemption) Agreement	Premiums paid by partnership are nondeductible. Disability benefits are received tax free by the partnership. Liquidation payments received by the disabled partner are • ordinary income to the extent they represent unrealized receivables, appreciated inventory, and depreciation recapture • capital gain to the extent they are received for the partnership interest (including goodwill if specified in the agreement) (no basis step-up)	Premiums paid by the corporation are nondeductible. Disability benefits are received tax free by the corporation. Redemption amounts received by the disabled shareholder are • ordinary income (to the extent of E & P) if redemption fails to qualify for sale-or-exchange treatment under Sec. 302 (no basis step-up) • capital gain if redemption qualifies for sale-or-exchange treatment under Sec. 302 (Sec. 303 unavailable) (no basis step-up)

CONTINUATION OF A DISABLED OWNER'S SALARY

The severe financial effect of the disability of the business owner or professional was discussed earlier in the chapter. The disabled owner's salary must be replaced in some manner for his or her standard of living to be maintained. The lost income can be replaced either by the business through a salary continuation plan or by the individual owners through personally owned disability income policies. If the business provides for continued salary payments to an owner, such payments should be made at least until the disability buy-sell agreement becomes effective or perhaps for the entire period of the owner's disability.

Types of Disability Salary Continuation Plans

Disability salary continuation plans for the owners and regular employees of a business fall into three categories. Two of these, *sick-pay plans and short-term disability plans,* provide benefits for a relatively short period of time if a participant is unable to work due to illness or injury.

Since most businesses can afford to continue an owner's or regular employee's salary for short periods of time without undue hardship, we will focus our discussion here on the third type of salary continuation program—the *long-term disability plan.* These plans can be either formal or informal and funded in advance or left unfunded.

Corporate Disability Salary Continuation Plans

salary continuation plan

Tax Benefits of the Properly Designed Plan. A formally establisheddisability *salary continuation plan* provides tax benefits both to the corporation and to the plan participants. The plan can be funded in advance either by the purchase of insurance by the corporation or by contributions to a savings fund.

Deductibility of Contributions by the Corporation. Salary continuation plans provided by corporations can be either insured or uninsured. Insured plans typically provide that the corporation pays the premiums for the insurance, while the employee is the beneficiary of the proceeds. Under this type of plan the premiums are a deductible business expense to the corporation. The deduction is limited by the reasonable-compensation test, taking the participant's premium costs and other compensation into consideration. An alternative design for insured salary continuation plans is for the corporation to be the owner and beneficiary of the insurance policy. The disabled participant is paid by the corporation and not directly by the insurer. Under this arrangement the premiums are nondeductible by the corporation.

A salary continuation plan may also be uninsured, in which case contributions to a savings fund are nondeductible since they continue to be unrestricted assets of the employer.

Contributions Excluded From the Employee's Gross Income. Employer contributions to fund a salary continuation plan, whether insurance premiums or deposits to a savings fund, are excluded from the participant's gross income. Therefore a properly designed plan will not create taxable income to a participant when the advance funding occurs.

Receipt of Proceeds and Payment of Benefits by the Corporation. If the corporation is the owner and beneficiary of the disability policies, the benefits are received tax free by the corporation when a participant becomes disabled. The corporation will be able to deduct reasonable salary continuation payments to the participant when the insurance benefits are used to make these payments. If the salary continuation plan is not insured, reasonable salary continuation payments made to a disabled participant are likewise deductible as an ordinary business expense.

Receipt of Salary Continuation Payments by the Employee. The plan benefits received by the disabled participant from either the insurer or the corporation are generally taxable income. There is a small tax credit under IRC Sec. 22 that can be taken against the federal income tax liability of an individual retired on permanent and total disability. The tax credit is equal to 15 percent of the salary continuation income up to a specified limit determined by the individual's marital and filing status. The credit is reduced gradually as the disabled individual's income increases and is eventually phased out completely. The low maximum overall limit of the credit, combined with the phaseout procedure, makes the Sec. 22 credit relatively useless for business owners or professionals with substantial income. The maximum credit and the phaseout thresholds are illustrated below.

Table 12-4 Maximum Credit and Phaseout Thresholds

	Maximum Salary Continuation Benefits Eligible for the Credit	Maximum Credit	Credit Phased Out as Adjusted Gross Income Exceeds
Single individual or joint return with only one disabled spouse	$5,000	$ 750	$17,500
Joint return with two disabled spouses	7,500	1,125	25,000
Two disabled spouses filing separately	3,750	562.50	12,500

Establishing a Formal Salary Continuation Plan. Tax rules define a salary continuation plan as an accident or health plan. The plan may cover one or more employees, and there may be different plans for different classes of employees. The plan may be either insured or uninsured, and it is not necessary either that the plan be in writing or that the employee's rights to benefits be enforceable. If such rights to benefits are not enforceable, benefits will be deemed to be received from a salary continuation plan only if a plan or corporate policy providing for the salary continuation payments in the event of disability actually exists when the employee becomes disabled. Knowledge or notice of this plan or policy must be reasonably available to the participating employee. Since the plan must be for the benefit of employees, shareholder-employees of a corporation are eligible, whereas sole proprietors and partners are not.

The payment of benefits by a corporation may have an adverse tax impact unless a salary continuation plan has been established. The possibility that the IRS will challenge the legitimacy of these salary continuation plans is amplified by the fact that most closely held businesses provide these plans solely for shareholders and perhaps a few key employees. For this reason it is recommended that the salary continuation plan be formally adopted by the corporation and provide the participants with enforceable rights. These actions will both help establish the status of the plan for the IRS and provide assurance to the participating owner-employees that the benefits will be received.

Avoiding Nondiscrimination Restrictions. Many types of employee benefit plans have nondiscrimination rules that must be complied with by the employer. Fortunately these rules are not applicable to salary continuation plans if benefits will be included in the employee's gross income. For this reason the salary continuation plans discussed here may be provided on a discriminatory basis. That is, the plans can be limited to owner-employees and key personnel. The corporation may also provide separate plans for different categories of employees. Therefore the closely held or professional corporation can provide a salary continuation plan for its owner-employees without making similar expenditures in behalf of regular employees.

ERISA Requirements. Salary continuation plans are considered welfare benefit plans for the purposes of ERISA. ERISA generally requires a written plan document and substantial reporting and disclosure requirements to plan participants and the Department of Labor (DOL). A salary continuation plan limited to highly compensated employees and key management personnel is exempt from most of the reporting and disclosure requirements. However, a written plan document must be provided to the DOL upon request. It is important to note that the requirements of ERISA pertaining to establishing a salary continuation plan are separate from those of the IRS.

Checklist for Establishing a Plan. Tax benefits may be lost if the corporation provides benefit payments to employees in the absence of a salary continuation plan. The corporation should, therefore, take the following steps to provide evidence that a formal plan has been established:

- Approve the plan at the board of directors meeting and document in the corporate minutes that the plan is established for the benefit of employees. (The plan may be limited to shareholder-employees.)
- For the purposes of ERISA adopt a written plan that includes the provisions for the receipt of benefits by covered participants. The plan should specify that any shareholders participating in the plan will benefit because they are members of a covered class of corporate employees.
- Provide notice of the plan to the participants.
- Provide for benefits to be (1) related to compensation and services performed and (2) received upon absence from work due to disability. This provision of the plan helps to establish for the IRS that the benefits are reasonable compensation for services performed.

Dangers of an Informal Plan. The employment conditions of the shareholder-employees of a closely held corporation are often established informally based on a mere understanding among the owners. In the case of the salary continuation plan the owners usually expect that a reasonable level of salary will be continued by the business during a period of disability. Unfortunately the IRS may take the position that a mere understanding or expectation is not a salary continuation plan. Courts will decide in favor of the IRS in these cases if the plan (1) is established after a disability occurs, (2) is administered inconsistently over time, (3) is not communicated to participants in advance, or (4) provides benefits that bear no relationship to services performed by the participants.

If the IRS is successful in its claim that no plan exists, the corporation will lose its deduction for benefit payments made to shareholders. These payments will be treated as nondeductible dividends and will be received as ordinary taxable income by the shareholder with no Sec. 22 credit available. Furthermore, benefit payments to regular employees might not be deductible as a reasonable business expense if no plan has been established. To avoid these results it is recommended that the owners of a closely held corporation follow the relatively easy steps of establishing the plan in advance.

Funding Considerations. A salary continuation plan can either be funded or unfunded. Generally speaking, it would be impractical for the small closely held corporation to self-fund a salary continuation plan in advance. A huge fund would have to be established immediately, since the occurrence of disability is unpredictable and a long-term disability could create an enormous liability to the corporation. The problems of providing salary continuation payments to a disabled shareholder out of current income were discussed earlier in the chapter. Since most closely held corporations cannot continue salary payments to a disabled owner indefinitely without causing a ruinous drain on the corporate finances, most formal salary continuation plans are funded with long-term disability insurance.

Advantages of Insurance Funding. The advantages of funding the salary continuation plan with disability income insurance include the following:

- The burden of determining when a disability has occurred and when payments should begin is transferred to the insurance company.
- The shareholders have assurances that their salary will be continued during a period of disability even if the business fails.
- The cost of the plan is predictable to the corporation. Corporate funds not required to continue the disabled shareholder's salary payments can be used to hire and train replacement personnel.

Corporate or Individual Ownership of Disability Insurance. The primary purpose of salary continuation plans is to provide for the maintenance of the shareholder's standard of living during a period of disability. It should not matter for this purpose whether the insurance protection covering this risk is provided for by the employing corporation or by individually owned insurance. However, the differences in the tax consequences of each arrangement should be considered. If the corporation provides the insurance and pays the premium, these premiums will be deductible by the corporation and the insurance proceeds will be received tax free by the corporation. The benefit payments funded by this insurance, however, will be taxable income (subject to the Sec. 22 credit) to the disabled participant. If the owner purchases individual disability income insurance, the premiums will be paid in after-tax dollars, but the benefit payments received upon a disabling event will be tax free.

Assuming the reasonable-compensation tests can be met, the corporation could provide the owner-employee with a bonus sufficient to provide the individual insurance premiums. The bonus would be deductible as an ordinary salary expense to the corporation and taxable as income to the employee, while the benefits would be received tax free by the employee. This may not be advantageous if the employee would have to forgo personal exemptions and deductions due to the tax-free nature of the proceeds. You should recall that the normal salary continuation plan provides taxable benefit payments to the employee. The relative tax brackets of the participating owners and the corporation should be considered before determining which method is appropriate.

EXAMPLE

Dr. Kilgare, aged 40, operates his practice as a professional corporation. He must choose between a corporate salary continuation plan and personally owned disability insurance. His 2004 salary from the corporation is $120,000, and the corporation retains $5,000 that may be used to (1) provide a bonus to Dr. Kilgare to cover his premium costs or (2) pay deductible premiums to an insured salary continuation plan with benefits paid directly to the doctor by the insurer. His income qualifies him for $5,150 a month in individual coverage, but the insurer will provide $6,350 monthly coverage if the corporation adopts a salary continuation plan. This higher participation limit reflects the fact that salary continuation payments provided by the corporation would be reduced by federal income tax when received by Dr. Kilgare. He and his wife have two young children. His personal exemptions total $7,800 per year, and he has $30,000 in itemized deductions (home mortgage, local property and state income taxes, and so on). He and his wife have no other income.

The illustrations for the "bonus" individual policy and corporate salary continuation plan are as follows:

Individual Insurance	Corporate Plan
Benefit: $5,150/month	Benefit: $6,350/month
Payment of premium: $2,100/annually; corporation must provide $2,917 bonus for the doctor to pay this premium (assuming a 28 percent individual tax rate)	Payment of premium: $2,600/annually
Bonus to Dr. Kilgare: $2,917 is necessary to pay premium (assuming 28 percent individual rates)	Tax saving on deductible corporate premium: $390 (assuming 15 percent corporate rate)
Corporate tax saving on bonus: $437.55 (assuming 15 percent corporate rate)	
Total corporate taxes: $312.45	"Total corporate $360"
Additional tax to Dr. Kilgare: $816.76	

After Disability

Annual disability payments	$61,800	Annual salary continuation payments	$76,200
		Personal exemptions and itemized deductions	37,800
		Taxable income	$38,400
Income tax	0	Federal income tax	3,758
Net income	$61,800	Net income	$72,442

As you can see, the tax-free receipt of individually purchased insurance proceeds is not always preferable to taxable corporate salary continuation benefits. This is particularly true if the insured has substantial deductions to take against taxable income.

Summary of the Tax Consequences of Corporate Salary Continuation Plans

The taxation of salary continuation plans depends on the type of plan and funding arrangement. The tax treatment of the various plans we have discussed above is summarized below.

Table 12-5 Tax Treatment of Corporate Salary Continuation Plans

INSURED	Formal Plan: Corporation Pays Premium and Participant Is Owner and Beneficiary of Policy	Formal Plan: Corporation Purchases Insurance and Is Beneficiary of Policy	Informal Plan: Corporation Gives Premium as Bonus to Employee Who Buys Individual Policy
Premium Payment or Contribution to Self-fund	• deductible by corporation if reasonable • not taxable income to employee	• nondeductible by corporation • not taxable income to employee	• bonuses deductible if reasonable compensation • premium payment not deductible by employee
Receipt of Insurance Proceeds	• taxable income to employee subject to Sec. 22 credit	• not taxable income to corporation or employee	• no effect to corporation • not taxable to employee- beneficiary (Sec. 22 credit unavailable)

Payment of Benefits by Corporation	N/A	• deductible by corporation if reasonable compensation • taxable income to employee subject to Sec. 22 credit	N/A
UNINSURED	Advance Funded		Unfunded
Premium Payment or Contribution to Self-fund	• nondeductible by corporation • not taxable income to employee		N/A
Receipt of Insurance Proceeds	N/A	N/A	N/A
Payment of Benefits by Corporation	• deductible by corporation if reasonable compensation • taxable income to employee (Sec. 22 credit available if valid plan)		• deductible by corporation if reasonable compensation • taxable income to employee (Sec. 22 credit available if valid plan)

SALARY CONTINUATION PLANS FOR UNINCORPORATED BUSINESSES AND S CORPORATIONS

Sole proprietors, partners, and more-than-2-percent shareholders of S corporations are not considered employees for the purposes of fringe benefits, including salary continuation plans. Contributions made by these business entities to fund salary continuation benefits for the owners will not be deductible by the business. Therefore premiums paid by the partnership will not reduce partnership taxable income. Partners will be taxed on their distributive share of partnership income, including funds expended for these premium payments. Partnership agreements should specifically allocate the premium costs to the individual partners to avoid any inadvertent premium subsidy among the partners.

Insurance proceeds on policies used to fund the plan benefits will be received tax free by the partnership. When the payments are made to a disabled partner, they are treated as guaranteed payment amounts and pass through as nontaxable income to the disabled partner.

Since the tax laws provide that a greater-than-2-percent shareholder of an S corporation is treated as a partner for fringe benefit purposes, salary continuation plans of S corporations will have results similar to those of partnerships.

Sole proprietors do not operate their businesses as a separate entity for federal income tax purposes. Premiums paid by a sole proprietor for disability income protection insurance are personal expenditures. The premiums will be nondeductible, but the policy proceeds will be received income tax free when the proprietor becomes disabled. Individual disability insurance planning will be discussed later.

Nonowner-employees of sole proprietorships, partnerships, and S corporations will be treated as employees for the purposes of salary continuation plans. Plans established by these entities will be treated similarly to corporations for tax purposes with respect to the coverage of employees.

INDIVIDUALLY OWNED DISABILITY INCOME PROTECTION INSURANCE

Both the magnitude of the disability risk and its impact on closely held business owners and professionals were well documented earlier in the chapter. The loss of income a disabled owner or professional suffers might be replaced by a business salary continuation plan, as discussed previously. If no salary continuation plan is in effect, or if the benefits from a salary continuation plan would be insufficient to protect the business owner or professional, personal disability income protection should be purchased.

Factors to Consider

Once it is determined that the business owner or professional needs individual disability income insurance, there are several decisions to be made. For example, the level of monthly protection to be purchased must be determined. Will the amount of insurance needed be available under insurer underwriting rules? Should a group policy offered by a professional's association or an individual policy be selected? Which policy provisions are most appropriate for the client, and should any additional optional riders be added to the policy?

The financial services professional should carefully explain the choices to the client since the selection of an inappropriate insurance plan could have disastrous results. For example, an inappropriate definition of disability could result in the client's failing to qualify for benefits when the client is unable to work at his or her former business or profession. The wrong policy choice could result in the client's coverage being canceled in the future after he or she has become uninsurable. Finally, the failure to consider the impact of inflation could cause the benefits available to the client to be inadequate to maintain his or her customary standard of living in the future.

Amount of Coverage Needed

A good starting point for determining the appropriate monthly benefit levels begins with a determination of the client's anticipated monthly expenses following disability. The income available to the client after disability should be subtracted from these expenses to determine the shortfall that must be filled. The insured should secure the coverage necessary to fill this gap.

Other Available Funds

Although the business owner or professional client often receives substantial income from the business or professional practice, not all this income may have to be replaced with individual disability benefits. The financial services professional should assist the client in determining the other sources of funds that will be available after disability. Overestimation of these other income sources may cause a shortfall between the client's anticipated needs and available funds. Underestimation of the other sources of funds will result in the expense of unnecessary insurance premiums. The other sources of funds available to a disabled client include

- unearned income from the client's investments
- earnings of the client's spouse
- salary continuation payments from the business
- Social Security disability benefits (since eligibility for these benefits is generally more restrictive than private insurance, such benefits should be relied upon only after careful consideration)
- disability benefits from private retirement plans
- funds received for the client's business interest if the disability results in a buyout

- funds normally expended for life and disability insurance premiums if waiver of premium is in effect
- reductions in living expenses since the disabled individual no longer has work-related expenses
- reductions in federal income taxes due to reduced earned income and the tax-free nature of private disability benefits

How Much Coverage Is Available. Insurers will underwrite disability income risks carefully. These policies are subject to participation limits providing that only a specified percentage (40 to 70 percent) of earnings will be insured. These participation limits reflect the fact that an insured does not need 100 percent of prior earnings following a disability, since policy benefits are received tax free and the disabled insured will no longer be incurring work-related expenses. Insurers feel that coverage above these participation limits will provide the insured with less incentive to undergo rehabilitation and return to work.

There is also an overall monthly benefit limit that cannot be exceeded even if the insured qualifies for more under the percentage-participation limits. This maximum limit has been increasing over time because of demand from the high-income market for disability products. Even high monthly benefit limits may restrict the amount of coverage available to some highly compensated business owners or professionals, particularly those affected by lower benefit limits available in their occupational class.

These participation and maximum-benefit limits are often applied by insurers to the total coverage of the individual applicant. When underwriting individual policies, the insurance company will check the other coverage already in force on the applicant and make appropriate reductions in the participation limits available to the applicant. For this reason the client should consider the appropriateness of other coverages in force. For example, if disability income insurance is used to fund the buy-sell agreement or salary continuation plan, this coverage might reduce the monthly benefit that the client is eligible for individually. As discussed earlier, the practices of individual insurers differ regarding the application of participation limits on the aggregate coverage on an insured. The financial services professional should coordinate the business disability insurance with personal coverage so that participation limits will not prevent the client from securing adequate individual coverage.

Options Available to the Disability Client

The types of policies and policy options available to the business owner and professional seeking personal disability income coverage are voluminous. This discussion is not intended to be exhaustive of all possibilities but will emphasize a few key issues.

Definition of Disability. The business owner or professional typically performs a specialized service for most of his or her income. The disability policy should protect this individual in the event that a disability renders him or her unable to perform the usual specialty. The insured should purchase a policy with an own-occupation definition of disability. Although an own-occupation policy is the most expensive form of coverage, it should be selected if the client would find it offensive to be forced to work in another occupation.

In some cases, insurance companies will issue specialty letters with the contract guaranteeing benefits if the insured is unable to perform a particular specialty. This is critical to the business owner or professional employed in a particularly unique specialty. Insurers have recently been less likely to issue specialty letters in some occupational classes, such as physicians, where specialty letters were quite common in the past. Please be aware that own occupation without a specialty letter, or some lesser definition, may be all that is available for certain risks.

To reduce the cost of the disability coverage, it is common to provide an own-occupation definition of disability for a period of time (2 to 3 years). Following this period the policy will shift to a less favorable definition, such as "any occupation for which the insured is reasonably suited." This contract provides the client with time to adjust to a new suitable occupation following a disability. Some contracts will continue to provide reduced benefits if the new occupation provides less income to the insured than does his or her original specialty.

Some insurers use a slightly different disability definition that is based on a loss of earned income. For example, a total disability might be deemed to occur when there is a reduction in earned income of 75 percent due to an illness or injury. Partial disability benefits may be payable for smaller reductions to earned income under this type of policy.

Residual Disability. Does an own-occupation policy fully protect the business or professional client against disability income loss? Unfortunately the answer is probably not. Unless residual disability benefits are included, the own-occupation policy will terminate benefit payments immediately if the insured returns to work in his or her former occupation, even if the insured returns to work on a part-time basis or at a reduced salary. Since the typical business or professional person will return to work only in his or her former occupation after recovery, the own-occupation policy will penalize the insured who returns to work without immediately attaining prior income levels.

residual disability benefit

Most disability income policies offer a *residual disability benefit* option to provide an incentive for the insured to return to work. This option, also referred to as an *income replacement or recovery benefit,* provides for reduced benefits when the disabled insured suffers a partial loss of earned income.

The coverage provided by these options is based on the drop in net income while the insured is disabled. Insurers vary on benefit provisions, but most residual benefit policies will provide benefits only when the disability reduces the insured's income below 80 percent of the base-period income level. A typical policy will provide a residual disability benefit based on the following formula:

$$\text{Benefit amount} = \frac{\text{loss in net income}}{\text{base} - \text{period net income}} = \text{maximum full disability amount}$$

Again, insurers vary as to when an insured becomes eligible for the residual benefits. The most liberal policies provide this benefit even if the insured has never become totally disabled but simply has a period of reduced income due to sickness or injury. On the other hand, most policies require the insured to be *totally* disabled for at least the policy elimination period before residual benefits are available.

The residual benefits are an important consideration to the business or professional client. The financial services professional should determine the client's needs before securing coverage. In many cases the client will express a desire to return to his or her former occupation after recovery from a disability, even if the return is on a limited basis. The client is best protected by an occupation policy containing residual benefits under these circumstances.

Residual Disability Benefit

- Provides a partial benefit if the insured can work only on a part-time or reduced-salary basis
- Usually pays a benefit only if the insured's income is less than 80 percent of what it was during a specified base period
- Benefits usually payable only after a period of total disability

Continuance Provisions. Policy continuance provisions specify the (1) length of the policy term, (2) ability of the insured to renew, and (3) ability of the insurer to cancel coverage or change premium rates. The type of continuance provision selected by the business or professional client will depend on the circumstance of the individual case.

noncancelable

In most cases the business or professional client will want coverage guaranteed for the normal working years. The best available contract for this purpose is one that is *noncancelable*, which provides that the insurer cannot cancel the contract prior to age 65 and guarantees the premium rate for the entire period. Recognizing the fact that business owners or professionals often work beyond the normal retirement age, most high-quality noncancelable policies allow the insured to renew coverage annually after age 65. The insured will generally be permitted to renew the policy for ages beyond 65 provided that he or she is employed full time. Some insurers are now providing coverage renewable annually for lifetime with premiums and claims procedures consistent with attained ages at renewal. Due to recent changes in the marketplace, noncancelable policies may not be available for all occupational classes.

Other types of continuance provisions provide fewer guarantees than the noncancelable contract. Policies with these provisions cost less than noncancelable contracts but might leave the insured without coverage in the future. Policies that are *cancelable, renewable at the insurer's option, or conditionally renewable* do not guarantee that the insurer will maintain coverage for the insured's working lifetime. A policy that is *guaranteed renewable* does guarantee renewal until age 65 at the discretion of the insured. Unlike the noncancelable contract, however, the premium rates are not guaranteed and will increase if the insurer raises premium rates for the insured's disability class. This policy provides guaranteed coverage at generally lower current premium rates than noncancelable contracts.

However, caution should be employed since the insured may be subject to drastic rate increases in the future.

Inflation Protection. Since a long-term disability contract is usually recommended for the business or professional client, the effect of inflation must be considered. Since the insurer participation limits restrict the amount of monthly coverage that can be purchased, these benefits will soon be inadequate if inflation forces up income levels and living costs. To mitigate this problem, the insured might initially purchase the maximum amount of coverage available within the participation limits. Overinsuring the disability client is not recommended. Even if the excess coverage is overlooked in the underwriting process, overinsured claimants sometimes have problems receiving benefits since such claims are viewed with suspicion.

If it is anticipated that inflation will create a need for increased benefit payments in the future, there are a few planning steps that can be taken to handle this problem. The financial services professional and the client can regularly update the coverage by purchasing new protection when the insured qualifies for additional coverage under the participation limits. This can be done systematically when the business disability insurance is updated.

Many disability policies provide some form of "guaranteed-insurability" option for an additional premium. Insurers vary in the operation of their guaranteed insurability options. These options basically provide the insured with the option to purchase additional coverage at specified dates in the future. Some provide a great deal of flexibility and allow limited increases at any time prior to a specified age (for example, 60). Insurers limit both (1) the allowable increase at each option date and (2) overall increase during the policy term. The benefit of this provision is that an insured whose income increases can qualify for additional coverage without providing evidence of insurability.

The alternatives mentioned above protect the insured for inflation prior to the occurrence of a disabling event. What happens after the disabling event? Unfortunately plans normally provide a fixed monthly benefit for the policy term, presumably age 65. If the insured is disabled at a young age, the fixed monthly benefit will quickly become inadequate during a period of significant inflation. Insurers now offer a cost-of-living rider to disability income contracts for an additional premium. This provision increases the benefits annually based on some index, such as the consumer price index, after the insured has begun receiving benefits. Insurers again provide annual and overall limits on the amount of cost-of-living increases permitted. For example, the insurer might limit the annual benefit increase to 7 percent and the overall increases during the policy term to a multiple (2 to 3) of the initial monthly benefit. This rider is recommended particularly for younger clients whose benefit is potentially long-term.

Plans of Professional Associations. Professionals will often receive direct-mail solicitation from providers of group disability income policies sponsored by their professional association. Although these plans usually offer favorable initial premiums and ease of purchase when compared to individual policies, they should be examined carefully since benefits purchased under these plans will reduce the coverage available to the client on an individual basis due to each insurer's participation limits. These plans can be a low-cost alternative for the professional seeking disability coverage but come up short in guarantees when compared to the best noncancelable individual policies.

The provisions of the group professional association plan that should be examined carefully by the financial services professional advising the disability client are

- *definition of disability.* Professional association plans typically provide an own-occupation definition for a period of years followed by any occupation for which the insured is reasonably suited by training, experience, and the like.
- *continuance provisions.* Most group association plans allow the insurer to discontinue coverage if the professional leaves the association or ceases to work full time, or if the association terminates the plan. Since these associations occasionally change carriers for their plans, an examination of the specific provision is important. Insurers will often offer conversion privileges to individuals when coverage is terminated. Unfortunately the rates to convert to individual policies are usually high. Furthermore, if the association has replaced the plan with a new carrier, this new carrier may or may not provide an open-enrollment period in which association members insured under the prior plan can replace their coverage without providing evidence of insurability. Finally, the premiums under these plans are typically not guaranteed, and rate increases are regularly negotiated between the sponsoring association and the provider.
- *benefit limits.* Participation limits are similar to individual policies, but the maximum benefit amount available under these plans is typically lower. This may not be a problem if the insured is

otherwise happy with the group plan since individual coverage can be purchased to fill the gap.

- *elimination period and successive disabilities.* Professional association plans do not typically have provisions for successive disability and will provide benefits only if the insured is disabled continuously throughout the elimination period. This provision discourages an insured from attempting to return to work during a period of recovery, and individual policies are usually more liberal in this regard.

A few insurers are now providing professional association plans with high-quality contracts similar to individual noncancelable coverage with the benefits of group premium rates and underwriting. Financial services professionals should examine the plan being considered by the client to prevent the purchase of an inappropriate policy. Some professional association plans will provide the professional client with a quality low-cost alternative to individual contracts. Other plans provide the client with an undesirable exposure to risk, and these plans should be avoided even at the lower cost.

BUSINESS-OVERHEAD-EXPENSE DISABILITY INSURANCE

A risk often overlooked by business or professional clients is the disability-related office-overhead-expense-continuation problem. A disabled business owner or professional will probably hope to return to normal working activities if the disability is temporary. Unless many office expenses continue to be paid during a period of disability, the recovered business owner or professional may not have a business or practice to return to.

business-overhead-expense disability insurance

This risk is particularly important for the professional operating a solo practice. The professional practitioner can lose clients, goodwill, valuable employees, and a favorable location if office expenses are not continued while the professional is disabled. The professional's career could be destroyed if he or she is disabled for even a short period of time. *Business-overhead-expense disability insurance* is available at a relatively low cost to pay these expenses during a disability.

Policy Provisions

The policy provisions of the overhead expense policy are similar to those of the disability income policy. The elimination period under these policies may range from 30 to 90 days, and many policies provide for retroactive benefits to the date of disability once the elimination period has been satisfied. The contracts are available on a noncancelable basis so that the insured who is willing to pay for this coverage will have guaranteed protection and premium rates for the policy term.

Policy Benefits

Business-overhead insurance is designed to provide for short-term disabilities with coverage limited to a period of 12, 18, or 24 months. Since the insured is covered for the expenses of his or her business or practice, an own-occupation definition of disability is used. The benefits are limited to a maximum monthly amount generally underwritten on the basis of the insured's income. Overhead-expense coverage is available even if the insured has reached the participation limits of his or her disability income contract. When the insured is disabled, *either totally or partially*, the policy reimburses the beneficiary for covered office expenses actually incurred. Many overhead-expense policies have an extended benefit feature providing that any unused benefit amounts can be carried over and paid by the insurer even after the disabled individual's benefit period had elapsed.

EXAMPLE

Roger Buck operates a thriving solo law practice and employs a part-time law clerk and a legal secretary. Roger carries $8,000/month of disability income protection insurance and $4,000/month of business-overhead coverage with a 12-month benefit period and an extended benefit provision. Roger becomes disabled and incurs $3,000 per month in covered continuing office expenses for the first year of disability. If Roger remains disabled after 12 months, the $12,000 of unused overhead expense benefits will be available until either (1) the benefits are used up or (2) Roger recovers.

Covered Expenses

The expenses covered under overhead-expense policies are those normally paid by the insured in the ordinary course of business. Among the expenses typically covered by overhead-expense insurance policies are mortgage or rent payments on business property, property taxes, utilities, cleaning and maintenance services, interest costs incurred to purchase equipment and furniture, insurance premiums including malpractice, professional dues, legal and accounting costs, and employee salary and fringe benefit payments.

Excluded Expenses

Excluded from coverage are costs associated with new purchases, salary payments to the insured or his or her replacement, and expenses not causing cash disbursements by the insured, such as depreciation or premium payments waived during the disability. Business or professional clients considering overhead-expense insurance should examine normal monthly expenses to determine whether any unusual payments are regularly made. The financial services professional should contact the insurer to establish whether these expenses are covered.

Business-Overhead-Expense Insurance

- The policy covers certain of the business's ongoing expenses while the insured owner is disabled.
- The elimination period is 30-90 days, but benefits may be retroactive.
- Benefit periods are 12-24 months.
- Coverage is available in addition to the insured owner's disability income coverage.
- The insured owner's salary, noncash expenses, new purchases, and perhaps unusual expenses are excluded expenses.
- Premiums are deductible and benefits are taxable as income.

Taxation

The taxation of the business overhead-expense disability plan differs from a disability income policy. The premiums for overhead-expense insurance are deductible by the insured as a business expense similar to property and liability coverages. Unlike individually owned disability income insurance benefits, the benefits from overhead-expense insurance are unfortunately taxable income to the insured. This should not be a major problem, however, since the benefit payments are used to pay regular business expenses that are generally deductible when paid.

CHAPTER REVIEW

Key Terms and Concepts

elimination period
trigger date
presumptive-disability provision
salary continuation plan
residual disability benefit
noncancelable
business-overhead- expense disability insurance

Review Questions

The answers to the review questions are in the supplement. The self-test questions and the answers to them are also in the supplement and on The American College Online.

1. Discuss which is more likely to occur: the premature death or the disability of a closely held business owner. [1]

2. Describe the problems a business owner's long-term disability creates for the healthy active business owners. [1]

3. A disability buy-sell agreement usually provides for the expiration of some specific period of time following the onset of a disability before a buy-sell becomes mandatory. What are some of the criteria that should be taken into account when determining this time period? [2]

4. Miles, Ned, and Ozzie are interested in entering into a disability buy-sell agreement for their respective interests in the MNO Corporation. One deterrent has been that they do not want to have to determine for themselves when one of them has met the definition of a disability. What alternatives can you suggest for removing the burden of making that decision from Miles, Ned, and Ozzie? [2]

5. Identify and distinguish between the definitions of disability that might be used to trigger a buy-sell agreement. [2]

6. One problem with a disability buy-sell agreement is the possibility that a disabled owner might recover during or after the elimination period. Discuss how an agreement might be designed to address
   a. successive disabilities
   b. post-buyout recovery [2]

7. In the event of a disability, what are the tax advantages of having an installment form of buyout? [2]

8. Describe the differences between disability income and buyout insurance, and discuss how these policies may be adapted to the disability buy-sell agreement. [2]

9. Explain how the financial underwriting of the typical disability buyout policy affects the purchase price selected for the buy-sell agreement. [2]

10. Explain how the life insurance funding for a buy-sell agreement for an owner's death may be coordinated with the disability buy-sell agreement. [2]

11. The Efflux Corporation has decided to establish a salary continuation plan funded with disability income insurance. The Efflux Corporation will pay all the premiums for the coverage, but it has not yet decided whether to have the insurance company make the payments directly to the employees or to the corporation. [3]
    a. If payments of disability benefits are to be made directly to the employees as policyowners, how are the premium payments treated for income tax purposes by (i) the Efflux Corporation and (ii) the covered employees?
    b. If payments of disability benefits are to be paid to the Efflux Corporation as policyowner, what will be the income tax treatment of premium payments with regard to (i) the Efflux Corporation and (ii) the covered employees?

12. The IRC provides a tax credit for payments received by a totally disabled individual. Discuss whether this credit is significant for a closely held business owner or professional receiving salary continuation payments. [3]

13. Can a salary continuation plan cover only stockholder-employees? Explain. [3]

14. What reasons exist for using disability income insurance to fund a salary continuation plan? [3]

15. Hal, an employee of an organization that has no salary continuation plan, is considering the purchase of personally owned disability income insurance. Describe the federal income tax treatment of
    a. any premium payments made by Hal
    b. any disability income benefits received from such insurance [3]

16. When either a proprietorship or a partnership has a salary continuation plan, explain the tax treatment of insurance premiums and benefit payments to
    a. the employees
    b. the proprietor or partner [3]

17. A business owner or professional often has need for individual disability income protection. What factors should be considered with respect to the following policy options:
    a. definition of disability
    b. policy continuance provisions
    c. cost-of-living riders [4]

18. Professional associations often sponsor group disability income plans. In what respect are these plans less favorable than individual disability income policies? [4]

19. Describe the purposes that business-overhead-expense insurance serves. [5]

20. What expenses are typically excluded from coverage under business-overhead insurance policies? [5]

MANAGING RISK IN THE CLOSELY HELD BUSINESS 13

Learning Objectives

An understanding of the material in this chapter should enable the student to

1. Discuss the process of risk analysis for a closely held business.
2. Describe the risk-management techniques that might be employed, and identify the types of risks that would be appropriate for insurance.
3. Describe how the workers' compensation program changed traditional employers' liability for personnel exposures, and identify the coverages provided by Parts I and II of the workers' compensation policy.
4. Identify the factors in determining the key employees of a business, and explain how the value of a key employee can be determined.
5. Explain how life insurance and disability income insurance can be used to protect the business from the loss of a key employee.

The proper planning for the risks facing the owners of a closely held business is undeniably essential if the business is to meet the owners' objectives. A successful business should provide a steady stream of income to the owners and possess adequate appreciation potential. The effective use of the tax and continuation planning techniques discussed earlier will help the owners reach these objectives.

The continuing financial stability of the business typically depends not only on the continued viability of its current owners but also on the existence of business property and the availability of key nonowner-employees. The loss of these physical and human assets by the business will result in a decrease in business income and/or increase in required business expenditures. Other potentially devastating business losses include liability claims against the business.

Large public corporations generally recognize the importance of handling risk and employ full-time risk managers to analyze business risk and implement a risk-management plan. Because small closely held businesses cannot afford to employ a full-time risk manager, this critical function is often left to the owners. These individuals, by necessity, focus their attention on the everyday operation of the business, and the risk-management function is therefore either ignored or performed inadequately. In some cases financial services professionals may be relied on by the closely held business to perform the risk-management function. Professionals who are not specialists in this area should inform the client of the critical nature of risk planning and recommend that appropriate professional help be secured.

ANALYZING RISK IN THE CLOSELY HELD BUSINESS

Risk analysis involves the identification and evaluation of risks faced by the business. The first step in this process is to identify the risks that could threaten the specific closely held business. Unless the risks are identified, appropriate planning cannot be accomplished and a potentially devastating loss could be suffered. The second step in risk analysis is the measurement of the potential financial impact of losses on the business and its owners.

Risk Identification

pure risk

Risk can be defined as uncertainty about financial loss from an exposure. A loss in this context is defined as the decrease in value of the business and/or its property. We will be concerned solely with *pure risk* as opposed to speculative risk.

A speculative risk is one that provides a chance for either gain or loss. An example of a speculative risk is the chance that a business will succeed or fail in the competitive marketplace.

A pure risk is characterized by the chance of a loss only. The chance that a business will lose income due to the disability of a key employee is an example of a pure risk. Risk and insurance management are typically associated only with pure risks.

The methods for identifying the pure risks facing a closely held business range from informal to highly sophisticated. Generally speaking, the more sophisticated the technique used to identify risks, the lower the possibility of inadvertently ignoring a risk exposure. Sophisticated techniques, of course, can become quite expensive in terms of both dollar cost and time consumption. Since many closely held businesses face similar risks, an experienced professional in this area should be able to identify the risks faced by a particular closely held business through the use of some basic inexpensive techniques. Among the methods commonly used to identify the risks faced by a business are the following:

- the completion of a questionnaire by the client providing information on business property and operations
- examination of the financial statements of the business. The balance sheet will identify the business assets carried on the books and assist the risk manager in the formulation of additional inquiries concerning business property. The income statement can be useful to identify the various sources of business income that will assist the planner in evaluating the financial impact of potential losses.
- the client's preparation of a business flow chart summarizing business operations. An understanding of the stages and interrelationships in the business operation will help identify most of the risk exposures.
- the personal inspection of the premises by the planner. The actual on-site inspection by the planner is a useful technique to determine risks that were not identified by the other techniques.
- an examination of any currently employed risk-transfer devices. An example of a risk-transfer device is, of course, the purchase of insurance. The risks that are already adequately managed will come to light in an examination of existing policies. For example, a closely held business may currently be holding insurance on the life of a key employee. If the insurance coverage is adequate, the key employee death risk is no longer a serious exposure.

Evaluation of Risk

The risk faced by a particular closely held business identified in the initial step of the risk-analysis process may or may not require eventual planning. The second stage of risk analysis is the determination of the potential impact of the possible losses identified in the previous step. If the chance of loss is remote and its magnitude small, a closely held business can probably ignore a risk. If the chance of loss is high but its magnitude small, the business is likely to provide for losses associated with this risk to be funded out of business cash flow. The most significant planning is required for a risk with a remote chance of loss with a potentially severe magnitude. This type of risk should not be retained by the business if other alternatives are available.

Sophisticated statistical techniques may be employed to determine the magnitude of the risks facing a business. Unfortunately the use of these techniques requires a substantial number of observations before the results are meaningful. As discussed above, most risk-transfer planning by a closely held business is associated with the low-probability and high-severity risks. Large corporations or insurance rating organizations typically have enough observations to develop significant estimates of probable loss for a particular business risk. This data is relatively useless for the small closely held business since the statistical principles of large numbers are inapplicable. That is, the observations of low-frequency losses in an individual small closely held business are infrequent, and estimated loss predictions are unreliable in these circumstances. This situation is analogous to the risks of death or disability of a closely held business owner discussed in previous chapters. Since probability statistics for these risks are inapplicable to a group with few exposures, such risks must be transferred through insurance risk-pooling principles.

To determine the magnitude of a potential risk, the most appropriate measures for the closely held business are maximum possible loss and maximum probable loss. The maximum possible loss represents the worst case scenario in which the loss is total. For example, the maximum possible loss associated with the fire risk faced by the owner of a building is its full replacement cost. This measure of a risk assumes that nothing of value will remain following a loss.

maximum probable loss

The *maximum probable loss* is the maximum loss that is most likely to happen if a loss occurs. For example, suppose a business relies on the sales of three key employees for its success. Assuming the salespersons do not travel together, the maximum probable loss associated with the key-employee death risk is the value of one salesperson, since it is unlikely that more than one will die at any point in time. The maximum possible loss in this case, of course, is the value of all three salespersons. The determination of maximum probable loss in a closely held business will depend on the subjective determination of the likelihood of various events. Since the law of large numbers also limits the usefulness of statistical probabilities with respect to the severity of a loss, maximum possible loss might be the most appropriate measure of loss for a typical closely held business.

Risk Evaluation

- Maximum possible loss: the largest amount that could be lost under a worst-case scenario if a peril occurs
- Maximum probable loss: the largest amount that is likely to be lost if a peril occurs

RISK-MANAGEMENT TECHNIQUES

To implement a plan for managing the risks in a closely held business, a decision must be made about the methods for handling the identified risks. Techniques for handling risks in a business can be categorized as risk avoidance, loss control, risk transfer, or risk retention. This selection process is critical since a loss suffered due to an inadequately managed risk might threaten the financial survival of the business.

Risk Avoidance

risk avoidance

The objective of *risk avoidance* is the elimination of a risk from the business. The business avoids the risk by either refusing to assume it initially or by abandoning a risk to which the firm is currently exposed. For example, a firm could discontinue production of a hazardous product to avoid the product-liability risk associated with that product.

Risk avoidance is accomplished through elimination, substitution, separation, and sensible planning. Elimination involves removing the source of risk from the firm's operations. For example, a business can avoid the automobile property damage risk by operating without a fleet of vehicles. Or, as mentioned in the example above, the firm could avoid production of a hazardous product.

Careful thought should be given to the elimination procedure since the technique might not be effective in avoiding the risk. For example, a business that leases property to avoid the property-damage risk associated with ownership may, in fact, be liable for property damage through the terms of the lease.

Substitution is the replacement of one thing for another. For example, a volatile chemical used in the production process may be replaced by a less hazardous substance that is just as effective in production.

Separation refers to the division of activities so that potentially hazardous combinations do not come into contact. For example, certain chemicals will cause explosion or fire if they come into contact. These chemicals could be stored at separate locations to avoid such a risk. A business could decide to split off a potentially hazardous business into a separate corporation, protecting the parent firm through the limited-liability concept.

Some risks can be avoided through careful planning. For example, a firm should attempt to have more than one supplier for key raw materials. Thus the loss of one supplier might not result in an income loss by the business. Risk avoidance is the most aggressive and effective method for handling risk if the sole objective is to eliminate risk at all costs. Risk avoidance requires careful thought since the risk-management process should generally not deter the firm from entering into or continuing a profitable endeavor merely to avoid risk.

Loss Control

Loss-control techniques are activities designed to reduce the possibility of loss or to minimize the magnitude of losses that actually occur. The techniques to meet these objectives are loss prevention and loss reduction.

Loss Prevention

loss prevention

Loss-prevention programs attempt to reduce the chance of loss for any risk that cannot be avoided. It is often impossible or impractical to avoid all the risks facing the closely held business. *Loss prevention* is designed to reduce the frequency of losses associated with these unavoidable risks. The inclusion of safety devices in the design of the firm's products is an example of loss prevention with respect to the product-liability risk.

Loss prevention is an important consideration in all aspects of business operations. Loss-prevention activities are generally more effective if instituted in the planning phase for the activity creating the risk exposure. For example, the prevention of fire loss to a building is more effective if the building is originally constructed to be fire resistant. The building materials, wiring, and ventilation design can be selected to reduce the chance of fire loss. The placement of safety devices on products will cost less if included in the original design.

An experienced risk manager is particularly helpful in the loss-prevention process. The potential impact of a loss and the costs associated with reducing its frequency must also be considered before instituting loss-prevention activities. For example, a retail store might find that employing additional store detectives will not be cost-effective for reducing shoplifting losses. Because loss prevention is generally more effective if the owners and employees of a business are highly conscious of its benefits, business owners should attempt to make the employees of a business aware of the importance of loss prevention.

Loss Reduction

loss reduction

The objective of *loss reduction* is to control the severity of losses that occur. That is, these techniques minimize the financial impact of a loss on the business. The planning techniques for loss reduction could include minimizing the loss as it occurs and salvaging damaged property after a loss. Examples of loss-reduction activities for fire losses include the construction of a building with fire walls, sprinkler systems, and fire extinguisher locations, and the location of the business premises adjacent to a firehouse or fire hydrant. Note that the loss-reduction activities do not involve the avoidance or prevention of losses. As these examples demonstrate, the activities are all designed to reduce the impact of a fire loss once the fire has started. Loss-reduction activities are extremely important since many potentially devastating losses can be minimized at manageable levels if proper planning is done.

Retention of Risk

Risks that cannot be avoided by business owners must be financed in some manner. Retention is the self-assumption of responsibility for financing losses. Loss-financing methods do not affect the frequency or severity of a loss but merely indicate how the firm will pay for a loss. The possibilities for risk retention in a closely held business are limited. The lack of statistical observations prevents the measurement of many risks faced by a closely held business. Generally speaking, high-severity losses should not be retained by closely held businesses. That is, any loss that would seriously interrupt the flow of earnings and interfere with the business's long-range planning should be transferred. Risks that might be appropriate for retention in a closely held business include

- high-frequency/low-severity losses
- losses that can be absorbed as a normal operating expense

- losses whose probability is so remote that no reasonable person would expend premium dollars to insure the risk (for example, flood insurance is not purchased if the insured property is not in a flood plain)
- uninsurable losses
- the deductible amount of insured losses

The owners of a closely held business are likely to believe that their business is too small to practice risk retention. These business owners do, however, actually practice extensive risk retention. For example, insurance policy deductibles are a form of risk retention. The deductible amounts fall into the category of losses that can be absorbed as a normal operating expense. Increasing deductibles can provide the business with substantial premium savings. Other risks are retained when the business owner ignores the risk or considers the risk too remote to be of any concern. It is widely believed that most small firms and business owners do not take advantage of potential savings available through risk retention. The effective use of loss-control activities along with risk retention may significantly reduce the insurance costs of the closely held business.

Risk Transfer

All risks that have not been avoided or retained are transferred by the business. The business may transfer risk to an insurer through the purchase of insurance or through noninsurance contracts.

Noninsurance Transfers

hold-harmless agreement

In the remainder of the chapter we will focus primarily on the transfer of risk through the purchase of insurance. However, the financing of a risk can be transferred contractually to another party, forcing that party to either retain or insure the risk. One such contractual arrangement is known as the *hold-harmless agreement*, defined as a contract in which one party assumes the liability for losses as an incidental obligation in a contract between the parties. For example, the owner of property is typically exposed to the risk of damage or loss to the property. However, this individual may be able to contractually transfer the property risk to a tenant when the property is in the possession of another.

Hold-harmless agreements are frequently used in the commercial setting. Sellers of products frequently attempt to include hold-harmless clauses in contracts for the sale of goods. The purchaser will not, of course, wish to relieve the seller of the risks associated with the product. Commercial law has developed a confusing set of rules that apply to the "battle of the forms." This battle occurs when the purchaser specifies different conditions in the purchase order than those the seller includes in the order acknowledgment.

The risk of loss for goods shipped between the seller and buyer can often be transferred, and the terms of the order should be quite clear on this issue. The risk of loss on goods shipped F.O.B. destination remains with the seller until the goods are received at the purchaser's location. Goods shipped F.O.B. point of origin become the purchaser's responsibility when placed in shipment. Business owners can negotiate these terms to effectively transfer the shipping risks to the other party.

Noninsurance transfers are common but present some problems. Since the contract language becomes quite complex, legal counsel may be required for the proper drafting of hold-harmless agreements. Furthermore, many contractual transfers of risk will be invalid. For example, a seller's hold-harmless agreement for the product-liability risk may be in opposition to public policy if it relieves the seller of product warranties mandated by law. Courts often invalidate contract provisions that are grossly unfair to consumers because of the unequal bargaining position between the business and the consumer. Planners should proceed with caution when using noninsurance transfers since an ineffective transfer leaves the business unprotected when a loss occurs.

Insurance Transfers

Insurance transfers involve a two-party contract between the business and the insurer that protects the business against the financial loss resulting from the insured risk. Only pure risks are appropriate subjects for insurance. For a relatively small premium charge the insurer will take responsibility for the risk of a loss. Insurers can accept this risk by pooling a large number of similar risks to take advantage of the predictability created by the statistical principles of large numbers. In general, only the following types of risks are insurable:

- The risk exposures must be homogeneous. A larger number of similar risks is necessary for the principle of large numbers to enable the insurer to estimate costs.

Risk-Management Techniques

- Risk avoidance
  - Elimination
  - Substitution
  - Separation
  - Sensible planning
- Loss control
  - Prevention
  - Reduction
- Risk retention
  - In full
  - Partial
- Risk transfer
  - Noninsurance
  - Insurance

- The loss must be fortuitous (that is, occurrence and severity are beyond the control of the insured).
- The loss should be definite in time and amount.
- The loss should not expose the insurer to an unmeasurable catastrophic result. For this reason war and nuclear risk are typical exclusions in insurance policies.

Losses that are unpredictable and would have a severe financial impact on a business should be transferred.

PERSONNEL EXPOSURES

Business owners who carry out their operations through employees face several risks. The liability exposure to third parties related to this risk was covered earlier. Other personnel exposures include the risk that the employer will incur expense and/or liability for employment-related illnesses or injuries suffered by the employee. Finally, the employer is subject to a loss of income risk should a key employee become disabled or die.

Workers' Compensation and Employers' Liability

workers' compensation

Workers' compensation is a statutory program specified by the laws of the various states. The workers' compensation program replaces the traditional negligence liability concepts in that the employer is obligated to provide a statutory benefit to employees incurring employment-related illnesses or injuries. The employee must accept the benefits provided by the statute and gives up the right to sue the employer under liability for illnesses or injuries covered by these statutes. Most relevant closely held businesses have a workers' compensation exposure since only a few small businesses will be excluded. The closely held business typically will not self-insure the workers' compensation exposure. In fact, several states require that the employer purchase insurance. For large businesses the workers' compensation risk is a candidate for retention where permissible, since the statutory benefits are limited by law and claim frequency is relatively predictable.

The basic workers' compensation and employers' liability policy contains two parts. Part I contains coverage for the workers' compensation recovery amounts equal to the liability imposed on the employer by the laws of the state. Coverage for additional states can be included in part I by specifically listing the states in the information page on the policy. If the closely held business has workers traveling to several states, a third part to the policy, known as *other-states insurance*, should be purchased. This policy section provides coverage to the employer for liability incurred to satisfy the workers' compensation requirements of another state. Such coverage is necessary since other states might have benefit limits higher than the employer's state of domicile.

Employee illnesses and injuries not covered by workers' compensation statutes are adjudicated under traditional liability concepts. That is, the employee must prove that the employer's negligence caused the illness or injury. The employer has the usual defenses applicable to general liability cases. Part II of the workers' compensation and employers' liability policy covers this exposure. The insurer agrees to pay all amounts, up to policy limits, that the employer becomes obligated to pay due to bodily injuries suffered by employees.

The Key Employee Risk

The success of a closely held business often depends on the personal services of key owner-employees and non-owner-employees. The loss of a key employee's services due to death or disability will probably result in a loss of income, at least temporarily, to the closely held business. In addition, increased expenses could result from these circumstances since a replacement employee may have to be recruited at a higher salary and require extensive training. This key employee exposure should be considered in the risk-management process.

key employees

The first step in handling this risk is to identify the key employees. *Key employees* have several characteristics distinguishing them from other employees, including the following:

- A key employee might have a specialized skill critical to the success of the particular closely held business. The skill may be possessed by potential replacements, but replacement employees might have to be recruited at higher salary levels.
- The key employee has a substantial customer or client base, and this employee is responsible for attracting significant amounts of business.
- The key employee might be a source of capital if the loss of this key employee would damage the credit rating of the closely held business.

Identifying the key employee might be more difficult than it seems. Initially the owners of a closely held business are generally material participants in the business and can be classified as key employees. Beyond the owners the key employee risk is often overlooked. The business owners might uncover this risk by considering the damage to the business that would occur if a specific managerial employee was absent for longer than the normal vacation period.

Valuing the Key Employee

Determining the key employee's value to the closely held business is even more speculative than the valuation of the business itself. The actual valuation method employed depends on the characteristic of the employee that creates the key employee status. Determining the value of the key employee who attracts substantial business might be relatively easy. The net income resulting from the business produced by the key employee in excess of the amount of net income that could be expected from a similarly situated less effective employee could be capitalized in some manner. Or if business goodwill is attributed to one key employee, the income level above the amount expected for a similar business can be attributed to that key employee. This income attributed to goodwill can be capitalized to arrive at a current value for the employee.

Traditional Approaches to Key Employee Valuation

There are several methods of valuing a key employee. Four of the most commonly used approaches are as follows:

- to apply some multiple to a key employee's salary
- to capitalize at some discount rate corporate earnings traceable to the key employee's efforts, skills, knowledge, talents, contacts, sales results, or other attributes
- to estimate the percentage reduction in the firm's going-concern value that would result from the loss of the key employee and to multiply that percentage by the firm's going-concern value (A variation computes the value of the firm's goodwill and the presumed value of its earning power over and above what would be expected and allocates a percentage of that goodwill as the assumed worth of the key employee.)
- to employ the unscientific assumption that the maximum amount of coverage an insurance company will issue on the key employee equals that employee's worth

EXAMPLE

A business currently has \$500,000 of tangible assets and generates \$100,000 a year in net income. Similarly situated businesses have a rate of return on tangible assets of 10 percent. In this case \$50,000 of income can be attributed to capital and \$50,000 of income can be attributed to goodwill and the management skill of the key employee. Returning to the capitalization methods discussed earlier in the business valuation chapter, we can capitalize the \$50,000 of earnings at the 10 percent expected return rate and reach a value for the key employee. The capitalization factor in this case is 10 (100 ÷ 10).

Net income attributable to goodwill x capitalization factor = value of goodwill resulting from employee

\$50,000 x 10 = \$500,000

In this case the key employee's value to the business is \$500,000.

The task of evaluating a key employee's worth to a company will always require some judgment and therefore can never be totally precise. Nevertheless, although the four traditional approaches described above have the advantage of simplicity, they all suffer from important conceptual limitations. For example, if a key employee's worth is only some multiple of salary, the employer should be indifferent, at least in a financial sense, to whether the key employee remains with the company or leaves it. Capitalizing the earnings attributable to the key employee or assigning some portion of the firm's going-concern value or goodwill to the employee (which was done in the example above) is based on an assumption that the key employee's worth will continue into perpetuity. The lack of a sound conceptual foundation for the simple assumption that the amount an insurance company will write equals the key employee's worth goes without saying.

The value of a key employee, particularly when more than one key employee is present, is usually more difficult to determine than was seen in the example above. The firm may have to consider various subjective factors to arrive at a proxy for the value of the key employee. For example, the firm should consider replacement salaries and the training required for a replacement employee to become effective. A simple approach might be adequate in many circumstances; however, many business owners may want to be more precise in valuing key employees.

A Sophisticated Approach to Key Employee Valuation

A conceptually sound approach to key employee valuation should

- be forward-looking (What will the key employee produce for the firm *in the future?*)
- take into account the *timing* of the key employee's contribution to the firm (which sounds suspiciously like a time-value-of-money question)
- recognize that the key employee's annual contribution to the firm may rise (or fall) over time
- take into account the fact that at some point (the employee's retirement date), the key employee's contribution to the firm will probably end, even if he or she doesn't die, become disabled, or resign before then
- recognize that except in rare cases, if the employer loses a key employee, that employee will probably have to be replaced (although there may be substantial added costs of various kinds associated with replacement)

The method of key employee valuation described below incorporates all of the features just outlined. If properly used and explained, it should provide the owners of a business with a readily understandable statement of the key employee's true worth to the firm and an accurate estimate of the loss should that employee die, become totally and permanently disabled, or resign prior to retirement. This method can be used as the basis for a set of plans (for example, life insurance, disability insurance, and a sinking fund) to hedge against that loss so that the business can remain financially whole—that is, neither better nor worse off. This method may also serve as a strong argument to an insurer's underwriting department to justify the issuance of a requested amount of insurance and can provide a useful guideline for such a department to use in evaluating applications for key employee coverage.

The key employee valuation method advocated here involves several steps. The business owner or a professional risk manager must estimate the following:

- the number of years that would be necessary to locate, hire, train, and develop a replacement for the key employee to the point that the replacement's value to the firm would equal that of the incumbent key employee. This number of years will be called the *planning period* (except for the rare cases in which the number of years until the key employee's retirement is smaller than this number).
- the firm's gross revenue (sales) for each year in the planning period
- the amount of the key employee's anticipated contribution to the firm as a percentage of the projected gross revenue for each year in the planning period
- the expected total compensation package of the key employee for each year in the planning period (including the cost of all employer-provided employee benefits and Social Security)
- the total direct costs of locating, hiring, installing, compensating, and training a replacement for the key employee for each year in the planning period
- the contribution a replacement would make to the firm as a percentage of the contribution the incumbent key employee would make for each year in the planning period

The data received from the list above will be used in a formula demonstrated in Table 13-1. From the data above the following steps must be taken:

- Compute the revenue attributable to the incumbent key employee. This is included in column (3) of Table 13-1.
- Subtract the compensation of the incumbent key employee and enter this number in column (5).

- Determine the relative effectiveness of a replacement employee (expressed as a percentage of the effectiveness of the incumbent) and multiply this percentage by the revenue attributed to the incumbent. Place this amount in column (7).
- Subtract the cost of the replacement employee (column (8)) and enter the difference (the net contribution of the replacement) in column (9).
- Enter the difference between the net contribution of the replacement employee (column (9)) and the incumbent key employee (column (5)) in column (10) to indicate the lost value to the business from replacing the incumbent.
- Discount the lost net contributions in each of the selected number of future years by a present value factor (column (11)) and add the present values of the lost net contributions to determine the actual value of the key employee.

EXAMPLE

Assume that Kenn Eisenman, aged 42, is the top salesman for Cherry, Inc., a small manufacturer of printing products. Marshall Cherry, the sole owner of the firm, tells you that gross revenue (sales) this year will be about $1.1 million and that he expects revenue to rise by about 10 percent per year in the next several years. Eisenman has been personally responsible for about 20 percent of the firm's annual gross revenue in recent years, a pattern that, according to Cherry, is expected to continue into the foreseeable future. Cherry also informs you that Eisenman's total compensation package this year, including salary, benefits, and bonus, is likely to be about $85,000 and will probably rise at the same 10 percent annual rate as gross revenue for the company.

Cherry estimates that if Eisenman were to die, become totally and permanently disabled, or resign, it would take 5 years to hire and train a replacement to the point where the new person would be able to contribute as much to the firm as Eisenman. Cherry tells you that a replacement would be worth only about 20 percent of Eisenman's current worth in the first year, but that the replacement's value would grow by about 20 percentage points per year. When asked what a replacement for Eisenman would cost, Cherry estimates that the initial direct costs would be as follows:

Costs of the search process	$ 5,000
Relocation expenses	5,000
Compensation package	65,000
Training and development costs	15,000
Total	$90,000

In subsequent years, Cherry says, this total would rise by about $10,000 per year due to increases in the replacement's compensation package and to the continuation of some costs of training and development. These items would more than offset the disappearance of the search and relocation costs.

The final piece of information you need from Cherry relates to the appropriate discount rate to use in calculating present values. A reasonable choice for this purpose is the rate of return the firm has earned in recent years on owners' equity. Cherry advises you that this figure has averaged 15 percent over the past few years, and he anticipates similar results in the future.

The information provided by Cherry has been used to fill in work sheet columns (1), (2), (4), (6), and (8). Simple calculations were performed to complete columns (3), (5), (7), (9), and (10).

To calculate the present value factors called for in column (11), use the following formula:

$$\frac{1}{(1+i)^n}$$

where:

i is the interest rate

n is the number of periods

The final piece of information you need from Cherry relates to the appropriate discount rate to use in calculating present values. A reasonable choice for this purpose is the rate of return the firm has earned in recent years on owners' equity. Cherry advises you that this figure has averaged 15 percent over the past few years, and he anticipates similar results in the future.

The information provided by Cherry has been used to fill in work sheet columns (1), (2), (4), (6), and (8).

n is the number of periods

Using the 15 percent given in this case, the present value factor for the first year, rounded to four decimal places, would be

$$\frac{1}{(1.15)^1} = .8696$$

The final step in completing the work sheet was to perform the calculations called for in column (12). The total of the figures in column (12) is a good approximation of the net loss Cherry will incur as a result of the loss of key employee Ken Eisenman. Eisenman's value appears to be almost $400,000. A contingency plan, such as key employee life and disability insurance (discussed below), to cover a loss in that amount should be developed and implemented.

Table 13-1 Key Employee Valuation Work Sheet

(1)	(2)	(3)	(4)	(5)	(6)
Input: Years Needed to Replace Key Employee	*Input:* Estimated Total Sales	Sales Attributable to Key Employee (2) x 20%	*Input:* Key Employee's Compensation Package	Key Employee's Net Contribution (3) – (4)	*Input:* Relative Value of Replacement Employee
1	$1.1 million	$220,000	$ 85,000	$135,000	20%
2	$1.21 million	$242,000	$ 93,500	$148,500	40%
3	$1.33 million	$266,000	$102,850	$163,150	60%
4	$1.46 million	$292,000	$113,135	$178,865	80%
5	$1.61 million	$322,000	$124,450	$197,550	100%

(7)	(8)	(9)	(10)	(11)	(12)
Sales Attributable to Replacement (3) x (6)	***Input:* Total Cost of Replacement Employee**	**Replacement Employee's Net Contribution (7) – (8)**	**Reduction in Net Contribution (5) – (9)**	***Input:* Present Value Factor (15%)**	**Present Value of Reductions in Net Contribution (10) x (11)**
$ 44,000	$ 90,000	($ 46,000)	$181,000	.8696	$157,398
$ 96,800	$100,000	($ 3,200)	$151,700	.7561	$114,700
$159,600	$110,000	$ 49,600	$113,550	.6575	$ 74,659
$233,600	$120,000	$113,600	$ 65,265	.5718	$ 37,319
$322,000	$130,000	$192,000	$ 5,550	.4972	$ 2,759
Present Value of Net Loss Due to Loss of Key Employee					$386,835

Key Employee Life Insurance

A business could purchase life insurance on the life of the key employee to cover the risk of income loss and/or increase in expenses resulting from the key employee's death. Term insurance can be purchased if the primary concern is the key employee's dollar value to the business. Decreasing term might be appropriate because the key employee exposure decreases as the insured approaches retirement, since the business can be expected to have his or her services for a fewer number of years.

The provisions of the Pension Protection Act (PPA) of 2006 provide new restrictions for employer-owned life insurance to prevent abusive circumstances involving life insurance coverage on employees' lives. If the employee does not meet specified status, and employee notice and consent requirements are not met, the life insurance proceeds will be subject to income tax to the extent the proceeds exceed the policyowner's basis in the policy. First, there is an exception for an insured who was an employee at any time during the 12-month period before the insured's death. Second, there is an exception for an insured who was, at the time the contract was issued, a director or highly compensated employee or highly compensated individual. Thus, key person coverage would generally qualify for traditional income-tax-free receipt of life insurance for the corporation-policyowner, provided the notice and consent requirements are met.[34]

---

34. The notice and consent requirements of this provision are met if, prior to the issuance of the contract, the employee

    1. is notified in writing that the employer intends to insure the employee's life and the maximum face amount for which the employee could be insured at the time the contract was issued,
    2. provides written consent to being insured under the contract and that such coverage may continue after the insured terminates employment, and
    3. is informed in writing that the employer will be a beneficiary of any proceeds payable upon the death of the employee.

    There are two other exceptions that should be mentioned. First, the provision does not apply (and the adverse income tax consequences are avoided) if

    1. the proceeds are paid to a family member of the employee or
    2. the proceeds are to be used by the employer to purchase the business interest held by the employee from the employee's estate.

Key employee insurance, however, is usually coupled with some other purpose such as providing a retirement benefit for the key employee. Permanent life insurance is typically purchased to meet this objective. The life insurance death benefit will be received by the business as indemnification for the income loss and/or increase in expenses resulting from the key employee's death. If the insured survives to retirement, the corporation can use the cash surrender value to fund a deferred-compensation retirement benefit. Another approach would be for the business to transfer the policy to the employee at retirement. The business should be the owner and beneficiary of key employee life insurance. This should pose no insurable interest problems since the business will suffer a pecuniary loss at the death of the key employee. The premiums for key employee insurance will be nondeductible, while death benefits will be received tax free. An additional benefit of key employee insurance is that no accumulated-earnings-tax problems should result since the accumulation of earnings to insure the key employee death risk will meet the reasonable-business-needs test. For incorporated businesses key employee life insurance may, however, increase exposure to the alternative minimum corporate tax.

Tax Aspects of Key Employee Life Insurance

- Premiums are not deductible for employer.
- Death proceeds are tax free to employer.
- There are no accumulated-earnings tax problems for reasonable coverage.

Key Employee Disability Income Insurance

The total and permanent disability of a key employee presents problems similar to those posed by the death of a key employee. The business will also incur an additional expenditure when salary continuation payments will be made to the disabled key employee. To cover the loss of income and increased expenditures resulting from a key employee disability exposure, the business could purchase and be beneficiary of a disability income policy. First, an appropriate elimination period must be selected. One approach would be to select an elimination period equal to the longest vacation or leave of absence that could be provided to the key employee without causing a financial strain on the business. The insurer-participation limits for disability income insurance policies might present a problem. Although the closely held business is the beneficiary of the policy, many insurers' underwriting rules will reduce the coverage available to the insured individually due to the coverage purchased by the employer. This may cause dissatisfaction with key employees who are unable to secure adequate individual coverage as a result of these participation limits. Disability income policies are currently available with high monthly benefit amounts that should alleviate much of the financial loss suffered by a business should the key employee become disabled.

CHAPTER REVIEW

Key Terms and Concepts

pure risk
maximum probable loss
risk avoidance
loss prevention
loss reduction
hold-harmless agreement
workers' compensation
key employees

Review Questions

The answers to the review questions are in the supplement. The self-test questions and the answers to them are also in the supplement and on The American College Online.

1. Discuss the procedures that might be used to identify the risks faced by a closely held business. [1]
2. Explain the difference between maximum probable loss and maximum possible loss. [2]
3. Describe the procedures that can be employed to manage the risks of a closely held business. [2]
4. Identify the types of risk that might be appropriate for retention by the business. [2]
5. Identify the characteristics of a risk that generally will be insurable. [2]
6. Explain how workers' compensation statutes have replaced traditional concepts of liability. [3]
7. What risks are covered by the two parts of the workers' compensation and employers' liability policies? [3]
8. What are the distinguishing characteristics of a key employee? [4]
9. Identify the traditional methods for valuing a key employee. [4]

10. Cobus, Inc., is a manufacturer of microcircuits. It has $5 million of tangible assets and had net earnings of $1.2 million in 2008. A typical rate of return for similar businesses is 15 percent. Much of the recent success of Cobus can be attributed to the skills of an engineer who developed a new product late in 2007. Using traditional capitalization techniques, determine the value of the key employee. [4]
11. Explain the shortcomings of traditional methods for valuing a key employee. [4]
12. Identify the factors that must be considered if a key employee will be valued using more sophisticated techniques. [4]
13. Explain why permanent life insurance might be appropriate for insuring the loss of a key employee. [5]
14. What might the employer do with respect to key employee life insurance if the insured key employee terminates employment? [5]
15. What problems might occur if both the employer and key employee desire substantial disability income coverage? [5]

accumulated taxable income • the portion of a corporation's income, which is beyond the expected needs of the business and therefore the tax base for the calculation of the accumulated-earnings tax

adjusted book value • an approximate fair market value that is arrived at by adjusting the value of assets and liabilities as carried on the books, adding a value for goodwill to the value of the firm's tangible assets

administrator • a representative of the decedent, appointed by the court in the absence of a duly appointed executor, who is designated to hold legal title to the estate's property

alternative minimum taxable income (AMTI) • the amount of a corporation's income that determines if the alternative minimum tax must be paid. The base is calculated by adding certain tax-preference items to the corporation's normal taxable income.

articles of incorporation • a document registered and filed with the state, describing such aspects of a corporation as the name and location, its purpose and powers, and the capitalization of the corporation. The corporation's legal existence is established by the filing of the articles with the appropriate state authority.

asset sale • the sale of a corporation in which the buyer may pick and choose the assets of a company he or she wishes to purchase, and the purchaser will gain a new cost basis for the assets. This type of sale may require action by the shareholders of the selling corporation, such as a majority (or super majority) vote by the shareholders of the corporation.

assignee in interest • the transferee of a partnership interest who is not admitted as a partner. Transferees might include the estate of a deceased partner, donees of gifts of the donor's interests, and third-party purchasers.

attribution • stock owned by one individual or entity but considered to be owned by another individual or entity for the purpose of determining how a particular transaction is taxed (also referred to as constructive ownership)

blockage discount • a discount allowed by the IRS when a large block of corporate stock is valued for estate tax purposes, reflecting the fact that the market would be depressed if a large block of corporate stock was offered for sale in a brief time frame

book value • a type of business value equal to the excess of assets over liabilities; not considered the "real" value, or fair market value, of the business

business-judgment rule • the standard by which the directors and officers of a corporation measure up to their fiduciary obligation to the corporation by exercising ordinary prudent business judgment, removing them from liability for losses

business-overhead-expense disability insurance • insurance that provides reimbursement for certain specified expenses to allow the business to remain viable until the disabled owner returns to work

bylaws • in a corporation, a document approved by the incorporators that describes duties and powers of directors and shareholders, the rules for shareholder and director meetings, and other corporate operating matters

capitalization factor • the inverse of the rate of return calculated for the capitalization procedure

capitalization of earnings • one of the most common methods of valuing a closely held business, based on the concept that the value of property is the value of the earnings stream it produces

closely held business • a business not traded on a securities exchange whose shares are not generally offered for sale. The business is controlled by a small group of shareholders who generally provide services for the business.

collateral-assignment method • the corporation loans the employee its share of the annual premium; the corporate amounts are secured by the assignment of the policy to the corporation

compensation planning • a plan designed to maximize the usefulness to the owners and key employees of any income earned by the business that will be paid for services of the owner-employees and other key employees

complete redemption • a stock redemption that qualifies as a capital transaction if a corporation redeems all the stock the shareholder owns. This results in complete termination of the shareholder's interest in the redeeming corporation.

consequential losses • losses that decrease the net income of a business as a result of a direct loss. A consequential loss may occur for two reasons: The gross receipts may be reduced if operations are curtailed due to a direct loss, or a firm may be subject to increased operating expenses as a result of a direct loss.

constructive receipt • a tax-timing concept that provides that income is taxed when it is available to a recipient without substantial limitations or restrictions. This availability must be avoided for nonqualified deferred compensation to be effective at deferring taxation to the participant.

corporate liquidation • dissolution of a corporation in which the corporation's properties are distributed to shareholders and the corporate stock is canceled in the process of terminating the corporation

cross-purchase agreement • a type of buy-sell agreement formed between the owners of a business that commits the surviving owner(s) to buy and the deceased owner's estate to sell the ownership interest of a deceased owner. A cross-purchase agreement can be formed between partners of a partnership, shareholders of a corporation, and members of a limited liability company.

cumulative voting • a method of maximizing the voting power of minority shareholders by providing that each share of stock receive one vote for each of the directors to be elected at the meeting. These votes can be accumulated by abstaining from voting for specific directors and then casting all the accumulated votes for one director position.

death-benefit-only (DBO) plan • a type of nonqualified plan designed to provide death benefits to a participant's heirs, usually by paying installment benefits at the participant's death, but occasionally in a lump sum to the participant's survivors

disability buyout insurance • specialty policies designed to facilitate a disability buy-sell agreement by providing for large lump-sum or installment benefits related to the value of the business. These policies, provided by a limited number of insurers, are subject to restrictive financial underwriting and policy maximums.

disability income protection insurance • insurance that provides income payments at the disability of an insured. If used to fund a cross-purchase buy-sell agreement, the individual owners will purchase disability income insurance on the other owners. If used in an entity or stock-redemption approach, the business itself will buy, pay the premiums for, and be the beneficiary of policies covering the owners.

discounted future earnings (DFE) • a method of valuation similar to the capitalization-of-earnings method but based on projected future earnings

dissolution • the point at which a corporation or partnership ceases as an entity or is dissolved

dividend coverage • the ratio of the sum of the pretax and pre-interest earnings to the sum of the total interest to be paid and the pretax earnings needed to pay the after-tax dividends

earnings and profits (E & P) • current or past earnings of a corporation that have not been distributed as dividends to shareholders and are carried on the corporate books

economic benefit • a benefit from a nonqualified deferred-compensation plan that is immediately taxable if the plan is treated as funded with the benefits set aside for the participants beyond the claims of the corporation's general creditors

economic benefit theory • the tax treatment of certain endorsement and nonequity collateral-assignment split-dollar plans under which the employee is taxed on the share of the employer's premium that provides pure insurance coverage to the employee

electing small business trust (ESBT) • a trust receiving S corporation stock by gift or bequest. The trust may have more than one current beneficiary, and the S election is made by the trustee rather than the beneficiary.

elimination period • the amount of time that must elapse after the onset of a disability before benefits are paid from a disability income policy or purchase must occur in a disability buy-sell agreement

entity agreement • a type of buy-sell agreement in which the business, as a separate legal entity from the owners, will purchase the interest held by any deceased owner's estate. As parties to the agreement, the owners commit their estates to sell their ownership interests to the business at death. In a corporation, an entity agreement is known as a stock-redemption agreement.

equity split-dollar plan • a variation on the split-dollar arrangement in which the employer's rights are limited to the actual premiums the employer paid and the excess cash surrender value vesting in the participant

estate freeze • a transaction in which a senior family member transfers property with substantial appreciation potential to a younger family member at a reduced transfer tax cost and retains an interest in the property without appreciation potential

executor • a representative of the decedent named in a valid will, who is designated to hold legal title to the estate's property

fair market value • used as a business valuation technique, the net amount at which a willing purchaser would pay a willing seller, neither being under any compulsion to buy and sell and both having reasonable knowledge of all relevant factors

family partnership • a partnership in which family members act as the partners, often splitting the partnership income among several people and placing some business income in lower tax brackets

first-offer restriction • a provision contained in many closely held corporation stock certificates requiring the shareholder to offer stock to the existing shareholders first, usually at an agreed price, before selling it to outsiders

general partnership • a partnership containing only general partners who are typically coequals in the ownership and management responsibilities for the business. Each general partner's liability for business activities is joint and several.

goodwill • theoretically, the earning power of a business in excess of a fair return on the business's tangible assets; its formula valuation is often used by appraisers and generally accepted by the courts

grantor trust • a common type of living trust in which the grantor is treated as the owner for income tax purposes, typically a revocable trust created as a probate-avoidance device

grantor-retained annuity trust (GRAT) • a trust in which the donor retains the right to receive amounts payable at least annually that are a fixed amount (an annuity) and the trust remainder is provided to remainder beneficiaries at the termination of the trust

grantor-retained unitrust (GRUT) • a trust in which the donor retains the right to receive amounts payable at least annually that are a fixed percentage of the value of the trust's assets determined annually, and the trust remainder is provided to remainder beneficiaries at the termination of the trust

guaranteed payments • fixed payments paid to service partners; these payments are like salaries and should reflect the efforts of partners who provide substantial services to the partnership

guaranteed renewable • the insurer must renew an insurance policy until the insured reaches 65 but has the option to adopt a new rate structure for future renewal premiums

hold-harmless agreement • a contract in which one party assumes the liability for losses as an incidental obligation in a contract between the parties

hot assets • a portion of the proceeds from a business sale that includes unrealized receivables and appreciated inventory items. This portion is treated as ordinary income to the estate, to which no basis step-up is available.

imputed interest • interest on an installment note that is regulated by a minimum rate of interest defined in the Internal Revenue Code. Imputed interest is imposed for tax purposes if an installment sale does not provide for an adequate rate of interest, and it is taxed over the installment period by a complex set of rules.

income in respect of a decedent (IRD) • income that was earned by a decedent but not constructively received at the time of his or her death

installment obligation • a purchase method of installment payments for a business interest, employed when prefunding is not the option of choice for a buy-sell agreement or if the life insurance funding proves to be inadequate. The buy-sell agreement specifies the details of the installment purchase, such as term and principal amount.

installment sale • a sale in which at least one principal payment is received in a year other than the year of the sale

insurable interest • a pecuniary interest in the insured in which there is a reasonable expectation of benefit from the insured's continued life or a financial loss from the insured's death

intangible assets • business assets that are not considered tangible and thus not included as assets on the unadjusted balance sheet (for example, customer relationships or production know-how)

interest-free loan • the treatment, under Sec. 7872, of an equity collateral-assignment split-dollar plan as a series of below-market loans, whereby the employee will not have income currently for the value of the insurance protection or any equity in the policy's cash surrender value but will have income from the forgone interest on the loan from the employer

key employee • an employee whose skills, customer/client base, or other attribute make him or her a valuable asset to the closely held business. A loss of the key employee may result in a loss of income and increased expenses.

limited-liability company (LLC) • a form of business enterprise in which business owners (members) have liability protection, and the company can elect to receive pass-through tax treatment for federal income tax purposes

limited-liability partnership (LLP) • a partnership in which all partners are sheltered from liability for partnership activities

limited partnership • a partnership composed of active participants (general partners) who retain personal responsibility for business operations, and passive investment partners (limited partners) who are at risk only to the extent of their investment in the business

liquidating trustees • surviving partners in a partnership that is dissolved upon the death of a general partner

liquidation (of a partnership) • the dissolution of a partnership upon the death of a general partner

liquidation rights • a legal interest against business property if the business is dissolved, which is held by the owners of a partnership, LLC, or corporation

loss prevention • a technique to reduce the chance of loss for any business risk that cannot be avoided

loss reduction • a technique to control the severity of losses that occur, minimizing the financial impact of a loss on the business

marketability discount • a discount in value of a closely held business, employed if a business interest lacks a ready market and cannot be quickly converted to cash

maximum probable loss • the greatest potential loss that may result from a business risk, dependent on the subjective determination of the likelihood of various events

member • a holder of an ownership interest in a limited liability company

minority discount • a discount in value for a minority interest, based on the lack of power to control the business

noncancelable • the insurer cannot cancel an insurance policy prior to the insured's reaching age 65 and must guarantee the premium rate for the entire period

not essentially equivalent to a dividend • a stock redemption that has undergone a "meaningful reduction" in a shareholder's interest in a corporation. This classification is determined by a subjective test by the IRS, which evaluates the particular facts of the redemption and allows the redemption to be treated as a capital transaction for tax purposes.

operating agreement • a contract drawn up by members of a limited liability company that states the terms upon which the organization will perform its business or services, similar to a partnership agreement. Modification is generally only allowed by the unanimous vote of the members.

option agreement • a type of restriction used to handle business continuation problems, stipulating that the surviving owners of the business will have the option to buy a deceased owner's stock at a specific price

own-occupation definition of disability • the continuous inability of the insured to engage in his or her regular occupation or profession due to illness or injury

partial liquidation • a distribution in which the distributing corporation is partially liquidated, qualifying it for treatment as a capital transaction for tax purposes. Qualification is determined by examination at the corporate level, rather than from the point of view of the shareholder receiving proceeds.

partnership • an unincorporated business that is run by two or more persons who act as co-owners of the business for profit

partnership interest • an intangible personal property right held by each partner once a partnership is formed and holds property. A partnership interest is considered personal property and is treated as such for inheritance tax and succession purposes.

pass-through entity • business organizational form whose items of taxable income, capital gain, tax-exempt income, losses, deductions, and credits resulting from business operations generally pass through as individually taxed items in relation to the owners' relative interests in the business. Pass-through entities include partnerships, LLCs (if partnership tax treatment is chosen), and S corporations.

personal property • property other than real property

personal-service corporation (PSC) • a corporation owned by shareholder-employees in which substantially all activities involve services in the fields of health, law, engineering, architecture, accounting, actuarial science, performing arts, or consulting. This type of corporation is subject to a flat rate of 35 percent on all corporate earnings.

presumptive disability provision • a provision that triggers automatic payment of benefits under a disability policy at the insured's loss of certain functions, such as complete loss of eyesight or loss of two limbs

professional corporation • a corporation whose activities involve the performance of professional services by professionals who are shareholders of the corporation

proprietorship • a business enterprise that is formed with one owner who owns the business assets, manages the business, and conducts business affairs. The business is not a separate legal entity, and assets and income of the business are treated as directly owned by the proprietor.

pure risk • a business risk that is characterized by the chance of a loss without the chance of gain

qualified payments • dividends payable on a periodic basis on cumulative preferred stock or comparable payments under a partnership interest to the extent that such dividends or comparable partnership payments are determined at a fixed rate

qualified subchapter S subsidiary (QSSS) • a permissible subsidiary of an S corporation, which causes all assets, items of income, deductions, and QSSS credits to be treated as if they belong to the parent S corporation

qualified subchapter S trust (QSST) • a type of trust eligible to hold S corporation stock that splits S corporation income among family members without relinquishing complete control of the stock

quorum • a designated minimum number of directors required to be in attendance for action taken at a board meeting to be valid

real property • land and anything permanently attached or affixed to the land

reasonable compensation • a compensation test that determines if a deduction from corporate income tax as an ordinary and necessary business expense will be permitted for the total compensation of a shareholder-employee. Amounts determined to exceed reasonable compensation will be treated as dividends, which are subject to double taxation.

recapitalization • a rearrangement of the capital structure of a corporation involving the exchange of all or part of a shareholder's stock for newly issued stock, pursuant to the plan of recapitalization

residual disability benefit • a disability plan that provides reduced benefits when the disabled insured suffers a partial loss of earned income, thus giving the insured an incentive to return to work (also referred to as income replacement or recovery benefit)

reverse split-dollar (RSD) plan • variation on the split-dollar arrangement in which the roles of the corporation and the executive are reversed—the corporation pays the pure insurance portion of the premium, and the executive pays the balance of the premium and controls the cash surrender value

risk avoidance • the elimination of a risk either by refusing to assume it initially or by abandoning it

salary continuation plan • a plan to replace the salary of a disabled business owner or employee, funded either by disability income insurance or by the business itself. When used in conjunction with a disability buy-sell agreement, the payments generally continue at least until the disability buy-sell agreement becomes effective.

salary reduction plan • an agreement between the employer and the participating employee either to reduce the employee's salary or to defer an anticipated bonus and provide that such amounts be received in future tax years (also called an *in lieu of* plan)

sale-or-exchange treatment • a value-for-value disposition of property, in which the seller receives capital-gains tax treatment for federal income tax purposes

savings fund • as one alternative to funding a buy-sell agreement, a fund created to accumulate enough money for a key employee or other purchaser to buy the business interest at the owner's death

Sec. 79 plan • group term life insurance benefit plan that gives the employer a tax deduction for premium payments made on behalf of a participant, provides up to $50,000 of coverage tax free to participants, and follows nondiscrimination rules provided by Sec. 79

Sec. 162 plan • executive bonus life insurance plan that avoids the nondiscrimination rules applicable to other fringe benefits by having shareholder-employees and executives who participate in the plan apply for, own, and name the beneficiary on permanent life insurance policies covering their lives, with the corporation paying the premiums through a bonus payment to the insurer or as a bonus to the executive

Sec. 303 redemption • a relief provision of the Internal Revenue Code that applies to estates in which stock of a closely held corporation constitutes a substantial portion of total estate assets. This type of redemption allows distributions to be treated as made in exchange for a capital asset and therefore eligible for capital-gains treatment, subject to certain requirements and limitations.

Sec. 6166 installment payments • if a qualifying estate holds a business interest that comprises a substantial portion of the gross estate of a deceased owner of a closely held business, an estate liquidity technique that allows the estate tax caused by the business interest to be spread over a number of years in installments

Sec. 754 election • a provision of the Internal Revenue Code that allows an adjustment in the basis in partnership assets for payments made by the surviving partners when a deceased partner's interest is purchased

self-employed business owner • proprietor, partner (or member in an LLC taxed as a partnership), and more-than-2-percent shareholders in S corporations

special-use valuation • an election available to value certain real property by taking into consideration how the property is currently being utilized instead of how it might be used if placed in its best and most profitable use

specific performance • a remedy provided by the courts when a valid buy-sell agreement has been breached for the sale of a unique property and money damages would be either difficult to determine or inadequate (also known as specific enforcement)

split-dollar plan • life insurance plans in which the premium obligations and policy benefits of a life insurance policy are split between two individual entities, usually an employer and employee, who share the premium costs while the policy is in effect and split the benefits at the death of the insured or termination of the agreement

split-dollar rollout • a split-dollar arrangement may terminate at some point during the employee's life, with the policy vesting in the employee and the corporation either being repaid for its contributions or providing the policy to the participant as a bonus

stock-redemption arrangement • a buy-sell arrangement that binds the corporation to purchase a shareholder's interest at the occurrence of certain specified events

stock sale • the sale of a corporation in which the buyer acquires the whole corporation with all its assets and liabilities. In this type of sale the buyer cannot incur direct liability for the corporation's debts, and the sale of stock does not affect the basis of the corporation's assets.

stock-transfer restrictions • a provision in a buy-sell agreement that sets forth any restrictions imposed on the shares of stock subject to the agreement, such as a first-offer requirement preventing a shareholder from disposing of stock to a nonparty without first giving the other parties to the buy-sell agreement the option to purchase the shares at a specified price

substantially disproportionate redemption • a stock redemption that qualifies as a capital transaction if a mathematical safe-harbor test is met. Requirements include a less than 50 percent ownership of the total voting power of the corporation by the shareholder after the redemption, which must also be less than 80 percent of his of her percentage ownership before the redemption. The shareholder's percentage ownership of common stock must also be less than 80 percent of his or her preredemption percentage ownership of common stock.

supplemental executive retirement plan (SERP) • a salary continuation plan designed to supplement the retirement benefits at levels both above and below the qualified plan limitations for key executives of a corporation

tax-free reorganization • the reorganization of a business, such as a sale of assets or a sale of stock, which does not incur tax to the seller/selling corporation at the time of the transaction, and in which the seller receives stock in the acquiring corporation at a basis equal to the seller's basis in the property sold

tenants in partnership • a form of property ownership in which each partner has an undivided interest in each specific partnership asset, giving each partner the right to use partnership property for partnership business

termination by operation of law • the termination of a business by the death, bankruptcy, or legal disability of an owner

trade creditors • parties to whom a business becomes indebted following the business owner's death

trigger date • the date a disability buy-sell agreement becomes operative after an elimination period following the onset of the owner's disability

voting trust • an arrangement in which trust settlors transfer shares in the corporation to the trust and the trustee votes the shares as provided by the terms of the trust. The trustee of the voting trust holds legal title to the shares, and the settlors receive voting trust certificates that demonstrate their continuing beneficial interest in the shares of stock.

wait-and-see buy-sell • a buy-sell arrangement in which the identity of the purchaser is not predetermined in the agreement but upon the first death of a shareholder

waiver of family attribution • by meeting certain Internal Revenue Code requirements, the avoidance of having stock owned by a shareholder's family attributed to the shareholder when all the stock is redeemed

weighted-average earnings • a calculation used to determine representative earnings in which the most recent year's earnings are given the greatest weight and earnings of the preceding years are given progressively less weight

workers' compensation • a program specified by the laws of various states that obliges an employer to provide a statutory benefit to employees incurring employment-related illnesses or injuries

zero-tax bonus plan • an arrangement most often used to provide a bonus to an executive to meet a specific benefit need in which the bonus is large enough to cover both the amount of the bonus and the executive's income tax liability (also referred to as a double-bonus plan or a tax gross-up plan)

INDEX

C

D

E

F

G

H

I

K

L

M

N

O

P

Q

R

S

T